Guotai Yu

ENGINES
OF FORTUNE

A TALE OF BUSINESS,
FAMILY, AND PERSEVERANCE

Translated from the Chinese by Jicheng Sun and Yingrui Gong

Proofread by John Drew and Hal Swindall

1 Plus Books

1 Plus Books

https://1plusbooks.com

Author: Yu Guotai

English Translation by Jicheng Sun and Yingrui Gong

Title: Engines of Fortune

Subtitle: A Tale of Business, Family, and Perseverance

2025 1 Plus Books®

Paperback Edition

Published and Printed in the United States of America

ISBN: 978-1-966814-12-2

Library of Congress Control Number: 2025908394

Publisher: Yan Liu

Book Design: 1 Plus Books

Suggested Retail Price: $24.99

San Francisco, USA, 2025

https://1plusbooks.com

email: 1plus@1plusbooks.com

CONTENTS

CHAPTER 1
SETTING OUT FOR BUSINESS

1.1 Enchanting Sight in Springtime

We intended to set out for the Tushan Commune Plastic Factory on the second day to deliver plastic strips. However, during a discussion that morning, the two drivers suggested we leave in the afternoon to save a day by reaching our destination before starting work the next morning after a one-night journey because it would take us 10 to 12 hours to cover 200 kilometers, driving a 25-horsepower tractor with an average speed of 20 kilometers, which could barely hit 25 kilometers per hour at full capacity. It was quiet and mild on the night road. I checked out and handled some business after unloading the goods so the two drivers could return home on the same day. They had hired the tractor of the production team to earn as much money as possible if they preferred it to the work point.

The two drivers, Little Zhao and Little Jing, drove the Taishan-24 tractor to the plant gate from the edge of a bay by the eastern part of the village and through the alleys at five in the afternoon. It was formerly a warehouse and noodle workshop for the production team, featuring a small courtyard with four rooms to the north, four to the west, and three open sheds to the south. In the 1960s, the rooms in the north were used as sheds for oxen and donkeys. However, by the 1970s, they had been converted into a noodle workshop, a sideline of the production team. Rooms in the west served as warehouses to store corn, wheat, and crop seeds, as well as concentrated feed for donkeys and oxen, and dried sweet potatoes for pigs. Three years before, I had removed two rooms and added an extruder for plastic processing to produce plastic strips, which was now my plastic processing plant.

The noodle workshop in the north was still operating smoothly. My warehouse, in the west and near the gate, was used to store the plastic strips from my new enterprise. Six female workers carried them out about seven to eight meters from the tractor at the gate. At the same time, Little Zhao and Little Jing, who were in their early twenties and full of energy, loaded them onto the tractor. They climbed aboard and jumped off the tractor effortlessly while I assisted them. After more than 40 minutes, the tractor was full of plastic strips.

After we had tied dozens of plastic strips tightly with two thick hemp ropes and hoisted them onto the vehicle, we washed our hands and got into the tractor to set off. From the gate to the main road, it was a two-kilometer dirt road full of bumps and potholes, which made the tractor shake constantly. The cabin frame was constructed with triangular iron, with the flat side facing outward. The sharp edges facing inward, poking our backs at every shake, forced us to support ourselves with our hands and hunch over. Still, we set off in high spirits despite the jolting.

The Taishan-24 tractor, produced by the Shandong Tractor Factory, was a highly sought-after commodity, as new ones were scarce and difficult to obtain. In the spring of 1980, I entrusted someone to buy a used one for 4,000 yuan while I was in Weifang, a major city in Shandong province famous for its kites. We initially used it for two years as part of our first production group. The tractor was contracted to Little Zhao and Little Jing after the 1982 economic reforms. It was the first time I had embarked on a long-distance trip to sell my goods and make money, so I was excited and thrilled. The more the tractor shook, the happier I felt.

The three of us chatted and laughed during the trip, discussing the production team's anecdotes and how to make money in the future. Hardly noticing, we passed over the Zihe River and through Miaozicun Village, located within the Weifang city limits. Then we climbed up Niujiaoling Ridge, situated at the northern foot of the Taiyi Mountains, 25 kilometers southwest of Qingzhou City, a necessary route from Zichuan District to Yidu City (now Qingzhou). The route featured winding mountain roads in an S-shape, with not one bend but three or four, to reach the mountaintop. The water in the tank boiled over three times while we climbed steep slopes on the sandy road. We stopped the tractor every time it boiled and did not start until the water temperature had dropped. I asked whether there was a problem with the water tank. Little Jing replied that the entire tractor had been thoroughly checked at the repair shop before our long journey, and everything had gone well. It was normal for the water temperature to rise when climbing uphill. It was downhill to Yidu after climbing the Niujiaoling Ridge, and it was late by then.

After passing through Yidu, we noticed that the tractor leaned slightly to one side. We stopped and found that one tire was flat, so we replaced it with a spare and continued. But what should we do if it happened again? Therefore, Little Jing ran into a yard beside the road to ask if there was a place to repair tires, but the answer was no. In those days, there were few cars and tractors, so repair shops were scarce, and even if we were lucky enough to find one, it would likely be closed. Quite luckily, though, there was a carriage shop. Should we stay there or not? If we continued our trip and another tire blew, we would have to spend the night on the road. Then, when Little Zhao carefully inspected them and found that one tire was lumped, we stayed at the carriage shop.

After we entered the courtyard, an old man walked over to the tractor from the west room and asked politely, "How many of you need a place to stay? Each one needs three mao (毛 , a monetary unit in China equaling 0.1 yuan) for one night." Little Jing, a quick-witted man, replied immediately, "Three." The old man pointed to the three rooms on the right and said, "Come here." Then he entered the room first and turned on the light. There were only five beds covered with straw mats without pillows or quilts. He asked if we wanted quilts, an additional two mao for each. After all, who would sleep without them? He mentioned that cart drivers usually brought their quilts with them. Little Jing said, "We need three quilts." The old man first brought a bamboo thermos, then returned with three quilts. In the dim light, it was difficult to determine whether they were blue, yellow, or a combination of the two. As Little Jing and Little Zhao unfolded them, an unpleasant odor filled the room. I touched a folded one and found it greasy, probably not washed for years.

Having drunk a glass of water, the two drivers looked disheartened, not saying a word. Before setting off, however, they were confident and said, "I'm sure we can stay here twice." Unexpectedly, the tractor broke down after less than half the way. Looking at each other and having no idea, we had no choice but to sleep there again because we needed to hit the road early upon hearing the cock crow.

It was the first time that I had ever seen this carriage shop. In the early 1980s, the main means of transportation in rural areas were carriages and donkey carts. I had never imagined cart drivers staying in a hotel whose windows had wooden frames pasted with paper, and two wooden doors were without glass. There were no chairs or tables, just five wooden beds with straw mats, which were worse than the watchman's shack at the wheat field in the production team.

The two drivers lay down, unable to sleep, but they felt it was more comfortable than sitting. However, I was unable to do that. I sat on the quilt, leaving one door half-open, and gazed up at the blue sky full of twinkling stars while the moon, visible in the east, was obscured by clouds. It was chilly in May, and I sat there for the rest of the night.

The previous year (1981), the household contract system, promulgated by the authorities, had been implemented in rural areas after the autumn harvest. Collectively farmed land had disappeared and was distributed to households based on the amount of land in each village, and then to individual households within those villages. Each man in our team was allotted four mu (亩 , a Chinese land measure equal to 0.0667 hectares), while each woman was allotted three mu. Households working in communes and factories of production teams without a labor force were not assigned contracted fields instead. As long as the production teams were not disbanded, their distribution methods, as well as the constitution of the People's Commune, remained unchanged. Work points depended on land cultivation and the wages of factory workers. Their grain was distributed as follows: 30 percent was based on work points.

In comparison, the number of family members determined the remaining 70 percent. The land was classified into different grades: the first for twice-harvest land yielding 800 jin (斤 , a unit of weight in China equal to 0.5 kilograms) per mu, the second for 700 jin, and mountainous land 400 jin. The output was a mandatory standard. The production team handed over public grain as agricultural tax once it had finished settling after completing two harvests, regardless of whether the crop was a bumper or a poor one. The surplus was handed over to the team and distributed to members without land, so that the production team system and the distribution system remained intact.

Factories in a commune and the production team operated as usual under the original management. Workshops in the production group could be individually contracted, with negotiations between both parties regarding the annual payment to the production team and the allocation of the remaining amount to the individual. It was stipulated in government regulations that factories within a commune and production teams could not operate under individual contracting, but rather through collective ownership.

In 1979, our sub-team set up a sideline workshop, transforming old plastic shoe soles into plastic strips and making semi-finished plastic products. I was one of the six workers, serving as the plant director and accountant in charge of waste procurement and product sales. After the final accounts at the end of 1980, our labor value was 1.04 yuan, 10 work points per person. Each male worker earned an average of 12 points per day, 1.24 yuan. As for the contract fee, the leader had proposed 3,000 yuan annually, but I suggested 5,000 yuan. He thought it was too much since it was too expensive to be contracted. Eventually, we agreed to sign a two-year contract. However, we encountered setbacks and felt defeated due to the first unsuccessful delivery.

Sitting on the bed with my back against the wall, I stayed up all night in a daze. It was dawn at five o'clock in the morning in May. The two drivers, lying under the smelly quilts, did not sleep well. After they got up, we continued our journey.

And so, at the beginning of the reform and opening up in 1982, we made another start, scared and anxious about the rare repair shops, afraid that the same accident would happen again. What if another tire blew? We left the carriage shop and drove, avoiding cliffs and taking downhill paths that were clear of pedestrians and vehicles. After about two hours, we found a repair shop by the roadside. It was past seven, but the shop had not opened yet. We parked the tractor at the door and waited there until the tire was fixed.

We had breakfast after the repair and then hurried to the Tushan Plastic Plant, which was still over 100 kilometers away. We could arrive in the afternoon and unload the goods, allowing the drivers to walk back home at night.

We encountered an uphill slope after a while. The tractor revved up to full power, but the water in the tank boiled over; thus, we had to stop to refill it. We prepared plastic buckets, and there was still a bucket of water left after we had poured the others in. Having added over half a bucket of water to the tank, we continued moving forward. Climbing the big slope, we could not see its end. Then, after traveling only a few kilometers, the water boiled over again. This time, we poured all the water into it, but it was not enough. Little Zhao and Little Jing grumbled to themselves that something was wrong with the tank and decided to find a repair shop. However, they couldn't see one by the roadside, so they had to go to the county of Changle for help.

We made frequent stops, filling the buckets with water from a small river by the roadside and adding it to the tank multiple times every few kilometers, so many times that I couldn't remember them. Finally, we arrived in Changle City. We were told there was only one repair shop, which we found after traversing several streets. The yard was small, with four open sheds and three main rooms. Two mechanics were sitting in the yard, drinking tea. After Little Zhao and Little Jing explained the overheated water tank, they approached the tractor, opened the engine hood, and inspected it. They concluded it was so rusty and clogged that it prevented proper circulation, so they spent over an hour removing the rust. Then, we added water above the tank to test the tractor, but it leaked heavily underneath. Upon closer inspection, the mechanics found two holes and removed the parts for repair.

The tank was placed on a rack. One mechanic held the welding torch while the other fetched welding rods. However, they were out of copper welding rods. One took off his work gloves and rode his bicycle to the hardware store to buy the rods, while the other continued smoking and drinking tea. After chatting with him, I learned that the Subdistrict office managed the tractor repair shop, and the mechanics would be paid as usual if they did not repair any vehicles for a day. When the rods were at hand, however, it was time for lunch. We begged them to finish their work before lunch since we were eager to continue our journey, but they intentionally ignored us.

They started at one o'clock in the afternoon, stalling for time and enjoying themselves as usual. Eventually, we left Changle at half past three, after the repaired tank was installed, with the sun about to set.

It became apparent that we would not reach our destination that day. We had not even covered half the distance, so we stopped where we were. As the saying goes, "One cannot drink hot corn congee in a hurry." Things were not going according to plan, but we had to accept it.

It was already dark as we entered Weifang. However, it was still early enough to find accommodation, so we intended to push on a little further. Around eight o'clock, we passed through a fairly large village and stopped. We were told that it was the headquarters of the Zhuli Commune, located in Shangyoucun Village (now affiliated with Xueye Street, Laiwu District, Jinan City). There were inns and restaurants, so we decided to rest for the night. The Inn of the Supply and Marketing Cooperative had a favorably large courtyard, with two rows of buildings for accommodation. Each room had four beds, along with tables, chairs, and clean bedding, all of which were identical to those found in the city. After dropping off our small luggage, we went out to find a restaurant for dinner.

As we left our room, we noticed two people standing beside our tractor, holding the bag and carefully examining the plastic strips inside it.

We approached them and asked, "What are you doing?"

"Are these yours?"

"Of course!"

"Could you sell them to me?"

Annoyed by the intrusive words, we ignored them and continued walking after a day and night of frustrating travel.

One caught up and said, "Let's discuss it."

"We haven't eaten yet; let's make it later."

"Which room are you staying in?"

"Room 205."

"We'll come to your room after dinner."

Eating and chatting, we thought about who might buy our goods in the meantime. Were they genuine buyers or just trying to get the price? This had dropped to 1,350 yuan per ton when Tushan Plastic Factory purchased two tons of plastic strips from our production group last time. Before leaving, the Factory director, Xu, had asked me if I could drop the price by 100 yuan per ton for the next delivery. After a lengthy negotiation, we eventually reached a deal at 1,300 yuan per ton. They said they planned to change products, so they would not force us to do business if we did not want to.

In the spring of 1981, the Commune Plastic Factory we supplied changed its products, no longer purchasing our plastic strips. I therefore traveled to several cities — Fuyang, Mengcheng in Anhui Province, Linyi, and Xintai in Shandong Province — visiting seven or eight factories over a period of more than two months. Still, I was unable to sell our products. Back then, buyers could not find sellers due to blocked information and automated phones, and vice versa. After collecting five or six tons of scrap plastic shoes, we produced over four tons of plastic strips in three months. Still, we were unable to come up with a viable idea for selling them. One day, while dining with a friend from a plastic factory, I heard about a plastic factory in Tushan Commune, Yexian County, that needed them, so I set off without hesitation. Changing four long-distance buses and spending a night in Weifang, I arrived in Tushan Town the next afternoon, past four o'clock. When I arrived, I had to wait for the factory managers, who were in a meeting. After half an hour, the meeting ended, and I approached the factory manager to pitch our strips. However, the manager burst into laughter.

"How much is it per ton?" he muttered. "What a timely rain!"

Considering it prudent not to ask for too much, given my limited experience managing a plant, I replied, "1,450 yuan per ton, my standard and reasonable price."

"Alright, it's a deal. How much do you have?"

"Around four or five tons."

He confessed that they had just finished their meeting and had been worried about their shortage of plastic strips, which was solved by my offer. The next day, they would send a truck to pick up the goods from our plant. Besides, he shared a connection with Cicun Village — he had often visited our No.1 Coal Mine for business. He was acquainted with directors Zhao and Tang, as well as the Party Secretary of the plant office. Xu, the factory director, was frank and straightforward. The goods we had produced over the past four months were transported by two trucks and sold satisfactorily, alleviating the urgent need to sell them.

As the business of Tushan Plastic Factory drew to a close at the end of the year, Mr. Xu came to me because they planned to change their production line next year to reduce the use of plastic strips. It was time for me to prepare for the changes, as two more suppliers were involved, which would reduce their prices. While dining, I discussed our upcoming delivery with two drivers. We were not sure how much the prices had dropped. One thousand three hundred yuan per ton was a decent price. The situation had been bad since I took over the contract.

The two buyers showed up as soon as we returned to our rooms. Introducing themselves as Section Chief Bi and Deputy Section Chief Liu, respectively, from the Wendeng No. 5 Plastic Factory, it was clear that they were in urgent need from their tone. I emphasized that the goods sent to Tushan were not available to them.

Mr. Bi pleaded repeatedly, "Please give us first, then we'll negotiate deliveries in the future." He asked for a quote: "How about 1,500 yuan per ton?"

I had no idea whether they would accept my quotation, which was 200 yuan higher than the one for Tushan, equivalent to half a year's salary for the workers, who earned only around thirty yuan per month.

After a brief pause, he agreed, "All right, that is settled then. Your word is your bond."

I then admitted that the truck had broken down and could not reach Wendeng District, Weihai City. Mr. Bi agreed to inform the plant and send a truck the next day.

Mr. Bi went to the post office the following day to make a long-distance phone call. In those days, it might take one, even three or four, hours to be answered. Liu took us to unload the plastic strips at a nearby warehouse of a production team, as we were not concerned about losing them or being deceived this time. Then, we returned to our rooms to wait for Bi, who arrived around 10 o'clock, stating that a truck would pick up the plastic strips the next day at noon.

Having loaded the goods and had lunch, the truck driver departed. Bi explained that we still had over 200 kilometers to go to Wendeng. The winding mountain roads went up and down, so I had to remember the route clearly at every intersection that we turned in Laiyang in Yantai, passing Fengjia Town and Nanhuang Town in Rushan District, Weihai City, arriving at Zetoucun Village in Wendeng District, Weihai City, finally entering the gate of Wendeng No. 5 Plastic Factory after seven in the evening. When Bi sent me to a hotel, a huge burden was relieved.

Wendeng No. 5 Plastic Factory, operated by the Zetou Commune of Wendeng County, specialized in black plastic covering for unfired bricks. If we could not offer the plastic strips on time, they would have to halt production the day after tomorrow. Bi informed me that they needed at least two truckloads per month without limitation on the quantity after the settlement, from which a long-term business relationship was established. He took me to the bus station on his motorcycle, and there was a long-distance bus from Zetoucun Village to Yantai.

1.2 Delivering Goods to Zetoucun Village

Having unloaded the plastic strips from Zhuli Commune to Wendeng No.5 Plastic Factory, Bi asked me, "Do old plastic sandals belong to the raw materials for the production?"

I replied, "Yes, mostly they do, with a few soles."

"Please cut them off next time, and don't make them into strips," he said.

I could not understand his dialect.

"How to fire (sounds like cut in the dialect) them off?"

I repeated this three times, so he gestured how to cut a sandal in half from the middle, from heel to toe. Load them into a truck directly after washing; their price was the same as that of the processed ones, saving on electricity and labor costs.

The factory in Wendeng produced black plastic cloth to cover unfired bricks for other factories, which was cost-effective due to the use of waste plastic. Spring was the peak season for production, so Bi told us that regardless of when and how many we delivered to them, they would accept all of them.

Old sandals accounted for two-thirds of the raw materials used in the production of plastic strips. In contrast, the plastic soles of cloth shoes accounted for one-third of the total. Therefore, it could save a lot of time not to process sandals. The soles, made from recycled waste materials, contained many impurities and had to be processed through an extruder to filter out the substances and convert them into strips before being transformed into other products. It took us six days to return from Zetoucun Village, purchase sandals, and process the strips. Having collected more than three tons, we loaded them into a Jiefang truck. This four-ton truck could only carry just over three tons since the plastic occupied a large volume.

In 1982, there were no self-employed truck owners in the long-distance transportation industry. There was a transport fleet in the industrial office of the township consisting of two trucks: a light 130 model with a load capacity of two tons, and an old Jiefang model with a load capacity of four tons. Both trucks had to be scheduled three days in advance and assigned a date in sequence with their application.

At four in the afternoon, the truck arrived at the entrance to the galvanizing factory at the south end of a small alley in the east of the village. My plastic plant was located over 100 meters down the alley and accessible only by tractor, rather than truck, so we had to use trolleys to transport the goods out for loading.

Four trolleys were prepared, and all eight workers from the plant, two men and six women, helped. The females used trolleys to deliver goods outside, while the two male workers and I loaded them into the truck. It was strenuous, so two of us carried one bag and threw it into the truck, with one worker arranging it. After finishing the first tier, one person could complete the second. Still, when we reached the third, two people were needed to lift the bags onto the truck, with three people taking turns on and off the truck. By the fourth, a table was placed under the truck, and bags were moved onto it. We stood on the table with two people lifting it onto the truck. However, by the fifth, the driver shouted that it was too high and we should stop, but half a tier more was made as heavily pressed bags were distributed on the sixth. They took a bamboo pole to measure the truck, which was just within the limits. There were still a dozen bags left, though we had loaded three and a half tons of goods. It was six and dusk when the truck was fully loaded.

The truck reached the village's east side on time, as we had agreed to depart at six the next morning. Three of us, two drivers and I, squeezed into a narrow cab of an old Jiefang truck from the 1970s, a copy of a Soviet Gaz truck. Still, it was quite comfortable despite the chilly morning weather.

We drove through Zichuan District, heading east, passing Heiwang Town to the east of Zichuan, crossing the Zihe River, and exiting Miaozicun Village on a sandy road to Yidu (Qingzhou). There was a sign on the side of the road at Niujiaoling Ridge indicating a slow speed ahead due to road repair. The road was too narrow to allow two cars to pass each other in opposite directions. No cars were on the road except for two tractors coming from the opposite direction. There were seven or eight large bends, with half of the road being repaired to accommodate widening. Halfway through, we stopped to wait for tractors and bicycles every few meters, which made a twelve-minute journey into an hour. The same went for the road downhill after that, and it did not become smooth until we reached Wulitang Village.

After passing Yidu, the sun shone directly into the cab, and it was hot with three people squeezed together. I asked the driver to stop so that I could climb onto the truck and lie on the plastic bags, which were quite comfortable as a makeshift bunk. I did not know how far we had traveled and fell asleep in a daze. The truck shook and then came to a stop after a few creaks. I was unprepared for slipping off the bags and falling into a ditch on the side of the road, with only half a meter of loose soil covering its edge and bottom. Being young and agile, however, I was safe and sound. The driver repeatedly apologized for braking when he met another vehicle and made a turn. Luckily, it was a soil ditch because my arms would have been injured if it had been rocky. I returned to the cab and continued the journey, as it did not matter whether it was crowded or hot.

It was approximately 450 kilometers to the Zetou Plastic Factory. We planned to arrive there around nine or 10 in the evening. However, by the time we arrived in Laiyang, it was already past seven, as we had been delayed for an hour on the narrow road from Zichuan to Yidu. For a while, I fell into a ditch. We were going to find a hotel as the driver was tired, and there were still over 150 kilometers left. Upon entering Laiyang, we came across a hotel with a parking lot and a restaurant.

Accommodation registration was completed. There was a restaurant at the entrance of the courtyard.

A waiter warmly greeted us as we entered, asking, "How many of you are together?"

"Three," I replied.

"Please have a seat. Sorry, we have already run out of lard, so cooking dishes will be difficult."

I said quickly, "Why not use pork to replace it?"

"Sorry, there's no lard (pork) at all," she answered.

"Don't be silly! Just use peanut oil to replace lard," I said.

The waitress, in her twenties, seemed a bit flustered.

"I said there's no lard (pork)."

"I meant peanut oil," I clarified.

She finally understood and burst into laughter. It turned out that in their dialect, the pronunciation of "lard" is the same as "pork." We all laughed along and did not care too much. Therefore, we ordered scrambled eggs and stir-fried tofu rather than lard (pork) to mimic the Laiyang accent. In those days, the types of dishes available in restaurants were limited, mostly consisting of stir-fried dishes with pork and vegetables such as radishes, scallions, celery, and scrambled eggs, which were popular during the spring in eastern Shandong. As a result, repetition would often occur when ordering seven or eight dishes at once. They were mostly stir-fried with meat in times of meat shortage.

We arrived at the Zetou Plastic Factory at 10 o'clock the next day. The driver returned to Zichuan with the goods unloaded and the receipts finished. I stayed in a hotel, waiting to get the payment the next day.

There was only one Supply and Marketing Cooperative Hotel in Zetoucun Village, located at a three-way intersection. Wendeng No. 5 Plastic Factory was located approximately 100 meters to its left. In comparison, the bus station was situated approximately 200 meters to its right, offering a direct long-distance bus service to Yantai every day. A wholesale market was in front of it — no single or double rooms, just four-person ones.

As soon as I entered my room, a young man with a bag in his hand came in, asking talkatively, "Bro, where do you work?".

"I work in Zichuan Plastic Plant."

"What products do you produce?"

"Plastic strips."

"I'm at Luwang Plastic Plant in Yexian County, delivering goods to the No. 5 Plastic Plant. Was that your truck unloaded at noon today?"

"Yes, it was."

We found out we were colleagues, which bridged the gap. He introduced himself as a paid salesperson at a village-run plastic plant in Panjiacun Village, Luwang Township, rather than a contracted one. He was waiting for the payment for the plastic strips that had been delivered the previous day. By contrast, my company was registered in the name of a village-run plant as there were no individual owners at the time, and it was also difficult to believe in the existence of private plants.

In the afternoon, we strolled around. There was a free market on the street, with over a dozen stalls selling fish and vegetables and various marine products I had never seen before. Little Pan, one of my roommates, explained that those resembling large earthworms were called truly delicious sea worms, stir-fried with garlic chives. Those resembling small bamboo joints were named razor clams, which were quite tasty for soup or scrambled eggs. I also recognized the sea crab that I had eaten in 1975. I had had a stomachache all night from them, rushing to the toilet several times during the day after, so I felt nauseous when I saw them. He mentioned that in the 1970s, the crabs were no longer fresh due to the long transportation, so eating them by the sea with a few slices of ginger was better. Having asked about the price, he bought three jin for nine mao and brought them to the restaurant to eat with a drink after boiling them in the hotel.

Then, we ordered stir-fried pork with scallions and scrambled eggs with razor clams, accompanied by Penglaige Daqu, a famous Chinese baijiu from Yantai in the 1980s, along with crabs. Despite our first meeting, we had a heated and pleasant conversation from which I knew Little Pan had been doing business half a year longer than I. We had both had dealings with No.5 Plastic Plant in 1981. They now intended to produce polyethylene (PE) plastic strips, which differed from the polyvinyl chloride (PVC) plastic they had previously produced. He knew better than I because I could only tell the difference by their hardness. Zetou Plastic Plant was preparing to produce plastic barrels made from PE plastic, possibly to store a type of paint I was unfamiliar with. After drinking two liang (两 , a unit of weight equaling 50 grams), he was mostly drunk. At the same time, I had only drunk half a jin without finishing a bottle of that Baijiu. We kept chatting until midnight and then returned to our room to sleep. The next day, I took the long-distance bus from Zetoucun Village to Yantai at 1 p.m. I caught the train from Yantai to Jinan at 9 p.m. and arrived in Zhangdian District at 6 a.m. after receiving the payment.

1.3 Running into the Third Young Uncle Sun

The plastic fabric sheeting produced by Wendeng No. 5 Plastic Factory had a strong seasonal demand. The brick plant began producing unfired bricks in March 1982, with a daily output of thousands to tens of thousands of pieces. As the unfired bricks were produced, they were immediately covered with plastic fabric sheeting, which continued until the rainy season in July. In the year's second half, brick production decreased, so the brickyard did not purchase plastic fabric sheeting that could be used repeatedly. We did not need to deliver plastic strips to it until we were informed of the reduced demand for that plant, a sharp contrast with the abundant demand in spring. Hence, there had been no business for two months from August to the autumn harvest and wheat planting.

One day at noon, I was sowing wheat with a drill in the contracted fields in the village. My mother came to say that someone was looking for me. Since the wheat fields were at the edge of the village, it only took me a few minutes to get home. The man sitting in my mother's room was Elder Brother Jiang from the neighboring village, a friend I had known for years who sold electric fans at the fan plant. A few days before, while dining together, we had discussed the sales of plastic strips. I had asked him for help in inquiring about any plants that still required plastic strips, as we had not received an order from Wendeng in two months. Today, he came to me specifically for the sale of plastic strips. The day before, Jiang had gone to Boshan Department Store to deliver fans and learned that there were two plastic factories in Boshan, Zibo No. 3 and No. 9 Plastic Factories. He recommended the former as it was larger in scale and offered a variety of products.

It was time to serve superb baijiu since friends were paying a visit, so my mother prepared a selection of dishes to accompany it. Then, I showed him around my small plant, about thirty meters from my house. Diagonally opposite the main gate were the warehouses of the production team. My plant had initially occupied only two rooms, but it had now expanded to four on the west. The previous month, two warehouses had been removed, with a plastic extruder occupying one and a half rooms at the south end. The plastic strips produced were stored at the north end. They had now accumulated over two tons, as there had been no deliveries to Wendeng for two months, so I did not dare produce too much. Therefore, Jiang urged me to visit the Zibo No. 3 Plastic Plant the following day.

Zibo No. 3 Plastic Factory was located on Qinglong Mountain. From the train station iron bridge, heading east and climbing up the cliff, it was about 20 meters to arrive here. The office building was two stories high, with the purchasing and sales department on the second floor. After asking around, I learned that the factory had undergone reforms, with each workshop operating independently under the responsibility system, purchasing raw materials and selling products. The factory management was decentralized, and waste plastic was processed in the third workshop. The director of the workshop was Mr. Liu, and a female clerk from the purchasing and sales department provided an explanation of all the details.

The third workshop was in the southwest corner. I found director Liu sitting alone in the office. After greeting him, I introduced my product — plastic strips — the semi-manufactured goods made from old plastic sandals and discarded shoe soles.

"I heard from a friend that your factory needs them," I said as I handed him the plastic strips. Director Liu examined them for a while, then asked, "Are there any other types of waste plastic mixed in?"

"We only use these two types, nothing else; I guarantee my products," I replied. "In my workshop, we only use old sandals as raw materials. We haven't used this type of strip before, but as long as they are made from sandals and plastic shoe soles, there is no problem."

"Director Liu, what products do you produce?" I asked.

"We produce plastic pellets for shoe factories to make shoe soles," he explained.

I understood that the rubber shoe soles I purchased were made from these pellets. "Director Liu, we collect rubber shoe soles, remove the fabric, clean them, feed them into the plastic extruder, filter them, and turn them into strips, so our products are compatible with yours," I added.

Director Liu remained silent for a few minutes before saying, "It is worth considering and very compatible. We have only been producing this product for two months. The workers in state-owned enterprises are unwilling to wash waste shoes, and collecting them from the waste company is also a struggle for the sales staff. We are facing difficulties."

I began to speak, but director Liu said, "I can help you solve this problem using our strips directly."

While I was talking with director Liu, a chubby, dark-skinned young man in work clothes came in without greeting director Liu, sat in a chair on the side, and poured himself a glass of water.

Director Liu spoke to him first, "Master Sun, this is Factory director Yu, who came to discuss business."

Master Sun glanced at me, sat on the chair, and did not move. I quickly walked over to him and shook hands, and he remained seated, extending his hand and giving me a gentle shake without leaving the chair.

"Mr. Yu, which village are you from?" director Liu asked me.

"I'm from Baixicun Village, the Commune of Cicun Village," I replied.

At this point, Master Sun raised his head, staring at me with widened eyes.

"What's your name?" he asked.

"Yu Guotai," I answered. When I said my name, Master Sun stood up, walked over to me in two quick steps, and grabbed my hand.

"So you're Guotai! I remember your nickname, but I will not call it in front of director Liu," he said.

I stood up immediately, and we looked at each other.

I could not remember the familiar face in front of me, which was enthusiastic, smiling warmly, and looking at me kindly as the owner held my hand tightly.

"I'm your Third Young Uncle Sun — Little San! I used to take you to play on Xiyejie Street when you were little," he said.

Oh, I had some recollection. Little San was three or four years older than me, and I had not seen him for over 20 years.

So I said quickly, "I remember now, little San Young Uncle, and you used to teach me to play the gudang (鼓档 , a glass wind instrument that is popular with kids in the north of China)," I said. "Elder Uncle Yu is in good health, right? Retired now?" he asked.

"Yes."

"And Elder Brother Yu and Young Uncle Chen are still working in Shanghai?"

He continued to inquire while director Liu stared at the two of us, a look of dumbfounded astonishment on his face.

Uncle Sun was the son of our old landlord in Boshan. In the 1950s, my grandfather purchased glass products from Boshan and sent them to Shanghai. He set up an office in the Boshan District and rented rooms from Third Uncle Sun's house. After the Public-Private Joint Partnership reform in 1963, we moved away after more than 10 years of residence. Before attending school in the 1950s, I often lived in their house. Sun's house was on Houqigoujie Street, a small courtyard with an east-west orientation. Grandpa rented three rooms in the west and two in the east. The Sun family lived in the north, occupying a four-room house. On the west side were central rooms (a one-story Chinese traditional house consisting of several rooms in a row) with five steps, high and wide, while on the north side were wing rooms, short and narrow. Uncle Sun's father was the same generation as my grandfather, so I called him Grandpa Sun. When we lived there, the Sun family had three sons: the eldest had started working, the second was in middle school, and the third was in elementary school, three or four years older than I and very mischievous. When he came home from school, he would take me to play on the street, and I would call him Third Young Uncle, following the family tradition. He used to be skinny, but he was now chubby, so I did not recognize him. Without mentioning Baixicun Village, he did not pay attention to me, but when he heard my name, he recognized me. We had not been in contact for more than 20 years, and despite the short distance, meeting an old acquaintance in a strange place was unexpected.

Uncle Sun was a workshop salesperson and a truck driver responsible for purchasing raw materials, so my plastic strips were guaranteed to be of high quality. As we chatted more, we grew closer. I wanted to treat him to lunch, but Third Uncle Sun disagreed. He would invite me to Julecun Restaurant near his hometown. We used to go there for meals in our childhood.

We needed to sign contracts at the No. 3 Plastic Factory, specifically for the plastic strips business in the third workshop. The contract department of the state-owned enterprise was responsible for reviewing and approving contracts, then submitting and settling accounts. All procedures had been smooth over the past two months. We supplied four to five tons of plastic strips every month, using a small tractor to deliver them three times a month. With the help of the Third Young Uncle Sun, I saved much trouble in my business. Through this relationship, director Liu, the deputy director of the workshop, the technician, and the chairman of the trade union all took care of us. I could not delay any longer, so I needed to express my gratitude by inviting them to a big meal.

To the south of the No. 3 Plastic Factory on Wulongcun Street, a new restaurant was located, which held the first private business license in Boshan. With the reform and opening up policy, individuals were allowed to open restaurants. Young Uncle Sun arranged this meal, and I footed the bill. The restaurant had opened just a few days ago, run by a retired chef from Julecun Restaurant with his son. They followed the restaurant's culinary standards. They added a few traditional dishes, surpassing the quality of Julecun Restaurant, which had been in operation since the 1920s, ranking as Boshan's largest restaurant before 1949 and in the top three before the Cultural Revolution.

The guests who attended today included the director and the deputy director, the chief of the financial section at the factory, the director of the factory office, Third Young Uncle Sun, the technician, and me, totaling eight people. There was a tradition in Zibo of several hundred years, where eight people would sit at a square table with eight yuankui chairs (元奎椅 , a traditional wooden chair in ancient China), showing respect for their guests. The restaurant owner innovatively served set meals instead of allowing customers to order dishes individually. For fifteen yuan per table, we were served 10 dishes. They revived traditional dishes like stir-fried sea cucumber with scallions, braised pork intestines, sweet and sour carp, deep-fried pork, Boshan tofu box, stir-fried pork kidney, quick-boiled meatballs, stir-fried beef tendon, stir-fried pork slices, and boneless pork mixed with cucumber. There were six appetizers, including peanuts and pickled cucumbers. Since there were good dishes, we needed to pair them with a good wine, such as a bottle of Lanlingdaqu, a famous Chinese liquor from Lanling, for 3.60 yuan. We discussed many things while eating, and most of us had not eaten several of these famous dishes before, some of which existed before the Cultural Revolution but were done away with, along with the "Four Olds" (old thoughts, old customs, old habits, old traditions) during the 10 years of upheaval, when bourgeois lifestyles were eliminated in favor of mass culture. When I was young and lived on Houqigoujie Street, I often ate traditional dishes such as stir-fried sea cucumber with scallions with my grandfather. Still, I had long forgotten about it after 20 years, as I broadened my horizons.

We had a great time drinking and eating. Director Liu could no longer stand steadily.

Third Young Uncle Sun held my hand for over 20 minutes, repeatedly saying, "I am going to visit Elder Uncle Yu; I miss him. If Young Uncle Chen and Elder Brother Yu return from Shanghai, I have to see them. I miss them as well."

He stood rooted at the restaurant's entrance and repeated his words a dozen times, maybe more, my hands trapped in his like a vow. Deputy director Zhang and Technician Little Wang finally managed to pull Third Young Uncle Sun away, and I was able to break free.

That afternoon, director Liu asked me to come to his office after I had delivered the goods and settled the accounts. Only director Liu was there when I arrived, asking me for a favor. This year, the entire factory implemented the workshop contract system, and four people in the third workshop had formed a contract. They worked tirelessly, but only received a monthly salary of around 40 yuan. As to the year-end bonus, they dared not expect it. Therefore, the four of them decided to make some money through a trick by invoicing for more tons of plastic strips than were delivered, such as delivering one ton and invoicing for 1.2 tons, then collecting the extra payment, deducting the taxes, and finally, their workshop receiving the remaining cash. In this way, neither side suffered a loss.

I asked, "What if the factory found out?" It would be a hard cheese for everyone. Director Liu was confident, as he was very familiar with the factory's financial management. The factory only cared about the amount of money spent on purchasing materials. It did not keep track of the quantity. There were more than 20 types of materials, and the prices frequently fluctuated. For example, the price of one material could be 1,000 yuan per ton this month but might rise to 1,100 yuan next month. They would not be able to detect it from the accounts. They could distribute bonuses in advance by making some money in the workshop. We had achieved mutual trust with Third Young Uncle Sun's help, so this favor needed to be done. In comparison, choosing other suppliers would involve a risk. Director Liu had many ideas about dividing a few hundred yuan among the four contracting leaders without being noticed.

However, the good times did not last long. Half a year later, director Liu informed me that deputy Factory director Sun had brought someone from our neighboring village the previous day to promote plastic strips, offering a price that was 100 yuan lower per ton than mine. Since Sun was the deputy director in the first place and the second-in-command of No. 3 Plastic Factory, responsible for production technology, we must show him respect.

Upon investigation, I discovered that three months prior, Liu Bin from Lijiazhuang Village had bought a plastic extruder and partnered with two others. Pooling just 1,000 or 2,000 yuan, they could start production with a simple process and no technical skills. Many people in the countryside had nothing to do under the rural land contracting system. They rode bicycles around villages, collected waste plastic, washed it, and delivered it to their plant. Last year, he had to visit various waste collection stations to purchase waste sandals and plastic soles. Still, this year, he was receiving deliveries every day at the plant. He therefore only needed to focus on production and sales. Producing plastic strips was easy for clever ones like him, and No. 3 Plastic Factory was only 20 kilometers away. With the help of friends and relatives, he quickly found the deputy factory directors. Lowering the price helped sales, and with so many people in the countryside with free time and eagerness to earn money, he could not afford to lose out.

A few days later, I received more news. Little Lu from Majiazhuang Village had also bought a plastic extruder and was preparing to start production. Sun, the old friend who used to deliver old sandals to me, told me about it. They had already posted advertisements, offering five mao more per jin for old shoes than I did, with the sales target being No. 3 Plastic Factory.

When I went to No. 3 Plastic Factory, Third Young Uncle Sun helped me understand the situation. The third supplier trying to sell plastic strips was a small business owner surnamed Lu. He had connections with the Boshan District Committee. Lu had approached the deputy district chief in charge of industry. Then he contacted the factory director, the first in command of No. 3 Plastic Factory. They still had to purchase from him even if the same price was offered. The contracting leaders in the third workshop were also helpless.

As the year draws to a close, No. 3 Plastic Factory has finalized its operating plan for the upcoming year. They would cancel the workshop's contracted system and switch to the factory director's contracted system. Some people had raised concerns about loopholes in the workshop's contracted system. Therefore, there was no room for hesitation. They needed to seize the opportunity to change production, introduce new products, and develop high-tech products, leading the way in the reform.

1.4 Manufacturing Plastic Pellets

In 1982, with the rural reform, small workshops and plants sprang up like spring bamboo shoots after the rain. Within two to three years, they spread everywhere, although lacking technology and relying on simple processes. Products that required investments of only a few hundred or a few thousand yuan were fiercely contested.

With the addition of two suppliers of plastic strips to Zibo No. 3 Plastic Factory, the three plants were engaging in a price war and competing for orders, so I could not supply them all; if I did, all suppliers would suffer losses. Therefore, preparations were made for an immediate production change. I had met Little Pan in Zetoucun Village two months before, where I learned that the PE plastic strips they produced had a strong market demand and favorable prices. Since there were no producers in the Zibo area, I could not wait and immediately went to Yexian County to inquire about the market situation.

Little Pan sent a telegram to me, waiting for me at home. Little Pan lived in Panjiacun Village, Luwang Township. When I arrived there, it was already six o'clock in the evening. After dinner, Little Pan broke down the turbulent shifts in the PE plastic strips market over the past year — prices swinging like a pendulum, demand vanishing overnight.

According to Little Pan's description, they used to produce PVC plastic strips a few years ago at Panjia Plastic Plant, which is similar to the products sent to Wendeng No. 5 Plastic Factory. Last year, they switched to producing PE plastic strips, which sold well at around 1,500 yuan per ton. They purchased scrap plastic at 500 to 600 yuan per ton; after deducting impurities, wages, electricity costs, and other expenses, the profit per ton was around 400 to 500 yuan. It made me excited, and my heart was racing with anticipation. PE plastic strips were used to produce paint buckets, and paint was a high-end product that had just entered the domestic market. Its demand would multiply by tens in the next few years. This type of strip was not only used to produce this particular type of bucket, but it could also be used as a raw material for various plastic buckets, meeting high social demand. The waste plastic bags and plastic film used to produce these plastic strips were everywhere, and the purchase prices were low. We could purchase them at 400 yuan per ton in areas like Zibo. After discussing it all night, we visited the Panjia Plastic Plant the next day to learn about the situation on-site.

Early the next morning, Little Pan came to pick me up on his Dajinlu bicycle, also known as the Golden Deer 28-inch bicycle, which was designed for males. The small plastic plant was three huali (华里 , a unit of distance equal to 0.5 kilometers) away from the hotel, located in a small courtyard. Upon entering the gate, a pile of plastic film waste was visible in the middle of the courtyard, approximately three to four meters high, with three workers collecting and packing the waste plastic from the ground into woven bags. Little Pan quietly explained the process to me: the sorted plastic was pushed to the wheat field on the right, washed clean, dried, and then moved back to their courtyard. He led me into the workshop, where there were three plastic extruders. Beside each machine were two workers grabbing washed waste plastic bags and film, and stuffing them into the machine with a small wooden stick. The extruded strips were about one meter long, and when pulled with force, they would stretch into a single strand, which was then laid on the ground. About 20 strands were bundled together, cooling down to a hardness similar to wood. The PE strips were soft, similar to belts. With the original extruder, the output per time was only half of the PVC plastic strips. I understood the process clearly and decided to start production immediately upon my return.

My small plastic plant consisted of a small courtyard with four rooms in the west wing and an office for the production team. The four rooms in the north wing were used for the production team's noodle-making workshop. My family lived in the rooms on the south and east sides of the building. The square courtyard was identical to that of the Panjia Plastic Plant.

Within a 5-kilometer radius of the surrounding villages, notices were posted for the purchase of waste plastic film and bags at three fen (0.1 mao) per jin. In just a few days, some people brought dozens of jin of waste plastic by bicycle. From then on, waste plastic was delivered every day. Within dozens of li, we became the first to purchase waste plastic film that had previously been discarded. In just over a month, the waste plastic in the courtyard had accumulated into a small mountain. The caretaker estimated that it amounted to over three tons.

Cleaning the plastic film was labor-intensive. It was transported to the river north of the village on a cart, washed, dried, and then brought back. Four workers could wash 200 jin in a full eight-hour shift.

After washing for over a month, Elder Uncle Wang, who grew vegetables by the river, came politely one day to say, "Child, you wash the plastic film upstream, and I water my cucumbers and eggplants downstream. This morning, many of them died. A few cucumber plants dying is no big deal, but if the fish and shrimp are poisoned, it's a serious issue, especially since people eat them. You can't wash plastic film in the river anymore."

I asked the workers who washed the plastic film. They had collected bags of raw materials from the pesticide factory, so they contained pesticides. They put them into the river to wash. The smell was strong, so I had to find a solution for washing the plastic film.

A well was dug in the courtyard to address the issue of disposing of waste plastic. Professional well diggers in the countryside would dig a well every three days. A bricklayer was hired to build a water tank, making it convenient and efficient to wash in the courtyard. However, another problem emerged: there was not enough space to dry the washed plastic, so it had to be taken to the wheat field for drying. When spreading the plastic out in the wheat field, the workers gave it a turn with a wooden stick. With a gust of wind, it scattered all around, prompting a chase and scramble for the two people trying to gather it, keeping them busy. Many pieces of plastic were blown away with wind speeds reaching force five or six on the Beaufort scale.

We still used the machine that processed plastic shoe soles to clean the plastic film and plastic bags. The plastic shoes were thick, and one worker sitting beside the machine slowly fed them in quite easily. On the contrary, processing plastic film and plastic bags required a two-person operation beside an extruder. One worker grabbed a large handful of them, which was not very heavy, with one hand and fed them into the hopper with the other, using a wooden stick to press them in. The two workers took turns, with one persisting until one bag was done, and then the second brought another bag. The extruded plastic strips were very light, weighing about half as much as those made with sandals. The output per shift was half of what it used to be with the original plastic strips, but despite the decrease in output, the price per ton of plastic strips increased three to four times.

After producing three tons of plastic strips, we sent them to Wendeng No. 5 Plastic Factory in a hurry. It had been over a year since we last did business with them, and Section Chief Bi was still in charge of procurement.

After unloading, Bi asked me when we settled the account, "Do you know the price?"

"I told you it was 1,450 yuan per ton over two months ago."

"Brother Yu, the market changes quickly and has dropped to 1,300 yuan per ton. If you are not a regular customer or friend, we will not accept the goods unless you contact us in advance to arrange payment. The warehouse is already overflowing with plastic strips."

I understood. It could not be compared to my first year of delivering. A year had passed, and prices were bound to change.

Bi was very polite, and as he saw me off from the office, he reiterated, "Make sure to contact us in advance for the next delivery."

Returning from Wendeng, I learned that a plastic products factory in Xintai County used strips like mine. I therefore took a bus from Cicun Village to Boshan, then transferred to a long-distance bus to Laiwu, which is currently a district under the jurisdiction of Jinan. Finally, I changed to another bus bound for Xintai. The country welcomed me with a sun already bruised purple, the kind of lateness that whispers you should not have come. The plastic factory was located in the suburbs, with a quaint name, Dongdongzhou, whose origin was unknown. There were no buses or three-wheeled taxis; only No. 11 bicycles were available, which meant walking on foot, a process that took over 40 minutes. Arriving at the purchasing department of the factory, I learned that the price of plastic strips was 1,260 yuan per ton, which was even lower than in Wendeng. This trip had been in vain, though, since they would not buy goods for the next two months.

The market changed too fast to keep up. In the first two years of rural reform, costs were rarely calculated; whether one earned more or less, there was always a profit to be made. By the end of 1984, without meticulous accounting, losses were inevitable. Since PE production had been ongoing for several months, it was time to calculate the profits.

When receiving a large amount of plastic, the caretaker placed it in a separate location and began sorting, removing various unusable waste plastics such as PVC and polystyrene, as well as items like boxes and bottles. This was necessary because some unscrupulous vendors would bundle the plastic together with a stone or brick in the middle. After sorting, washing, and drying, about 130 jin would be lost. By regulating the material receiving process, we unpacked large and small bundles, as well as big and small packages of waste plastic brought by vendors. We then sorted, packed, and weighed the plastic on-site, which significantly reduced the cost of a portion of the process.

Washing the waste plastic was no longer a collective effort; wages were paid based on the amount of waste plastic collected. One small pond was allocated for washing, with workers taking turns to wash and dry their respective portions. It reduced the previous cost by more than half.

I added another extruder, making it two machines with three workers. The price of waste plastic dropped by 100 yuan per ton. Overall, the cost decreased by over 260 yuan per ton. Even with the decrease in market prices, a profit was still made.

The number of people delivering waste plastic increased monthly, expanding to four or five surrounding townships, with the price dropping from three to two mao per jin. In the cotton-producing area of Huimin County under the jurisdiction of Binzhou, they promoted plastic film technology. After harvesting the cotton, they collected the waste plastic film. The plastic film in the 1980s was two to three times thicker than the film from a decade later. It folded into large pieces, measuring between 2 and 3 meters or 4 and 5 meters in length. They obtained our information, contacted us, brought samples, and offered the waste plastic film at 1.5 yuan per jin, 300 yuan per ton. This type of plastic film, made from homogeneous material, came in large pieces. In contrast, the plastic bags we usually collected came in various sizes and colors, making them troublesome to wash. Therefore, we no longer accepted waste plastic bags from vendors; instead, we collected their plastic film waste for recycling.

Within half a month, they had brought over five tons of used plastic film by four tractors. When they had brought the samples two weeks prior, they mentioned that the plastic film inevitably carried some dust, so they deducted 50 jin of dust per ton. They picked up a few sheets of plastic film from the tractor, shook them, and found no dust. After washing and drying 200 jin of film, we weighed it again and were surprised to find it only weighed 168 jin, with 32 jin of dust removed. Buying was thus not as profitable as selling all the time.

As the price of waste plastic decreased, so did the plastic strips, dropping to 1,100 yuan per ton. After using this plastic film, another month passed, and we posted a notice to continue collecting waste plastic at the same price. After advertising for over 10 days, however, no one came to deliver. I visited the homes of a few regular customers to inquire, only to find that before our factory had stopped accepting waste plastic, two new plastic plants had opened in Lingzizhen Town, under the jurisdiction of Linzi District, Zibo, in the nearby market area. They feared they could not collect enough waste plastic, so they increased the price by two mao per jin. The raw material price, therefore, remained the same despite the decrease in product price. What should we do?

A new situation arose: the clever young people no longer collected discarded plastic on the streets, but instead went to plastic product factories to collect the leftover materials, and to factories to collect plastic packaging bags. These waste materials did not require washing and were almost as good as new plastic raw materials, producing transparent and shiny strips of high quality, but the price could not be increased. In previous years, this plastic had been sold to waste companies, and state-owned enterprises did not negotiate prices; nobody cared whether they were selling more or less. However, over the past one or two years, with the market opening, many people had begun buying waste materials from factories, turning large factories into cash cows, which had driven the price of waste materials higher and higher. According to inside sources, the market for collecting waste plastics from large factories was promising, with much more volume than collecting from the streets and alleys. We needed to find ways to improve product quality and increase the prices of our products. Talking to several young people who collected waste plastic from factories, we shared the same opinion. They gave me ideas and suggested developing this market segment.

Five or six communes in the area had disbanded their production teams. My plant was the first to process products made from waste plastic, thus setting the standard. Over the past two years, the waste plastic market had entered a period of intense competition. In this period, we could not afford to lose battles and rely solely on strength;

we must free our minds, broaden our horizons, and seek new products.

It had been over six months since our last business with Zibo No. 3 Plastic Factory. It was time to visit some old friends and learn about product information. There was quite a coincidence when I went there that day: Director Liu, Third Young Uncle Sun, and Salesperson Little Wang were all in the office of the third workshop. After a brief discussion, lunchtime arrived unnoticed. We gathered around a large table, catching up on personal matters and discussing products.

They mentioned that Zibo No. 3 Plastic Factory had launched a new major product: high-end sponges for sofas, produced by foam machines imported from West Germany. They were currently debugging the machines and would soon start production. They had also introduced a minor product, the household plastic water pipes made from plastic pellets produced by Sinopec Qilu Petrochemical Company. Since the second half of last year, the price of plastic raw materials had increased. Plastic water pipes from south of the Yangtze River had entered the Zibo market, undercutting the prices of plastic pipes produced in the north. It was reported that small private factories located south of the Yangtze River mixed waste plastic with raw materials during the production of plastic water pipes, thereby reducing the cost of raw materials while maintaining a similar quality of the finished product.

Upon hearing this, I became excited and immediately interjected, "What about using the new leftover materials — large plastic bags that haven't been exposed to sunlight or dust — to make pellets?"

He answered affirmatively, "You can select large packaging bags that have only been used once, free from water and dust. The pellets made from these new leftover materials are slightly inferior in quality to new pellets, but can still be used."

"I have a source for obtaining leftover materials: large plastic bags. Is it difficult to produce pellets from them?" I inquired.

"Not difficult," director Liu replied with an expression indicating that the process was not too challenging.

Continuing the conversation, I explained the production of PE plastic strips over the past six months. The process was simple, requiring only one extruder, but there was almost no profit. I had already considered giving up the production of plastic strips. Currently, I had not explored any new products. Director Liu then asked about the market situation for purchasing large packaging bags. I estimated that purchasing four to five tons per month was no problem.

"That can be done," a confident director Liu replied. "I have learned that there are no factories in several surrounding counties that use waste plastic to produce pellets."

Salesperson Little Wang interjected, having traveled extensively around Shandong Province for business and being very familiar with the plastic market.

"That's great. Where can we find technicians or engineers?" I asked director Liu.

Director Liu smiled, "There is someone with the same surname as you, Engineer Yu. He is an undergraduate and very proficient in plastic machinery and processing. Yu has visited many plastic factories across the country. He has a good character and is willing to lend a hand. You can pay him a fee for his assistance, and he'll be able to help on a weekend."

That was fantastic news. After thinking about a new product for two or three months without any progress, there was finally some progress by accident. That day, I did not come to seek a product specifically but to see old friends and relax. How fortunate!

"Director Liu, let's have a drink. Young Uncle Sun, let's have a drink."

I was delighted, but I drank too much and could not return home, so I stayed at a hotel.

The next day, I met Engineer Yu in the second-floor office of No. 3 Plastic Factory. Introduced by director Liu, we had the opportunity to get to know one another. I discussed in detail my ideas about producing pellets, the source of raw materials, factory buildings, and machinery.

After listening, Engineer Yu confidently said, "It can be done. I have seen pellet machines in both large and small plastic factories. With a few modifications, using leftover materials will work well. It can be done."

We agreed to visit my plant's workshop and plastic extruders next Sunday and design the production process.

On Sunday, Engineer Yu visited the workshop and inspected the extruders. The workshop was 10 meters long, consisting of three rooms, with enough space for our layout. Three extruders were needed, two for the first pass and one for the second, to extrude materials into strips and cut them into pellets. However, only two extruders were available, so another one needed to be acquired. Engineer Yu promised to devise a design plan promptly and contact a mold factory to produce the strip die. The extruded plastic strips were to resemble noodles in shape. Engineer Yu was familiar with the mold factory and urged me to purchase another extruder.

The standard plastic extruder, the minimum size available from a manufacturer in Laiwu, was priced at 13,000 yuan. Still, there was not enough funding to purchase it. I was unable to find a manufacturer that produced machines for extruding waste plastic. The first extruder we used was self-made by the commune's plastic factory, and the second one was made by a local locksmith based on a rough sketch. Then, I purchased steel pipes from a trailer yard in Boshan, made a screw barrel at the Kunlun Dong Fang Hong Factory with the help of a classmate, crafted a screw shaft at a coal machine factory, and acquired a gearbox from a motor factory in Boshan through an acquaintance, all of which cost over 2,000 yuan. The manufacturing method of the second extruder, with a larger size of two cun (寸, 1 cun equals 3.3 centimeters), followed the same process as before.

The production process designed by Engineer Yu involved aligning two extruders side by side, with their outlets facing the third extruder. The extruded strips from the first two machines would directly enter the third extruder, which would then extrude them into strips through the grinding head, similar to noodles. The thin strips would then enter a water trough over three meters long for cooling before being fed into a pelletizer to be cut into pellets the size of mung beans. After finishing the design for the pelletizer, Engineer Yu headed to the tool factory to make the cutting tools.

Engineer Yu explained the operation steps to us, emphasizing that the two aligning extruders would operate simultaneously for the first pass. Due to uneven feeding caused by waste plastic, the output from two machines ensured a consistent supply of thick strips, which the third machine then used to produce thin strips. The water temperature in the trough should not have exceeded 70 degrees Celsius, with water continuously being added to maintain the desired temperature. If the temperature of the plastic strips was too high, they could not be cut into pellets. Three to four sets of cutting tools for pellets needed to be prepared, with changes made three or four times per shift and tools sharpened as needed. Engineer Yu gave us a detailed explanation.

Despite thorough planning, challenges arose along the way. The Coal Mine Factory fabricated the shafts, the Dong Fang Hong General Factory fabricated the drums, and the Boshan Factory processed the die heads. The pelletizer was small but complete in parts, which needed the reducer, grinder roll, and cutting blade. I found seven or eight processing factories. In the 1980s, individual and commune factories were not qualified to process metals, so we all depended on the state-owned factories. A state-owned factory had multiple standards. First, we needed to obtain approval from the factory director, arrange things with the workshop director, and request that technicians review the drawings. Then the work, which usually should be finished in one day, would be delayed for three days. Actually, it would be good if the work were completed within a week. Nonetheless, the mechanical setup of the pelletizer was eventually completed after two months, which we had planned to accomplish in one month.

After the mechanical setup was completed, Engineer Yu took a day off to supervise the production. With the highest-quality raw materials, the extruded plastic strips closely resembled those produced by a noodle machine, meeting the highest standards. After cooling in the trough, the strips were rolled onto a turntable that was as thick as the diameter of a bowl and fed into the pelletizer to be cut into individual pellets. The cutting blade operated when there were many strips on the turntable and stopped when there were fewer. The trial production on the first day was successful, producing over 20 kilograms of pellets. Continuing on the second day, Engineer Yu stayed overnight to personally instruct us on how to operate the machines. Over 50 kilograms of pellets were produced on the second day, and they were slightly yellowish compared to the original pellets. With this production method, they could fetch a good price on the market.

Based on Engineer Yu's design, each shift could produce over 100 kilograms, producing a monthly output of three to four tons. They already had three tons of raw materials in stock, enough for one month's production. With these two products, another extruder was planned for extruding waste strips at full capacity. At that time, it was the largest waste plastic processing plant in four or five townships.

There had been frequent power outages this year, although not too often; sometimes, though, they occurred once every three to five days. When we started producing pellets in those days, there were power outages every day, with no notification, set time, or pattern — they just stopped when they wanted to and came back on when they wanted to. Sometimes, the power went out at eight and came back on at nine. Sometimes, it would go out at 10 and come back on at ten-thirty. Workers would work for half an hour, then the power would go out. Then they waited half an hour for it to come back on, but sometimes they waited an hour, and it did not come back on until the workers had just gone home.

Power outages had a significant impact on plastic processing, particularly during the winter months. The plastic extruder's plastic was heated to 80 or 90 degrees. However, the plastic cooled down in the machine if the power went out. It was slightly reheated and continued to produce after over 10 minutes or half an hour. If there were a power outage for an hour, the temperature would drop. When the extruder was restarted, it took half an hour to heat up again. If the power went out once a day at noon, they could manage to keep working, but if it went out twice, they could not continue.

The pelletizing process designed by Engineer Yu was successful, offering the potential for increased production capacity. He installed another gearbox based on the feed rate, increasing production by thirty percent. With two extruders operating side by side, there was a surplus of thirty percent in the extruded strips. He also planned to install a larger extruder set to achieve a monthly output of 10 tons. Plans might change, but adaptation might not, as unpredictable power outages could disrupt production schedules.

A visitor arrived one day while I was drinking tea in the office. Judging by his appearance, he was from the south.

"What's your last name, my boss?" he asked.

There was no specific term for "boss" in the north.

"My last name is Yu. May I ask which company you're from?"

"Rui'an Plastic Weaving Factory in Wenzhou."

"I haven't heard of Rui'an, but I know Wenzhou."

After a brief exchange, I invited the visitor to sit down.

"It is a county next to Wenzhou in Rui'an City. According to a friend's introduction, you produce pellets here."

"The output is small."

"May I have a look?"

"Of course."

Communicating in Mandarin seemed laborious for the man from Wenzhou, with each word carefully pronounced. We did not talk much, and I led him to the workshop to inspect the pellets stored there, which were not in a separate warehouse.

Over 10 bags of pellets, weighing less than half a ton, were stored in the corner of the wall. Upon arriving in the workshop, Rui'an's friend picked up a bag of pellets and exclaimed, "These look great! How much are they?"

"2,200 yuan." I gestured with two fingers.

"I'll take them all."

"I'm sorry, they're already sold."

"Can we make a deal for future production? The price is

negotiable."

I ignored his request, as the production capacity could not meet demand due to power outages. There were also several bags of unprocessed downstream materials stacked in the corner.

He noticed them and asked, "Are these the raw materials for making pellets?"

"Yes, they are."

He scooped up a handful from the bag, looked closer, and asked, "How many do you still have?" "Over two tons."

"Can I buy them at the same price as the pellets?"

"Of course," I replied, feeling pleased, though I couldn't immediately answer and stalled for a moment. "Our regular customer urgently needs pellets, and a contract has already been signed."

"How about this? I'll pay an extra 200 yuan for freight, and you were responsible for sending them by train."

"Let's discuss it back in the office."

I could not agree immediately. After dawdling for half an hour, we signed the agreement. Three days later, the goods were collected from the plant, and payment was made. I was responsible for delivering them by train.

Back in the day, if we wanted to deliver goods by train but did not have connections or know someone important, our goods would not go anywhere. Once, I reached out to my old classmate, a former Red Guard comrade from the Cultural Revolution era, who was now a team leader at the Boshan Freight Station, to handle a shipment for me. I contacted him a day in advance, specifying what goods were to be sent, the receiving station, and confirming the time. The tractor arrived at the freight yard, and the goods were repackaged and weighed. The entire process was completed in under an hour. The small business owner from Wenzhou was very satisfied, and we agreed that they would take all the materials left.

An issue with an unstable power supply arose, causing us to cease production of plastic pellets due to increased orders from the Wenzhou client.

The production process for waste plastic was straightforward, and the raw materials were readily available, however. Several nearby villages set up processing plants, but the profit margin was less than 5 percent. The labor intensity was high, and the work was dirty and tiring. Unable to continue, they sought new products, abandoning the waste plastic processing industry.

Waste plastic processing lasted for three years and ten months for me, from January 1982 to October 1985, during which I produced PVC strips, PE strips, and pellets. Three years after I switched production, waste plastic processing took off in 1988. A plant in Shanghai had developed specialized machinery for processing waste plastic. After cleaning the waste plastic, it did not require drying. Still, it went directly from the water tank to the extruder and was cut into pellets directly from the die head. Production increased four to five times, and the number of processing plants increased to dozens. Waste plastic was imported from abroad and transported to various processing plants from Tianjin Port and Qingdao Port, becoming a major local industry. Following the tightening of environmental regulations in 2010, the cleanup of waste plastic processing plants was postponed until 2015. However, that was a story for another time, a mere insignificant page in history.

1.5 Being Rich and Glorious by Labor

In 1981, before the autumn harvest, the district government in Zibo convened a meeting called the "Three Cadres Meeting" (cadres from the production team, Commune, and District) to convey the content of the document on contracted fields in rural areas. It seemed somewhat sudden, with no public opinion before the meeting. Many years later, it was revealed in articles that the central leadership had been debating for over a year whether to continue along the old path, reserving people's communization, or to distribute land to households. In the end, the facts in the countryside spoke for themselves. For Anhui

Province and Sichuan Province, after over 20 years of insufficient grain production, every household now had a surplus of grain due to land distribution for just one year.

The "Three Cadres Meeting" of the Commune of Cicun Village was held in the commune's auditorium (cinema) and lasted two days. They studied Vice Chairman Deng Xiaoping's speeches and central documents, clarifying the theme: it was not to dissolve production teams, but to distribute responsibility fields and contract land to individuals. After planting responsibility fields, free operation and a free market were allowed. People could engage in handicrafts and grow some cash crops. Production would no longer be organized by production teams, allowing individuals to have complete control over their labor.

In 1982, the countryside underwent many new changes. Bricklayers organized spontaneously to build houses in the countryside. Each artisan earned 1.2 yuan per day, while helpers earned 0.8 yuan per day. Carpenters, meanwhile, made furniture to be sold at markets. Several people organized factories to roast melon seeds. Some even traveled to Guangzhou and Zhejiang to sell electronic watches. Within a year, there were households with an annual income of 10,000 yuan, an astronomical figure at the time. Workers' wages were around 30 yuan per month for over 20 years, unimaginable since the industrial and commercial reforms and the people's communication in 1958. In just one year, the land remained unchanged, and the old houses and streets in the countryside remained intact; however, the people's spirits had changed significantly in that short time. They walked faster, spoke more forcefully, and dressed more stylishly.

In January 1983, the Party Committee and the People's Government of Zichuan District convened a grand meeting to promote diligence and prosperity in the countryside, creating momentum and public opinion for a wave of hard work and wealth.

Each village recommended candidates in two categories: those from households with an annual income of 5,000 yuan and those from households with an annual income of 10,000 yuan or more. The

Commune of Cicun Village selected two 10,000-yuan households and ten 5,000-yuan households. There were dozens of such households, many of whom hid their wealth, still apprehensive.

The Commune of Cicun Village dispatched a double-row truck, with the Party Secretary of the commune and the director sitting in the driver's seat. In contrast, the delegates sat in the rear cargo area. Another Jiefang truck carried the secretaries and directors of the villages. They left at noon and attended a three-day conference after arranging accommodations in the Zichuan District. The delegation from Cicun Village stayed at the Traffic Hotel, which was east of the Zhangdian-Boshan Expressway.

The conference opened grandly in the district auditorium, with the deputy Secretary of the Municipal Party Committee, the deputy director, and all the district leaders seated in two rows. The meeting, which had been expected to last a day, continued for two and a half days.

After the Secretary of the Municipal Party Committee had delivered reports, most of the time was spent on delegate speeches, sharing experiences in becoming prosperous. The first speaker was a young woman in her twenties from Erlicun Village Commune who had taught herself sewing techniques. She made pants at home first, starting by herself and selling a dozen pairs at the market, which sold very well. Later, she bought three sewing machines and hired a few female workers. They could make over a dozen pairs of pants daily, selling them at stalls at the Xiguan Bridge market in Zichuan District. They sold out every day. Therefore, they expanded production, adding over 10 sewing machines, and the workforce grew to over 20, enabling them to produce more than 2,000 pairs a month, which were sold to Jinan and Tai'an. They earned over 15,000 yuan a year, probably even more, but she did not want to say too much.

Other speakers included a tractor driver who plowed the fields during the farming season and used transportation during the off-season, loading stones, bricks, and coal, earning over 20 yuan a day. A repairman also opened a shop to repair bicycles and wooden carts, employing one or two assistants and earning between 500 and 600 yuan a month. Individuals opened grocery stores selling tobacco, alcohol, sugar, tea, and daily necessities. They were already allowed to run shops independently, no longer under the sole control of supply and marketing cooperatives. The grocery store owner said he had earned barely 3,000 yuan instead of the expected 5,000 yuan this year. The Party Secretary of the commune came to visit, asking him to explain how he coped with the pressure and managed the meeting procedures. He was one of the first batch of individual retail points to obtain business licenses in Zichuan District. It served as an example to guide rural small business owners and revitalize the economy. It was no longer engaged in speculation and profiteering because the government provided strong support.

The next day, the delegates were divided into discussion groups. Over 40 people from the Commune of Cicun Village squeezed into a small conference room in the auditorium.

Secretary Jia of the commune began by saying, "The purpose of this meeting is to make everyone understand that Vice Chairman Deng's call for some people in the countryside to get rich first is completely correct. The 'big pot' distribution system and egalitarianism can only hinder the development of productivity and are not true socialism. We must take a socialist path with Chinese characteristics. Distributing land to households has transformed our rural areas in just one year. Every household has surplus grain and money. The enthusiasm of the masses has been mobilized. Everyone keeps a sense of competition. They will also strive to be rich if others get rich. All of them get rich together. Use your brains to think of ways to make money."

Secretary Jia's words were down-to-earth, and everyone felt relieved and confident after this meeting. They were not afraid of being accused of practicing capitalism.

"Comrades, move forward boldly and confidently. The good days are still ahead of us," Secretary Jia added.

After Secretary Jia finished speaking, the applause lasted a long time, emanating from the heart of the audience and being much stronger than at previous meetings.

Representatives at the conference gave speeches, including Master Zhang, who repaired bicycles and was also the head of a household worth 10,000 yuan in Cicun Village. He was the first to give a speech, introducing a method for earning money over the year. Initially, he opened a bicycle repair shop, which had limited success. He broadened his thinking: bicycles were difficult to buy at the time, and could be purchased with industrial product coupons. Therefore, he assembled bicycles by seeking personal connections because buying parts is easier than buying a whole bicycle. He asked a friend to buy a bicycle frame from Boshan District, asked his relatives to buy wheels from Zhoucun District, and bought tires from Hongshan Town, Zichuan District. It required him to purchase all the bicycle parts from more than 10 places. He assembled a bicycle and sold it for over 30 yuan higher than the market price. Besides, he also took over assembling bicycles in the Supply and Marketing Cooperative, earning more than 10 yuan as a result. The Supply and Marketing Cooperative workers had secure jobs, and no one wanted to work more. He learned to repair motorcycles and tractors, and he developed a comprehensive repair shop by repairing bicycles, hiring five workers, and earning over 10,000 yuan a year, which truly made his a 10,000-yuan household in Cicun Village.

CHAPTER 2
SOARING OF THE SWAN WASHING MACHINE

2.1 Getting Started with Coatings

Business at Wendeng Plastics No.5 Factory came to a halt. Several small factories producing polyethylene plastic strips had sprung up near Zetou (a town under Wendeng District, Weihai City), engaging in fierce price competition, so I decided to withdraw. There were still over 5,000 yuan in outstanding payments, which Section Chief Bi promised to settle in full.

As I exited Bi's office, someone called from behind, "Elder Brother Yu! Elder Brother Yu!"

Turning around, I saw Little Pan from Yexian County (now known as Laizhou County) running over.

"Are you still delivering goods?" I asked him.

"A delivery came yesterday, just settled the accounts," he responded as we walked out while chatting. "Have you seen the plastic barrels produced by this factory?" Little Pan suddenly asked.

"I've been delivering plastic strips for over half a year and haven't seen their products."

"Let me take you to have a look," Little Pan suggested, turning right, and I followed, heading toward the last workshop of the factory. Inside were two blow molding machines, which produced blow-molded square-shaped plastic barrels, similar to oil drums, as well as round barrels. He picked up one of the round barrels and said, "These are used to hold something called coating; the coatings just hit the market a few years ago."

After inspecting these barrels, we headed out.

We bumped into section chief Bi at the gate; he was going to the town to do some shopping. Little Pan and I returned to the hotel together.

As we chatted along the way, I asked Bi, "What are the uses of coatings in your company's barrels?"

"They're called wall coatings and are used for painting rooms. Spread from abroad, it is similar to paint. It gives the walls a smooth and bright finish. Thus, in the future, it will be used for painting both the interior and exterior of houses. The hotel where you two are staying was painted last month, and it's already being used in cities."

After a few minutes of conversation, we arrived at the hotel entrance; Bi went to the shop, and Little Pan and I went inside the hotel.

Walking through the hotel's corridor, the bottom part of the wall, one meter high, was painted apple green, while the upper part, two meters high, was creamy white. The newly painted coating looked beautiful. I repeatedly touched it with my hands, feeling its smoothness, which was almost like that of a piece of glass.

I had known Little Pan for over two years; we were both peers and friends. He had helped me start the polyethylene plastic strip business. We had not seen each other for over half a year, so we had a few drinks at noon. As we discussed all my twists and turns and tough challenges over the past six months, the more we chatted, the more excited we became. Little Pan's start of the polyethylene strip business was smooth, but its shutdown was swift. In the first few months of collecting waste plastic, we lacked experience, which led to us being deceived by petty dealers, resulting in many impurities. After repeated hassles with things like washing plastics, we did not earn much money by the year-end settlement, despite the business having seemed very profitable beforehand. Sorting out the waste plastic and getting into production had proceeded smoothly enough. However, as external sales began to pick up, the market changed drastically, and prices plummeted. Switching to plastic pellets also went smoothly with the help of a benefactor. Unexpectedly, though, we were now struggling due to the power supply issues. The waste plastic business was dirty and exhausting, and I did not plan to continue in it. What product should I pursue next? Where should I search for it? Searching for a product with a long market lifetime, one could not quit after a year or two; the uncertainty was unsettling. Little Pan was a salesperson who received a salary and had little resonance. My experiences over the past two years felt like a fairy tale to him.

He kept persuading me, "Elder Brother Yu, where there's a will, there's a way. The road gets wider as you go, and success lies in human effort, overcoming all odds."

My heartfelt words moved him to have three drinks. Little Pan could not hold his liquor well, so his speech became slurred, but his mind remained clear.

"Elder Brother Yu, whatever product you want to pursue, I'll help. I'll give you a hundred percent support, no more outsourcing semi-finished products, it's too restrictive."

"Younger brother Pan, I want to switch to another product to expand, but where do I look? I can't find anything!"

"I'll help you find it, help you get into it; I'm not drunk; these are my true feelings."

Little Pan became more spirited as he spoke; he could not drink or eat. Back at the hotel, Little Pan stood up, swaying to the door, one hand holding onto the door, the other touching the wall several times, saying, "The hotel was painted recently, right? Elder Brother Yu, we have a product now; let's produce paint; the paint market is huge, it's massive."

Looking at Little Pan, looking at the paint on the wall, emboldened by alcohol, I agreed to Little Pan's suggestion without hesitation.

"Younger brother Pan, let's start producing coating; let's do it."

Back in the hotel room, sitting on the bed, speaking my mind freely, starting a coating production business was still just a thought. Little Pan sat on the chair drinking water, suddenly stomped his foot, slapped his thigh, and jumped up.

"We've got it, we've got it, Brother Yu, you've inspired me; I remembered something; it seems our communal Chemical Machinery Factory produces coating equipment; I'll go back and ask."

"The sooner, the better."

A few days later, I received a letter from Little Pan in which he mentioned that his fiancée's brother worked at the Chemical Machinery Factory. To gain a deeper understanding of the market situation, I should visit Yexian County for a face-to-face discussion. The Chemical Machinery Factory was a county-owned enterprise located in Luwang

Town, Laizhou, Yexian County. It was only two kilometers from Little Pan's village. His fiancée's brother, surnamed Wang, was the head of the manufacturing department. After a warm meeting, he took me to the manufacturing workshop to see the complete machinery and equipment for producing coating and explained the process. Back in the office, Chief Wang presented a stack of materials on global coating production, including production volume, consumption, average per capita consumption, and annual sales volume by city.

Developed countries had an average per capita consumption of 2.5 kilograms, two kilograms, or one kilogram. It was not just used in office buildings and hotels; ordinary households also used it. It has just begun to sell in cities within our country, and only prefecture-level cities have had sales outlets this year. Our country's per capita consumption was only 0.02 catties; the market was huge, and whoever got in early would dominate the market. We would therefore start Shandong's first coating machinery production factory. After purchasing the entire set of equipment, the machinery factory provided installation services to ensure the quality of the products. They guided the purchase of raw materials, while we only focused on sales. It sounded very tempting and appealing, and I planned to conduct market research before making a decision. After returning from various county markets, I found that there were no sales because the small grocery store owners were unfamiliar with the product. After hearing from a friend, I discovered a coating machine manufacturer in Jinan, located on West Wuli Paifang Street. I went to Jinan, found the machine factory near the street, and got a manual. I learned that the Jinan market was similar to what Section Chief Wang had introduced, with the paint machines being launched last year and just gaining traction this year. The paint machines were about 5,000 yuan more expensive than those from Luwang Machinery Factory. Still, the equipment was largely the same.

I decided to give up on the plastic strips. In the past few months, two more factories had sprung up in Cicun Township, Zichuan, Zibo, bringing the total to four, thereby crowding the market. Although

Uncle Sun helped out and Section Chief Liu was enthusiastic, market competition was inevitable and unchangeable. Therefore, I decided to start producing coatings.

However, there was insufficient capital for paint production. Buying the machine required 20,000 yuan; another 20,000 yuan was needed for packaging barrels. I approached Little Qi, a credit officer at the Credit Cooperative, and he helped secure a loan of 20,000 yuan. It was a significant personal loan from the township credit union. Still, with the funds sorted out, I was ready for action.

I made another trip to Luwang Chemical Machinery Factory. I found Section Chief Wang and negotiated the purchase of a complete set of paint machines. While he could set the price, there was still a formal process to follow. I found deputy factory manager Liu, who was in charge of operations, and negotiated a discount of 1,000 yuan per set. We signed an agreement under which I was required to pick up the goods in cash.

Upon returning, I arranged for a check. I used a Yuejin light truck from the electric porcelain accessories factory to transport two tons of coal to Section Chief Wang's house, planning to arrive within a day. When we arrived at his house, it was already six o'clock in the evening. After unloading the coal, we prepared dinner. Still, the driver, Little Shi, was unable to find a suitable parking spot. It was the peak of the snowy season, with temperatures around -3 or 4 degrees Celsius. Starting the truck was a big problem, so we found a downhill road. Section Chief Wang prepared a sumptuous seafood meal. Sated from good food and drink, we retreated to the truck an hour later.

Little Shi drove while the four of us pushed from behind. Going downhill was not too difficult, but the truck would not start after two attempts. We finished going downhill, then pushed with all our strength on the flat road. After another attempt, the truck still would not start. Exhausted and half sobering up, we could not push anymore. Only then did Little Shi, the driver, realize what was wrong. The engine was frozen. We poured hot water over it after Section Chief Wang brought two pots of hot water. After pouring the hot water over the engine, we pushed again. Within five meters, the engine finally roared to life. We returned to the guesthouse, planning to install the machine the next day.

The next day, after completing the machine handover procedures, we had a forklift to load the machine onto the truck. Some items were being moved in the workshop, and another customer was buying other machinery, so we had to wait. By noon, everything was loaded, and we applied for the exit permit. However, the finance department encountered a problem — the bank stamp on the cash cheque was unclear, so the local bank would not accept it.

We needed to find section chief Wang to explain the situation. With an introduction from a friend, we assured them we were not scammers. I found the factory manager, and with section chief Wang's guarantee, I stayed at the factory as a hostage. At the same time, Section Chief Wang accompanied the delivery of the machine. After the exit permit was processed, the paint machine truck was allowed to leave. I stayed in the factory's guesthouse and was unable to leave the premises. As I later learned from Little Pan, someone from the security department had been tracking me. Section chief Wang retrieved the check, and only then could I leave the factory.

Before starting production, I had already recruited four salespersons. My friend Little Pan gave up his previous job to help with sales. Elder Brother Zhao had been helping me sell plastic for over a year. He had the necessary sales skills, so he switched to selling paint. Little Zhao was articulate and had worked temporary jobs in government departments, so I poached him for sales. Uncle Sun, who was related to me, was willing and capable of doing the job. The four salespersons were assigned to four different sales areas with no overlap. Little Pan covered the eastern area, including the Linzi District in Zibo, Yidu (now known as Qingzhou), Changle in Weifang City, and Weifang itself. Little Zhao covered the northern area, including Zhangdian and Huantai in Zibo, as well as Boxing and Binzhou. Elder brother Zhao covered the southern route, including Boshan, Laiwu, and Tai'an. Uncle Sun covered the western route, including Wangcun,

Puji, Zhangqiu, Longshan, and Diaozhen County. Keeping up with the trend, we printed business cards. After visiting various print shops in Zichuan, we found only one that could do it — Qianjin Printing House. We held a meeting to set sales targets: 600 tons in the first year, with each person responsible for selling 150 tons. We deployed a network-style approach within the sales range, ensuring no small grocery store or construction company was overlooked. We purchased a truck for delivery, aiming to deliver two tons per day within a 100-kilometer radius. We made a round trip the same day, striving for a successful first year.

With the product on the market, it needed a name. We could pick any name since there were no registered trademarks that year. After pondering for two days, we decided to delve deeper into the color white and named it "Swan." The pure white feathers of a swan were universally loved, after all. We officially named it "Swan brand wall coating." For a new product, advertising was essential. In those days, there were no TV commercials, and people rarely read newspapers. We purchased plywood and hired an artist to create a design that was simple yet effective. The son of Teacher Ren, a graduate of the Academy of Fine Arts, who was unemployed at home, readily agreed to help. With a broad vision as a fine arts graduate, he sketched a layout in just over an hour. A large swan flew from a lake towards the blue sky with its head held high. After he sought my opinion, I fully agreed. After half an hour of brainstorming, we settled on a concise, direct, and complementary slogan that matched the artwork: "White clouds, blue sky, green water, red palms — presenting you with a colorful world." We bought thirty sheets of plywood, one for each advertisement board. We delivered them to major sales points in counties and towns, hanging them in places where passersby could easily see them.

After the Chinese New Year, we launched our campaign in all four directions, and within two months, we had set up over 100 sales outlets, making good progress. All the sales outlets were consignment-based. At each location, we left approximately 10 barrels for larger outlets and 5 or 6 for smaller ones. For over two months, we only made deliveries, setting up these outlets without settling accounts or collecting payments. Placing the paint at the sales points was akin to stocking our warehouse. If it were sold, we would receive payment; if not, we would retrieve it. While this sales approach faced initial resistance from some customers, after over half a year of relentless promotion and explanation, the residents began to understand the paint better. Both businesses and new buildings began using our coating for their painting needs. Even ordinary households started adopting it. After the autumn harvest and sowing, the high season came; people used it to decorate rooms for weddings in slack seasons, and before the Chinese New Year, many households would repaint their old homes. We seized this opportunity, with our sales team working diligently while the factory focused on production. Ensuring that each sales point remained stocked was crucial, so a daily delivery of one truckload was made to each. We thus aimed to achieve our sales target for that year.

2.2 A Severe Cold Snap

As November arrived, winter set in, prompting us to reorganize the paint storage. We gathered the sales team for a meeting to discuss the storage of coatings during the winter. The experienced coating production masters explained that at zero degrees Celsius, the coating thickens but remains usable; however, at around minus five degrees Celsius, it becomes too dense for application. Therefore, during the winter, all coatings at sales points must be stored indoors, away from the elements. We visited each sales location to ensure this instruction was clear and followed without exception. The sales team immediately assured us of their commitment to fulfilling the task. Until November 10th, the weather remained relatively mild, resembling that of previous years. However, from the 15th onward, the temperature dropped to close to zero degrees Celsius. During that era, people paid little attention to weather forecasts, and information was scarce. Severe weather warnings were broadcast only once and not repeatedly. On the

12th, a cold north wind blew, followed by a day of strong winds on the 13th. By the morning of the 14th, the temperature had plummeted to minus 10 degrees Celsius, a first in several decades. In the 1980s, automated phone systems were not yet available in counties and townships, and information communication relied heavily on personal visits. Immediately, the sales team set out to assess the condition of the paint at each sales point.

One, two, or three days passed, and most of the paint was found outdoors, exposed in the yards. Responsible shop owners had stored their paint indoors. However, many petty dealers neglected this precaution and did not feel a personal connection to the product. However, whether indoors or outdoors, the paint was still considered company property. It could not be sold or returned to the company. It was estimated that about two-thirds of the paint had frozen.

I reprimanded the sales team for their negligence and lack of thoroughness. They complained that while many owners had initially agreed to the storage instructions, some needed to rearrange their shops to accommodate the paint: the following day, an unforeseen cold snap had hit. The cold snap had arrived unexpectedly early, catching everyone off guard. These were all first-year businesses, so their sense of responsibility and experience were evenly divided, leaving us to ponder the next steps.

The frozen paint was gradually brought back and categorized into two types: that left in the yards was frozen solid, resembling blocks of tofu, while that in sheds was semi-solid, akin to thick porridge but still pourable. We first tackled the latter category of semi-solid paint.

In the coating production process, we used two reaction kettles. Water was added to the kettle and heated to 95°C; the raw materials were then added and mixed. The mixture was then transferred to a grinder and ground to a 200-mesh consistency before being packaged. When the kettle was two-thirds full, water and additional materials were added. The quality of the coating produced remained consistent. The kettles were positioned about one meter off the ground, making it strenuous for two workers to lift the barrels onto them. This slow process caused delays, especially considering the limited space in the workshop. When retrieving the paint, we could only accommodate about 20 to 30 barrels in the workshop, leaving only a narrow passage.

The sales team reported the presence of frozen paint at various sales points, totaling approximately 650 barrels. About 150 barrels were semi-solid and could be reprocessed immediately, while the remaining 500 were frozen solid. These could not be poured out of the barrels and had to be scooped out manually, one spoonful at a time. We could only fit about 300 barrels in the yard, leaving us nowhere to store the rest.

Five rooms were used for paint production, originally belonging to the production team's donkey sheds. Since the production team had been disbanded, these spaces were unused. Considering the convenience of transportation, we converted them into paint production facilities. We identified two or three vacant rooms in the vicinity, with the only suitable location being the space adjacent to the workshop. This area, measuring over 300 square meters, was bordered by a wheat field on one side and a dirt road leading to the village on the other. Of the five sheds, three were used for reaction kettles and grinders. At the same time, the remaining two served as warehouses for raw materials such as polyvinyl alcohol, titanium dioxide, and pigments — all of which were expensive. Two temporary sheds were erected to store additional materials, including light calcium carbonate and talcum powder, at a total investment of 5,000 yuan for an Old Taishan truck used for transportation. However, loading and unloading the truck with barrels was cumbersome due to the narrow passage.

Each ton of paint contained 33 barrels, and over 20 tons were damaged by freezing. To accommodate the new paint, we needed additional barrels. Under normal circumstances, we would add 200 barrels each month to maintain supply. However, we had to increase this number due to the recent incident. After careful calculation, we decided to add 700 to 800 barrels. No. 4 Plastic Factory was our regular supplier, but it was unable to meet our immediate needs. After receiving the notice, the No.4 factory sent 300 barrels, and the salesperson came with the truck to return the barrel money. We already owed for two previous batches and needed to settle the old debts along with this one. I explained this special situation and encountered difficulties with Little Li, a salesperson from the No. 4 factory, whose barrel payment would be settled after a week. However, Little Li disagreed and quarreled with me. State-owned factory salespeople were tough and regarded themselves as highly skilled. They felt embarrassed to deliver barrels to individual businesses without immediate payment. Little Li insisted on loading the barrels onto the truck to return them. But I urgently needed them and could not immediately give him the money. Without the payment, he could not take the barrels back. We used woven bags for loading the barrels, with five barrels per bag. Little Li grabbed a bag and tried tossing it onto the truck, but I held it firmly. I inadvertently jerked the bag in the struggle, causing Little Li to knock over a water jar. Enraged, he lunged at me, but one of our workers, Old Zhao, intervened and pinned Little Li to the ground. I quickly restrained Old Zhao, realizing that we were in the wrong. The driver from the No. 4 factory shoved Little Li back onto the truck and sped off.

As the situation worsened, I needed to borrow money to purchase barrels, ensuring normal production. I approached Little Qi, the credit officer at the credit union. Little Qi explained that as the year-end approached, no more loan quotas would be available until January of the following year. Desperate, I borrowed 2,000 yuan from my good friend, old Chen, and another 1,000 yuan from my old classmate, Zhang. Borrowing 1,000 yuan was quite challenging back then. I urged the sales team to collect bills in various denominations, including 100 yuan, 200 yuan, and even a few dozen yuan. It was crucial to ensure there were no shortages in the market.

Since barrels from the No. 4 factory were no longer available, we had to find an alternative supplier. When Little Zhao, one of our salespeople, heard about it, he mentioned that the Fu Family Factory in Zhangdian, a nearby town, had just started production. Yesterday, Old Zhao had also mentioned that a plastic barrel factory in Zhangzhuang village, Zichuan, had just begun operations, so we decided to visit Zhangzhuang first. We took our paint delivery truck to the Dongshan District, where Zhangzhuang Village was. Four factories were lined up alongside a small river, with the plastic barrel factory in the center. Upon entering the factory, Mr. Zhang, the factory director, warmly welcomed me. The factory had only been operational for about 10 days, and I was their first customer. Director Zhang eagerly offered cigarettes, poured tea, and took us on a workshop tour. He immediately conducted a strength test on the barrels before exiting the workshop. He filled a barrel with water, tightly sealed the lid, and had a worker climb onto the flat roof of the guardhouse with the barrel on his shoulder. The barrel was deliberately dropped from over three meters, but remained intact. Director Zhang then placed a barrel on the ground and repeatedly stomped on it. To my amazement, the barrel showed no signs of damage.

With a smile, director Zhang asked, "Are you satisfied?"

"Yes. Now, let's talk about the price," I replied.

"Five yuan and 50 mao per barrel, five mao cheaper than No.4 Plastic Factory," Mr. Zhang offered.

Content with the deal, we concluded our business without further discussion.

Back in the office, director Zhang brewed Laiwu Old Dry Oven tea, which he had not had in years and which emanated a strong aroma that filled every corner of the room.

"Director Zhang, I didn't plan to purchase plastic barrels today or bring a check. Let's start with 200 barrels. You can deliver the remaining 300 barrels in three days, and I will pay half of the payment upfront. Is that acceptable?"

Sitting beside the tea table, sipping Old Dry Oven tea, I tentatively tested director Zhang's attitude.

"That's negotiable. Director Yu is a reasonable person. Let's have lunch first; there's no rush to load the barrels."

Director Zhang did not miss any opportunity to entertain customers, especially those who were the first to receive deliveries since the factory's inception. Pretending to leave, I felt director Zhang's hands firmly grip my shoulders.

"You can't leave. Today, we'll taste the whole lamb from Zhangzhuang. Not eating means not being a friend, and if business isn't concluded, there'll be no barrels."

"Alright, alright. I'll go along with director Zhang's suggestion."

It was the first time I had heard of eating a whole lamb. Entering several old stone houses, we found ourselves in a room with several small tables. Zhang and his team of five were joined by two of my associates, making a total of eight guests. Two small tables were pushed together to accommodate us all perfectly. After a short smoke break, a lady brought in a large aluminum basin and placed it in the center of the table. Each of us was handed a bowl, and director Zhang, taking the lead, began serving. The stew contained lamb head, meat, intestines, and blood. Once we were well-fed and had conducted business, we left with 200 paint barrels, resolving our shortage.

The paint left in the yard had frozen solid over the winter, becoming as hard as rocks. Rolling on the ground, the barrels made loud banging sounds, and scooping the paint out with a spoon was impossible. We decided to wait until the following year for it to thaw naturally. Roughly estimated, there were still over 400 barrels of frozen paint remaining.

By April, the temperature had risen to over 20 degrees Celsius. Still, the frozen paint remained solid, similar to rubber in texture and resistant when pressed. It was not until June or July, when temperatures climbed to over thirty degrees, that we decided to resume action.

By June, however, with temperatures reaching over thirty degrees, the frozen paint still showed no signs of softening despite the heat. We understood the reason for this: the first-generation paint formula the machinery factory had taught us used genuine materials. However, the adhesive and filler added according to the formula caused the paint to solidify more than expected.

As the scorching July sun beat down, we laid the frozen coatings out in the yard, hoping they would soften. But even after a day of exposure, the frozen coatings remained unyielding. It seemed impervious to the sun's rays. It was time for a more drastic approach.

Unable to scoop it out with spoons, we used sharp knives to cut the coatings into small blocks. These were then transferred into empty barrels. However, incorporating the frozen coatings into the production process proved challenging. While the new paint flowed smoothly, the thawed paint took significantly longer to melt, resulting in a production delay of over two hours. Digging out the coatings from the barrels had become an additional step in the production process, with workers paid five yuan for each barrel dug out. We worked tirelessly until October to complete the transformation of the frozen coating.

2.3 Second Formula Revision

Seven or eight more paint factories emerged a year later in the surrounding four or five townships. Requiring an investment of only 2,000 or 3,000 yuan, they could easily produce with simple equipment, such as a large iron pot, and deliver it with small handcarts or donkey carts. Therefore, those factories slashed prices drastically. Although my factory was more like a workshop, it had a higher cost structure, with sales staff, accountants, workshop production team leaders, vehicles, and drivers. How would we survive if we didn't keep up with the market, even with a good product? There was no turning back from the arrow.

The saying goes, "It never rains but it pours." The prices of the two main raw materials for paint began to rise. Polyvinyl alcohol increased day by day and was also in short supply. Two months ago, the price was 2,700 yuan per ton; now, it has risen to approximately 7,000 yuan per ton. Titanium dioxide quickly followed suit, increasing from 2,300 yuan per barrel to 5,000. Product price increases failed to keep up with the soaring raw material costs. While we announced a price increase of three yuan per barrel at our sales points, the materials continued to rise, forcing us to operate at a loss. Paint factories were all trying to find solutions. The old formula could not keep up with the changing times. Adjustments, price cuts, perseverance — those who persisted would have the last laugh. We could not give up halfway.

Little Pan learned from the Chemical Machinery Factory that Section Chief Wang knew an engineer surnamed Liu in Jinan who had a formula for cost reduction. We arranged to visit Mr. Liu's house on a Sunday to ask for the formula. Mr. Liu's house was on an old street named Kuanhousuo Street. (In the past, it was known as the four famous streets in the south of Quancheng Road in Jinan.) When we arrived at Mr. Liu's house around 11:00 a.m., he welcomed us warmly. He was even younger than I, probably under thirty.

Without any explanation from us, Mr. Liu got straight to the point: "I developed this formula over a year. I worked on it myself on Sundays. I won't sell it unless through friends."

We could not proceed without knowing how many connections we sought, while being kept in suspense. All we could do was listen attentively. Finally, we had it. The revised formula involved reducing polyvinyl alcohol by half, adding cellulose and cornstarch, eliminating the expensive titanium dioxide, and replacing it with a whitening agent developed by Mr. Liu. The other materials were slightly modified, resulting in a 30 percent reduction in cost. The transfer fee was relatively low, at just 2,000 yuan. However, the whitening agent had to be purchased from Mr. Liu, as it was not available on the market because he had developed it himself. We had to come regularly for the whitening agent. This was Mr. Liu's way of making money.

Following Mr. Liu's formula, the quality of the produced paint was not inferior. It had good adhesion and even better whiteness. We immediately released it to the market, turning losses into small profits and gaining market share.

A month later, our salespeople reported that the coating had an unusual odor. I immediately went to Manager Bi's hardware store in Mingshui County. Manager Bi had a good reputation and was honest; he could provide me with a genuine assessment. He explained that there were no issues when the coating was sold within three to five days. However, if it sat for more than half a month, customers noticed a strange odor when they brushed it onto the walls. I had detected a slight odor when I opened several barrels of paint that had been sent half a month before. We were unable to sell it; we had to withdraw it immediately.

I briefly explained the situation to Mr. Liu over the phone. I arranged to visit him in Jinan the following Sunday to modify the formula. Mr. Liu was a regular worker without formal training at a professional school and struggled to articulate explanations over the phone. We agreed to meet in Room 303 of the Jinan Association for Science and Technology, near Minzu Market.

I arrived at Minzu Market in Jinan and found the association. Mr. Liu was inside, accompanied by another person. Mr. Liu introduced him as director Zhang from the Association for Science and Technology. I clearly explained the situation with the paint, including its condition, odor, and customer feedback. Mr. Liu remained silent, but director Zhang spoke up. He explained that the odor from the coating was due to the moldy starch. The formula developed the previous winter had not thoroughly incorporated this aspect. The preservative properties of formaldehyde would have had little effect on the starch, but adding a food preservative could solve the problem. Director Zhang apologized profusely, acknowledging their oversight. He and Mr. Liu worked together; one focused on research while the other promoted the product and connected with buyers.

What to do with the spoiled coating? It was a loss to throw it away. Given our small-scale operation, we could not afford to lose money for half a year. Director Zhang remained silent for over 10 minutes, then pulled out a notebook from his drawer and flipped to the middle, reading a few pages.

"Adding some light calcium powder, also known as lime powder, can eliminate the odor," he said after a pause. After another few minutes, director Zhang added, "Next week, I will go to your factory with Mr. Liu to make some adjustments to the formula and find a way to dispose of the spoiled coating."

After the May Day holiday, we recalled all the unsold coatings as the weather warmed up. We exchanged the spoiled coating for new ones. The frozen coating from the previous year had just been dealt with. Over 200 barrels of smelly coating were in the courtyard, leaving only a narrow passageway. This confirmed the saying that "Misfortunes never come singly."

With the revised formula from director Zhang, we increased production by one ton per day to replace the spoiled coating. We were unable to expand our influence due to this misfortune; we had to quickly turn the market situation around. The market competition remained intense, and it was uncertain who would ultimately prevail.

On a Sunday, Mr. Liu and director Zhang came specifically to adjust the formula for the spoiled coating. For each reaction tank producing one ton, we only added half a ton of new materials and half a ton of spoiled coating, which was slightly tainted with an odor. We added three bags of lime powder and a package of stabilizers brought by director Zhang from Jinan. After experimenting and operating all afternoon, the coating produced through the mixture showed no difference in appearance. It exhibited smoothness, whiteness, and adhesion without anomalies when applied to the wall. The experiment was successful. We planned to use up all the spoiled coating within 10 days.

This minor setback affected only a few sales points, with minimal impact on the market. Salesmen reported that surrounding coating factories have raised prices again, adding three yuan per barrel. However, we insisted on not raising prices. We used the formula from Jinan, suffering only minimal losses. We held on for a few days. The adjusted formula gradually improved our market sales by increasing the whiteness of the coating. Each barrel was priced at fifteen yuan in the first round of coating listings. We adjusted the price five times within a year, starting from 18 yuan per barrel, then increasing to 22 yuan, 25 yuan, and finally to 30 yuan per barrel. It doubled from the initial price, while raw material costs had tripled or quadrupled. While other companies were raising prices, we did not; instead, we opted to avoid a price war.

As winter set in and the agricultural off-season began, living standards had improved. Only the bedrooms in old rural houses had ceilings, while others were left exposed to the elements. The dust settled on the exposed beams and rafters, which were unsanitary and untidy. During that winter, people had started using plastic woven fabric to create makeshift ceilings. Before painting, they stretched the fabric tightly and secured it around the edges with wooden strips. It was both aesthetically pleasing and practical, not to mention inexpensive. However, a problem had arisen with coating the fabric. The plastic cloth, marked with fine lines, was smooth and lay out mid-air. Due to the poor adhesive properties of the coating, most of it adhered, but a significant portion fell off. This was laborious and wasteful, so customers demanded a solution to this problem. If we could produce a specialized coating for ceilings, it would sell even better, and we could raise the price. However, expecting people to use one type of coating for walls and a different one for ceilings was unrealistic.

One morning, I sat at my desk with furrowed brows, gazing at the sycamore tree in the courtyard where two small birds were chirping incessantly. While I was considering whether to go to Jinan that day, a stranger walked in. He wore a blue jacket and brown leather shoes, and had a half-crew cut hairstyle. Without sitting down, he handed me his business card — Professor Wu Ziqiang from the Department of Materials Science at Wuhan University of Technology. I stood up from my chair and shook Professor Wu's hand, introducing myself, "Yu Guotai." Professor Wu sat down on the sofa, exchanged a few pleasantries, and then began elaborating on the situation regarding the coating, covering national sales, development prospects, and coating research. He spoke eloquently while I remained calm.

Could it be possible that a university professor from Wuhan had come all this way to sell coating formulas? There were too many scammers in society nowadays. Sensing my skepticism, Professor Wu did not beat around the bush. He was straightforward, saying he had come to discuss long-term collaboration with enterprises. If I had any intention of cooperating, we could discuss this further. If not, he would leave immediately without discussing formulas or money. Professor Wu was very frank; I felt he was not a scammer. After a successful discussion, we agreed to cooperate on a long-term basis. Since we had such a successful meeting, I brought up the immediate problem of the coating's poor adhesion to plastic cloth, which urgently needed a solution. We agreed that I would go to Wuhan University of Technology and conduct experiments in Professor Wu's laboratory. This was our first meeting, and the method of cooperation would be determined during my stay in Wuhan.

Wuhan University of Technology is located in Wuchang. I entered through the main gate, and the guard directed me straight ahead to the Department of Materials Science building. Professor Wu's laboratory was on the third floor. I arrived at the appointed time to find Professor Wu waiting for me. Professor Wu immediately began the experiment without any small talk, reducing the formula to 2,000 kilograms of coating. He carefully measured various materials, heated the beaker to 95°C, and stirred it rapidly. After about two hours, the sample was ready. We applied it to plywood, and the whiteness and adhesion were excellent, with a 10 percent reduction in cost compared to mine. It had market competitiveness. With a profit-sharing arrangement in place, I decided to collaborate with Professor Wu on a long-term basis. We would not pay any research fees; settlements would be made every six months. Payment would not be made for each formula revision; however, it would be based on market development and growth. Professor Wu should research and modify formulas as needed and introduce new varieties, such as a premium exterior coating. With Professor Wu's laboratory serving as our research base, we thus established a long-term partnership.

We immediately signed a contract agreement. During our first meeting, I also mentioned the problem of poor coating adhesion to plastic cloth. Since I had not explained it clearly and had not brought the plastic cloth with me, I brought it this time. I asked Professor Wu to modify the formula to improve adhesion. Professor Wu briefly glanced at the plastic-woven cloth, then paused for a moment. He said he would modify the formula and conduct experiments in the laboratory the next day.

We began producing small batches of coating according to the formula from Professor Wu. We received positive feedback upon our market release. The effect on the plastic-woven cloth ceilings was unexpected; the paint adhered completely without dripping when the brush or roller touched the woven cloth. Market sales increased significantly, and we raised the price by three yuan per barrel.

During my second visit to Wuhan, I thanked Professor Wu. We did not discuss paint this time; instead, we discussed the Yellow Crane Tower, the Wuchang Uprising, Zhang Zhidong, and the Hanyang Rifle. Wu looked at me with newfound respect and took me on to tour of the East Lake and Wuhan University. The two of us rode bicycles and explored Wuchang together.

2.4 Ghosts Pounding the Wall

Wangcun Jian'an Company operates twelve construction sites across cities such as Zhoucun, Zhangdian, and Jinan. They are all major clients with an annual paint consumption of several hundred tons. However, after contacting them a few times, it became apparent that the quality was not up to par, leaving us unsettled. With the second formula taught by Teacher Wu, we could provide our targeted key clients with 100 percent quality assurance by absorbing the increased costs. We decided to contact the supply department of Wangcun Jian'an Company.

We had met director Yang of the supply department several times before. While they had used dozens of tons of paint on small construction sites, but not utilized it on large projects. This time, when we approached director Yang and expressed the technical expertise from Wuhan University, ensuring 100 percent quality assurance, he agreed to a trial run. After October, there would be a large-scale usage, with most projects set to be completed by the year's end.

If this trial met the users' requirements, all the construction sites in Zhoucun, Jinan, would switch to our product. Director Yang was now well aware that Swan Coating Factory, within dozens of kilometers, was the largest coating factory around.

Feedback from the construction sites in Jinan indicated that the coating quality was satisfactory. Director Yang agreed that we could supply in batches, with notifications on the quantity required. It could be anywhere from 300 to 500 tons. Over the past two years, he had met the largest client of the coating factory, so we went to director Yang's home to express our gratitude.

The date was set. One afternoon, production team leader Fourth Uncle and sales department head Uncle Sun rode on motorcycles carrying cigarettes and baijiu to visit director Yang's home. Director Yang had left work early, and the banquet was ready. His elder brother accompanied us. We drank heartily, without discussing work, just chatting. Director Yang and I were the same age and went to school in 1958. We participated in the Great Leap Forward Movement (1958-1960), with him carrying ore and me carrying bricks. All classmates lined up for meals. After that, I went to Zibo No. 10 Middle School for junior high school, while director Yang attended Zibo No. 8 Middle School. During the Cultural Revolution, many of us went to Beijing and Shanghai. We gradually hit it off with chit-chatting. Unknowingly, as the banquet peaked, his elder brother insisted on two more drinks. Not wanting to lose face, we drank, but I drank more, while Fourth Uncle and Third Uncle Sun drank less. We had agreed before coming that we would ensure a safe return on motorcycles for the ten-plus-kilometer journey.

The banquet ended at eight in the evening, and director Yang escorted us to the door. I sat on the back seat of Uncle Sun's Jialing motorcycle. At the same time, Fourth Uncle rode another motorcycle ahead, leading the way along the dirt road back home.

Unknowingly, I fell asleep on the motorcycle. Uncle Sun kept shouting, urging me not to sleep. When I finally woke up and held onto his waist, determined not to sleep, the motorcycle suddenly tipped over, throwing me into the roadside ditch. As I climbed out of the ditch, I heard them shouting and pulling a young man riding a bicycle. Feeling my face wet, I touched it and found blood. When they heard me shout about bleeding, they let go of the cyclist and checked my face and wound. Fourth Uncle shouted that this guy should accompany us to treat the wound. In that split second of commotion, the cyclist ran away. They chased him. Where could he go? Both of them got on their motorcycles and went after the cyclist.

Standing on the roadside, I became clearer in my mind. Recalling the accident and their shouts, I pondered. The cyclist must have been drunk, too, swaying on his bicycle as he approached from the opposite direction. Who collided with whom? The motorcycle tipped over, and the bicycle skidded several meters away. We had been eating in greater numbers, while the other party was alone. Naturally, the fault lay on his side, and we must insist on compensation. I thought they would return after chasing the cyclist for a few minutes, but it felt like a long time had passed. Why hadn't they come back?

I suddenly felt abandoned by them, thinking they had gone home without waiting for me. Not wanting to wait any longer, I decided to walk home alone. It was only about six or seven kilometers, which I could cover in less than an hour. So, I started walking toward home, feeling that the road was narrow with walls on both sides. It was pitch black around me, but I could vaguely see a light ahead. I hastened toward it, walking quickly and continuously without encountering any vehicles, pedestrians, houses, or fields. The corn by the roadside had started to tassel. I felt like I was on the road home, with no inclines, cliffs, or turns, just a straight path ahead. I did not know how long I had been walking. Suddenly, a flash of light appeared before me — the gate of the fan factory, with lights on both sides. I stopped and looked carefully. Yes, it was the gate, and I recognized the security guard, Old Chen. I asked him to lend me a bicycle to ride home, but he shook his head and refused. The next day, Old Chen told my younger brother that I had been drunk last night, with one foot wearing a shoe and the other only a sock, staggering around, insisting on riding a bicycle, but he had not let me.

Continuing forward, I kept pondering. It did not make sense for me to come from the direction of the fan factory. The place where I fell was directly north, but the fan factory was to the south. The distance from where I fell to my home was about three or four kilometers, while the factory was about two or three kilometers from my home. I had walked in a big circle, with a total distance of over five kilometers. Why had I walked so far without realizing it? I had kept walking without feeling tired, just eager to get home. But when I saw the fan factory and continued forward, my legs suddenly stopped moving. My foot without a shoe hurt badly, and my face throbbed. I tried, but still failed to recall which road I should take.

Suddenly, it sounded like someone was talking. It was nice to hear someone's voice at midnight. The further I walked, the louder the voices became. When I could hear them clearly, I recognized them as Fourth Uncle and Uncle Sun.

I hurried a few steps and shouted, "Hey, you two! You dropped me and ran off, and now you're here chatting!"

They saw me and ran over from an abandoned lime kiln.

"Thank God we found you! We were so worried," Uncle Sun said, while Fourth Uncle echoed, "Couldn't find you; how were we supposed to get home?"

They approached me and jumped with joy.

From the lime kiln to home, it was still over one kilometer. The three of us walked slowly, reminiscing about the night's romantic journey. Uncle Sun checked his watch — it was 3:10 in the morning. I had fallen off the road around nine in the evening, so we had walked for more than six hours. Which way had we come from? They recounted their search for me.

When they had caught up with the cyclist and turned him back, they returned to where I had fallen in less than 20 minutes, but I was gone. Since finding me was the priority, they did not bother about the cyclist and had ridden to Shiniucun Village. It did not take long, so they had turned back, with one person walking along the road with a flashlight. They had suspected I might be sleeping in the roadside ditch, so they returned to the original spot but could not find me. They then rode their bikes back along the small road, thinking I might have taken the side road among the newly tasseled corn, which would have made the journey slow. With the flashlight illuminating the path, they had reached Dabaixicun Village, then circled back toward Shiniucun Village. From Shiniucun Village, they had returned to the intersection and headed south toward Cicun Village, but had found no sign of me. They had then split up at the crossroads — one heading west toward Xiwangcun Village, the other east toward Kunlun Bridge. One went to Lingzi Mine intersection, the other to Kunlun Bridge. However, neither of them could reach those places by running.

They had therefore returned to Shiniucun Village and found their way along the road until they had reached our village.

They had knocked on my bedroom window and asked, "Has Guotai returned?"

My family had replied, "He has not come back. Where did he go?"

They had lied, saying, "He's drinking at old Sun's house."

After that, they had returned to the road. It was already midnight. What should they do? They then retraced their steps and rode back along the road, finding Shiniucun Village and finally, the river valley! They had searched through streets and alleys, even found Xu's house, but could not find any sign of me. Finally, they sat on the lime kiln, feeling worried.

They asked me to think hard about which road I had taken or if I had slept in one place the whole time. I was fully awake now and remembered walking along one road without turning. Suddenly, it became clear before me — the gate of the fan factory, about 10 meters away. The gate's lights were bright and should have been visible from 100 meters away. It was like waking up from a dream, seeing the gate appear before me.

"You must have met ghosts pounding the wall!" Uncle Sun

repeated.

It was like the legend of "ghosts pounding the wall," a local saying in Zibo, known as "zhāo dàng" (招档). When drunk and confused, you may see a little ghost carrying a lantern, guiding you to a forbidden place. If you encounter light or a rooster crowing along the way, the little ghost disappears, and you wake up. I had heard stories like this from adults when I was a child, and tonight I felt as though the ghost was haunting me.

In the second year following this incident, a friend, two years my junior, had a similar experience. He was drinking at a friend's house, and when he had finished and went home while he was only slightly drunk. His friend's house was about two kilometers away, so he walked home. All the drinkers saw that he walked back to his house. At twelve that night, however, his wife found his friend's house and thought he was still drinking. His friend explained that he had already gone home and was not drunk. But what had happened? Then, many friends and relatives went out to search for him all night. Finally, he was sent back by a motorcyclist at breakfast time the next day.

My friend came back and told his story. As he walked forward, he saw a small light ahead and followed it without looking around, simply walking straight ahead. It was still dark, but he thought he heard a few rooster crows. When the light went out, he found himself in front of a large reservoir. He turned around and saw a village, so he walked toward it and met someone, asking where he was. It turned out to be the Mengshan Reservoir. How had he gotten there? It was 17.5 kilometers from his home, and he had walked all night. A kind person had used a motorcycle to take him back.

There are many such stories, but this was my own experience. My friend's experience at Mengshan Reservoir remains unexplained to this day.

2.5 Paint Revolution

I received a letter from engineer Liu in Jinan inviting me to attend a product promotion event organized by the Jinan Association for Science and Technology on October 10th, 1983.

The event was government-led, with participation from major universities and colleges. It was the first time such an event had been held since the reform and opening up began, and it introduced new and fresh products. There were many visitors to the Science and Technology Association. After wandering around for a while, I could not find any suitable products to engage with. Since there were no new paint-related projects, I finished the visit at 11:00 am.

Engineer Liu arranged for us to have lunch at Go-Believe (狗 不 理) Restaurant in the Grand View Garden, which was conveniently close to the Science and Technology Association. It was a second-floor room with eight guests. I only knew engineer Liu and director Zhang. During the meal, I conversed pleasantly with director Zhang about paint. He was interested in it because he had graduated from the Chemical Engineering Department of Shandong University and had studied paints and coatings. Director Zhang mentioned that since last year, he had been considering a major reform of the paint industry, which would be a significant step forward. We agreed to meet again the following Tuesday to discuss the reform plan for paints.

As promised, I visited the Jinan Association for Science and Technology. Director Zhang welcomed me with a cup of tea and a newspaper in his office. The Jinan Association for Science and Technology's work environment seemed relatively relaxed. I could work on other tasks during work hours. After offering me a cup of Longing tea, director Zhang presented his two-step plan. Firstly, he proposed developing scented paints with fragrances such as apple, orange, and banana. When applied to a room, these paints would emit a fragrance that lasted over six months, with a minimal cost increase of around 50 yuan per ton of paint. Therefore, a 200 yuan increase could raise the selling price. It was suggested that the formula be patented for exclusive production, given its excellent market prospects. When I asked director Zhang rhetorically how paint can remain fragrant for half a year when it normally emits odor for about 10 days at most when brushed onto the wall. Director Zhang interrupted me, saying he would explain later.

He then discussed the research on anti-mosquito paints. These paints can kill mosquitoes and flies within minutes of application, making them ideal for use in restaurants, schools, and hotels. The effect of repelling mosquitoes and flies would last for over a year. I asked if the paint would essentially act as an insecticide. Director Zhang explained that insecticide sprays applied to walls lose effectiveness within a day. At the same time, their research on this paint showed it remained effective for at least a year.

Director Zhang sipped Longning tea and methodically continued his explanation. He mentioned his former classmate, who had graduated with a master's degree and returned to Shandong University to research sustained-release medicine. This field involves adjusting medication that is typically taken three times a day to once a day by incorporating a corrosion inhibitor. He suggested adding similar medicine to paints, allowing fragrances or anti-mosquito paints to release slowly over a year. This could be a revolutionary reform in the paint industry.

Director Zhang provided thorough and profound explanations. I listened with great interest. He had already contacted his former classmates twice over the phone and agreed to help with the research. He was determined to persevere despite the challenges ahead. If the paint revolution succeeded, production would be scaled up, and the products would be sold nationwide.

I was somewhat skeptical about the anti-mosquito paints. However, I agreed to start with the scented paint and proceed with anti-mosquito paints once the first phase was successful. Our priority was the development of scented paint, and director Zhang helped us find fragrance manufacturers.

Following the plan, I visited the Jinan Daily Products Chemical

Plant, which produced toothpaste and snowflake cream, to inquire about industrial fragrances. The chemical plant is in Huangtai, north of the cigarette factory. I considered trying it out to see if I could get one. I entered the gate and found the supply and marketing section. However, they refused to sell to us, stating that they imported fragrances from Guangzhou for their own use and did not sell to external parties. Despite my repeated requests, they remained firm. I found that dealing with state-owned enterprises was challenging. Simply approaching lower-level officials would not suffice. It was necessary to reach out to those with actual authority. If their approval could not be secured, a few days' wait would be required. Director Zhang secured approval from the head of the supply department three days later.

On my second visit to the Jinan Daily Products Chemical Plant, I entered the office of the Supply and Marketing Section. I met the same two comrades I had met for the first time. I explained the situation to one of them. The head of the section approved the purchase of two pounds of fragrances, and they took me to the warehouse, where I chose apple and orange. The process took us only half an hour; we successfully acquired the fragrances from the time we entered the factory to the time we made the purchase.

The following Sunday, director Zhang came to formulate the recipe. After learning the formulas from Teacher Wu in Wuhan, we acquired all the necessary experimental equipment, including scales, beakers, and mixers. Director Zhang arrived at my office at 10 o'clock, and we experimented with two different processes. In the first process, we heated water to 95°C using an alcohol lamp. We added polyvinyl alcohol, starch, adhesive, fragrance, and light calcium carbonate to create a sample. In the second process, we added fragrance to the finished paint and stirred it evenly. In one case, the fragrance was added during production; in the other, it was added afterward. We applied both samples to two wooden boards and observed the results. When I asked director Zhang about the lack of sustained-release agents, he said that his former classmates were busy with other matters and had not had the chance to research them.

We left the boards in the Sun for a few minutes until the paint had dried. We then smelled them repeatedly and found that the smell was similar in both cases. Hence, we could not tell which process was superior. Director Zhang also could not answer, either, admitting he did not know when the sustained-release medicine would be available. We decided to continue experimenting and wait for the sustained-release medicine.

The paint applied to the room without sustained-release medicine still smelled good a few days later. It worked well, so we started by producing scented paint without sustained-release medicine. We agreed to mix one kilogram of fragrance into one ton of paint and sell it on the market to gauge the response.

We produced one ton of scented paint, printed promotional posters, and distributed them to seven or eight sales points, awaiting market feedback. After two weeks, the largest sales point in Boxing County sent a message requesting that I visit. This store was in the center of the county and was owned by Mr. Lu, who explained that a customer had purchased three barrels of scented paint. After painting the bedroom, the fragrance filled the room, but the customer felt uncomfortable after sleeping in it. The neighbors talked about this: "The scent does not dissolve for several months, they wonder whether it is harmful or beneficial to the body, and what is contained in the paint ingredients? There is no explanation." Moreover, the customer wanted the paint back. Mr. Lu had to offer three barrels of regular paint free of charge to cover up the fragrance. He explained that while solving the issue with the three paint barrels was relatively easy, promoting the product proved to be challenging. Many customers were not interested in the fragrance, and the five-yuan price increase per barrel was also a deterrent. Mr. Lu thus shared his thoughts from the perspective of a distributor and a friend.

Mr. Lu's insights were enlightening. I visited various sales points to understand the market's response to the new product.

I accompanied the delivery trucks on their routes, visiting several sales points in Yidu, where one sold only one barrel of scented paint, and another did not sell any, with no feedback received. In Wangcun town, five sales commission agencies were given one barrel each. Still, only one barrel was sold, while the rest remained unsold. In Zhangqiu County, a commission agency in Mingshui Town sold one barrel, and one at Xiuhui sold one barrel, with one barrel remaining unsold. The feedback from the commission agencies was that customers were not interested in the new product, and when asked, they thought the price was too high. We decided to wait and observe the market for a while.

As winter approached, only five barrels of scented paint were sold out of the one-ton production, indicating poor market demand. Director Zhang urged me to accelerate the research on insect-repellent paint, as the process was complex and required several experiments.

Manufacturing anti-mosquito paints was challenging, as they could not use conventional insecticides. Director Zhang developed a formula using raw materials commonly found in insecticides. However, obtaining these materials through legitimate channels required approval from the Public Security Bureau, which could take up to six months to process. Trying to purchase them directly from the factories was futile, as even the factory directors could not authorize the sale without proper documentation. The only way was to obtain a small amount from the workshop secretly, with only the workshop director involved to maintain confidentiality. Fortunately, I had a middle school classmate who worked at a pesticide factory, although I could not recall his name. Twenty years after graduation, I contacted him, and he had obtained half a kilogram of the necessary materials. I went to pick it up and invited seven or eight old middle school classmates for lunch. We reminisced about our school days during the Cultural Revolution.

With the anti-mosquito raw materials acquired, I went to Jinan to discuss the next steps with director Zhang. I brought a two-row truck to transport him from the Jinan Association for Science and Technology. Shandong University's old campus was in Huangtai, right through the city center. When we arrived at Shandong University, it was already 11:30 a.m. We met with my former classmate and talked over lunch. Director Zhang spoke for several minutes, detailing his long-term vision and market prospects. While my classmate listened attentively, he did not respond. I introduced the paint factory's equipment and the market's experience with operating paints, and we discussed the business extensively. It was the first time I had met my classmate, and he spoke very slowly. He acknowledged the comprehensive and detailed introduction that director Zhang and I had given him and expressed his understanding of it. He pointed out the gap between our discussion of the sustained-release medicine and wall paint, emphasizing that our ideas could not be realized as we had imagined. He advised us to focus on procuring the raw materials for anti-mosquito paints and a few kilograms of paint ingredients, and to work out the production process. He cautioned against rushing, stating that if we could not achieve it this summer, we could try again next year. He did not commit to whether he could realize director Zhang's envisioned new product.

I could not always urge progress; director Zhang was more anxious than I. His grand plan had been drawn, new trademarks registered, patents obtained, and a new packaging design had been created, all accompanied by the elegance of high-grade paint. He then doubled the price, and the province pushed open sales, namely, marketing the country. Within two or three years, the output value exceeded 100 million yuan. When director Zhang was chairman, I was the general manager, and the paint business was experiencing rapid growth.

The second meeting was scheduled by graduate students in director Zhang's office; we did not inquire about the experimental situation of the slow-release agent, as the graduate students spoke first. The role of the slow-release was to combine the subject and object of a piece of slow-release agent that did not dissolve in the scented, mosquito, and fly paint. For example, retardant molecules, added to the paint molecules, slowly release the fragrance. However, the fly killer could not be done at present. At the first meeting, out of fear of upsetting old classmates, I did not speak out; medicinal slow-release agents in Europe and the United States had been studied for over a decade, and our research aimed to build upon the work of others. You two imagined that the product could not be done.

My graduate student classmate's words shattered director Zhang's grand plan and brought me back to reality. After accompanying director Zhang on this journey for several months, I realized that although we had ventured into the peach blossom forest, we had returned to our humble hut.

2.6 Shiqian Ditch

This set of coating equipment had been in use for three years without any mechanical failures, indicating its excellent quality. One day at work, my initial reaction was that the paint pot was not draining, and the chemical pump was not functioning. After dismantling it for inspection, it turned out that the valve was broken. I immediately went to buy a new valve, as the demand for goods was then high, leading to overtime production. Boshan is the national pump production base, offering a wide range of pump varieties. I therefore rushed to Boshan with my worn-out truck and the broken valve. After visiting several water pump shops, however, I was unable to find the specific valve I needed. Then, the owner of a specialty pump shop recommended a chemical pump manufacturer and suggested that we visit them.

This factory was located in Yaotu Village, Beiboshan Township, a village-run enterprise about 20 kilometers from Boshan. We explained our purpose to the enthusiastic sales staff upon arrival, who promptly took us to the warehouse. After comparing the broken valve, we concluded that they did not have the specific valve or pump we needed. Since the market in Zhangdian, where the Zibo Municipal Government was located, was larger and offered a wider range of mechanical equipment, we headed there. Despite searching the chemical pump and valve market in Zhangdian, we still could not find what we were looking for.

In the 1980s, when information was limited and the internet did not exist, we had to visit manufacturers directly to obtain the necessary details. Therefore, we headed to the production factory in Luwang Village.

The factory was located on a small hill, approximately three to four kilometers from Luwang Village. Little Pan, who had purchased the complete coating production equipment, including two stainless steel reaction pots and a grinder, introduced us to the whole set of coating production equipment. A chemical pump would pump the well-mixed coating from the pot into the grinder, where it would be ground to a 200-mesh size in a rotating drum filled with glass beads before being packaged in barrels. After touring Zhangdian until around three in the afternoon, we rushed to catch the long-distance bus to Weifang, which still had one more departure for the day. When we arrived in Weifang, we found that no more buses were heading towards Yantai, so we had to stay at the workers' hostel. I always stayed at the workers' hostel whenever I had to transfer to Weifang. The hostel had a large courtyard for parking cars, a restaurant, and a bathhouse, and offered affordable prices. Additionally, it was conveniently located near the long-distance bus station, just across Weihe Bridge.

The next afternoon, we got off the bus at Shahe Town. There were no public buses to Luwang, so we went to the bicycle cooperative next to the bus station. Tickets to Luwang cost one yuan, and the drivers, mostly middle-aged and elderly, provided a safe and steady ride. Sitting on the bicycle's rear rack, we bobbed along the road for about an hour until we reached our destination.

We arrived at the Chemical Machinery Factory afternoon, and the workers would start at two. It would not help to be in a hurry, so we sat under a tree and waited until it was time to start work. The factory specialized in batch production of coating machinery and maintained a stockpile in its warehouse. After completing the paperwork, making the payment, and collecting the goods, we finished everything by three o'clock. I explained the urgency to director Wang, who arranged for a truck to drop me off at the roadside in Shahe. Standing by the roadside, waiting for a bus, I hoped to catch one to Weifang and visit Zhangdian to return home by the next morning. I waited until five o'clock, but there was no car, so I could only stay in Shahe. I was just about to leave when a Huanghai bus arrived; I waved for it to stop and asked where it went.

"Zibo?"

"Get on the bus."

Just as I boarded the Yantai to Jinan long-distance bus, the attendant asked, "Where are you going?"

"Zhangdian."

"We do not go to Zhangdian, where the road is under repair; we go to Jinan from Hutian to Zichuan."

"Great! Zichuan to Jinan must go through it; I will get off there."

"Where is the enterprise?"

"Ten kilometers west of Zichuan, I will notify you when we arrive, and you can stop the bus on the side of the road."

"Wonderful! I'll be able to go home tonight."

As one in the morning approached, the bus stopped in front of the Business Cooperative Credit Union. Looking at my watch, I realized it was already past midnight. Various government departments from the town were stationed at the cooperative, about seven kilometers from my coating factory. I had cycled this route many times during the day, but it was the first time I had cycled it at night.

Carrying the valve, which weighed over 10 kilograms, I turned two corners, crossed three streets, and left the cooperative area, heading south along a mountain road. The road was not particularly hilly, just a slight incline. As I walked along the slightly flatter section of the road, with cornfields on either side, I could hear leaves rustling in the wind. Walking on the dark road, I felt afraid but pushed forward.

After climbing a short slope and making a turn, the road became gravelly. Looking ahead, I could see that I was nearing Stone Shallow Ditch. Locals referred to this stretch of road as Shiqian Ditch, a small and shallow gully. As I walked along the gully's edge, my head suddenly buzzed, and my whole body gave me goosebumps.

When I was younger, I had heard many stories about Shiqian Ditch, where a female ghost known as the White Daughter-in-Law was said to reside. Before the Liberation, there were stories from neighboring villages that someone would meet her at midnight near Shiqian Ditch. They said she would suddenly jump out and scare the person to the ground with her long white hair, protruding teeth, and green eyes before robbing them of their belongings.

Even after Liberation, a story from 1952 emerged of someone encountering her. Late one night, after drinking heavily, a man named Zhang encountered her on his way back from a friend's house. Despite her attempts to stop him, Zhang, encouraged by the lack of belief in ghosts in the post-Liberation era and fueled by alcohol, kicked her into the ditch and ran home as fast as he could.

As I remembered these stories, I realized I had entered Shiqian Ditch. This stretch of road, shaped like a bow, had a stone wall over two meters high on the north side, with the road running below it. On the south side was a shallow depression about two meters deep, which would fill with water during the summer rains. The road twisted and turned, with three small bends, uneven terrain, and loose gravel and sand. In the era of production teams, this road was repaired twice a year: once in the spring, when crops were being planted, and once before autumn to address any damage from rain. When the land was divided among households, the soil in these mountainous areas was only a few decimeters thick, prone to flooding when it rained and quickly drying up when it did not, making it unattractive for cultivation and leaving the road repairs neglected.

Carrying the valve, which still weighed over 10 kilograms, made every step feel slippery, and my heart pounded. I remembered the story of Lu Xun kicking ghosts from my fourth-grade textbook and reminded myself that ghosts did not exist; they were merely creations of human imagination. Pushing myself to be bold, I pressed forward without looking back. But I could not shake the feeling that someone was behind me, since I seemed to hear footsteps. When I turned to look, no one was there, and everything seemed normal. Upon reaching the middle stretch of Shiqian Ditch, I felt a great deal calmer. There was no White Daughter-in-Law here; it was all just a joke.

"Hoo, hoo, hoo, hoo meow...." The distant hooting of an owl startled me and made me shudder. My feet slipped, and I tumbled into the ditch. Falling to my hands and knees, I crawled along the bottom of the ditch, the valve rolling more than two meters away. As I stood up and surveyed my surroundings, I realized I was no longer afraid. Confirming that there was no White Daughter-in-Law, I retrieved the valve and climbed up from the shallow south side of the ditch. Passing through a patch of sweet potato fields, I found my way back to the original path, quickening my pace as if running until I had passed Shiqian Ditch.

A straight path led south, crossing a small river and passing through an area called Jiahou, indicating I was close to Xiaobaixi Village. I searched the edges of three fields but could not find the path. The more I panicked, the more elusive it became, and all I could see were fields of sweet potatoes. I gave up the search and continued westward, reaching an apple orchard. Surrounding the orchard was a path heading south, which I followed until I faintly saw a village ahead. When I realized it was Dabaixi Village, I felt a sense of relief. Even with my eyes closed, I could find my way home. With a sigh of relief, I felt the weight of the valve, and the sweat on my body dissipated, replaced by a cool breeze.

After returning home and showering, I noticed a sore spot on my calf where I had scratched it. Although I had not felt any pain during the journey, the wound had dried up by the time I arrived home. Finally, I was able to relax and fall asleep.

2.7 Financial and Tax Inspection

In the 1990s, most of the village-run enterprises underwent restructuring. In some areas, the contract responsibility system was implemented, where whoever handed over more profits to the village would operate the enterprise. In other places, the enterprises were privatized and sold to individuals. At the same time, the village only collected leasing fees and water charges. However, they still referred to the collective enterprise as an external business and managed it by the township government. The term "private" was discriminated against because enterprises were required to attend collective enterprise meetings, convey higher-level documents, and undergo regular inspections.

Township enterprises in the Zichuan area remained unchanged. Economic Committees were established in the township. The director was typically a deputy secretary (the third in command), taking charge of economic matters. The Economic Committee was an economic entity, meaning a large company. The director was the general manager, and the township secretary (the first in command) was now the chairman; the Economic Committee appointed the heads of the factories. Project product changes and operating rights were all overseen by the Economic Committee director. Major matters required approval from the chairman. The committee had seven deputy directors and established departments, including personnel, finance, operations, product development, procurement, auditing, political work, and village-run enterprises. With a complete structure, it operated in an orderly manner. There were two-story office buildings, dozens of offices, and working cadres. Apart from running factories, various economic entities, including gas stations, guesthouses, trading companies, and clinics, were also operational.

With such comprehensive management departments, enterprises underwent annual financial inspections and audits. The previous Tuesday, the Village-Run Enterprises Department had held a meeting for enterprise leaders to arrange matters related to the district government's financial and tax inspection. Deputy director Zou, who was in charge of village-run enterprises on the Economic Committee, conveyed deputy District mayor Xing's speech. The speech highlighted that, under the unified leadership of the provincial government, the municipal government, led by a deputy mayor, formed a joint group comprising the Finance Bureau, Tax Bureau, Audit Bureau, and Financial Office to conduct financial and tax inspections. Every year, there would be an annual financial and tax inspection for township and village-run enterprises in the city. Relevant government departments at all levels, as well as township and village enterprise managers, were required to study and understand the relevant documents and important speeches of the Party Central Committee, the State Council, and provincial and municipal leaders, actively cooperating to fulfill the tasks assigned by the higher authorities. Three requirements were put forward: first, we should seriously study relevant documents of the municipal government and understand the spirit of deputy mayor Shi's speech; second, we should conduct a self-examination and self-correction, identify and resolve problems, and complete this task positively; third, we should strictly prohibit all forms of misconduct, including special treatment, gift-giving, improper practices, and going through the motions. The meeting should end after the superior documents and the leader's speech had been conveyed.

Deputy director Zou assigned specific tasks. This year's inspection was given more importance than in previous years, with a focus on counterpart checks rather than each enterprise inspecting the financial staff of others, as had been the case in previous years. Each district county conducted cross-checks. For example, financial personnel from Zichuan District went to Linzi for inspection, Linzi went to Huantai, and Huantai went to Boshan, with a citywide rotation. This way, mutual cover-ups, personal relationships, unclear accounts, and trivializing issues could be avoided. If any problems were found, they had to be addressed accordingly.

For example, discrepancies between inventory and records had been a common issue in the past. There were 100 tons of goods in the factory's storage. However, 150 tons of goods were written on the warehouse slip. Records were meticulously fabricated, making it difficult to detect discrepancies at first glance. Each enterprise kept two sets of books — one for internal use and one for external presentation, ensuring meticulousness in the latter. If problems were discovered, fines would be borne by them. The time of the inspection team's arrival was not yet known. When they arrived, it would be best for factory managers not to be away on business but present at the enterprises to deal with problems promptly and minimize losses. Deputy director Zou's speech was sincere, practical, and detailed. They awaited further instructions after the meeting.

The inspection team has arrived. The inspection team from Huantai inspected township enterprises in Zichuan and split into two groups to visit Cicun Town. One group inspected township-run enterprises, while the other inspected village-run enterprises, with deputy director Zou leading the team for the village-run enterprises. The group leader and members were from the Huantai County finance department. Deputy director Zhou was responsible for arranging the reception and resolving various issues and interpersonal relationships. Our village had four village-run factories to be inspected before noon. Then, it moved to the neighboring village in the afternoon. After inspecting two villages, the inspection findings would be summarized in the afternoon. Each group consisted of nine members: one leader and eight team members who worked in pairs, conducting the inspections in the village committee office. Each factory accountant brought one year's financial records to assist with the inspection. The team members were diligent and responsible, meticulously checking every entry, including invoices, receipts, and accounting vouchers, leaving no stone unturned. Their scrutiny was even more meticulous than that of the Inland Revenue Department. The accountants promptly clarified any areas of confusion, and any problems found were meticulously recorded in their notebooks.

Deputy director Zou accompanied several factory directors from our village to another office. They chatted over tea until around eleven o'clock. They asked director Zou where to eat lunch. Director Zou replied that the town's Economic Committee had made unified arrangements, so there was no need to bother enterprises.

Deputy director Zou returned briefly and called for a meeting with the four factory directors. During the meeting, he discussed the inspection findings. He pointed out that the Electrical Fittings Factory had the largest scale and highest sales revenue among the four factories, but had several issues. These included unrecorded transactions, discrepancies between outgoing and incoming goods records, and serial numbers that could not be traced. In total, there were more than a dozen items with problems. The Electrical Fittings Factory had a higher output value than the combined output of the other three smaller factories. The smaller factories had fewer documents and certificates, and several issues were not discussed in detail. The accountants provided each factory with a list of identified issues to address, and corrective actions were implemented individually for each factory. Fines were assessed based on predetermined standards, totaling over 70,000 yuan for the four factories. The larger factory was fined two to three times more than the smaller ones. After hearing this, the four factory directors expressed dissatisfaction with the significant increase compared to previous years. They asked deputy director Zou to provide solutions and suggestions to minimize the burden.

After the discussion, the deputy director Zou took a sip of tea and cleared his throat before explaining his delay. He had been negotiating with Chen, the leader of the inspection team from Huantai, to minimize the fines. As the inspection team leader, Chen mentioned that the municipal government had set higher targets for each district county this year, with a 10 percent increase from the previous year. The amount set must be met; there was no room for reduction. If we paid less, other enterprises would receive more severe penalties. Chen refused to compromise despite repeated negotiations. It was a coincidence; five years before, Zou and Chen had been classmates in the city's accounting training courses, where they studied and attended lectures together. We caught up with our classmates, paid half of the fine, and then discussed the nature of friendship. However, after subtracting half of the fine again, the total came down, resulting in a payment of only slightly more than 20,000. Everyone was satisfied with it; it was slightly higher than last year, costing a few hundred yuan more. When deputy director Zou retold his negotiation story, everyone was relieved; the factory directors were busy pouring water for director Zou and handing out cigarettes.

To show our appreciation, director Sun said, "Which restaurant should we go to?"

Manager Li from the stone factory quickly said, "There's a new chain restaurant from Jinan in Zichuan, 'Xiang-E Jiujia,' a restaurant with specialty dishes from Guangxi and Hubei. Let's go try it out."

Everyone started discussing enthusiastically, and the atmosphere became lively.

After director Zou allowed everyone to finish speaking, he continued, "I understand everyone's mood, but the inspection team will be leaving this afternoon, and tomorrow is Sunday, so we will not have a meal. I discussed this with Team Leader Chen, and everyone is satisfied with how this year's situation was handled. We want to express our gratitude. Each person can buy a small gift without spending too much money."

Team Leader Chen was honest and informed me that they had already purchased T-shirts and other shirts in the previous villages. After some discussion, each male comrade would receive a windproof lighter costing over 300 yuan. In comparison, two female comrades would purchase cosmetics totaling over 2,700 yuan. We would skip dinner that night to save money for the banquet in Zichuan. Director Zou's speech left everyone satisfied. Director Zou and Team Leader Chen worked together in excellent cooperation.

The financial audit was completed. It went through the formality with much crying and little wool, or the loud thunder but small raindrops. It was rare for the four factory directors to gather together, making it a challenge to dine with director Zou. We opted for the highest-grade restaurant in town, Jiangnan Jiujia Restaurant. Deputy director Zou sent the inspection team away and arrived promptly at six o'clock. Deputy director Zou, the four factory directors, the village CPC secretary, and the accountant gathered together. The specialties filled the table, including meicai kourou (pork with salted vegetables), jiaoyan paigu (pepper salt spareribs), beef, and donkey meat, along with a bottle of the Yunmen Jianiang wine and a case of Tsingtao beer. Accompanied by deputy director Zou, we aimed for an even bigger victory next time.

A van came when I opened the newspaper and read the headlines in the office at noon. Two people exited the car, walking confidently with solemn, measured steps and looking around as they made their way towards the office. Their demeanor was unusual and did not seem like a regular business inquiry. I stood up from the sofa and greeted them, but they did not respond or sit down. They scanned the office with their eyes for a minute or two before sitting on the sofa.

I asked, "Which department are you from?"

They replied, "The Inland Revenue."

After I had offered them tea and cigarettes, the taller ones introduced themselves: "We are from the Kunshan branch, just here to take a look. This is our director Hu, who was transferred from Beigou a few days ago."

Another slender person added to the conversation. I extend my sincere greetings to them.

Director Hu asked, "How is the production? Still running smoothly? Is the accountant at home?"

I said, "Yes, he's at home."

The slender man stood up and continued, "Have you received the notice? We are conducting a routine inspection and will return last year's accounts to the branch. We'll come to the branch to collect them next Tuesday."

Upon receiving this information, I quickly informed Accountant Wang, who packed last year's accounts and vouchers into a cardboard box and loaded them into the van. Director Hu only had a glass of water and stayed for about fifteen minutes before leaving,

A month prior, a notice had been issued regarding the financial and tax inspection. The financial audit had been completed, and the inspection team had arrived to review the accounts and determine the amount of fines. To date, there had been no news on how the tax inspection would be conducted. However, they suddenly visited today and removed the account books while requesting the accounting vouchers. It is uncertain what new requirements they might have.

In previous years, during tax audits, they were always found to be associated with any company, regardless of whether it was state-owned, collective, or an individual enterprise. Due to an unwritten rule, the amount found did not necessarily have to match what should have been paid. The higher-level department set the target. In the first half of this year, each district's tax bureau was required to collect a specific amount, which was then distributed to each branch. Meeting the target was crucial, and it became more challenging every year. The audit rules and scope of the audit changed annually. While companies were unaware, the tax officers were well-informed. They could determine the amounts of fines to impose on a company. Both business owners and tax officers were familiar with this practice. Both collective and individual enterprises kept two sets of books. If your books are audited, fines might be imposed based on the findings. The fine amount was determined by the social connections of the company's managers.

Three days after taking the accounts, the Kunshan Inland Revenue Department notified us to visit director Hu's office at 9 a.m. the next day.

"Factory director Yu, there are quite a few issues found during the inspection, about a dozen or so. I've made a list for you and the accountant to see."

When I entered the director of Bureau Hu's office and sat down, director Hu took two sheets of paper from a folder. I looked at one, and the accountant looked at the other. A shipment of goods was not accounted for, and only two tons were invoiced, but no tax had been paid. There were also two cars, totaling 130,000 yuan in value, which had to be paid in back taxes. I knew the latter; I would deal with it myself.

"Director Hu, this payment for the truck is a payment for goods, and it's already been taxed, so why do we have to pay additional tax?"

I felt it was reasonable to question.

"Factory director Yu, was the transaction for the cars? Were they sold to someone else?"

"Yes, they were sold to someone else. This is the sales amount. Our factory doesn't produce cars."

"Buying and selling require paying taxes. Whether it is production or purchasing from others, you must pay taxes as long as you sell products. Do you understand?"

Director Hu's tone grew increasingly higher with each sentence, sounding increasingly angry. I could not ask any more questions; the Inland Revenue Department was following the law. Upon examining the fine notice, the amount was found to be 1,2362 yuan.

"Go back and prepare the money. It should be paid next week. If it's late, there will be a late fee." Director Hu said confidently.

"If we can't afford it, director Hu, please consider it."

"Do your best. If I can help, I will be happy to. I have a meeting at ten." Director Hu said as he stood up.

Accountant Wang and I took good notice and left the office.

"Damn, he's so ruthless."

I cursed softly; only Accountant Wang could hear. During last year's tax inspection, the accounts had not been taken. Director Du looked through them in the office and fined us only 3,000 yuan. Du was my cousin's comrade in arms, but he had been transferred this year, and Hu had taken his place. It had been three years of tax inspections, with fines not exceeding a few thousand yuan each year, the most being 5,000. This year, it was more than 10 times that amount, so we needed to find a solution quickly.

The factory director, Li, was an old friend of mine. He found out where director Hu lived and told me that InzoneMall had just launched shopping vouchers, which were more convenient than gifts. He advised me to buy two vouchers and send them to director Hu.

Director Hu lived in the suburbs of the city. He had a single courtyard, which was easily accessible. At eight o'clock in the evening, Accountant Wang and I walked to the end of the street and found the house number. We knocked on the door, and a middle-aged woman answered.

I asked, "Is this director Hu's house?"

She replied, "Yes, please come in."

Director Hu was sitting on the sofa and stood up to greet us, saying, "Please have a seat."

Director Hu appeared tired and slightly intoxicated after our initial greetings.

I presented the shopping vouchers, saying, "Here is a shopping voucher. Feel free to buy something small."

As I attempted to leave, director Hu grabbed my arm and attempted to return the voucher to me. Director Hu retrieved it and pushed it back into my pocket before ushering us out the door, insisting that it was unacceptable. I took it out and threw it onto the sofa. Director Hu retrieved it and pushed it back into my pocket before ushering us out the door, insisting that it was unacceptable.

I realized that three or four factory directors had sent gifts to director Hu, and director Hu had accepted them. When I gave him a gift, however, he did not accept it, and he refused it quite firmly, most likely because we were unfamiliar with each other. Paying according to the ticket had never been like this. If I delayed, my colleagues would say I could not handle things and lacked competence. Therefore, I found another way. I sought the help of director Liu, who was enthusiastic and had been friends with director Hu for five or six years. They had known each other since before director Hu was transferred to Kunshan. Director Liu said that director Hu had strong self-esteem and enjoyed making friends over drinks. If he had been treated once, it would be easier to discuss things later. In the meantime, I should raise the issue of the fine that occurred a few days ago, which could then be resolved more easily. Director Liu promised to arrange a banquet within three or four days.

The restaurant was in an unmarked alley and appeared to be an ordinary family courtyard from the outside. It was my first visit there, and I found that it was quite upscale, with prices comparable to those of a three-star hotel, as arranged by director Liu. Director Hu invited three colleagues, and I purchased four T-shirts, one for each person. Director Liu told me that there was an unwritten rule in the Inland

Revenue Department about entertaining guests.

"If the unit you are in charge of invites you, I will ask a few of my colleagues to join. When the unit I am responsible for hosts guests, I will invite you to join us and give each person a gift. If you know familiar people, please get in touch with them in advance. The gift is not important. When we are familiar with each other in the future, we don't have to be large-scale in treating people, and it's fine to act individually in various forms."

There were six diners and two female servers pouring wine and water. The host and I poured a glass for each person. After the ceremonial drinks, the female servers encouraged more drinking. The restaurant's tax bureau officials were regulars, and the servers were familiar with them. They drank freely; if one drank, the other had to drink, clinking glasses and exchanging them differently. The first to falter was a petite waitress. She could not hold her liquor, swaying and leaning against the wall as she left the scene, followed by cheers from the table. After drinking to about 80 or 90 percent of his capacity, director Hu raised a toast to the two directors, insisting they drink together. It was unacceptable not to drink; he could not lose face. After downing the drink, he could barely stand. His colleagues could only lie down and leave the scene when they drank another glass! Unable to sit still and maintain manners, they slipped out to pay the bill.

"You continue drinking!" they said.

The next day, I met with director Liu for tea to discuss our next steps.

Director Liu bluntly said, "Now is the time for gifts. Last night, we had a very good time drinking, and we should keep it up."

Since director Hu had not accepted the shopping vouchers, what should we send? Director Liu knew that director Hu liked collecting different stones, so I immediately went to arrange them.

On Monday, Accountant Wang and I hurried to director Hu's office. He had just opened the door and invited us to sit down, making a cup of tea for each of us.

"Director Yu, you are good at drinking. Last night, you finished a bottle by yourself."

"I'm sorry, director Hu. I left early; otherwise, I would have made a scene after drinking too much."

Director Hu took two sheets of office paper from the left side of his desk and looked at them for a few minutes, muttering to himself.

"Where to start? The car? The inventory?"

He scribbled on the paper with a pen.

"Director Yu, I've removed some unimportant items. I've calculated the rest."

Director Hu took out a calculator and punched in some numbers.

"It adds up to over 13,000. Is that okay? Take this, and there's nothing else I can do."

"That's fine, that's fine. Thank you, director Hu."

"Once you have collected the fines, request that accountant Wang deliver them here. If this method meets your requirements, it is acceptable."

Director Hu said as he opened the door, "Little Zhang, come here."

Shortly after, a lady in a tax collector's uniform stood before director Hu's desk. He pointed to the paper, drawing lines and making marks.

"Fix this number, print it, stamp it with the official seal, and bring it over."

The tax audit had been completed, and my factory had fulfilled its duties. Director Hu poured each of us a glass of water, smiled, and pointed to accountant Wang.

"You should be more careful in the future. It is obvious when there's a discrepancy in the accounts. You cannot show on the books that you sold a truck and recorded it as a sale of goods. The sales and receipts must match. In the future, you have to avoid taking detours."

Accountant Wang nodded repeatedly. After a brief conversation, the lady in the tax collector's uniform brought the printed payment receipt and handed it to director Hu. After a glance, I signed it, he signed it, and we each kept a copy. Director Hu escorted us out of the office, shaking hands with us. We said our goodbyes and returned to the factory.

2.8 Participating in the People's Congress
2.8.1

The loudspeakers on the streets blared repeatedly. Today, the villagers were convening a general meeting to elect their village head and representatives to the People's Congress. I listened attentively from my office. It was the first time the villagers had directly elected their village chief. I actively participated, aiming to select a competent village committee and representatives to the People's Congress that would meet the villagers' needs. It is a fresh experience to see how the election process works.

The election meeting was held in the courtyard of the village committee office. Two small tables were set up in the middle, surrounded by dozens of villagers. They stood in groups of three or five, chatting and laughing, creating a lively atmosphere. Most present were elderly or homemakers, with few employed or working outside.

From the era of production teams to the reform and opening up in the 1980s and 1990s, village-level elections were not conducted among all villagers at the village level. The village party branch secretary and the town party committee appointed positions; elections were formalities. The process involved holding a party member meeting, announcing appointment letters, and passing them with raised hands. The branch secretary, village head, and committee members were appointed without proper procedures. This habit persisted for many years. That day was the first election, and the common folk were at a loss regarding how to proceed. Voter cards were distributed at the entrance — one per person over the age of eighteen. I received seven voter cards for my mother, my younger brother, and others in three families. I stood for over 10 minutes and returned to the office before the meeting began.

Upon my return to the office, I received a call from the machinery factory of the Mining Bureau. Director Sun was scheduled to visit at noon to see the new products. I immediately arranged for the courtyard to be cleaned, the workshop to be tidied up, and selected new product samples to be selected. Once the preparations were completed, director

Sun and his entourage arrived. I was therefore unable to participate in the election, as I had to receive important guests.

While I was preparing to accompany director Sun to the restaurant, Village Committee Member Zhang and Party Group Leader Little Zhao unexpectedly entered the office carrying a cardboard box.

They greeted me cheerfully, saying, "Exercise your voting rights!"

"Where are the ballots?" I asked.

"Here," Zhang replied, holding a bundle of them. "How many for your family?"

"I have several voter cards, so give me a few. Let me count... one, two... seven."

He took seven and counted seven from another packet and handed them to me. Then, Zhang counted out another seven from another bundle and handed them to me. As I looked at the ballots, I saw the names of the incumbent village committee members, the candidates for the People's Congress, and even my name.

"I can also be a representative," I muttered to myself.

"Who else, if not you?"

Zhang urged me to mark the ballots quickly.

"Could you please make a trip for me?" I said, marking the ballots while conversing politely with Zhang.

Due to the insufficient number of participants in the election, mobile ballot boxes were arranged to visit each household. The task had to be completed by noon, and the report would be made to the town. I stood and finished marking the ballots, and Zhang left hurriedly.

After director Sun left, I napped in the office for an hour. As soon as I finished drinking a glass of water, Village Party Secretary Chen and Zhang, the committee member, arrived.

Secretary Chen exclaimed, "Congratulations on being elected as a People's Congress representative. Here's your certificate of election."

"But this is your appointment; how could I be elected?"

I took the certificate and invited Secretary Chen to sit down.

"The appointment is not yet complete, but the procedure is complete, and all the villagers chose it anyway," Secretary Chen said casually, sitting comfortably on the sofa.

Zhang continued, "The election went smoothly without any mistakes. The villagers were very conscious and followed the intentions of the town government leaders, selecting the village head and representatives to the People's Congress. The town's top leaders are very satisfied."

I had to say a few words, too, going along with the flow: "With the correct leadership of the Party and the town government leaders in charge, wherever they direct, the common people will follow. That's for sure."

Secretary Chen continued, "In three days, the town-level elections will be over, followed by the town People's Congress convening. You cannot be absent from the People's Congress. The town mayor and deputy mayor are to be elected for the first time since the country's founding. The leaders attach great importance to it, fearing mistakes. The representatives are elected through discussions between the town leaders and the village committee. They are reliable and loyal. We believe you will support the town's work. Secretary Li of the town asked us to inform everyone first to prepare mentally and conduct the People's Congress well."

Secretary Chen, who had been the branch secretary for over a year, now spoke with an official tone.

Secretary Chen was a year older than I, and he was a childhood friend and neighbor of mine. Our houses were about 20 meters apart, both from landowning families. He was a grade ahead of me in school, excelling academically and politically. When I graduated from primary school, the school reserved three seats for students, as per the Party's policy, who could be educated well despite their low-income family backgrounds. Before the Cultural Revolution in 1966, I passed the entrance exam for Zibo No. 4 Middle School. After graduating, I returned to my hometown and worked in the fields. Before the Cultural Revolution, my grandfather had shed his label as a landlord and become a rehabilitated member of the People's Commune. When the Cultural Revolution came, there was no distinction between those who had had their labels removed and those who still wore them. When filling out forms for family members, under the "Background" section, it was still "Landlord." The removed labels were reattached. It was thus more challenging for children to pursue education, find employment, or form relationships. Some old classmates had not received their graduation certificates for six or seven years and had not participated in the school's Cultural Revolution. They farmed at home instead. They could work hard in the production team, but could not hold significant positions or even become timekeepers. It was not until after the Third Plenary Session of the Eleventh Central Committee in 1978 that one of them became the accountant for the production team. After the dissolution of the People's Commune in 1983, he became the accountant for the brigade. In 1994, he became the secretary of the village Party branch. Twenty years ago, I had never dreamed of becoming a Party branch secretary.

It was quite natural for me to become a representative. In contrast, my old classmate became the secretary because of our close relationship.

The next day, the town government leaders would hold a symposium with the elected representatives from the San Shan area. The area comprised seven villages with 20 representatives and seven village secretaries. Secretaries were not representatives, but the village heads had to be. The symposium would be held in the conference room of the Majiazhuang Village Committee. At 10 o'clock, the leaders arrived. Secretary Li led the way, followed by the mayor, the deputy Secretary, the deputy mayor, and the Office director. All the town leaders were present. The seats in the meeting room were arranged neatly according to the officials' ranks. We took our seats and awaited the leaders' speeches.

In his forties, the township Party Secretary, Li, who had a healthy complexion and high spirits, greeted everyone warmly, without the formality of a government meeting. He pulled his chair closer to the representatives. Today's meeting was informal, serving as an opportunity for the leaders to meet with representatives. It would be a joke if the secretary did not know the representatives. The Sanpianshan area was vast, comprising four distinct areas within the town. As the town's leader, it had the largest population and industrial output value. One was also the first stop for inspections. This People's Congress meeting would be the first to address the format and procedure of inspections since the country's founding.

In the previous sessions, representatives were appointed by the leaders. But this time, candidates were put forward by various levels of leadership, and the common people elected them. The election of the town mayor and deputy mayor was a crucial item on the agenda for this People's Congress. Representatives would vote, and the candidate who received the most votes would be elected. The mayors were all cadres dispatched by the higher authorities and were not elected, regardless of their appointment. It was important to note that they were all government cadres. Their superiors had an overall plan for their promotions. The allocation of mayors and deputy mayors in each town had been arranged properly. It was important to note that their speeches had been edited for grammatical correctness, sentence structure, and vocabulary to ensure accessibility and clarity. It was expected that the representatives would possess a high level of political consciousness and literacy and would not make uninformed choices. Two new deputy mayors had been transferred here and were being introduced. This was done by mayor Wang, who stood up and bowed to the assembled crowd. He was previously the deputy director of the district government office, with extensive political experience, an honest character, and a strong work ethic. And this was deputy mayor Liu, formerly the deputy mayor of Chuanghe Township. He therefore had experience working in townships. Wang said, "Representatives are familiar with these three deputy mayors, so I would not introduce them individually."

After the secretary had finished speaking, mayor Guo delivered a speech. The country promoted democratic elections, starting with direct elections at the village level. Every eligible citizen had one vote to elect village heads and committee members. The first step was to implement this system at the village level. The central government was not yet considering direct elections at the town level because it would lead to chaos, as the common people were not yet at the required level of understanding. But this step should be taken eventually, since representatives must be elected at the town and township levels. Our mission was to fulfill this historic task. This was a significant responsibility entrusted to us by the Party and the government. Today, we provided information on the procedures that would be followed step by step during the meeting.

The deputy mayors expressed their determination to serve the people and enterprises wholeheartedly, dedicating themselves to being the people's servants.

One representative was selected to speak. Old Zhang, sitting next to the Office director, stood up. He was a veteran cadre from Hexi. The municipal Party Secretary's speeches and the district government's documents would be studied and comprehended, he announced. We would fulfill the glorious task assigned to us under the strong leadership of the town Party Committee and the government. We would not cause trouble for the leaders or present them with difficult problems. The representative became increasingly impassioned, veering off-topic. A village secretary beside him nudged him several times, signaling him to stop. Eventually, the representative's speech came to a halt.

At noon, the Office director announced the symposium's conclusion. There were four tables with interspersed seating for town leaders and delegates, with two leaders at each table as the main host and the deputy host. The Office director had arranged everything meticulously, and the seating arrangement was impeccable.

The Secretary proposed a toast: "Good afternoon, everyone. Today, we gather to exchange ideas. Let's drink to the successful holding of the town's People's Congress and the fulfillment of the task entrusted to us by the Party."

The banquet proceeded in a lively atmosphere. Secretary Li suggested finishing a glass in one gulp. Everyone did so. Sanshan

Hotel was the highest-class restaurant in town, featuring chefs from Boshan who prepare famous dishes and serve Zibo's renowned liquor, Yellow River Loong Wine. The mayor proposed a second toast for a united and successful congress.

2.8.2

The first session of the Fifth People's Congress of Yaowu Town was held in the auditorium of the town's middle school. The preparatory meeting was opened at 8:00 a.m., with the selection of officers for the General Assembly. The staff read out the list of presidium members, and approval was signified by raising hands. The list of conference secretary-generals, checkers, and vote counters was announced as the second item. Approval was given unanimously by raised hands. The presidium members were invited to take their seats, and the venue erupted in applause.

Everyone stood up and sang the national anthem. The solemn opening ceremony of the first session of the Fifth People's Congress of Yaowu Town began with this majestic tune.

The mayor delivered the government work report. The previous year had been challenging due to complex international and domestic situations. However, under the correct leadership of Mao Zedong Thought, Deng Xiaoping Theory, and the Three Represents, and under the correct leadership of the Party Central Committee and the provincial, municipal, and district Party committees and governments, they had made significant progress in town construction by vigorously implementing the five major strategies of Yaowu (窑坞) and focusing on fighting three major battles. They had made exemplary progress in town construction, achieving significant results. Last year, the town had completed a fixed asset investment of 1.55 billion yuan, a 25 percent increase over the previous year. Tax revenue had reached 120 million yuan, with local fiscal revenue totaling 69.52 million yuan, a 21 percent increase over the previous year...

They had focused on two key projects during the comprehensive battle and promoted the construction of basic infrastructure. They had invested 100 million yuan in upgrading and renovating two town-level roads. They had also ensured social stability and safeguarded people's livelihoods, vigorously promoting the construction of a harmonious society and developing projects that enhanced them.

This year was crucial for deepening reform and laying the groundwork for a new start. The officials would work to accelerate the development of rural areas, enhance the development environment, actively promote project construction, and attract investment....

The mayor continued to his fellow delegates that Yaowu's construction had entered a new stage. They must forge ahead with determination, deepen their reforms, be practical and realistic, conduct in-depth investigations, face no difficulties, and be unafraid of risks. They must enforce laws in a standardized manner, governed by law, be upright and selfless, and serve the people diligently.

Yaowu's development had reached a new historical starting point, with promising prospects and arduous tasks ahead. Under the strong leadership of the town Party committee, they had to gather the wisdom and strength of the people of Yaowu. They would carry forward the past, seize the moment, and compose an even more brilliant and magnificent new chapter.

The mayor's report was powerful and resonant, and the venue fell silent, with only the mayor's clear and melodious voice echoing throughout. The report lasted 40 minutes.

The staff then read the town's financial budget report. The overall budget execution of the town included public expenditure, education expenditure of 1.2 million yuan, scientific and technological expenditure of 300,000 yuan, and urban and rural community expenditure of 1.23 million yuan, totaling expenditures of 3.73 million yuan. There was also public budget revenue, including local tax revenue of 52 million yuan, various special fund revenues of 1.7 million yuan, and other sources, totaling 73.32 million yuan. The budget for the year had thus achieved a balance between revenue and expenditure. The financial budget arrangements included public service expenditure of 1.5 million yuan, representing a 2.5 percent increase; scientific and technological expenditure of 400,000 yuan, a 30 percent increase; and education expenditure of 2.1 million yuan, a 90 percent increase. The total expenditure was 86.88 million yuan. The town's public financial budget had indeed relatively balanced revenue and expenditure.

The financial work for the new year was challenging, and they had greater responsibilities. They were determined to implement the resolutions of this congress under the correct leadership of the town Party committee and government, under the supervision of the town People's Congress and all sectors of society. The mayor called on the audience to be inspired, work solidly, and satisfactorily complete all financial tasks, making new and greater contributions to all undertakings in the town.

2.8.3
Representatives gathered for group discussions. Each area formed a group, with the Sanshan District convening in a small meeting room on the second floor. The head of each district acted as the group leader. The discussion focused on the mayor's government work report and the government's financial budget report. After a few remarks from the group leaders, they asked who would speak first. No one responded, so one of them pointed to the seats in the front row and said, "Let's start speaking from here. Such an important report, it is not possible to say a few words. The head of the town government's report spoke to the hearts of our people. It outlines grand plans and three major campaigns, emphasizing increases in industrial output value and improvements in people's livelihoods to achieve a moderately prosperous society within three years. It's excellent." Following the content of the first speaker, the second and third speakers climbed higher on the same pole, discussing lofty goals, five key projects, and the three major campaigns. As the discussions continued, some ran out of things to say.

After the silence, the group leader said, "Let's suggest some reasonable proposals and urgent matters that need attention. Everyone, please share your thoughts."

A representative suddenly realized, "The dangerous bridge in the north of our village, the town promised to repair it last year, but it has not been done yet. It needs to be fixed immediately."

Another representative added, "The road connecting our village to the town is full of potholes, making driving impossible". It needs to be repaired immediately."

Representatives competed to speak, discussing various issues, from kindergarten repairs to village squares, and expressing their opinions passionately. As one representative finished speaking, another would immediately take over. The two recorders were sweating profusely, their hands trembling as they struggled to keep pace. However, they were determined to complete everything accurately, which pleased the group leader. The mayor stood for a few minutes, promising to take all suggestions seriously and implement them promptly after the meeting.

A plenary session was held in the afternoon to explain the election procedures. This election law was formulated according to the "Organic Law of the People's Congress of the People's Republic of China and the Organic Law of Local People's Congresses at all Levels."

The system of people's congresses is the fundamental political system of our country. It is the basic form through which the Chinese people exercise people's democratic dictatorship and achieve self-governance. The Congress completed its election tasks. This session of the Congress elected one mayor and five deputy mayors.

The moderator read out the work resumes of the mayor and deputy mayors and explained the election process. According to the election law, a mayor and an equal number of candidates would be elected. Six candidates for deputy mayor were nominated, including the current five deputy mayors and the director of the Agricultural Committee. Everyone took this election seriously, as instructed by the higher authorities, to elect a new leadership team for the government.

After the meeting, group discussions were held to elect the mayor and deputy mayors. The group leader explained the procedures for equal and differential elections, and the representatives engaged in discussions eagerly. Most deputy mayors were unfamiliar with each other and lacked understanding of the situation. Hence, the selection process was somewhat challenging. The separate meeting rooms were chaotic for a while. Still, when Secretary Li and two deputy mayors joined the discussion, the atmosphere gradually calmed down.

Secretary Li greeted everyone warmly, standing among them instead of taking a seat.

"I'll say a few words," he began. Secretary Li explained that this was not the first Congress in the town; there had been four previous sessions. However, this was the first time the mayor and deputy mayor were being elected. Before the Congress, he had reminded everyone to uphold democracy while maintaining the Party's leadership, to exercise their representative rights, and to comply with the government's arrangements. He emphasized the Party's policy of democratic centralism and the importance of conducting the election flawlessly. He openly mentioned the case of a failed Congress in another county due to secret collusion and factionalism, resulting in the unexpected defeat of the incumbent mayor's re-election bid. Secretary Li emphasized the importance of vigilance and urged everyone to contribute to the success of this Congress. He concluded by expressing his trust in everyone to conduct the Congress and successfully elect the town's leadership team.

The audience applauded enthusiastically, and Secretary Li made no further comment, instead announcing that three other groups would also need to participate.

The discussion continued. After Secretary Li had left, the group leader, Liu Jiazhuang, spoke briefly. He had been the secretary of the old village branch for over 20 years. He was known for his seriousness and sense of responsibility. He never spoke lightly. The group leader mentioned that before the Congress, the secretary and the mayor had spoken to them repeatedly, stressing the importance of the election work. They emphasized that any mistake in this election would be considered a failure, such as not electing the designated deputy mayors or electing other alternates. Those elected as alternate deputy mayors would be reassigned, and if elected deputy mayors failed to meet expectations, it would reflect poorly on the leadership's capability. As trusted representatives, they could not afford to make mistakes. The group leader urged everyone to follow the instructions carefully.

The first day of the meeting came to an end. The group leader informed everyone to collect souvenirs from the organizing committee, with each representative receiving a Flying Swallow towel blanket, a renowned product from Zibo. The banquet would be held at Longxing Hotel, starting at 6:00 p.m. sharp, with guests arriving by 5:30 p.m..

The Longxing Hotel, which the Credit Cooperative occupied, had opened in the building a month prior. After the cooperative moved out, the building was sold to Mr. Meng. One of the halls could accommodate 10 banquet tables.

The arrangements made by the organizing committee were meticulous and thoughtful. With 10 tables set up, I was seated at the fifth table. There was carefully arranged seating for each representative and official. The secretary, the town head, and the deputy secretary, along with the other three secretaries, sat at the head of each table, accompanied by nine people, one at each table. They were joined by six deputy town-heads, the director, the head of the office, the head of urban planning, and the head of the agricultural committee. Representatives from various departments, including the Public Security Bureau, the bank, the school, the hospital, the court, and some staff members, filled the remaining seats.

Deputy mayor Guo delivered a toast, "Good evening, everyone. After a long day of meetings, I salute your hard work! Today's meeting progressed smoothly, with many valuable suggestions regarding the government report. This election has instilled confidence in everyone. With your high level of political awareness and excellent ideological consciousness, I am confident that you can fulfill the honorable task entrusted to us by the district party Committee and the Government. Let's toast to the successful completion of this session's town government leadership election and a fruitful future."

The second day began with the third plenary session, which focused on the election of the mayor and deputy mayors. The moderator reiterated the election procedures, explaining that the ballots were large red tickets. Representatives could vote in favor, against, choose another candidate, or abstain from voting. Those in favor would mark an "O" in the space provided, while those against would mark an "X" above the candidate's name. Abstentions did not need to be marked. The staff began distributing the ballots while the deputy Secretary and deputy mayors, who were not participating in the election, stood on both sides of the aisle and observed the representatives as they cast their votes.

A ballot box was placed in the meeting room. Voting began, starting with the supervisors and then proceeding to the presidium. Representatives lined up to cast their votes. After a few minutes, voting was closed, and the observers, scrutineers, and supervisors publicly counted the votes. The count was complete, with over 80 ballots processed in just under 10 minutes.

Once the counting was finished, the chief vote counter reported the election results to the presidium. Of the 83 delegates present, 83 ballots were received. The results were as follows: Guo, the mayoral candidate, received 83 votes; Wang, one of the deputy mayoral candidates, received 77 votes; Li received 81 votes; Liu received 79 votes; Zhang received 71 votes; and Chen received 80 votes. The Chairman of the Presidium, Secretary Li, announced that all six candidates for mayor and deputy mayor had been elected, prompting a round of applause.

Secretary Li spoke again, praising the collective efforts of all representatives for their unity, adherence to revolutionary traditions, and fulfillment of the Party's and the people's expectations, which ensured the successful completion of the Congress agenda. He expressed satisfaction with the election of the new town government leadership team. He described the Congress as a united and victorious event. Finally, he thanked all the representatives and declared the Fifth Session of the Yao Village People's Congress officially closed.

CHAPTER 3
THE STORY OF BEVERAGE BOTTLES

3.1 Encountering Plastic Bottled Beverages

Mr. Liu sold paint in Weiguzhen Town, Zhangdian District, Zibo, Shandong Province. He operated a sundry shop on Weigu Street. I had not been there for two months, but Mr. Liu had entrusted the driver of the paint truck to pass along the message, urging me to come for a drink. He enjoyed making drinking buddies. One day, with nothing much to do, I filled a truck with paint, unloaded most of it at surrounding grocery stores, leaving a dozen barrels, and finally arrived at Mr. Liu's sundry shop. After unloading the paint, Mr. Liu had already prepared four or five dishes. Mr. Liu enjoyed cooking and excelled at preparing several dishes. He could drink half a Jin (about 530 milliliters) of Wuhedaqu (乌河大曲 , a kind of liquor in Shandong Province). I invited two friends to accompany us.

Each person had two glasses of liquor, and we started playing finger-guessing games (划拳 , a finger game for fun while drinking). Suddenly, Mr. Liu's son came in from outside, holding a plastic beverage bottle.

One of the drinking buddies pointed at the bottle in the kid's hand and said, "My brother-in-law's factory produced this."

"Is there a beverage factory in Weiguzhen Town?" one of the buddies asked.

"There are beverage and plastic bottle factories," the friend replied. "My brother-in-law only produces beverage bottles."

"Where are the other beverage factories?" I joined the conversation. "I heard there's one in Linzi District."

The paint had been in production for over two years and was already on track. However, transportation limitations in the region made it difficult to scale up operations. Paternal Uncle Sun, skilled in mechanical molds, had ample experience. We were considering introducing a new product.

I asked the friend, "How's the market for beverages?"

"Kids love drinking them. It is much better than eating ice pops," he replied.

"How about your brother-in-law's beverage bottle production?" I continued to inquire.

"The beverage factory comes to pick up the goods, but production is intermittent. They work for three days and rest for two. It is hard to buy plastic raw materials," my friend answered.

I had processed waste plastic for three years. I had seen the production of plastic barrels in a plastic factory, which was a straightforward process. Upon hearing this information, I became interested. Taking advantage of the lively atmosphere, I continued chatting with my friend.

"Brother, I'm thinking of producing beverage bottles. Can I compete with your brother-in-law?"

"The market in Zibo is so big. Whoever has the capability can enter. The problem with beverage bottles is not the market; it is who can buy plastic raw materials. Bottles sell well, but plastic raw materials are hard to come by," the friend replied candidly.

We drank two glasses consecutively. The table was filled with spirited young drinkers. Mr. Liu was the first at the table to get drunk, while the two guests were just entering their prime drinking state. I could no longer hold on and quickly left.

Four or five days later, I received a telegram from Mr. Liu: "Come to my shop urgently for a discussion. Don't delay."

I was puzzled. Liu just sold paint. Anything matter? How hurried he was!

In the 1980s, taking the bus to contact the business was troublesome. I had to change buses three times to get to Weiguzhen Town. I could not drive an empty truck to drink with Liu, but I could go with a delivery truck. No matter how urgent it was to meet with Mr. Liu, I still had to contact other clients while delivering the goods. After loading a truck with paint, I headed for Mr. Liu's sundry shop, ensuring not to delay the two matters.

Following the usual routine, I finally unloaded the paint at Mr. Liu's shop. Just as I had finished unloading, the man who had accompanied us in drinking earlier arrived on his bicycle with another person following behind. After sitting down for a few minutes, he got to the point. My brother-in-law and I discussed the beverage bottle we had discussed last time. He no longer wanted to continue, feeling horrible about going out, unable to build social connections, and struggling to afford plastic raw materials. He wanted to sell the entire set of machinery and molds. Since Mr. Yu was interested, we decided to talk it over. Both sides were in agreement. With the idea of producing beverage bottles in mind, I did not expect the opportunity to come so soon. We agreed to inspect the machinery first and then discuss the details.

The beverage bottle factory was located east of Weigucun Village in a warehouse used by the production team. It was currently producing beverage bottles as before. There were three workers, one plastic extrusion machine, one air compressor, and two sets of molds, all of which were visible. After standing next to the molds for a few minutes to observe them, I gained an understanding of how they worked. There were two sets of molds for the cycle work. Compressed air was blown into the molds with one set, and the molding process was completed. After a brief cooling period, the mold was opened in just over 10 seconds, and a bottle was taken out while the other set of molds had already produced another bottle. The two sets of molds could produce seven to eight beverage bottles per minute, and the process was very simple.

We continued drinking at Mr. Liu's sundry shop and discussed transferring the beverage bottle equipment. My drinking buddy calculated the cost of each piece of equipment: the plastic machine, the air compressor, and the molds, totaling 6,800 yuan. We acted as both the seller and the buyer, with Mr. Liu's drinking buddy serving as the mediator. We concluded the discussion and decided to celebrate the deal with another round of drinks.

Upon returning, I introduced the situation with the beverage bottle equipment to my Paternal Uncle, Sun, and he was very supportive. Our conditions were favorable. I had business relations with Zibo Plastic's Third and Fourth Factories, and I got along well with the factory directors. Two factory directors were cadres sent down by the municipal plastic company. With their connections, buying plastic raw materials would not be difficult. I also had a relative in the township enterprise bureau. Paternal Uncle Sun knew the cadres with power in all walks of life. Purchasing plastic raw materials should not be a big problem. There were workshops on the east side of the paint workshop, where a small factory had recently vacated, leaving five factory spaces available. These were originally the courtyard houses of the production team, quite spacious. The investment was not large, and with available funds, there was no need for borrowing. We were ready to get started, and we would begin as soon as possible. I telegrammed Mr. Liu: "We'll be in Weiguzhen Town on the sixth day of the month to discuss the equipment transfer. Please wait."

After three rounds of negotiations, we finally settled on a price of 6,000 yuan. The Taishan 130 light truck carrying the entire set of beverage bottle equipment returned three days later.

We cleaned and organized the workshops, hiring a tile worker to pour cement on the floor, paint the walls, and install a ceiling. Hygiene was the top priority for producing beverage packaging. After half a month of intense preparation, a small workshop for producing beverage bottles was ready.

On the first day of operation, firecrackers were set off at 8:00 a.m. By noon, over 1,000 bottles had been successfully produced, and production was running smoothly.

3.2 Purchasing Plastic Pellets Three Times

The material used for beverage bottles was high-pressure polyethylene pellets, produced by Sinopec Qilu Petrochemical Company or imported. In 1987, raw materials such as steel, diesel, and plastic were allocated during the planned economy era, and purchasing them on the market was not easy. High-pressure polyethylene pellets were priced at 2,600 yuan per ton by the state and could not be sold at a higher price on the market. Three to five departments were allocated plastic raw materials, including the Plastic Industry Bureau, the Material Bureau, and the Chemical Industry Bureau, among others. Under these bureaus, state-owned and collective factories could obtain plastic raw materials. However, township enterprises had to resort to other methods, leveraging connections and using their influence to procure raw materials. Thus, selling would not be a problem, and money could be made immediately. Despite the simple principle, acquiring raw materials proved to be so complex and troublesome that we exhausted every effort to obtain plastic pellets.

When I delivered paint to Jinlingzhen Town, Sinopec Qilu Petrochemical Company came to mind. The Hui people of the production team in Jinlingzhen Town had their farmland occupied by Sinopec Qilu Petrochemical Company. Laborers under 50 years old in the village became company workers. Mr. Ma was the manager for paint sales. His son, daughter, and neighbors all worked at Sinopec Qilu Petrochemical Company. Mr. Ma mentioned that some even held cadre positions there. That day, when visiting Mr. Ma, I inquired about the possibility of purchasing high-pressure polyethylene pellets.

Under my desk, there was a set of high-grade tableware. I put it in the truck and gave it to Mr. Ma. Upon arriving in Jinlingzhen Town, I first visited Mr. Ma's general store at about 10 o'clock in the morning. Before being returned to me, the truck needed to unload paint at three other locations. Carrying the tableware, I entered Mr. Ma's office.

"Mr. Ma, we have not seen each other for half a year. I come to see you."

"Welcome, welcome! Just come! You needn't bring a gift."

"It's a local specialty from Boshan District, not much to offer, just household plates and bowls."

"Thank you. Please have a seat." Mr. Ma invited me to sit down.

As we sat on the sofa and sipped tea, we started chatting. Although we had built a business relationship for more than two years, it was the first time we had sat together to chat.

I broached the topic: "Mr. Ma, how long has it been since the Hui people's village was established?"

"It's said to date back to the Ming Dynasty, but there are no historical records. Jinlingcun Village's residents were divided into two production teams, one for the Han and the other for the Hui people. The Hui people resided to the south of the road, while the Han people resided to the north. This village was the most concentrated area of Hui people in Zibo. The farmland of Jinlingcun Village had all been taken over by Sinopec Qilu Petrochemical Company. Our county was concerned with the Hui people, arranging all non-disabled laborers to work as workers and allocating them to Sinopec Qilu Petrochemical Company's subordinate factories. The Han people moved to the outskirts of Zhangdian District, where a portion of land was allocated for farming. The Han people still worked as farmers, while the Hui people in our village enjoyed the benefits, becoming state workers."

Mr. Ma became increasingly enthusiastic as he spoke, and I could not get a word in edgewise.

Seizing a moment when Mr. Ma took a sip of water, I quickly asked, "Where do your son and daughter work?"

"My eldest son works at the power plant, my youngest son at the fertilizer plant, and my daughter seems to work at the polyethylene plant. I do not understand the name of her factory, and I do not ask. It is hard to keep up with young people because their customs have changed. When a young man from the Hui people celebrated a wedding, instead of hosting a banquet and serving alcohol, he cooked a large pot of stew made from chicken, duck, beef, and lamb. Each person received a bowl of rice for lunch, and it was refilled as needed. There were no stir-fry dishes. Nowadays, young people learn from you. When there's a celebration, they lay out a big feast. But there's one tradition they still adhere to — they don't eat pork."

"Mr. Ma, regarding the custom of not eating pork, what's the reason behind it?"

"It's hard to explain. It is a rule that has been passed down for thousands of years. Anyone who eats pork violates the rule."

Mr. Ma had come to urge me to deliver goods to my factory twice before. Therefore, I had invited him to dine at a restaurant, but he declined. The teacups in my office were boiled in hot water, and when tea was poured, he did not drink it; instead, he used his water cup.

As the conversation continued until around eleven o'clock, the truck for unloading paint returned. Since we had not yet reached the main topic, I needed to find an opportunity to address it.

"Mr. Ma, what does your daughter do at the polyethylene plant?"

"Oh, she's a warehouse keeper handling deliveries."

"And what about your son-in-law?"

"He's a small section chief in the procurement department."

As we continued talking, dinner time approached, but I could not eat at the Hui people's home.

"Mr. Ma, I have a favor to ask of you today. I have just launched a new product, beverage bottles, and the material requires polyethylene, produced by the polyethylene plant from Sinopec Qilu Petrochemical Company. It is quite a coincidence that your daughter and son-in-law work at the polyethylene plant. Could you help me purchase a few tons of polyethylene raw material? Any quantity will be OK."

"Sure, I'll ask them to help," Mr. Ma readily agreed.

"Please! I'll come by another day."

I left, but Mr. Ma unexpectedly pushed me back onto the sofa.

"You can't leave. Let's have a meal. My wife has prepared it; all dishes cater to the Hui people's taste."

"Mr. Ma, our customs are different. Is it appropriate?"

"Please help yourself; we're not strict about it."

I could not refuse his hospitality, so I sat down to dine.

On the dining table were four dishes: braised beef with brown sauce, double-boiled lamb soup, scrambled egg with tomato, and cucumber salad. Mr. Ma's wife continued to cook in the kitchen. On the table was a bottle of Xizunteniang wine (牺尊特酿).

"Try this, director Yu. It's a new wine just released by Linzi Distillery."

I had heard about it; they had unearthed a bronze artifact in the Linzi District from the Spring and Autumn Period of the Qi State, called Xizun (牺尊), of which only one existed in the country. It was a national treasure that was housed in the National Museum. The Qi Heritage Museum in Linzi District displayed a replica, but using it as a brand had a different impact. Mr. Ma did not drink, and neither did my salesperson, so I drank alone. After an hour, I quickly drank a catty (about 53 milliliters) of wine in Xizun, and the banquet ended.

Half a month later, I received a message from Mr. Ma informing me that I could pick up a ton of polyethylene pellets.

Then, director Ren of Zibo Plastic Third Factory agreed to help me purchase two tons of polyethylene pellets. The plastic company allocated production plans every month, typically in the first week. I arranged to visit director Ren's home on Sunday afternoon. He lived in the dormitory building of the plastic company.

I bought two sets of gifts, each consisting of two bottles of Wuliangye liquor and two packs of Peony brand cigarettes. I first delivered one set to director Ren's home. After sitting for a few minutes, director Ren led the way to the home of Mr. Wang, the deputy manager responsible for planning at the plastic company. The director Ren left me at the door and went back. He could not go with me. Director Ren had already communicated with Mr. Wang, so when I arrived, there was no need to discuss buying plastic pellets; I was only there to deliver the gifts.

Knocking on the door, I asked, "Is this Mr. Wang's home?"

"Please come in."

Mr. Wang handed me a cigarette and poured a glass of water.

"I'm a friend of director Ren."

"Old Ren mentioned you to me."

"We've been friends for many years. Before director Ren moved to Zibo Plastic Third Factory, we had already known each other when he was at the plastic company. We're even closer now that he's at Zibo Plastic Third Factory."

"We have business with Zibo Plastic Third Factory. Director Ren mentioned needing several hundred kilograms of polyethylene pellets, which will be delivered in three days."

"Thank you, director Wang."

I could not sit for long, as prolonged conversation could lead to leaks. After drinking a glass of water, I took my leave.

On Monday, I visited the planning department of the plastic company and met Mr. Ming, the head of planning. I handed him the introduction letter from Zibo Plastic Third Factory and identified myself as a salesperson from the factory. Then, I obtained the allocation order for high-pressure polyethylene pellets and hurried to the billing office on the first floor of a five-story building opposite the long-distance bus station. After paying and getting the invoice, I proceeded to pick up the goods from the warehouse of Zibo Zhongbu Chemical Co., Ltd.

With the allocation order in hand, I rushed to the billing office. Sitting in the truck, I carefully unfolded the two-layered document, which stated a weight of 2.5 tons. I had a conversation with Mr. Wang a few days ago. He could help me purchase half a ton of plastic pellets and give two tons of them to Zibo Plastic Third Factory. I did not think much of it; I was aiming to pick up the goods by noon.

Four or five people were in line at the billing counter, which was not too crowded. Two or three people were wandering around. When I was one person away from the counter, I felt someone crowding behind me. Looking back, I saw a tall young man standing close. When it was my turn, I handed the allocation order over with my right hand and held my briefcase with my left. There was an empty oil drum next to me, so I naturally placed my briefcase on it, preparing to put down the allocation order with my right hand and take out the cash. Just as I placed my briefcase on the oil drum, before the clerk could take the allocation order, my briefcase disappeared in the blink of an eye. I quickly turned around to see the tall young man who had stood close behind me, grabbing my briefcase and running four or five meters away. I pointed at him and shouted, "Robbery! He stole my bag!" As soon as I took a step forward, someone blocked me.

The young man ran outside the door, jumped on a bicycle, and ran south. As I shouted, the driver and the salesperson sitting nearby ran over, and we three ran after the bike.

We chased him and shouted, "That is the thief on the bike ahead. Stop him! Stop him!"

The pedestrians on the road turned their heads or leaned forward, but no one reached out or stopped the thief. Otherwise, the thief would have been arrested immediately. Also, being just two meters away, the driver could have reached out and grabbed him. However, the thief pedaled faster and faster while the pursuer ran slower and slower. The thief turned into an alley, and we followed him. However, four or five small alleyways diverged from each other, much like a maze. We three strung behind a few hutongs, turning left and right without seeing the bicycle.

Sitting on the roadside stone, panting heavily, we looked at each other. My money for the plastic pellets had been stolen in broad daylight. However, thankfully, I still had the allocation order in my hand. Tomorrow! Tomorrow I would come again. I would buy the plastic pellets.

Li Yinjian, my classmate in middle school, who was one year younger than I, used to sit in the classroom adjacent to mine. We were familiar with each other, as we often played in the same school courtyard during breaks. He was from Kunlunzhen Town and was assigned to work at the Silk Mill in Zhoucun District after graduation. He managed to transfer to Zibo Plastic Fourth Factory, along the Zhangdian-Boshan Expressway in Kunlunzhen Town. After transferring to work here, we had met up for drinks once. He was the deputy head of the sales department at Zibo Plastic Fourth Factory, a cadre position in a small state-owned factory under the plastic company, and he took pride in it. Working in his hometown meant he had many friends and acquaintances, and we often interacted with each other. When it came to producing beverage bottles, I could seek his help and try to buy plastic pellets.

One day, Li Yinjian called me and said he had a way to purchase plastic pellets. Having worked in Zhoucun District for 10 years, Li Yinjian was well acquainted with many people in factories, mines, and society. He was not an ordinary person. Today, he visited the Zibo

Plastic Fourth Factory. Here, he mentioned an old friend he had known for many years who could purchase the pellets. Li Yinjian promised to give him a little extra money as a reward for his efforts. He would discuss it with me in person. The details were not discussed over the phone, so we arranged to meet next Monday at noon at the southeast corner of the Zhoucun Train Station in Xiaozhaocun Village, Li's friend Zou Sihai's home.

In 1987, when I went on business trips, I rode my bike from the factory to Cicun Village. I went to the Post and Telecommunications Bureau to find my old acquaintance, Little Li. I parked my bike in front of the bureau, took the bus from the bus station at the gate to Wangcun Village, and then transferred to Zhoucun Bus Station. I could arrive in Zhoucun District around 10:00 if everything went smoothly.

I inquired at the Zhoucun Bus Station and found it was 2,500 meters from Xiaozhaocun Village, which required a "reverse donkey ride." The tricycles for hire in Zhoucun District featured a three-wheeled vehicle with two wheels in front and one in the back, with a seat in the front and the driver pedaling behind the passenger. This was the reason for the idiom. I got on one, enjoying the wide view ahead without looking at the driver's back. After about 10 minutes, I arrived at Xiaozhaocun Village.

Xiaozhaocun Village was not large, with only three or four streets. I asked an older man for directions and was warmly guided to Zou Sihai's home. It was a simple rural courtyard with four rooms facing south, clean and refreshing. When he heard a guest had arrived, Mr. Zou greeted me in the courtyard. He was tall, about the same age as me, and spoke with a smile, leading me into the house.

Zou Sihai was very talkative and had been friends with Li Yinjian for seven or eight years. When Li had worked in Zhoucun District, the two often drank together and played finger-guessing games. After Li returned to Kunlunzhen Town, they had less contact with each other. However, Zou tried his best to complete the assigned tasks and had found a way to obtain two tons of high-pressure polyethylene pellets.

Zou was straightforward and did not beat around the bush. He said he could buy the pellets through a friend and would pay a little extra as a favor. Zuo casually mentioned spending 500 or 600 yuan each time, but he was not specific about the amount. For two tons of pellets, he added an extra thousand yuan. He said he would do his friend a favor if I agreed; if I declined, it would mean no deal, and two other friends were waiting to buy. He would give me the pellets first. They would be ready for pickup around the fifth or sixth day of next month, and I would receive a call for confirmation. Zou explained the matter of the pellets in a heat.

I was secretly delighted. Two tons of plastic pellets could not be bought on the market, even with an additional thousand yuan. I bid farewell and returned to the bus station, the matter settled. After waiting at the roadside for a few minutes without seeing a reverse donkey ride, I walked back, carrying my small black bag. Following the main road, I crossed the railway overpass and returned to the bus station after 40 minutes. Zhoucun District used to have dozens of small and large state-owned factories, making the bus station a must-stop for express buses. The bus station was on the square, with people coming and going. With dozens of restaurants to choose from, I randomly selected a clean and bright one. I ordered two dishes, pork trotter jelly and Zhoucun hotpot. I was served beer in a white bowl and drank three of them. I then returned to the factory in high spirits.

Li Yinjian called me to say I could meet Zou Sihai at the Zhoucun Bus Station at noon to pick up the pellets. At a quarter past nine the next day, I arrived at the southeast corner of the Zhoucun Bus Station. Zou arrived on a Yamaha motorcycle, and he led the way, with my Taishan mini-truck following behind. After turning two corners and not going far, Zou parked his Yamaha motorcycle next to a large gate and told me to wait there while he went to pick up the order.

I exited the truck and felt like I had been here before. Looking at the doorplate, it read "Zhoucun District Bureau of Material Supply." The previous month, I had come to buy pellets but returned empty-handed. One day, when I visited my cousin's house, his cousin-in-law came. I was visiting my aunt, and he was visiting my aunt's husband. We had met before, and when we drank together, he introduced himself as working at the Bureau of Material Supply, overseeing oil, chemicals, plastics, and more. I continued with my cousin's topic, mentioning my interest in buying pellets. My cousin's cousin-in-law readily agreed, saying it was not a problem to arrange several tons. Upon hearing this good news, I happily drank three more cups of coffee. According to the agreed-upon date, I went to the Material Supply Bureau. The doorplate on the cousin's office read "Office of the director," the top official at the bureau. Upon entering and taking a seat, the staff offered cigarettes and poured water for them. My cousin sat firmly behind his large desk. When I mentioned buying pellets, he stood up, slapped his forehead, apologized profusely, and said I was too late. The high-pressure and low-pressure polyethylene plastic pellets from the previous day, totaling over 20 tons, had been sold out, and no more were available. He expressed his apologies again. Better luck next time! Better luck next time! I hoped we would have the chance to meet again and succeed. I had come with hope, but I returned disappointed.

Pacing on the road out front, I reflected and understood.

Zou came out of the Office of the director, hopped on his Yamaha, and gestured for me to follow him to pick up the goods.

Six months into the production of the beverage bottles, operations were running smoothly, and sales were progressing well. I purchased high-pressure polyethylene pellets, of which nearly 80 percent of bottles were manufactured.

3.3 How Beverages Were Produced

Beverage bottle production had been ongoing for three months, but I had never visited the factory. There was nothing else to do that day, so I tagged along with the delivery truck to visit the beverage factory. We loaded the truck half with paint and half with beverage bottles. After delivering the paint, we made our final stop at the beverage factory, located in Liujiazhuang Village, Dawuzhen Town, Linzi District, Zibo.

The Dawuzhen Town Supply and Marketing Cooperative Store,

which sold paint, was located near the beverage factory. Walking about 20 meters to the north and turning into an alley, we could see the beverage factory, which used to be the production team's warehouse. The warehouse consisted of six rooms with a small courtyard. The gate was large enough to accommodate trucks. Once the beverage bottles were unloaded into the warehouse and the salesperson had settled the bill, I headed to the workshop.

The factory director led the way into the beverage workshop. There were three rooms dedicated to the production of beverages. In the middle of each room were two homemade filling machines, each similar in size to a small drill press. Workers sat on footstools, a kind of little bench, with the filling machine in front of them. A small bucket with a switch underneath and a plastic tube sat beside the machine on a one-meter-high table. To the worker's left were beverage bottles in plastic woven bags, and to the right was a willow basket. The worker twisted the switch, holding an empty bottle with their left hand and aligning their right hand with the plastic tube. The bottle was filled and placed in the basket in less than a second. The workers did not wear masks or gloves. The liquid had to be filled to the brim when filling the bottles, causing the hands to become wet as it flowed out. The floor and table were covered in spilled beverages. The workers wore rubber shoes to work, with aprons tied around their chests.

Once a basket was filled, the transport workers moved it to the west end of the room, where two homemade sealing machines were located, and the operators sealed the bottle caps. I stood by and watched. The manual sealing machine was quite handy. Taking a bottle of beverage, the operator gently placed it on the ground, leaving about a centimeter of space at the bottle's mouth, ensuring the perfect length. On the workbench, a mold on the table fit perfectly. Taking a pair of heated pliers, the operator applied force with both hands, squeezing for a few seconds. The bottle was sealed tightly, without scorching or leaking from its mouth.

Besides the sealing machine, a worker affixed labels listing only apple, orange, and lemon juice, with no brand name, factory name, factory address, or phone number — four products. Three-wheeled carts waited at the door for delivery, with demand consistently outstripping supply.

I asked the factory director, "Where are the beverages made?"

"Follow me," he replied.

To the east of the three rooms were three large barrels, similar to those used in the countryside for storing grain.

The factory director explained, "This barrel produces apple juice, that one makes orange juice, and the other one makes lemon juice. These three are the best-selling on the market. There is a well in the courtyard, from which water is drawn and poured into barrels for sterilization. Then, fruit essence, sweeteners, and preservatives are added. A barrel of fruit juice is ready in about 10 minutes with a wooden stick, stirring it." The factory director continued, "Although it seems simple, we strictly follow the recipe for production. Regardless of how many days have passed, the taste must remain consistent. I spent 10,000 yuan on the recipe, and I am the only one who knows it. If the recipe were known, anyone could make it."

The factory director's words made sense.

He said, "We produce for seven months a year, starting in April and ending in October. The peak sales period is four months. During July and August, customers queue up for delivery. Each factory's juice recipe differs, so we cannot skimp on ingredients. Children can tell which brands are good and which are not. After more than a year of production, the brand has become established."

I kept asking, "What products are made during the off-season when production stops?"

The factory director led me to a room on the west side of the building.

He said, "This used to be the office of the production team, but now it's used to make snacks."

There were two tables with two boards — one for making "taosu," a kind of crisp biscuit, and the other for making cakes. Two workers were kneading dough.

"Currently, pastry sales are slow, but they peak in winter, complementing the beverage production. During the Mid-Autumn Festival, we make mooncakes busily for a while, with seven or eight workers working overtime every day."

The factory director became more energetic as he spoke.

"I've been running this snack business for five years, and it's been very profitable. The juice business took off last year."

After my beverage and snack factory tour, the salesperson settled the accounts and completed the formalities. We bade farewell to the factory director and proceeded to the Hutian Chemical Factory to load light calcium carbonate, the raw material used in paint. The delivery of paint and the pickup of raw materials were both completed in one day, ensuring that sales and production remained on track.

3.4 The Closure of the Beverage Bottle Business

In the second year of producing beverage bottles, as the reform and opening up deepened, the planned economy gradually transitioned to a market economy. The supply of raw materials expanded, enabling free buying and selling. Plastic pellets, no longer requiring connections or allocation orders, followed market prices and became readily available. This small industry of beverage bottle production flourished overnight, with seven or eight factories popping up in surrounding towns and villages. Due to the raw material shortage of the previous year, the market shifted from buyers to sellers. Countless beverage factories sprang up, transforming the landscape from door-to-door deliveries to a market of multiple competitors vying for orders, marking a year of significant change.

In 1987, I had supplied six beverage factories as their only supplier. In 1988, it became two or three suppliers. Whereas payments were made promptly upon delivery during the previous year, negotiations on pricing began this spring, followed by discussions on payment terms. Some delayed payments for one batch, while others held off on two. I determined to keep going despite the strain.

Sales had been smooth during the year before, but we had to venture beyond Zibo this year. Leveraging my advantage of having a delivery truck, I bundled beverage bottles with paint deliveries, charging only for the freight of the paint. In contrast, the bottles hitched a ride for free, a self-promotional strategy. Venturing beyond the market in Zibo, I sought buyers near my paint market.

In Hejiacun Village, 1,500 meters away from my paint factory, three partners ventured into the production of beverage bottles. Lacking transportation advantages, without trucks or tractors for delivery, they barely made a profit after factoring in transportation costs. One managed production at home, while the other two were delivered by bicycle. I encountered them several times while sitting in my car. Their bicycle had a homemade iron frame on both sides, extending approximately 1.5 meters in width and depth. Bags were hung on both sides, matching the handlebars, with the rider sandwiched between them. A large bag was placed on the rear seat, completely enclosing the rider, making it impossible to see the rider from the truck's driver's seat. Strong winds could knock over the bicycles; once, I stopped and asked where they were headed.

They replied, "Fengshuizhen Town in Zhangdian District."

It was more than thirty kilometers there and back in just a day.

We added a beverage factory in Wulitang Town, Qingzhou City, arranged by the salesperson. We delivered paint there, securing one payment batch and delivering the second batch before settling the account for the first. According to the salesperson, this factory was larger than several in Zibo, producing not only one type of beverage but also high-quality glass-bottled beverages. The Wulitang beverage factory doubled its output in July, the peak production season. I wanted to visit, but circumstances prevented me. By the end of July 1988, the salesperson reported that the second batch had not been paid. The factory promised to get a third batch while settling the previous two. After waiting for days and following the usual delivery routine, there was no notification for the third batch. When the salesperson left, the gate was shut tight; production had ceased. The older man at the gate said they were stopping production for just four or five days; the machinery had been removed, and they did not know why. The factory was rented, and its whereabouts were unknown. They owed over 6,000 yuan for two batches.

In 1988, the industrial and commercial sectors, as well as health departments, intensified enforcement, particularly on small food factories, with beverage factories under closer scrutiny. "Three-No" (no date, no production permission, and no factory address) enterprises faced increased pressure. Juice, pastries, and sodas were the main focus, with inspections expanding from July onwards. I was therefore cautious about doing business with beverage factories. Despite the checks, the factories continued production, however. I visited several of them, and the owners explained that inspections were only superficial. They were tipped off in advance and would shut down when the inspectors arrived, resuming production as usual after they had left. They worked at night and did not work during the day.

From August, inspections took a different approach, targeting the market by confiscating Three-No-Beverages and fining fixed stores. There was propaganda in society telling the dangers of "three-no" products, claiming they were harmful and did not meet hygiene standards. This led to a decline in the purchasing power of beverages and a rapid downturn in beverage factory production. We swiftly scaled back our beverage bottle business, settling accounts and collecting overdue payments.

Since starting the beverage bottle business in 1987, I carried out a year of normal operations in 1988. By the end of 1989, I had ceased operations at the last two beverage factories. This small venture came to an end.

CHAPTER 4
IN REMEMBRANCE OF GRANDFATHER

4.1

After getting up and finishing my tooth brushing and face washing, I went to my grandfather's room to check on him before having breakfast and headed to work. This habit had been formed over the past decade. In the past three or four years, my grandfather had gradually begun walking slowly and with difficulty. He could only walk around the room after getting up. Since the Chinese New Year in 1989, on the sixth day of the first lunar month, he could not eat and lay in bed for over 50 days, relying on glucose and medication to sustain him. One morning, I stood by his bed for over 10 minutes, feeling that he was more spirited than usual. I called out "Grandpa, Grandpa" a few times, and he moved his lips slightly, opening his eyes to look at me with a joyful expression. I had not left home for over 10 days. If I had to attend to urgent matters, I would rush back the same day.

One day, I rode my motorcycle to the Zichuan district and bought a few triangular belts, some screws, and two grape seedlings. At around 10 o'clock, on my way home, when I reached the downslope at Wudao Ridge, Uncle Zhao from our village waved at me from afar, signaling me to stop.

I pulled over, and Uncle Zhao said to me, "Your grandfather passed away over an hour ago. You should go back soon."

"Okay, I will."

With a pounding head, I collected myself, mounted the motorcycle, and hurried back. I could not wait to step inside the house. Running into his room, I saw my grandfather lying straight on the bed, his face waxen and his eyes tightly shut, lips sealed. I knelt beside the bed, saying, "Grandpa, Grandpa...." Tears streamed down. I clutched his withered hand, a hand with only a layer of skin left, devoid of any flesh on the bones. For over 50 days, he had not eaten a grain of rice, relying solely on medication; his flesh long withered away. If I had known that he would pass away today, I would not have left home even if I had had a momentous occasion. You had stopped speaking and opening your eyes for over 10 days. I knew this day would come in the darkness of night and the brightness of day, but I never expected it to be today. Yet this morning, his spirits had been unusually high. He had opened his eyes, tears seemed to well up, and his lips moved slightly. I had called "Grandpa" a few times, and he seemed to understand. Unhoped for, this was his last surge of vitality. I had forgotten that term. I had never expected him to take his last breath today, with me not by his side.

When I knelt by the bedside, memories flashed before my eyes. At five, I climbed Kunlun Mountain with my grandfather, took a train to Boshan District, and watched the Peking opera called Eighteen Arhats Fighting Wukong. As the curtain fell, he had lifted me high, letting me shake hands with the actor of Sun Wukong on stage. At Julecun Restaurant, there was always a seat for me at every banquet, and servings of my favorite fried meat. Whenever I had a cough and struggled to breathe, he would carry me to Qianqigou Street to visit Yamashita Clinic for Japanese injections and medication. At ten, we went to Shanghai. We watched an acrobatic show called "Trapeze" at night, sitting on open-air benches at the stadium. When my shoe fell three meters deep, he crawled under the bench to retrieve it for me. Pulling a handcart, we went to the Shanghai railway station to pick up goods. He pulled ahead, and I pushed from behind. In 1966, during the Great Cultural Revolution, I stayed with classmates at Shanghai No. 2 Cotton Mill, a factory on the outskirts of Zhabei District. It took a two-hour bus ride to get there. At night, you brought biscuits and White Rabbit candies for us to share.

At nineteen, you left this house and ventured alone in Suzhou and Shanghai. On the streets of the former, you endured slaps from Japanese soldiers. Crossing Nansi Lake by boat, you encountered river bandits who robbed you clean. Selling goods on the streets of Shanghai, you dealt with thugs who extorted money back and forth. After the liberation in 1949, in the new democratic Shanghai, national industries and private businesses flourished, and your Yongshengtai grocery store (永昇泰料货店) continued to grow stronger each year. You experienced the Public-Private Joint Partnership in 1957, the Great Leap Forward in 1958, which caused three years of natural disasters, and the Cultural Revolution. You experienced forty-six years of winds and rains, sunlight and hardships. In 1974, you returned to your hometown, surrounded by descendants, carefree and happy, spending your twilight years joyfully. Leaving home for 62 years, you have returned, still in this house.

I thought, "Rest in peace, Grandpa! Tonight, lying quietly, I will stay with you; tomorrow, I will spend the day with you, and the day after, reluctantly, you will depart for the Western Paradise."

4.2

On the sixth day of the first lunar month in 1989, after breakfast, my grandfather asked my third-youngest brother to go to the Township Grain Depot to buy a month's supply of grain for him. None of us agreed because it was the first day of work for the grain depot, and we had no grain shortage at home. Moreover, my grandfather no longer cooked for himself. My father had retired and, at home, took care of him considerately, delivering soup and dishes to his room punctually for every meal, sparing him the trouble of worrying about food and vegetables. Despite our objections, my third brother did not decline and rode his bike to buy the grain. It was 2.5 kilometers to the grain station, taking him an hour to go back and forth. After more than two hours, my third brother returned, saying he had lost the grain purchase certificate on the way and could not find it after retracing his steps. I encouraged him to apply for a new one a few days later, since the current grain purchase certificates were useless and the grain coupons were about to be abolished. My grandfather did not say anything. He did not touch the steamed buns at lunchtime and only drank a few sips of porridge. Thinking that my grandfather might be angry, I tried to persuade him to eat, but he shook his head in refusal. It was not because he was angry about losing the grain purchase certificate that he refused to eat. Still, it was difficult for him to swallow the steamed buns. In the afternoon, he had trouble swallowing water. Lying on the bed with his eyes closed, he spoke when asked where it hurt or what discomfort he felt. Shaking his head, he indicated there was no pain or discomfort. And he did not eat dinner.

My uncle, a doctor, was conveniently resting at home that day. He came over immediately, took my grandfather's pulse, measured his blood pressure, and diagnosed a minor cerebral hemorrhage, ruling out a stroke. He suggested going to the district hospital the next day. My uncle was well acquainted with the doctors there. Dr. Wang, the head of the internal medicine department, was a medical school classmate of his. They consulted with two experienced doctors, and my grandfather was diagnosed with a minor cerebral hemorrhage, causing pressure on the throat area. He was to receive injections for a few days without hospitalization, returning for intravenous drips.

The medicine was brought back from the district hospital. After seven days with no improvement, my grandfather could only drink a few sips of milk, which trickled down his chin slowly after being put in his mouth, as he could not swallow it. We again consulted Dr. Wang, who stated that if there were no improvement within seven days, the only solution would be to increase the dosage of the medicine. Still, it was uncertain whether it would work, and the site of the cerebral hemorrhage might have solidified. In the 1980s, without advanced CT scanning equipment, my grandfather could only be treated following the doctor's diagnosis.

My grandfather had three children: one son and two daughters. My father, already retired, cared for my grandfather day and night while my siblings and I took turns helping out. My eldest aunt lived in Jinan. She rushed back on the seventh day of the first lunar month as soon as she received the telegram. My second aunt lived in Lanzhou, Gansu Province, and she returned two days after I left. The whole family took turns looking after my grandfather. He lay in bed, unable to string a sentence together, speaking intermittently and unclearly, but he was not confused. He understood what was going on and seemed content.

My grandfather had been ill for over a month with no signs of improvement. Several treatment plans were attempted, but none proved effective. He had no sense of pain. He could not sit up alone, so we would sometimes turn him over in bed and help him sit up for a while. He could respond with some mouth movements when called, showing that his brain was still active. The elderly neighbors came to visit and chat with us. They said he had lived a good life, had helped his fellow villagers a lot, and now, he would not suffer from his illness. They believed that Heaven was sensible.

4.3

From my earliest memories, my grandfather had rarely stayed at home. He would return for about 20 days once a year during his annual leave. On June 8, 1974, we received a telegram from my father informing us that my grandfather was critically ill and hospitalized in Shanghai, urging us to come quickly. That same afternoon, I took the long-distance bus from Boshan District to Jinan. My eldest aunt lived east of Jingyi Road in Jinan, near the train station. Her husband's friend worked at the train station and could buy train tickets with seats. I boarded the 23rd express train from Beijing to Shanghai that evening, arriving the next day. It was my first time traveling on a reserved-seat train. My grandfather was admitted to the Hongguang Hospital, located east of People's Square, on Middle Tibet Road.

My grandfather lay on the hospital bed with a pale face and low spirits.

When he saw me, he had tears welling up in his eyes, and he said only one sentence, "You have come so quickly. Is everything well at home?"

"Grandfather, rest assured. Everything is well at home. I received the telegram yesterday at noon and rushed here from Jinan by express train," I replied.

Seeing my grandfather's demeanor, I refrained from saying more. He had been in good health when I had returned to my hometown earlier this year, lively and full of spirit. He walked without procrastinating and referred to discomfort in his stomach, planning to bring my grandmother to Shanghai after the Spring Festival.

My grandmother sat up on the bedside while my father stood nearby, recounting, "The night before last, your grandfather went to bed. In the middle of the night, he started having stomach pains and vomiting blood. He filled a basin with blood and vomit. Mr. Wang, a neighbor, heard your grandmother calling for help, carried your grandfather to the hospital, and then came to my dormitory on Yan'an Road to inform me. Your grandfather received hemostatic treatment that night, and the bleeding stopped. He has improved these days. The doctor advised him not to get out of bed for a few days and to rest; then they'll conduct further examinations on his stomach."

The doctors took an X-ray picture of his stomach a week later and revealed a tumor. But they could not determine whether it was benign or malignant. Further tests were necessary to confirm the diagnosis before a treatment plan could be formulated.

At that time, gastroscopes had just been acquired from Japan, with only two in China: one in Beijing and the other in Shanghai, making them the most advanced equipment for stomach examinations in the country. The hospital arranged a gastroscopy, but we had to wait 40 days due to the long queue. The hospital refused to perform surgery without a high degree of certainty.

The Hongguang Hospital, formerly known as the "Red Cross Hospital" before the Cultural Revolution, was a district-level hospital in Shanghai. Looking from the roadside, it was a whole building. Upon entering the main gate, the outpatient department and pharmacy were visible. Further inside, through a small door, a three-story building enclosed a courtyard. The second and third floors housed the inpatient wards. My grandfather was on the second floor, where only one person was allowed to care for the patient. Anyone who wanted to visit him needed to get a visitation card. Each visitation card allowed two people to visit, so if more than two people wanted to visit at once, two would go in first, then two more would go in after they had come out. It seemed quite miraculous at the time, but it was a cumbersome process.

It was not until after 2000 that most hospitals in China implemented this system. According to Shanghai's locals, this was how hospitals in Shanghai operated before Liberation.

The inpatient ward was a large room with corners and turns along the floor, rather than being square. My grandfather's room had twelve beds and separate washing and toilet facilities. The toilets were unisex, each with a cubicle and a door to close. The floors were made of wood and were cleaned twice a day by the janitor. We brought our bamboo mats and towels to sleep on the floor during night shifts, and they were remarkably clean — no dust was visible when touched. Visitors had to change into slippers before entering, and the hospital was entirely enclosed, shielded from wind and rain, and astonishingly clean everywhere.

My grandfather had been retired for two years, living in his own house at No. 3 Longmen Road. During the 1970s in Shanghai, owning one's own house made it easier to find a spouse, as property ownership was highly desirable and sought after.

While waiting for the gastroscopy appointment, my grandfather's condition remained stable. He did not experience pain or vomiting anymore and only took medicine three times a day. My grandmother cooked at home, and I delivered meals to the hospital three times a day. The house on Longmen Road was near Wusheng Road in People's Square, about 500 meters from the hospital. We would walk along Wusheng Road, turn into a small alley, and then walk to the end, where we would reach Middle Tibet Road. The Hongguang Hospital was located just more than 10 meters to the right. The doctor checked the inpatient ward during the lunch break, so I had two hours free. After lunch, while my grandfather napped, he no longer needed someone to accompany him. Therefore, I had a whole afternoon to wander the streets.

Getting out of Hongguang Hospital and going north along Middle Tibet Road, there was a triangular building that had been converted into a workers' cultural palace before the Cultural Revolution. They screened movies irregularly in a large hall with over 200 seats, similar to outdoor cinemas in rural areas, with tickets costing 10 mao each. In contrast, the cinema charged two mao for each screening. In 1974, color television had already appeared in Shanghai City. In one of the halls, they occasionally showed *The Legend of the Red Lantern, Sha Jia Bang*, and documentaries, all for a five-cent ticket. Color TVs were emerging then. We had lived in the Shanghai No. 2 Cotton Mill during the Cultural Revolution. In the evening, TV programs were shown at the canteen. TVs were square boxes that could display movies, which was quite a new concept. My classmates had not heard of them before, so this expanded their horizons.

Not far from Fuzhou Road, I sometimes visited bookstores. Before the Cultural Revolution, many books were considered harmful, with only Bright Sunny Skies left on the shelves. Mountains in Impulse and How the Steel Was Tempered, a translation of a Soviet book, had just been published. It was my first time seeing Dead Souls, translated by Lu Xun, so I bought a copy. Lu Xun's works were plentiful, including Hesitation, Old Tales Retold, and Stories of Lu Xun, by Shi Yige. I bought a copy of Morning Glow and several volumes of Learning and Criticism. I spent more time reading but bought fewer books. My grandfather was hospitalized, and our finances were tight, with my father's salary and my grandfather's pension barely covering our living expenses, leaving little room for extra book purchases.

Most of my time was spent around People's Square and People's Park. There were many cinemas nearby, including the Grand Theater, the Dashanghai Theater, the Battle Theater, the Peace Theater, and the Music Hall, totaling over a dozen. The Grand Theater charged the highest ticket prices, so I watched movies there only twice. Watching movies was the best form of entertainment back then.

When it was time for the gastroscopy appointment, my father hailed a taxi to go to Changning Hospital for the procedure. Dr. Guo was introduced on the signboard outside the hospital corridor's endoscopy room. He was the chief physician of the internal medicine department, who had been trained in Japan in gastroscopic imaging techniques. Gastroscopy was the world's most advanced equipment for stomach examinations at the time. From entering the endoscopy room to leaving, it took an hour. The nurse instructed my father that my grandfather could eat only liquid food and had to lie still for three days. It was a minor surgery, and the diagnostic report would be available in a week.

When the diagnostic report came back, it confirmed a malignant tumor. The doctors at Hongguang Hospital were already certain of this, based on their X-ray imaging, which had already identified it as malignant. Before the gastroscopy, the doctors did not tell the patients for sure, only hinting at the possibility. They informed my father that the sole treatment option was surgery to remove the tumor. They could not predict the outcome. It would either be eradicated or recur several years later. With no other choice, we prepared for the surgery as advised by the doctors.

The tumor was removed and sent to Long March Hospital for pathological testing. A week later, the results came out. It was a benign tumor with no cancer cells. The doctors immediately informed all relatives. At ease, we continued the post-operative care. My grandfather recovered soon and returned home.

He was discharged after the National Day, with doctors advising that he rest at home for two months before he could go out for a walk. Although it was not cancer, it was still a major surgery, with three-quarters of his stomach removed. After my grandfather was discharged, my grandmother did not feel well and wanted to return to our hometown urgently. Grandfather Chen, a hometown fellow from Shanghai, was returning to his hometown for a visit, so he took my grandmother back with him. On the second day after returning home, she suffered a stroke and could not get out of bed. My father rushed back from Shanghai to take care of her. I stayed with my grandfather in Shanghai to help him recover from his illness. In contrast, my father stayed in our hometown to accompany my grandmother to the hospital. With two family members ill, one in the north and one in the south, separated by 1,000 kilometers, we finally returned to our hometown at the end of December.

My grandfather had left home at the age of nineteen to seek his fortune in Suzhou and Shanghai. He returned to our hometown at 64, having spent 65 years away. Reluctantly, he returned home. Having grown accustomed to life in the south, he might have stayed in Shanghai for a few more years if he had not fallen ill.

4.4

While my grandfather returned to my hometown, my grandmother lay in bed, delirious, shouting nonsensically. My father had participated in the Peasant Association for Anti-Japanese National Salvation in 1947. When the landless landlords, armed as Home-Returning-Corps, came back for revenge, they could not catch my father, but instead tied up my grandmother, hung her from a tree, and beat her. This traumatic experience left my grandmother mentally unstable for some time. However, her physical and mental health were excellent for over 20 years after liberation. Following this stroke, elderly neighbors remarked that her shouting and flailing arms were reminiscent of her ordeal with the Home Returning Corps. My mother and aunts took turns caring for her day and night while my grandfather grew increasingly despondent. After several months of treatment, my grandmother's condition improved, and she regained stability. She could walk around the house and eat normally. After my aunts left, we had to return to our normal work routines. Only my grandfather remained by my grandmother's side day and night, caring for her for three years until my grandmother passed away in 1977. After her death, my grandfather lived alone in the northern room, rarely leaving the house and occasionally walking in the courtyard.

My grandfather had grown up in this place. Even though he had been away from it for over 40 years, our family remained rooted here, so he returned for a visit every year and maintained connections with relatives and neighbors. Upon retirement, my grandfather returned to his hometown. Logically, he should reintegrate into rural society and gradually adapt to his surroundings. He remained aloof despite returning for a few years; however, he seldom smiled or spoke. The living environment in the rural areas had improved in the 1980s. With the dissolution of production teams, elderly villagers gathered to play cards and chess during agricultural downtime. However, my grandfather abstained from such activities and rarely strolled outside, finding little common ground with fellow villagers.

He had things in common with only three or five people, including his brother, who was my second grandfather, and who often went to his room every few days to talk with him. These discussions centered around family and friends' updates, local news, and village gossip. My second grandfather talked more, while my grandfather spoke little, preferring to listen — three retired men whose family names were also Chen frequently visited him. One had worked with my grandfather for nearly thirty years. After retiring to the village, he often visited my grandfather's home to talk about Shanghai. He shared common interests with my grandfather, allowing them to converse for a long time. Another Grandpa Chen, who had worked in Shanghai in the 1950s and returned to Shandong Province in the 1960s, often visited my grandfather to talk about Shanghai in the 1950s after the liberation in 1949. There was also a grandfather named Chen who had retired from Boshan Shoe Factory. Our two families were neighbors, separated by a courtyard wall that was more than one meter high. The two families were like brothers from the previous generation. He often chatted with my grandfather, sharing news and anecdotes from their experiences. He was well-versed in social news. He would discuss which leader was liberated and became a cadre, and how criticizing Song Jiang, a leader in Outlaws of the Marsh, was essentially criticizing someone else. He knew so little news from outside the village that others could not get a word in when he talked.

My grandfather seldom talked about his past experiences. For older people, when they were idle and not working, the content of their conversation was mostly a matter of young people's experiences. He had spent more than 40 years in Suzhou, Shanghai and other cities, from the warlord era, the Japanese occupation for eight years, the civil war, to the movements of "three evils" (corruption, waste, and bureaucracy) and the "five evils" (bribery, tax evasion, stealing and deceiving national property, jerry-building, and stealing state economic information), the Great Leap Forward and the Cultural Revolution, so most of his life had been a turbulent and extraordinary time. However, he never shared his past with his children. Sometimes, we heard him tell others about taking trains, ships, and encountering devil soldiers and bandits before the liberation. He did not say a word about his post-liberation experience. He did not comment on the Cultural Revolution, neither endorsing nor condemning it. Instead, he listened to others when they talked.

Grandfather seldom talked about his past experiences. Older people were idle and did not work; the content of their conversations was mostly about their youthful experiences, which they had navigated through the five hurdles of wind and waves. More than 40 years in Suzhou, Shanghai, and the south of the Yangtze River, from the warlord era, eight years of Japanese occupation, the civil war, after the combat against corruption, waste, and bureaucratism, the Great Leap Forward, and the Cultural Revolution, most of his life has been a turbulent time, an extraordinary time. He never told his children about the past. He sometimes listened to him tell others about the train, the ship, the devil Zibing, and the bandits before 1949. The experience after 1949, not a word, the Cultural Revolution, do not say good, do not say bad, do not show his feelings. When others spoke, he just listened to them.

Only one night did he and I have a long conversation. After Lin Biao fell to his death in Wendur Khan, my grandfather came back to visit his relatives and was in a good mood, and we talked about the event. My grandfather told me that one's fate can be predetermined by the eight characters of the moment and the date of a person's birth, as per Chinese tradition: the ten Heavenly Stems and the twelve Earthly Branches. The strokes of their names could also determine their life. Before liberation, he had bought a book that described a person's name and strokes. Their names were written in traditional characters, and the number of strokes could determine the trajectory of their lives. Lin Biao had nineteen strokes in his name, indicating a tumultuous life. Mao Zedong had 28 strokes. The book was viewed favorably, and my grandfather had read it several times. He said this book was not compiled after the time of Mao Zedong and Lin Biao. This type of book has been published and circulated for centuries. I was skeptical; it was the first time I had heard of such a book. My grandfather said it was not sold in the bookstore after the liberation, but he kept a copy and retrieved it a few years later. In the 1980s, when the reform was initiated, Xinhua Bookstores had such books, which were also sold in street bookstores. After the twentieth century, when newborn children were named, I looked for professional masters to name them. I compared them, and the names given by the masters were consistent with what was said in the book. My grandfather said Lin Biao was determined to be the successor at the beginning of the Cultural Revolution. He analyzed Lin Biao's strokes and predicted that after Mao Zedong's death, Lin Biao would not be able to take over and might be replaced. My grandfather could not tell anyone; he just let me wait and see. Unexpectedly, he became the successor so soon and died in two years.

Grandpa Chen had worked in Shanghai with my grandfather before 1949. He was stationed in the Boshan District office after the 1949 liberation to purchase glazed wares. Before the Cultural Revolution, the office was closed, and he went to work in Shanghai. When I returned to visit my relatives, I visited him.

When we talked about my grandfather, he clapped his hands, saying, "Your grandfather was too careful, too cautious, and the regulations set by the government were completely followed."

He remembered the accounts clearly, lest anyone catch his mistakes, and he did not forget to pay all of his taxes. From the struggle against the "three evils" and the "five evils" to cracking down on economic crime and corruption, no matter what kind of sports, there was no problem at all with his store. Although the development was slow, it was fine. In 1957, the industrial and commercial transformation was carried out, and the public-private partnership was established. Grandpa Chen could not express things completely, and he would often leave half a sentence unfinished, leaving room for conjecture. He said, for example, that the new democracy was good. We spent five or six years of good life. Prices were stable, and society was prosperous.

Fried peanuts were five fen a pack, pork was three fen a catty, and two people drank half a catty of wine for one yuan. When it came to happiness, he would stomp and clap his hands.

Once, he said, "When your grandfather came back from Shanghai, the little furnace craftsmen in Boshan District rushed to treat us and made an appointment with me several days in advance. We went to Julecun Restaurant every day to eat sea cucumbers and shark fins."

The small bosses who did glass handicrafts were called small furnace artisans by the Boshan people. My grandfather sold their products in Shanghai and returned once or twice a year. The little furnace artisans dared not slack off, and Grandpa Chen naturally shone brightly among them. After the formation of public-private partnerships, small furnace artisans merged to form state-owned factories and implemented a wage system. My grandfather worked for Grandpa Chen in the Boshan District for three months in 1963. I visited Boshan District with my grandfather several times, but no one invited us.

My father seldom talked about what happened before my grandfather retired. Once, I asked my father how much my grandfather's retirement pension was. He told me 39 yuan. When my grandfather returned to his hometown, the retirement fee was deducted from his salary, and my father sent back 40 yuan. In the 1970s, he lived in Shanghai. He maintained a basic standard of living that was higher than that of ordinary workers in Zibo. On and off several times, I heard my father say that my grandfather's salary before the Cultural Revolution was 78 yuan. When the Cultural Revolution began, he took the initiative to reduce his salary by 10 yuan; his retirement pension was then calculated based on this revised salary. Following the public-private partnership, there was still some leftover capital, and the

Cultural Revolution came to an end. I had visited Shanghai with my grandfather in 1960. I worked in a small shop in Shanghai, with four salespeople, located in a large space measuring approximately 50 to 60 square meters. This was my grandfather's raw materials store.

During the Cultural Revolution, my grandfather was neither in power, nor a capitalist, nor a member of the working class. How to put food on the table? I casually filled in a term in my grandfather's column about his identification before the Cultural Revolution when I was in primary school. No one asked the staff and workers about it. We could not write about it casually during the Cultural Revolution. I wrote to ask my father about it, who told me my grandfather was an industrialist. It was a good name, not related to any of the red categories (militaries, revolutionary cadres, workers, poor peasants, and lower-middle peasants), or the black categories (landlords, rich peasants, anti-revolutionaries, bad guys, and rightists), but a standing aside class. Before the Cultural Revolution, he oversaw a small store. The manager was merely nominal, not coming to work, so my grandfather managed the small company by himself, including four or five employees. When the Cultural Revolution began, a person was sent to take charge, and my grandfather became an ordinary salesperson, with his salary reduced to more than 60 yuan. He was not inferior, but he felt half short. He could not speak out about his upset, but left it in his heart. Approaching retirement age, he was depressed for a long time and had stomach problems. In 1974, he underwent most of a gastrectomy and was forced to return to his hometown.

In 1972, my grandfather returned from Shanghai to our hometown on leave, staying longer than usual. Engaging in conversations with relatives, he mentioned that he seemed to have retired. It was inconvenient for his children to ask why he did not return to his hometown after retiring. In the Spring Festival of 1974, he returned to Shanghai and took my grandmother with him. My mother said he had lived there for a year, seemingly reluctant to discuss retirement or settling permanently in our hometown, preferring to remain in Shanghai.

4.5

Grandfather had entered a private school at the age of eight, studying diligently and developing a strong memory. The private school teacher taught students the ancient rites of marriages, funerals, and other ceremonies, which were intricate and lengthy, making it difficult for children to remember them all. Grandfather married at eleven, with his birthday falling on the 28th day of the twelfth lunar month. In those days, even if it was only two days before the New Year, it was counted as one year older, so his actual age at marriage was less than nine years old. Grandmother was seventeen at the time, six years older than him.

Back then, our family owned over 100 mu (approximately 67 hectares) of land and operated a liquor factory. The wedding ceremony was grand and magnificent, following the customs of ancient large wedding ceremonies. A "ceremonious wedding" referred to the elaborate procedures followed by wealthy families. In contrast, a "simple wedding" was more convenient for poorer households. Despite being only eleven years old, at the wedding ceremony, my grandfather was required to perform the rituals of a ceremonious wedding, including 24 formal kowtows and salutations, during which the groom was not allowed to make a single mistake. This lasted for over an hour. Despite being under nine years old and facing dozens of spectators, my grandfather maintained a dignified demeanor, executing the rituals flawlessly from start to finish, like an adult. Relatives, friends who attended the wedding, and neighbors praised the event. This story circulated in the surrounding villages for several years. I have heard it recounted by elderly villagers on multiple occasions.

Grandfather excelled in performing the rituals at his wedding, and he was also an outstanding student in school, eventually becoming something similar to a monitor. He studied the Four Books and Five Classics but did not attend a school in the city. He was skilled in various tasks, from assisting adults in running a hotel to planting crops in the ground. However, at the age of nineteen, he lost a large sum of money due to gambling, leading to the closure of the liquor store. In frustration, he left home and headed south, seeking a new life. He initially went to Suzhou, where he worked as an assistant alongside fellow villagers, and later ventured to Shanghai independently. However, my grandfather seldom spoke about this period, so I knew little about it.

As far back as I can remember, my grandfather would return during the busy farming seasons to visit his family. Before 1958, our family still cultivated thirteen mu of land. When I filled out forms for school, I had to write about the amount of land we had before liberation and before it was collectivized by the People's Commune. I would list it as 13.5 mu. During the wheat harvest, we would hire laborers and short-term workers to help. After returning, he could still handle all kinds of farm work. After harvesting wheat and planting corn in the spring, he would return to Shanghai. My father's visits home took place during the Spring Festival, by contrast.

In 1963, my grandfather worked for Mr. Chen in the Boshan District for several months. In the autumn, we cultivated private plots. Our family had one-fifth of a mu of a cornfield at the village's southern end. Grandfather husked the corn and tied the cornstalks into bundles. When I was thirteen, I also helped my grandfather. Grandfather taught me how to tie the cornstalks and plow the land. When working on the farm, my grandfather's farming work was no different from that of experienced farmers, who used the same techniques as he did. I followed behind, holding the hoe and rake, assisting with various tasks. When planting wheat, we first dug trenches, applied fertilizer, sowed the seeds, and then leveled the ground with a rake. The wheat that grandfather planted looked the same as our neighbors' fields. Besides the busy farming seasons, Grandfather would also use his visitation leave when home repairs were needed.

In my hometown during the Republican era, my great-grandfather ran a liquor store and distillery, with the shop in front and the factory in the rear. It was a square courtyard with four rooms in the north, three rooms each in the east, west, and south wings, surrounding a spacious central courtyard. A large backyard was between the south and west wings. There were six large sheds on the east and west sides, three walls on each shed and pillars in front, an open-air brewery, and a few additional small rooms. As far back as I can remember, my grandfather and father were in Shanghai, and my aunts were married, leaving only my grandmother, mother, younger brother, and me at home. The front and back courtyards required annual repairs to the old walls and buildings. Each year, during the grandfather's visit, any leaking roofs or damaged walls would be repaired with the help of relatives and friends, all of whom were coordinated by the grandfather. Major renovations required preparation in advance and would take up my grandfather's whole holiday.

Around 1964, in the spring, Grandfather returned to repair the one-and-a-half room at the east end of the north wing. The northern part was a hall with a roof made of small, traditional green clay tiles, which fell out of use after the liberation, so the skills to make them were lost. This room had been leaking for three or four years, with the issue progressively worsening each year. The plan was to reuse the original small tiles, saving money and preserving the original appearance. If we replaced it with new steel tiles, it would cost a lot of money; replacing it with straw would turn it into a thatched cottage, which would not match the walls below. Local artisans in our village lacked the skill to hang small tiles, and there were none available in neighboring villages for kilometers around. Grandfather walked 20 li (about 10 km) to Suwang Village to invite Master Xuan, who had learned the craft before liberation. At that time, Master Xuan was in his fifties and brought two apprentices to our house. I took two days off from school to help. We removed the small tiles from the roof, cleaned them, and categorized them into three groups: large, medium, and small sizes. They were arranged in rows on the roof. The old felt on the roof had rotted away, so we replaced it with two new beams, covered them with new reed felt and sorghum stalks, applied a mixture of yellow mud and lime, and then began hanging the tiles. We hung five or six rows of tiles daily and completed the project in five days. The small tiles were neatly arranged, resembling a newly constructed roof. After completing the repairs, Grandfather was reassured and returned to Shanghai.

That summer, a rare, heavy rainstorm — a once-in-a-decade event — caused flooding and reservoir breaches. The heavy rain lasted for three consecutive days. The recently repaired north wing, which had been leaking bit by bit in previous years, now had a minor leak inside due to the heavy rain outside. My grandmother and mother used washbasins and buckets to remove the water outside. The effort my grandfather put into repairing the roof was in vain. My grandmother hired artisans from our village to replace the small tiles with thatch, turning the tiled roof into a thatched one.

Two rafters of the north wing's roof broke the following year, requiring major repairs. My grandfather returned to oversee the project. We used the original small tiles to repair the house, saving money. However, after completion, we paid more for the artisans' work than for buying large steel tiles, making it a failed attempt at being thrifty. As usual, my grandfather returned in the spring and, through Mr. Chen from Boshan, bought large steel tiles from the Shuihe Tile Factory. It was common in those years to rely on personal connections when purchasing goods from state-owned factories. With the help of artisans from our village, we replaced the small tiles with large steel ones in the three main rooms. Four craftsmen and seven or eight laborers swiftly completed the task in two days, saving time and effort. My grandfather was very pleased with the result. From the completion of the repairs in 1965 until the demolition of the three rooms in 1989, the roof never leaked a single drop of water.

When I graduated from middle school in 1968 and returned home, I undertook various construction projects, including repairing the house, renovating the interior floor, rebuilding the courtyard walls, and constructing pigsties. I handled all these tasks myself without informing my grandfather via letter. As my grandfather grew older and no longer needed to labor, he would visit occasionally and always expressed satisfaction with the renovations around the house.

4.6

I had begun writing letters to my grandfather when I was 10 years old. During that summer vacation, I accompanied my grandfather to Shanghai for three months. We lived in the attic of a shop; when I could not go out to play on the streets, my grandfather would teach me how to write letters. That year, I entered the third grade and could write sentences with the characters I recognized. My grandfather said writing a letter is like expressing oneself in everyday conversation. Just write down whatever needs to be conveyed clearly, just as you would speak. If you can write a few sentences, then write a few sentences. When I returned home in October, I had started learning to write letters to my grandfather. I faithfully wrote down what my grandmother told me, even though my sentences were not always smooth. However, my grandfather could still understand them and praised me in his replies. Despite spending many years away from home, my grandfather often wrote letters to the family, and my father would write back to him. In 1948, when my father went to Shanghai, neither my grandmother, aunt, nor mother could read or write. Therefore, my grandfather wrote letters to the family, and my grandmother found someone to read them and write replies on their behalf. Sometimes, she would ask my other grandfather, and at other times, she would ask Mr. Zhao next door. Although simple, having someone read the letters and then speak about family matters to compose a reply was always a hassle. They hoped I could go to school soon, learn to read, and write letters myself.

I started writing letters in third grade, but I had not yet learned practical writing, so I did not know how to write them effectively. I would start with the greeting, write "Grandpa," and then write some sentences. My grandfather's letters had many characters I did not recognize, even though they were written in a neat hand. His letters contained many traditional characters, some of which were in semi-cursive script. When my grandfather returned, he taught me the characters I did not recognize from his letters, allowing me to understand them better. By the fourth grade, we had started learning practical writing in Chinese class. We were taught how to write letters, with the teacher emphasizing that the greeting in a letter, instead of "Grandpa," should be "Grandfather." The teacher also taught us to write "Hello, Grandfather." I had seen letters from my father to my grandfather, starting with "Dear Father", and letters from my uncle to my grandfather, starting with "Dear Father-in-Law". Thus, I also learned to write "Dear Grandfather". At the end of my father's letters to my grandfather, he would write, "Yours sincerely". By the time I reached the fifth grade, I could no longer write "I hope you can have a healthy body," so I changed it to "Wishing you peace and well-being" and wrote it until my grandfather retired.

My fountain pen handwriting was decent but not uniform. In this, my grandfather had a great influence on me. After graduating, I returned to the countryside and worked as a school teacher for two years. I practiced my fountain pen handwriting in my spare time. During the Cultural Revolution, fountain pen copybooks were unavailable. My grandfather's letters were mostly written in semi-cursive script, with some in grass script. My grandfather once told me that his handwriting, using both brush and pen, was an imitation of Liu Zongyuan's font. The character 我 (I) was frequently used in his letters. My grandfather's style was to omit the horizontal stroke at the top of the character 家 (home) and add a diagonal stroke instead. For the character 老 (old), my grandfather stylistically connected the strokes, sometimes writing many characters in a single stroke, creating a lively and flowing script. In my spare time, I would take out my grandfather's letters and practice handwriting by imitating them. Some characters were exactly like his in my imitation, while others could not capture the elegance of my grandfather's handwriting. Influenced by him, I gradually developed a liking for semi-cursive script, even turning some characters into grass script.

During the early stages of the Cultural Revolution, when my grandfather returned home for a visit, he brought back a copybook of cursive script. Published in the 1950s, it was the first time I had seen it, and my grandfather asked me to practice writing from the book. He told me he had read through it many times and practiced the characters from the book. He said that not every character needed to be learned; I should pick the ones I liked and felt comfortable writing. If a character looked strange or awkward, I should not bother learning it. He advised me to start with a regular script, even using a fountain pen, and practice stroke by stroke. Only after mastering regular script should I move on to semi-cursive script. I should not practice cursive script too much because others might not understand it if I write it excessively.

My grandfather primarily used semi-cursive script in his letters, with only a few characters in Cursive Script. I flipped through the book several times and practiced Cursive Script for a long time. The book consisted of five-character verses, with some phrases rolling off the tongue. One memorable phrase was " 六手示为禀 , 七红即是 袁 ". The character "six" (六) combined with "hand" (手) formed the Cursive Script "submission" (禀), while the characters "seven" (七) and "red" (红) formed the Cursive Script "yuan" (袁). I have kept this book for 50 years, and it still sits on my bookshelf. Since the 1980s, it has been widely available in bookstores.

My grandfather brought back many copybooks, including those of Liu Gongquan, Ouyang Xun, and Yan Zhenqing, as well as other renowned calligraphers. He loved calligraphy and was good at writing with a brush. Throughout his life, he never had the opportunity to write extensively. In his early years, he struggled to make a living. In his later years, during the Cultural Revolution, he fell ill after retiring from his career. I only saw couplets written by my grandfather; I never saw him write a full piece of calligraphy with a brush.

4.7

My grandfather left his hometown for over 40 years, leaving my grandmother alone to toil at home. Before liberation, she had to manage tens of mu of land and take care of several children, living in constant anxiety. Local ruffians extorted money in the village, and miscellaneous troops in society exacted grain. After liberation, life became more stable. From my earliest memories, my grandfather was very concerned about my grandmother's life, from dressing to eating and wearing wool sweaters and pants in spring and autumn. In those days, pure wool was used, with no synthetic fibers, and winter cotton jackets were lined with camel hair. In my childhood memories, when I went with my grandmother to Boshan, Zhangdian, and Jinan, some people wore wool sweaters, but wool pants were rare.

I slept with my grandmother from the age of five. In the morning, my grandmother made two bowls of lotus root powder, adding a few pieces of rock sugar to each bowl, one for each of us. After starting school, I recognized West Lake brand was the lotus root powder, and Yu Chu was the rock sugar brand. My grandmother also made a cup of glucose water. Powdered glucose has high nutritional value, so she made two cups every day without fail. During the three years of natural disasters (1959-1961), to ensure we had enough to eat, my grandfather sent biscuits home to us, since our supply of glucose was interrupted for two years. In 1962, normal life resumed, and my grandmother continued to drink lotus root powder and glucose every day until 1974, with my grandfather regularly sending them to her.

During the years when my grandmother was in good health and my grandfather had returned, our large family of seven or eight people would eat together at a square table. My grandfather did not drink much and ate little. He would just sit down with us. During meals, everyone sat properly, not picking at the dishes on the plates. My grandfather never ate leftovers. After my grandmother fell ill, meals were served separately, with my grandfather and grandmother eating alone. After my mother had cooked a meal, she would bring it to my grandparents' room. From a young age until retirement, my grandfather did not have the habit of drinking alone. At banquets, he would drink two or three small cups of alcohol; sometimes, he would get drunk after drinking three liang (about 150 ml) of wine. After my grandmother had passed away, my grandfather ate alone, pouring himself a glass of wine, about half a Liang, twice a day. When my father retired and returned home, he enjoyed cooking, meticulously preparing three meals daily. Sometimes, he would make Southern dishes and serve them to my grandfather, then clean up after him and eat by himself. My father had enjoyed drinking since he was young. He would not drink at lunch on workdays, but had to drink in the evenings. After retiring and staying at home, he drank at both lunch and dinner. Both my grandfather and father shared the same dining habits, and the people of Shanghai had adopted them as well. They each had three small dishes per meal. They did not even fill one plate when combined; sometimes, even then, they could not finish everything.

When my grandfather retired and returned home, he did not have many new clothes. From my earliest memories, he wore Zhongshan suits. He brought back an old wool coat and a half-length wool coat, both of which were purchased in the 1950s. My father mentioned that in the 1950s, when my grandfather returned from Shanghai to his hometown and got off the train in Jinan, he stayed overnight at his elder aunt's house, wearing a wool coat. It was quite conspicuous on the street. Upon leaving Jinan Railway Station, it felt like returning to the countryside compared to Shanghai. He wore the wool coat only twice, left it at his elder aunt's house in Jinan, and never wore it again upon returning home. If he had worn this garment on the street, the villagers would have secretly spoken ill of him. When he returned from visiting relatives, he dressed modestly, spoke with the same accent, using a local dialect, and had no Shanghai accent; he also showed no sense of returning home with honor.

After my grandfather's stomach surgery, he recovered well for two or three years. He could eat normally, walk, and speak with strength. One morning, just as I got up, he called me into his room, and I saw him struggling to take each step. He said his left arm and leg felt numb, and he could not control his leg when walking, his left hand could not be raised, and he had a problem with half of his body — a stroke. When my grandmother had a stroke, I used a small wooden cart to push her to Si Weicun Village to find a rural doctor for acupuncture. After two months of treatment, the effect was beneficial, enabling her to transition from being unable to get out of bed to walking. The old doctor was from a landlord family in his seventies. He had been called back home from the county hospital before the Cultural Revolution. The village secretly arranged for him to work at the clinic where acupuncture cost one yuan per session. I then used the small wooden cart again to take my grandfather for acupuncture. After seven or eight sessions, he recovered without medication or intravenous drips.

After recovering from the stroke, my grandfather's health was excellent, with no sequelae. He visited my elder aunt's house in Jinan twice and my second aunt's house in Lanzhou once, staying for more than a month each time. He also visited Shanghai once, staying for more than two months. For three to five years, his health remained good. Around 1984, however, he began to feel tired when walking, but medical examinations revealed no issues. Despite injections and medication, there was no significant improvement.

My uncle, my grandfather's son, had graduated from medical school before the Cultural Revolution and was skilled in medicine. When my grandfather fell ill, he received treatment at home, making it convenient and timely. Medical expenses were fully reimbursed, as retired workers in Shanghai were entitled to full reimbursement of their expenses. From the village clinic to the town hospital and then to the district hospital, the reimbursement bills were not discounted, with every yuan reimbursed in full. My grandfather went for treatment once a month, and the reimbursement bills were sent to his workplace in Shanghai. The medical expenses were returned by mail within 10 days, making medical treatment as convenient as when he was working in Shanghai.

After my grandfather had returned from Shanghai, he found walking increasingly difficult and stopped traveling far from home. Each year, his condition worsened. Despite consulting specialists and receiving intravenous therapy at the district hospital, the effects were not significant. He felt no pain or discomfort but still found it difficult to walk. In the two years leading up to his passing, he rarely left the house and would often walk around inside.

In 1989, my grandfather passed away at the age of 80, and so was considered long-lived for his generation. Having spent his life in the economic center of China for over 40 years, he had experienced neither great rises nor falls, leading a plain and ordinary life. Retiring to his hometown in his later years, he had lived a quiet life. In his final years, he suffered from illness, but without too much pain, with a household full of descendants and a contented mind.

He had a pleasant Chinese New Year. On the sixth day of the first lunar month, my grandfather insisted on sending my third brother to the Township Grain Depot to buy the allocated grain. My third brother obeyed, rode his bicycle there, and returned after two hours, but lost the food coupon. The destinies of great figures and ordinary folks differ: the former may leave with great fanfare, but the latter may pass away unnoticed. From the sixth day of the first lunar month in 1989, my grandfather refused to eat either rice or vegetables for over 50 days and passed away peacefully.

CHAPTER 5
ODE TO THE TRUCK

5.1 The Taishan Light Truck

When the coating factory started production, I had to buy a truck because the daily production of two to three tons of coating was delivered to the market. In the 1980s, there was no individual truck for transportation, and it was not easy to hire vehicles from state-owned collective transport companies. Buying a new truck was, therefore, a challenging and costly endeavor. There was no market for used trucks, making the acquisition of one even more challenging. When we were at a loss, the village-owned rubber factory decided to sell an Old Taishan light truck for 5,000 yuan, which perfectly suited our needs, so we bought it.

The truck had been in use for eight years, with nearly half of the cabin covered in rust, and the cargo compartment was too damaged to be windproof. On its first day, it broke down halfway; the starter motor was not working, so we had to manually crank the engine to get it started and drive it back to the factory. The hand crank was a crucial tool we could not afford to be without. Starting the truck became a daily routine.

No major clients were purchasing coating sales; the sales network was dispersed, with seven or eight distribution points in each county town, one or two in each township, and three or four in larger townships. To the north: Nanding, Zhangdian, Huantai, Boxing, and Binzhou. To the east: Zichuan, Yidu, Changle, Weifang, Changyi, and Yexian County. To the west: Wangcun Town, Zhoucun Town, Puji Town, Qingcheng Town, Mingshui Sub-District, Xiuhui Sub-District, Diaozhen Town, and Pinglingcheng Village. Some sales points were set up in the south but did not last long, including Boshan, Laiwu, Tai'an, Hezhuang, and Fanzhen. Both objective and subjective factors contributed to this; the salespeople were not diligent enough, and the business was not conducted thoroughly. Once, when we visited a construction site in Laiwu, we were unable to locate the site manager after unloading the goods, and we had to reload the truck and return.

Just after the factory was established, we encountered a fortuneteller who used the Six Yao divination on the street of Zichuan. Out of curiosity, we attempted to gauge the prospects of the coating business. After tossing six coins six times, marking several lines on the paper, some positive, some negative, the first pair of third, fourth to sixth, and correcting several times, he concluded that business was smooth in the east-west direction. Still, there were some obstacles in the south — it was not advisable to expand in that direction. At the time, we treated it as a mere amusement, not taking it seriously. We assigned a salesperson to focus on developing business in the southern counties and towns. However, within a year, we faced setbacks at every turn. I contacted the sales points and even ended up losing money. The venture came to a premature end after a year. It remains baffling how six old coins, tossed six times, could supposedly predict fortunes and the future. Despite our efforts at the southern sales points, we could not afford a complete failure, even if we were unable to win a sale.

With over 100 sales points scattered around nearby towns, delivering goods daily and returning raw materials, we were fortunate to have this old, faulty Taishan truck. On mornings when the truck would not start, which was quite normal, we would push-start it, and once it got going, it would run smoothly throughout the day. The hand crank was indispensable, and it was normal to crank it three to five times daily. In the winter, we would pour hot water into the engine to warm it up and start it. Every morning, Mr. Chen, the gatekeeper, would prepare two pots of hot water. Only when the driver poured it over the engine would the truck get started. Once, when we went to deliver coating to Shahe, a town having three sales sites more than 200 kilometers away, the truck broke down upon arrival. After unloading the goods, we were unable to start the truck. The salesperson cranked it a dozen times, but it would not start. We even shook four times in half an afternoon. After unloading the last batch at the sales point, the salesperson and the driver switched positions to crank it again, but the truck still malfunctioned. With assistance from people at the sales point, we had to push the truck to a nearby inn. The next morning, the salesperson called a mechanic to fix the truck, explaining what had happened the previous day. The mechanic adjusted a few screws on the battery and tightened a few bolts. When the driver turned the key, the engine roared back to life.

The spark plugs on the truck often malfunctioned. Since we could not obtain branded products, we had to settle for knockoffs, which often failed after less than 100 kilometers, typically resulting in snapped steel plates, timing belts, and other issues. Then there were some unexpected incidents — once, when we returned from delivering coating to Yidu Sub-District while descending from Niujiaoling Mountain onto a flat road, the truck gradually slowed down without the brakes being applied. Even when the driver pressed the accelerator, it would not move. Sensing that the accelerator was not working, he stopped the truck and discovered that the fuel tank was missing. We retraced our route and found the tank five kilometers back, lying in a ditch by the roadside. Despite being an old and sick truck with countless problems, it continued to surprise us with new issues that even veteran mechanics had not seen before.

For coating sales, the off-season and peak seasons were clearly defined. The peak season was in March, April, and May, following the Spring Festival, and in the second half of the year, from October to December. A month before the Spring Festival, there was so much demand that we did not have enough vehicles, so we had to find tractors to deliver the goods. The off-season occurred during the busy farming season, specifically from June to August. The salesperson accompanied the delivery truck, settled the accounts for the sold goods, issued a receipt for the goods just delivered, and collected the empty barrels. We used the remaining time to run the market, eliminate problematic customers, and acquire new ones as needed.

At that time, telephone numbers between towns, villages, and enterprises were all three digits. Baixi Coating Factory's phone number was 140. Since the semi-programmed phone number system was introduced in 1985, each township has been assigned a six-digit phone number. When you called from the local, you had to dial the programmed number in the village first. After the phone was connected, you asked the operator to dial 140. Zibo was ahead of most towns and counties where semi-programmed phone numbers were unavailable. We were accustomed to it and did not use the phone for business.

Each telegram had a telegram number. For example, 2016 represented Zichuan District, Cicun Township, Baixi Coating Factory. Sending a telegram could therefore save 10 words. Business contacts relied on telegrams. We received telegrams for goods daily, sometimes as many as four or five per day, during peak season. Before 1985, telegrams were sent together with newspapers. Sometimes, like letters, they took three days to receive. Only urgent messages were received on the same day. After 1985, the township and individual industries experienced rapid development. Telegrams were an important tool for business communication. Each township post and telecommunications office dispatched a dedicated person to deliver telegrams, once in the morning and once in the afternoon. There was no difference between ordinary and urgent points. Sending a telegram cost 0.5 yuan.

The coating factory received a telegram from old customers. The content was concise: "2016, send white 20, green 10, blue 5, Zhang in Wei Gu." They were all urgent, "Express Bai 15, LAN 5, Zhao." After understanding, we hung them on the wall, then arranged the truck delivery according to the order. Sometimes, we send an urgent first or a truck to the west, covering Wangcun and Puji Towns; to the north, covering Nanding, Zhangdian, and Huantai. Boxing County, with seven or eight sales agents, needed a truck sent singly, and so did Yidu. We sent goods to the clients who first sent their telegrams to us. For the rest, the scattered, small customers, we delivered a few barrels to each household.

Yet, even with all its flaws, this Old Taishan truck proved indispensable. After just two days without issues, things did not feel quite right. Leaving it behind, I knew one thing had become clear — coating was not easy.

5.2 Annual Inspection of Vehicles

Having been used for delivery for two years, we found that after the Taishan light truck underwent various repairs and maintenance, it proved to be stronger than a tractor. After paying the road maintenance fee, there had been no government inquiries. One day, a written notice arrived from the tractor management station stating that the vehicle needed its annual inspection. All vehicle units were advised to prepare accordingly, with the specific time to be notified later.

When the notice arrived, it instructed us to visit the tractor station the next day to submit our driver's license and vehicle registration certificate. With 10 days' notice, vehicles were not allowed on the road. We decided to repair the engine, rewire the truck, and completely refinish it. Failure in the annual inspection would result in the confiscation of the driver's and vehicle licenses.

I contacted the automobile repair shop. Our neighbor, Uncle Zhao, worked at the repair shop of the Mining Bureau's small vehicle fleet. He arranged with the shop manager for the repair shop to work overtime, aiming to complete the repairs in six days and finish the coating job in two. The repair shop for small vehicles had excellent skills. It specialized in repairing dozens of trucks from the Mining Bureau, focusing solely on internal jobs. This was a private job for personal vehicle owners, who did not issue invoices, and the repair fees went directly into their pockets. The plan was to complete the repairs in eight days, but strive for seven.

After repairing the truck, I drove it back and spent a day inspecting it myself. I cleaned off the mud and grease underneath the truck body and washed all six wheels with a brush until they were spotless. The headlights were carefully checked; during routine deliveries, all headlights were rarely on at the same time. Sometimes, only one of the small lights worked, and it was normal for the turn signal to malfunction. Inspection of the lights was a major aspect of the annual inspection. After the inspection, the truck was driven a short distance to check if any issues arose. If any did, it would be repaired again.

The vehicle's annual inspection was conducted at the wheat field north of Cicun Village. All forty-two vehicles in the township were inspected in two days. For vehicles from factories, the factory manager had to be present. In contrast, for vehicles owned by self-employed persons, the owner had to attend to show importance to the inspection. They could cover any unexpected costs and send some money that the drivers could not agree on. At the township tractor station, where the annual inspection was held, the group leader collected an additional 20 yuan per vehicle during fee collection, without issuing receipts, to entertain the inspection staff and leaders with meals, cigarettes, souvenirs, and other items. For vehicles with significant issues, special arrangements were made.

The forty-plus vehicles were divided into two rows, neatly lined up at the wheat field, waiting for the inspectors. At nine o'clock, a jeep arrived, with four people descending from it — there was no doubt they were the inspection officers. The comrades from the township tractor station's inspection team greeted them and exchanged pleasantries. The inspection began under the leadership of the group leader.

The first item was checking the lights. The driver entered the truck, and the inspector directed them to turn on the headlights. If there were no problems, inspectors checked the low beams, turn signals, and windshield wipers and inspected the rear, turn, and fog lights. Any failures were recorded. The next step was inspecting the engine. The hood was opened, and the engine started: "Bang, bang, bang." After running for a minute or two, it finished. The engine's appearance was examined, and if the coating was deemed unsatisfactory, it was noted down as below standard according to the inspectors' impression. They also checked the radiator, gearbox, and the entire internal part of the vehicle for oil stains and dirt, meticulously inspecting each component. The inspector's judgment was relied upon, and there were good reasons for whether the vehicle passed or failed.

By noon, six vehicles had been inspected. Inspection continued after lunch.

A banquet was held for lunch, with a deputy town mayor, town-owned factory managers, the inspection group leader, and other leaders in attendance. They first got acquainted, then socialized. The factory managers had prepared good wine and cigarettes in their bags. They made arrangements in advance to handle certain details of the inspection. It was not only the group leader; each team member could decide whether each vehicle would pass or fail. For the old vehicles, many years ago, finding faults was too easy. Although the lights had been checked twice the day before, at noon the next day, after a little bump on the road, one of the lights was not working — completely normal. The inspectors were familiar with the way of the world, so they marked "pass" on the inspection form, which was also normal, and no one questioned it. Without connections, if your vehicle required extra inspection, it would cost 50 yuan. If anyone did not pull strings for inspection at noon, there was always the next day.

According to the inspectors, the lights were inspected in the afternoon, followed by an assessment of the interior cleanliness of the vehicles. The exterior of the vehicles would be inspected at noon the following day, followed by a road test and brake inspection in the afternoon.

For the inspection of the exterior condition of the vehicles, two people were observed, with one person recording the observations. At the same time, the other checked the chassis, driver's cabin, and cargo area. If any aspect failed, it required rework or a new coating job. When inspecting the exterior, the inspectors had greater authority and discretion. They did not announce whether a vehicle passed or failed on the spot for each one, but did so only after all inspections were completed.

My old Taishan 130 vehicle smoothly passed through the initial stages during this inspection. Six workers and one manager were at the repair shop for the Mining Bureau's small vehicle fleet. The manager had driven for over thirty years before liberation, mostly in coal mines. With just a few engine noises, he could accurately deduce most problems. They were proficient in truck circuits and the skills needed to repair sedans. At the inspection site, none of the lights posed a problem. The entire vehicle's appearance, with its sedan-like coating, stood out among the inspected vehicles. When the inspectors approached my truck, without a word, they marked it as passing. Other parts were meticulously repaired. The repair costs I supported were distributed among the workers; the manager did not take much. The quality of repairs by the workers was significantly better than that done at individual repair shops. Today, the vehicle's driving and braking were flawless as it hit the road.

After the exterior and condition inspections, these trucks needed to run a few kilometers on the road to check the engine's performance and brakes. With over 40 vehicles and two inspectors, inspecting all trucks would take three days. For the sampling inspection, whichever vehicle was selected would go on the road. As for the vehicles that were not selected, the inspections were deemed complete. The vehicles were lined up in two rows. The team leader randomly chose five vehicles from the front row, ranging from the fifth to the ninth, and five from the back row, from the front and rear. These 10 vehicles would go on the road. After the team leader announced the selection, the other vehicles were considered to have passed. The drivers of the vehicles that were not selected cheered with joy and drove home! The annual inspection was passed!

My old Taishan 130-model vehicle was not selected for the road test, but it passed the annual inspection. Problems should be fixed promptly during the preliminary inspection, when the inspection team is in the next township. After all inspections were completed, driver's licenses and vehicle registrations would be issued five days later. It would be delayed by seven or eight days if it could not be issued within the five-day timeframe. If the vehicle had failed the second inspection, pulling strings and offering gifts would be necessary. If you cannot obtain the certificates, the vehicle cannot be driven on the roads.

5.3 The Truck's Troubles

Little Pan's business covered over 20 sales points in Yidu, Changle, Changyi, and Shahe Luwang in Yexian. When delivering coating to Shahe and Luwang, which were over 200 kilometers away, considering the transportation costs, there was no profit to be made. A type of raw material filler, talcum powder, was used in the coating, located 10 kilometers east of Shahe in Hongwei Township (now Shentang Town). In 1985, there were no distribution trucks, so we could only use bicycles for delivery, which incurred considerable transportation costs. However, by delivering the coating to Shahe and Luwang and bringing back talcum powder, we could save on talcum powder transportation costs. Little Pan's business was doing well, selling coating for two yuan more per bucket than in Zibo. On average, he made two to three trips a month, and the talcum powder could be used for coating, so there was no need for separate transportation.

When traveling to Shahe and Luwang, the truck could carry at least 70 buckets due to the long distance. In the Zibo area, it could carry only 40 to 50 buckets. We would depart in the morning and arrive in the afternoon, unloading the coating the same day and loading the talcum powder back to the factory the next day. Paternal Uncle Sun accompanied the driver while Little Pan waited in Shahe.

At one o'clock in the afternoon, an urgent call came in: the truck had overturned into a roadside ditch. Fortunately, no one was injured, and the damage to the truck was not significant, but all the coating had spilled into the ditch. Since I was out for something else, I received another call at four o'clock when I returned in the afternoon, informing me that the truck had been towed to the roadside station. Several road curbs were damaged, and the roadside station wanted to impose a fine. I brought the truck and the fine to the Changyi roadside station the next day.

I borrowed a truck with a double-row seating driving compartment from the fan factory. I arrived at the Changyi roadside station at noon.

I was fined 300 yuan for the curb damage and had the overturned truck towed back to the factory.

The driver had only been driving for a little over a year and lacked experience. He had veered onto the roadside curb and flipped into the ditch to avoid a large trailer. It was a deep, dirt-filled ditch, and the truck slowly tipped over. Although the windshield fell off, it did not break. All 70 buckets of coating rolled into the ditch, leaving none behind. The cabin was slightly deformed, and several rusty iron plates around it cracked upon impact. The lower part of the cabin needed welding. However, the engine could still start, the headlights were intact, and the truck could still move, although the entire cabin needed repairs.

We took the truck to the township repair shop, where the mechanic inspected it. Welding the cabin and recoating would cost 1,200 yuan. I had bought the truck for 5,000 yuan three years ago, and now it would not fetch more than 2,000 yuan on the market. The market had undergone significant changes over the past three years, with many new trucks replacing older models. Considering only welding and no other repairs, I pondered it. I decided to do it myself, which would cost at most 500 yuan.

Paternal Uncle Sun was knowledgeable about machinery and willing to use his brains to repair it. We discussed and decided to remove the cabin, find an electric welder, and weld it back in place in one day. I could handle the coating myself, without going to an auto repair shop, and be self-reliant in overcoming the difficulties.

We began with the truck's wiring, with Paternal Uncle Sun taking the lead and the driver providing assistance. Lacking understanding of the truck's wiring, we followed the design, dismantling one connector at a time and marking them as 1, 2, 3, 4, and 5 to ensure accurate reassembly. After dismantling the wiring, we used the same method to remove the steering wheel, seats, and doors. Although it was a bit clumsy, we finished in three hours. We borrowed a hand-operated hoist and easily moved the cabin to the ground.

We invited a gas welding master from the ceiling fan factory, who brought a complete set of tools, oxygen cylinders, and carbides. He was highly skilled and hardworking. He finished welding the cabin in half a day, from one o'clock in the afternoon to five-thirty o'clock, much quicker and neater than an auto repair shop. He did not charge hourly fees, and we would often drink with him in the evening.

We coated the grease the next day, which took a whole day. On the third day, installation was straightforward due to our disassembly experience. We easily installed everything, and attaching the windshield required some effort, but it was done securely. When we started the engine, it performed better than expected. After settling the bill, we spent less than 300 yuan. Poor people save their lives, and broken trucks have their repair methods. A few days later, in the afternoon, we delivered the coating. Since no coating was available at the site, we sent a bicycle to Luocun Town Chemical Factory to fetch a load of light calcium. It was over 20 kilometers away, taking more than two hours for a round trip, leaving us ample time in the afternoon. With the driver staying at the factory alone, the apprentice had to leave for a short time. In the past, when driving the old truck, two people went out together, with the apprentice loading and unloading, helping with repairs, and keeping an eye on the truck. I had nothing to do that afternoon, so I accompanied the driver to Luocun Town Chemical Factory to fetch light calcium.

Light calcium production was tight and often out of stock. After delivering the coating, we stopped by Luocun Town Chemical Factory and Hutian Light Calcium Carbonate Factory on the way back to pick up light calcium. We had to make several trips to deliver the light calcium to Mingshui and Puji since there was no return trip with light calcium along the way. On that afternoon, we sent a truck to Luocun Village.

Luocun Town Chemical Factory began production less than a year ago, with a limited number of business relationships. When we went to load the truck, there was no queue. We arrived at the factory around two o'clock, got the invoice, loaded the truck, and finished loading two and a half tons by three o'clock. As we drove away, the cabin creaked and groaned, but the welding job this time was very sturdy, and it did not sway, which was reassuring. The noise came from the chassis. It started creaking after driving over 10 meters from the factory onto the road, around a bend, and up a small slope. Climbing the hill for three to four minutes on the road, the driver muttered that the engine temperature had suddenly risen. Pulling over to the side, he opened the hood, and steam rose from the radiator. It was out of water. Bending down, the driver carefully observed and found two cracks in the radiator's cooling copper pipes. The radiator's bends were larger than the harder fan blades, and they had scraped the pipes open. Within minutes, the water had completely leaked out.

After waiting for it to cool down, we drove to Luocun Town and found an auto repair shop. After removing the radiator, the mechanic examined it. Two cracks on one side and four or five on the other were very thin and easily broken. How about a weld? The driver replied that disassembling the water tank once is troublesome. The mechanic went to get a copper welding rod, rummaging through a wooden box until he found one. However, one rod could only weld one crack at a time. "Is there no one selling this thing nearby?" the driver asked.

"You can only go to Zichuan to buy," the mechanic replied.

It was already four-thirty, and riding a motorcycle would take over an hour. Welding could not be completed today, and a 20-kilometer trip meant we would not be able to return to the factory in time.

Without programmable phones or mobile phones back then, if a delivery that was supposed to return the same day could not make it back, the vehicle would have broken down. This happened often when the distance was thirty to 25 kilometers, but there was no rush. It was commonplace, and we got used to it. Without this opportunity, we would not have stayed at the Luocun Town Supply and Marketing Cooperative's hotel. Over the course of these decades, we have only stayed there once.

5.4 New Truck Often Returned to Factory

The old truck had been in use for four years. The cost of repairs could have bought a new truck. Moreover, it was beyond repair. The cylinder head and block were aging, and the gearbox could not be engaged easily, even after trying several times. The driver's cabin had been repaired repeatedly. Borrowing money to buy a new truck, I would never buy an old truck again.

I decided to buy a small light truck from Zibo Automobile Factory, located in Zichuan District. Buying a new truck with the help of friends could save money. The factory director's hometown was Liuwazhuang Village of Cicun Township, making it easy to find acquaintances. I quickly found the head of the Production Department, who contacted the sales manager in Binzhou. Buying a truck from Binzhou could save over 1,200 yuan compared to purchasing it directly from the factory, and it would also help the sales manager meet their sales targets. It was a win-win situation. The cargo box needed to be elongated to accommodate coating drums. After waiting about half a month, Binzhou issued the invoice, and we picked up the truck from inside the Zichuan factory.

When it was time to pick up the truck, I took the driver and found a friend with a large truck to take us to the automobile factory. After completing the procedures for picking up the truck, we drove the new truck back to the factory with great satisfaction.

We had covered half of the journey back to the factory when we reached Five Ridge Mountain Road. This small mountain road had five distinct ridges to traverse. As we approached the fourth ridge and prepared to ascend the third ridge, the driver tried to shift gears, but the plastic triangle bracket on the gear lever snapped. This bracket was located next to the gear lever, adjacent to the steering wheel. The handle under the steering wheel, which connected the steering wheel and the shift lever, was a plastic tripod   — a circular plastic piece. Its breakage caused the gear lever to move erratically. Sitting in the passenger seat, I held the gear lever with my left hand. When putting it in gear, we had to keep it straight; if it were crooked, we could not engage the gear. I turned sideways, clutching the rod in my left hand, and we finally entered the factory. Upon arrival, I found that I was unable to open the passenger-side door. The driver tried to open it from the outside without success. Unlike the old truck door, which could be forcefully opened with a few hits from a hammer, the new truck could not be manipulated in a similar manner.

The next day, we went to the automobile factory's after-sales service department. After explaining the truck's issues, the staff burst into laughter. One jokingly remarked, "Just left yesterday and returned to visit the home. How affectionate." After tinkering with it for over an hour, they managed to fix it.

When a new truck was running, it needed to run on the engine; during that period, the speed should not exceed 40 kilometers per hour, and it required running for 2,000 kilometers. After this, the truck could be driven at full speed. There were no regulations against speeding violations at the time. After driving for a few days, the driver noticed that the steering wheel began to shake at 50 kilometers per hour and vibrate severely at 60 to 70 kilometers per hour. Since the truck was still under warranty, we returned to the automobile factory. After analysis, the factory mechanic determined that the front alignment was not properly adjusted. After it had been adjusted, we took it for another test drive to see if the steering wheel still shook.

After applying the coating for a few days, the steering wheel's vibration decreased slightly but remained present. When driving at 60 to 70 kilometers per hour, the vibration was slightly less severe than before. We had no choice but to seek further assistance.

The steering wheel vibration issue remained unresolved, and there was a "peng peng peng" sound coming from the engine. Initially, the noise was minor, so we did not pay much attention to it. However, a week later, it sounded like a tractor.

We returned to the automobile factory's after-sales service department, where the staff immediately identified a leak upon starting the truck. Upon inspection, they also found a small crack in the engine's exhaust pipe. Since the service department was unable to handle the repair, they sent a letter requesting assistance to the First Automobile Works Engine Factory in Changchun. The service staff wrapped several layers of glass cloth tape around the crack, reducing the noise, which did not affect the truck's normal operation.

Two First Automobile Works Engine Factory technicians arrived and opened the truck's hood. Two people talked.

"Such an obvious exhaust pipe defect was not found when loading the truck, and the people in the assembly workshop did not take the work seriously. The test can also reveal that the exhaust pipe sound is abnormal. They take the salary but waste their time. We go back to the factory report. This is the fourth exhaust pipe accident this year."

They inspected the engine and then came to my office. They politely informed me that the exhaust pipe was damaged and could not be repaired; it needed to be replaced. We returned to the factory and mailed the exhaust pipe to Zibo Automobile Factory. When the factory workers finished replacing it, it was about half a month later. In the meantime, we could still use the truck without any impact.

The Zibo Taishan light truck had inherent flaws, including a few major ones, as well as frequent minor issues. This truck delivered paint, hauled raw materials, and ran for 10 years before finally coming to a stop. Despite its shortcomings, it served faithfully, making significant contributions to my coating factory.

Years later, Zibo Automobile Factory seized the opportunity to undergo rapid transformation. They switched from gasoline to diesel engines, branding their vehicles as "Light Rider Agricultural Vehicles." This swift development led to an increase in their annual production from 2,000 gasoline vehicles to 30,000 diesel vehicles. A few years later, they abandoned the agricultural vehicle label and rebranded it as T. King Truck, experiencing even greater production growth. Production soared to 60,000 to 70,000 vehicles within two or three years, making the Zibo Automobile Factory a source of regional pride. But that is another story.

5.5 Overnight at Menglianggu

The Zibo Mining Bureau Leasing Station settled accounts with our factory. It provided us with a Jinbei double-row seat truck. This state-owned factory vehicle, which had been in use for five years, had just passed its annual inspection. From the outside, it appeared to be about 70 to 80 percent new. Thanks to good relations with the station chief, we agreed to offset 5,000 yuan with this vehicle. We later spent another 2,000 yuan to pass the inspection. In 1993, a double-row truck could be considered a limousine to drive to the unit to conduct business or pick up guests. The truck was invaluable in small enterprises.

When we purchased a 16-type lathe from Linyi Shengjian Machinery Factory, I decided to use the Jinbei van to transport it, marking the first time we had used a double-row truck for such a task. The journey to Linyi was over 200 kilometers. Since it was a mountainous route, we planned to complete it in two days, which was quite tight for a same-day return.

We tried to start the truck for work, but the engine would not turn over, despite my several attempts over several minutes. Finally, we started it by calling for a few people to push it to the door and jump-start it. This failure to start the engine was not uncommon; however, such minor issues did not impact our work.

We took the truck to a repair shop as we entered the urban area of Laiwu. At noon, when we tried to start the truck again after lunch, it failed to start once more. There was also a considerable distance to travel. The mechanics at the repair shop checked the wiring and replaced the spark plugs, fixing the issue within an hour. We hurriedly resumed our journey, determined to reach Linyi by the end of the day.

As we drove along the provincial road after passing Xintai, the road narrowed and became less congested with fewer vehicles. As we ascended a hill near Xintai, the driver attempted to shift gears, but a clattering sound ensued, and it took two or three tries to engage a gear.

"What's happening?" I asked the driver.

"It seems like something is blocking the lever underneath. It was unaffected, and we could also have a try," the driver replied.

As the truck climbed the mountain road, the noise grew louder and louder with each passing shift. We could barely shift gears twice, so we pulled over.

After pulling over, the driver crawled under the truck to inspect. The connecting point of the horizontal lever seemed deformed, with a possibility of breakage. What to do? There were no factories between counties, and industrial development was lacking, resulting in a lack of nearby repair shops. Returning to Xintai and retracing our steps was not cost-effective, and the city of Mengyin was ahead of us. There must be a solution ahead of us. We decided to continue forward.

After starting the truck, we were unable to shift gears. No matter how we adjusted it, we could not engage a gear. The engine stalled, and the driver crawled under the truck, holding the horizontal lever in place. At the same time, the trainee sat in the driver's seat, operating the gear lever. With some knowledge of trucks, the driver was holding the bar under him and slowly putting it into gear. Then he returned to his seat, started the engine slowly, and proceeded with caution.

With thirty kilometers to go until Mengyin, we could not afford to have the lever break. With no repair shops along the way, we proceeded cautiously. Shifting gears gently, we stopped the truck whenever we could not engage a gear, and the driver manually shifted gears under the truck. This process was repeated several times. With a speed of only 20 kilometers per hour, we finally reached Mengyin. We found a repair shop, but it was already closed. We decided to return the next day.

We arrived at the repair shop at eight o'clock the next morning. The mechanic inspected the truck and said the lever was close to breaking. Since they did not have a new one, we had to weld it and get a replacement after returning it. After the repair was done, we continued our journey. We asked the boss, who said there were more than 80 kilometers to Linyi. We would be there by noon, load up the lathe, and return in the afternoon.

As we left Mengyin, although the mountain roads were not steep, there were frequent sections that required both uphill and downhill travel. The gear-shifting problem persisted despite the repair. The mechanic who had welded the lever did not seem to have top-notch skills. The driver had to work underneath the truck whenever we could not engage a gear. We reached Qingtuo Town by noon. After lunch, as we left Qingtuo Town, the lever finally snapped with a "click." The truck broke down by the roadside. We stared blankly at each other, worried about what to do next. Mengyin's repair shop was untrustworthy, and we were unsure how to obtain a tow truck.

We asked pedestrians along the road if any tractor-trucks were available. A kind person advised us to negotiate the price with the tow truck driver first, as there were many dishonest operators in the area. Qingtuo had a tow truck, so we went there. The driver walked to Qingtuo, which took over an hour to reach. He found a reliable tow truck operator. With hooks and ropes in place, and without any deception, the tow truck took us to the Qingtuo repair shop for 50 yuan, a fair price.

This repair shop specializes in fixing tractors, not trucks. After explaining the truck's issues, the mechanic was hesitant. But he seemed genuine, not boasting. After pleading with him several times, saying that the driver could give a hand and guidance, he agreed to try his best to fix it.

The repair shop consisted of two small rooms and a small courtyard, run by the mechanic alone. The courtyard was occupied by a truck, leaving no space for the tow truck to park. Removing the components from the chassis without the pit for repairing trucks was difficult, even a simple task with the pit in place.

We spent the night at the Qingtuo Supply and Marketing Cooperative's hostel. The next day, the driver helped the mechanic. They got under the truck and spent over an hour removing the two rods. Welding the rods proved challenging for the mechanic, as welding tractor parts differed from welding a truck's. The truck's rod was as thick as a thumb, and the weld had to be smooth. Despite the simple job, welding took over an hour. Once it had been repaired, it was almost time for lunch.

We reached Linyi and found the Shengjian Machinery Factory, but it was already past three in the afternoon. The factory, a prison workshop, had ceased business after three o'clock.

We spent the night in Linyi and returned to the factory the next morning. After completing the paperwork and paying cash, we entered the workshop to install the lathe. As we opened the workshop door, the prisoners stared at the out-of-town truck, respectfully approached the vehicle, opened the wing board, cleaned the dust off, and prepared to install the lathe.

Before installing the lathe, we found the workshop director, the squadron leader. We offered him two packs of cigarettes and briefed him on welding the truck's rod. The welding job done at Qingtuo Tractor Factory was not satisfactory, and we worried that the rod might break again on the return journey because the truck was loaded with a lathe. The Shengjian Factory was a large establishment with many skilled workers. We asked the driver to remove the rod and the squadron leader to help re-weld it. The squadron leader, a prison cadre, was delighted to purchase a lathe for his workshop. He readily agreed because the prison factory also prioritized efficiency. Since the lathe could not be sold, he deducted a bonus from his salary. He found the most skilled welder, who redid the welding job that had been repaired in Qingtuo, ensuring it was as good as new.

After installing the lathe and re-welding the rod, we left the Shengjian Factory at 10 o'clock and hit the road.

The return journey was smooth, with no further issues with the truck. After four days on the road, we returned to the factory just before nightfall.

CHAPTER 6
SYMPHONY OF HYDRAULIC PROPS

6.1 Entering the Gate

I often walked past the Zibo Municipal Government Building. I had entered it before to find the city-level leaders. The first time, I had to muster up the courage to enter the municipal government to discuss business with the Bureau of Mines. I approached the gatekeeper, explained who I was looking for, and he made a phone call.

After a few "hmms," he nodded and said, "Go ahead, second door on the east side of the second floor." I was looking for the deputy director of the Municipal Government, accompanied by my elder male cousin from my uncle's family.

The second door on the east side of the second floor was there. I pushed it open, and the deputy director had just started his work. After exchanging pleasantries, I explained the purpose of my visit. The Mechanical Factory of the Bureau of Mines had a processing business, and I had the capability and machines to do it. However, it required approval from the department's leadership. Deputy district director Ning, recently assigned by the city, had a good working relationship with director Sun, the person in charge. With a nod from Ning, this business could be facilitated. After I finished speaking, the deputy director smiled and said, "Little Ning was once my subordinate and had worked under me for seven or eight years." He took the letter from the table, wrote a few lines, and handed it to me. I glanced at it; it roughly said, "My younger male cousin is contacting the Bureau of Mines for processing business; please assist." With the letter in hand, a huge weight was lifted off my shoulders. I had been pondering the issue for over a month, seeking solutions in vain. Still, it took only a few minutes to resolve it. The deputy director was approachable, enthusiastic, and efficient, accompanying us to the door.

The paint business had been operating smoothly in recent years, with sales areas within a 100-kilometer radius. A truck delivered the goods, the salesperson settled the accounts, and everything was proceeding as planned. Expanding the business meant increased transportation costs and higher fees for empty drum returns, further squeezing profits. Venturing beyond the 100-kilometer operating circle and finding new products was not easy, either. During a class reunion, an old classmate, Liu, told me that underground coal mining had been using a new piece of support equipment in recent years — hydraulic props. These props were recycled underground and required periodic maintenance. State-owned units found the maintenance troublesome, and coal mines avoided minor tasks, outsourcing them to external units. It had started last year as a new industry with low investment, high profits, and relatively simple maintenance. The challenge lay in establishing contacts. Coal mines were large entities, and despite the simplicity of the mechanical processing, competition was fierce, relying heavily on relationships and connections in the background, making it difficult for newcomers to enter.

After the reunion, Liu asked if I could handle hydraulic props maintenance. I had a workshop, and a few tens of thousands of yuan in investment for machinery was possible. Still, I was troubled by the lack of business. Liu was willing to help me with this maintenance work. He boasted that we could manage it. He knew the manager of the leasing station responsible for managing hydraulic props in the Bureau of Mines, which handled the processing work of repairing these props, falling under the leasing station's jurisdiction. Liu's home was 0.5 kilometers away from the leasing station. Although Liu and the station manager were not close friends, Liu was familiar with him, and they often played drinking games together and boasted about their accomplishments. Liu had confidence that we could manage it. As Liu and I arrived at the station manager's office one afternoon, we noticed he was leaving at that moment. We briefly discussed the maintenance of hydraulic props with him. However, he shook his head and waved his hand, indicating he did not want to communicate with us. It irritated Liu, and he half-jokingly half-cursed the manager. We left the office feeling upset about the situation.

Two months later, Liu informed me that a new station manager had been transferred from Xishan Mine, urging me to make contact. It is a good opportunity — my elementary school classmate and lifelong friend was the Party Secretary of Xishan Mine's district. The new manager used to work as the mine shaft manager under him at Xishan, and they were drinking buddies. One Saturday evening, this classmate took me to meet the new station manager. Over three cups of liquor, we bonded instantly. The new station manager had just taken office for a week and was not yet familiar with the business, so we could not act rashly. The former acting station manager, now the deputy station manager, was responsible for overseeing these local operations. The three of us brainstormed, devising a plan that would satisfy both the successful execution of the business and the deputy station manager's acceptance without resistance. The new station manager came up with an idea: the direct superior of the leasing station was the Production Department director, Sun. As long as we had director Sun's approval, the deputy station manager would not dare to intervene. The new deputy District director, Ning, who was appointed by the city, was a close friend of Sun. We needed to find a way to reach Ning and ensure everything would fall into place. With this plan, we took action step by step, each step connecting seamlessly. As long as we reached the new deputy district director, Ning, success was assured.

To achieve our goal smoothly, we needed an introduction from someone with a connection to the deputy district chief. Approaching him directly without any strings attached might not have worked out well. Therefore, we knew about an older male cousin who worked at the municipal government. I pretended to be his younger male cousin to enlist his aid in contacting the dispatched cadres.

With the letter from the "elder cousin director," I went to the district government the next day. The new deputy district director, Ning, was on a business trip and would return in three days. When he returned, he would not be at the district government office but stationed in Donggao Town, where he had ongoing responsibilities. If we needed anything, we would find him in the town.

Three days later, I arrived at the Donggao Town government in my Jinbei van after a 75-minute journey. The office had two floors, and deputy district director Ning was in the third office on the first floor, reading documents alone. In brief, I explained my purpose. However, I was unable to be entirely frank, adding a touch of artistry to my explanation. "A few days ago, at my elder male cousin's home," I casually mentioned the Bureau of Mines' minor business and asked for his help. He mentioned that he was unfamiliar with the Bureau of Mines, adding that the deputy district director, Ning, had been dispatched to Zichuan and could assist. The deputy district director, Ning, was very accommodating; even though he was not familiar with the Bureau of Mines, he was still able to facilitate things. After I finished speaking, I handed over the letter.

Ning read it and asked with a smile, "Who is in charge of this business at the Bureau of Mines?"

"Director Sun, from the Production Department," I promptly replied.

"Oh, we're old friends, no problem," he said, and then wrote a few lines below the letter from my elder male cousin, handing it to me and asking me to pass his regards to Sun.

Ning was straightforward and efficient in his words. I put the letter in my pocket, took two cartons of cigarettes from my bag, and placed them on Ning's desk. He politely declined.

"No need to be so formal," he said as he accompanied me to the door.

It had taken less than 10 minutes from entering to complete the job.

Sitting in the car, I carefully read the few lines at the end of the letter. "Director Zhang from the municipal government office was my former superior, and our relationship was extraordinary. The director's younger male cousin is contacting you regarding the processing and maintenance business of the factory under your department. Please assist in handling it, and I will visit to express my gratitude another day."

A comedy had just concluded, and the grand drama was yet to unfold.

The office area of the Zibo Bureau of Mines was quite exquisite, featuring small Western-style houses built by Germans and a cluster of villas, each with its unique style. The production department was located in the middle; I entered it, and there were irregularly shaped rooms, twists and turns, and director Sun was in the last room. After Sun finished reading the letter, I asked about the business of repairing hydraulic props, and Sun said it could be considered. He was not very familiar with the work at the leasing station, so he said he would visit the next day, finalize the details, and visit my factory. These intermediate processes needed to be completed: the first step was on-site inspection, the second step was a meeting for discussion, and the third step was approval, so preparations were necessary.

Although Sun agreed, he also needed to follow the instructions of his superiors. Considering there's no room for error, some packaging was needed. My factory did not look like a typical factory. The workshop covered the area of an ordinary rural residence, with seven rooms and a courtyard of just over an acre, a relatively small space. The personnel who came for inspection included the department's director, the chief engineer, the factory director, the leasing station manager, and the heads of state-owned enterprises. After inspecting my factory, although they did not say it to my face, they left with a concealed smile. They were unhappy with my factory when they agreed to pass it. The neighboring electric porcelain accessories factory covered 10 mu (approximately 1.65 acres) of land and had four workshops, each 20 meters wide, which could be considered a decent machinery factory in the countryside. I planned to conduct our activities using their facilities.

I found the director of the electric porcelain accessories factory, Zhao, and straightforwardly asked to borrow their factory. Zhao readily agreed, "Sure, I'll lend it to you immediately."

"I have a small project: bring the leader of the Bureau of Mines here. You will play the role of the director of Baixi Machinery Factory, and I will play the role of the director of a subsidiary factory. We'll rehearse and prepare for the reception."

Zhao had had many experiences and had dealt with the heads of large state-owned factories; he was skilled at this performance. With everything settled, we waited for the notification to arrive.

We were to be inspected on a certain afternoon when the notification came. At the same time, I waited on the road outside the factory gate, and two vehicles arrived: a sedan and a yellow minivan, each carrying seven or eight people. Upon entering the gate, Zhao led the department director, Sun, through the lathe and punching machine workshop, introducing them as they walked along. Zhao said the village-operated enterprise aims to enrich the villagers through projects, needing support from state-owned large factories. Sun and the other leaders nodded and murmured in agreement, looking satisfied. An afternoon appointment was made without much inquiry, and a banquet was arranged. There was a clean restaurant in our village serving authentic farmhouse dishes. Sun agreed, saying they would eat farmhouse dishes.

Factory director Zhao and I accompanied director Sun, who was seated as the primary guest, along with others, who sat in order. Following a historical tradition, the seats opposite the door were for guests, with the host sitting with their back to the door. In the 1990s, there was no concept of a round table separating the host and the guests; the host sat in the middle, and the guests sat on either side. As we sat together for the first time, each person received two cups of liquor after the polite greetings. The atmosphere at the banquet was initially not lively. Director Sun suggested that everyone share stories about the seating arrangements of the main guests at banquets, after an additional cup of tea was served to each person.

Director Sun took the lead and shared his story with us as follows.

Around 1987, a Soviet delegation inspected the Bureau of Mines. They first visited the Wangzhai Coal Mine, where director Sun served as secretary and mine manager. After the inspection, Sun hosted them in the evening. When treating foreign guests, Sun had to go to the bureau's hotel, with the best rooms reserved, not at the mine's guesthouse. Sun tried to give the head of their delegation the seat where Sun sat now, but he refused. Sun insisted, but he still would not sit, and Sun could not. Sun informed the interpreter that guests who had traveled from afar should sit in the middle seats.

The interpreter relayed this, and the head of the delegation urgently said a lot in Russian, and the interpreter explained, "He says that this seat belongs to whoever paid for it, which is the host's seat. So, are we footing the bill tonight?"

Everyone burst into laughter. There were significant differences between Eastern and Western banquets, and Sun had to sit in the middle.

"I won't be footing the bill tonight," joked Department director Sun, before continuing his story.

That night, we drank Moutai liquor, with the highest standard dishes from the restaurants of the Bureau of Mines. The Soviets drank as much as they were persuaded, glass by glass. They did not need any persuasion to eat; they used spoons and knives together, expressing satisfaction with a thumbs-up as they ate. The interpreter kept saying how delicious everything was. The dishes were finished before the liquor ran out, and we asked for more. The Soviet elder brothers were pleased and took over the role of persuading us to drink. We could not back down; after rounds of persuasion, the Soviets got drunk. They thought they had better alcohol tolerance than we Chinese and wanted to joke with us. The drinking partner I chose was a local booze star known for downing a catty of liquor without getting drunk. The four big-nosed Soviets were eventually carried back to their rooms. Later, we discovered that the Soviet Union was facing severe supply shortages during those years, unable to provide meat or vegetables, a situation even worse than in the 1970s in China. Department director Sun became more spirited as he spoke about his story.

As the drinking atmosphere picked up, Department director Sun, I, and Zhao downed two more shots, with Zhao ending up sprawled on the table. I could still stand steady. With such delightful circumstances, the inspection went smoothly, and everything was approved unanimously.

Two days after the inspection, the new station manager called and invited me to the leasing station to discuss the maintenance of hydraulic props. I arrived as agreed, and the new station manager informed me that a meeting had been held regarding my matter. The Department director, Sun, personally arranged it, making it very clear.

"It's a matter of relatives from the municipal government leader, so carry out the business without anyone interfering."

At the meeting, the deputy station manager, Wang, was passive and did not express his stance; Sun reprimanded him.

"Tomorrow, you can come to fetch the hydraulic oil cylinders, starting with repairing the cylinders."

Finding the department director, inspecting, and holding meetings took seven days to complete.

The hydraulic props used in coal mines required maintenance every few months. Once removed from the shaft, their non-broken components must be cleaned, and the broken ones must be repaired. My business was repairing oil cylinders within hydraulic pillars. Before taking over the business, two factories in Tai'an were responsible for cylinder repairs. Deputy station manager Wang had close ties with these factories and did not allow me to participate in their operations. However, he could not stop me from entering the leasing station gate this time.

Deputy station manager Wang was a key figure. Before the new station manager arrived, he was the acting station manager, knowledgeable about technology and familiar with the business. The former station manager was taken over by department director Sun, who used to visit once or twice a week, with actual management in the hands of deputy station manager Wang. With the reorganization of the Bureau of Mines, Sun no longer held the part-time role, and a new station manager was dispatched. The new station manager was an outsider, so his work still relied on the deputy station manager Wang. With my business coming in, Wang failed to prevent it, and maintaining good relations with him was necessary. I had encountered resistance in his office the previous month, but I had to visit again regardless.

My old classmate discovered where deputy station manager Wang lived. It was on No. A Qiangou Street, Yanshan City. I was familiar with this street; my grandfather's office was located on Hougu Street, adjacent to it. The street was just a few dozen meters long, and we could easily find Wang's place. Usually, the deputy station manager Wang lived at the factory, returning home only on Saturdays.

Finding No. A Qiangou Street, I climbed five steps to enter a small quadrangle courtyard; the eastern two rooms were deputy station manager Wang's residence.

I knocked lightly on the door, asking, "Is director Wang at home?"

"Oh, director Yu, please come in."

The room had two beds, a small table, and two small stools, crowded into just over 20 square meters. I sat on the edge of the bed, and the deputy station manager's wife poured me a glass of water, then promptly left upon realizing we were discussing business. As I began to discuss repairing the oil cylinders, Wang steered the conversation elsewhere, evading the topic. When we could not communicate, I needed to leave quickly. Just as I was about to get up, Wang put the bag I brought in my hands. Inside were four bottles of liquor and four cartons of cigarettes for good luck. In those days, liquor was not sold in boxed gift sets; instead, it was carried in woven bags. Wang firmly refused to accept them, pushing the liquor into my arms. I had already tossed the cigarettes onto the bed; I could not toss the liquor, so I had to carry it. Wang went back to the bed to get the cigarettes as I walked over 10 meters out.

The business began by pulling back old oil cylinders, repairing, welding, grinding, and copper plating them through multiple processes to meet the standards of the new oil cylinders, which were then returned to the leasing station.

Upon a friend's recommendation, I learned about repairing oil cylinders in Tai'an. Despite the simple techniques, the standards varied, requiring the technicians from the leasing station to ensure peace of mind.

The leasing station had two technicians responsible for inspection. Without inviting or visiting them, any flaws in quality would surely be detected under a magnifying glass. In a state-owned unit, networking was paramount.

Liu had a solution: to arrange for the technicians to come to the factory on Sundays, their day off, to guide the cylinder repairs and assist in the inspection. Of course, they would not work for free, so offering them compensation was a fair and reasonable approach. The two technicians readily agreed, like Zhou Yu and Huang Gai, who meant a consensual deal by both sides, as a symbol of pleasant cooperation.

On Monday, when the delivery arrived, the two technicians put on airs and treated me indifferently. They scrutinized a few minor issues that did not affect acceptance, dawdling for over an hour, and giving me some strange looks. They reported to deputy director Wang that the first batch of cylinders sent by Baixi Mine Machinery Repair Factory met national standards and were of high quality. Deputy director Wang nodded in agreement but gave me a reluctant glance. With the two technicians inspecting many times on Sunday, how could they not be qualified? The first delivery was a great success, and everything went smoothly.

Deputy director Wang attached great importance to newly established business units and personally inspected them on several occasions. For one thing, he was meticulous. For another, he put on airs as the leader and looked for flaws. But the two technicians responded flawlessly, eliminating any trace of problems. Although deputy director Wang had authority, he had to heed the words of his two subordinates.

My business was repairing oil cylinders, not producing them. The first step was to pull cylinders from the leasing station, and the more cylinders pulled, the more money earned.

The leasing station originally had two small factories for repairing cylinders; now, with my addition, there were three. The original two were both from Tai'an, with family ties, and they did not compete or fight over the number of cylinders — they just took what they were given. The two became wary when I arrived as the newcomer with powerful backing. They increased their efforts to cultivate relationships with department heads. The distributor responsible for distributing cylinders had good connections with the two Tai'an factories. There were some tricks up their sleeves, which I was well aware of. The station manager had instructed that the cylinders be distributed evenly among the three of them. Still, the distributor favored the other two from Tai'an, using various tactics to allocate more cylinders to them. As a newcomer, I could not randomly accuse the distributor without evidence, as stirring up trouble would make future work even more difficult. Sometimes I had to grin and bear the unfair in silence.

The distributor lived in a single house with a courtyard next to the leasing station. I visited twice to give him gifts, but he adamantly refused to accept them. Trying to negotiate through friends did not work much either — it was like trying to pry open a rusty lock. My friend replied that the distributor followed the station manager's instructions, distributing cylinders fairly and justly among the three. It was a minor issue, but it was hard to resolve.

Repairing old cylinders involved grinding, welding, grinding again, polishing, and finally, copper plating in Tai'an, which was done once a month. One day, when I went to Tai'an to deliver cylinders for plating, the salesperson accompanied me. As we approached the Qingshi Pass, we noticed a truck stuck in a ditch alongside the narrow, winding road. The truck was loaded with cylinders, and several people were standing nearby. It seemed like the truck was moving slowly while climbing up the road, which might have caused it to get stuck. Upon closer inspection, we realized that the driver and salesperson were acquaintances from the factory in Tai'an, where they had been repairing the cylinder. We stopped to help tow the car. In those days, everyone carried a tow rope. After securing it, the people in front pulled while those behind pushed.

As soon as we pulled the truck up, the distributor from the leasing station rushed over, shook hands with the salesperson, and pulled him aside, whispering, "Tomorrow is Sunday. Our family is going to visit Mount Tai. You cannot tell anyone when coming to the leasing station.

I follow Little Ma's truck to Tai'an. If the station manager finds out, I'll lose the job."

Little Ma was the salesperson from the Tai'an cylinder repair unit. The distributor was visiting Mount Tai. It did not need to be said explicitly — the business unit would cover all food, accommodation, and entertainment expenses. Word got around the leasing station, and the distributor's job would be fired. The distributor's job was neither wealthy nor poor, and many people wanted to take over.

When my salesperson returned and told me about it, we decided to keep quiet and not utter a word.

Coincidentally, when I went to the leasing station to pick up the cylinders after encountering the Qingshi Pass incident, the distributor greeted us with a smile and sent us off with one as well. It was obvious that we were getting more cylinders than before.

I made a wise decision to give gifts and entertain the distributor, which helped put his mind at ease. On my next visit to his house, he readily accepted the gifts. The distributor insisted on paying the bill during a small banquet with four people at a restaurant. I wondered if my salesperson should allow him to do so. No one mentioned anything about Qingshi Pass during dinner. We seemed to have moved on and were ready for the next show.

6.2 New Technology in Taiyuan

There's a new technology for repairing oil cylinders. Director Sun returned from Taiyuan after attending an appraisal meeting, where he detailed this new technique during a feast. Oil cylinders are coated with a layer of wear-resistant coating. After processing, the smoothness is better than that of copper plating, and the acid and alkali resistance is approximately two to three times longer; it can also help save costs. The panel had already appraised it and was ready to promote this new technology. Information had been sent to mining bureaus nationwide, and they were encouraged to visit Taiyuan to learn more about the initiative.

Among the appraisal team, led by director Sun, was a technician named Little A, with whom I had become friends over the past two years. He asked for leave to take me to Taiyuan.

In 1992, a train ran daily from Zibo to Taiyuan. We would board at nine in the evening and arrive in Taiyuan at six the next morning. We asked someone to buy sleeper tickets five days in advance, but they could only get one. Therefore, we took turns sleeping.

The unit behind the new technology for oil cylinders is a subsidiary of the Shanxi Hydraulic Abrasion Research Institute. The courtyard is vast, but the office consists of only three rooms. The person in charge explained the new technology in detail. After rough machining on a lathe, the old oil cylinders are coated with wear-resistant and anti-corrosive coatings, extending their lifespan by two to three times compared to the old ones. The new technique had a promising outlook when the copper plating technique was gradually eliminated. After the introduction, we toured the processing workshop and saw the newly sprayed oil cylinders.

We took a van to an arsenal outside Taiyuan and entered a small workshop. The arsenal was not performing well, as it was processing articles for civil use and taking on private jobs. Research institutes provided technology and the arsenal of manufactured products. The processed oil cylinders, about a dozen of them, had shiny black interiors. Today was an off day, and the staff explained the spraying method and grinding process. The technical staff of the arsenal developed three specialized pieces of equipment: a spraying machine, a heating and holding furnace, and a grinding machine, along with three sets of specialized tools. In the workshop, little A and I carefully inspected the specialized equipment with the technical staff from the arsenal.

Upon returning to the Shanxi Hydraulic Abrasion Research Institute, the person in charge revealed the prices. A complete set of machinery cost us 50,000 yuan, and the technology transfer fee was an additional 50,000 yuan, totaling 100,000 yuan. Suppose we sign the agreement and pay a deposit of 20,000 yuan. In that case, the equipment will be delivered within two months, with no room for negotiation.

As we left the office and strolled around the courtyard, we calculated the value of their equipment. The spraying machine, tooling, and heating furnace were worth over 10,000 yuan. The specialized equipment could not be used for other processes. If it failed, it could result in a loss of 2,000 to 3,000 yuan, with a risk of 90,000 yuan. When we came, no agreement had been signed anywhere throughout the country. Whether coal mines would accept it was still uncertain. The agreement could not be signed, and we headed for home.

It was my first time in Taiyuan. The Yingze Avenue in front of the train station was wider than Beijing's Chang'an Avenue. It was grand indeed. The Wuyi Square was even livelier, packed with people. We had some time to explore before our return to Zibo at 7 a.m. the next day.

As we walked and observed, a middle-aged man with a green backpack standing near the green belt in the middle of the square waved to us. We ignored the stranger and quickened our pace.

But he walked faster, blocking our path, saying, "Gentlemen, let me practice physiognomy for you."

Interrupting halfway on the road for physiognomy? Darned. I waved him off, saying we were not interested, and moved on. He insisted, saying he would charge us if the reading was good and would not if it was not. Ignoring his words, we walked away. He continued to follow.

"Of course, you will read well. You can't earn money if you don't say something good."

I pushed the middle-aged man away and walked forward.

He continued to follow, saying, "I say good things if it is truly good, and I say bad things if it is truly bad. You can believe me if I say accurately. In reverse, I will not take a cent. I'll be honest."

My friend, Little A, suggested we listen to him out of boredom, saying it was only 30 yuan each, so we had nothing to lose. All right, the three of us stood under the shade of a tree, ready to hear either fairy tales or ghost stories from Pu Songling's Strange Stories from a Chinese Studio.

The middle-aged man stared at me intently for over two minutes before speaking.

"Your ancestors were well-off, from a scholarly family with some reputation in the village. Your family is harmonious, and you have been successful. Your father has one brother, and you have three brothers. Am I right?"

I replied, "You guessed correctly."

He said, "You're not here just to wander around; you're here to connect with a product that can be profitable."

I interjected, "I've decided not to pursue it."

He said, "Whether you pursue it or not, it is destined. By May or June next year, it will come to fruition. If it does, you will earn a significant amount, believe it or not. And when you do, remember to thank me. Your physiognomy looks quite good; give me an extra 10 yuan."

The man wanted 40 yuan in total, which I reluctantly handed over. Little A listened to the middle-aged man with fascination, wanting to read his face. But the man refused to read for little A, saying no matter how much he paid, he would not read his face. With that, he left. Little A felt disappointed and remained gloomy even after returning to the hotel.

After returning from Taiyuan, no one mentioned the new technology anymore, and it gradually fell into oblivion.

Six months later, director Sun called on a May afternoon to discuss the use of new technology. Taiyuan was on the line, and the equipment and technology fees had been reduced. He asked me to come to the Production Department immediately and discuss whether to proceed.

Riding my Jialing motorcycle, I arrived at the Production Department in half an hour. Director Sun detailed the situation in Taiyuan. After two phone calls, he urged the Mining Bureau to act quickly. The equipment fee remained 50,000 yuan, but the technology transfer fee was waived. They would help with installation, debugging, and training, ensuring the delivery of qualified products. There was no technology fee; they only charged 50,000 yuan for the equipment.

But there was one condition: we had to use their powder for spraying, which cost 50,000 yuan per ton.

Director Sun was a member of the product appraisal team and had a say in this matter. Whether or not to use the Mine Bureau rental station was his call. Whether or not to make the product available was also his call.

When I asked director Sun whether the rental station would install this product, he earnestly replied, "I will call you to come to my office. Do I need to spell it out for you? Seize the opportunity. Occupy the market first; if others join in a year later, you'll miss out on a good opportunity."

On the morning of June 2nd at 6 o'clock, I disembarked from the train at Taiyuan Railway Station. Personnel from the Shanxi Hydraulic Abrasion Research Institute were sent to meet me at the station and arrange accommodation at the hotel before heading to the institute. The terms discussed were generally the same as those said by director Sun. After signing the agreement, the mechanical equipment would be delivered in three months, with production scheduled to begin in September. I had inspected the equipment but had not visited the arsenal. We were the third unit to sign the agreement.

The installation in September and the three months of preparation were tight. Upon returning, I arranged the workshop: three lathe rooms, three oil cylinder spraying rooms, three sandblasting rooms, and three oil cylinder grinding rooms. About a month before signing the agreement, the south neighboring zinc plating factory moved to a new factory building east of the village. It left behind a dozen dilapidated factory buildings built around 1969, which could not be called factories; they were all shabby sheds. There were three good houses, which used to be the wheat-threshing floor warehouse of the production team. It was quite a coincidence. There would not have been this small dilapidated factory if they had not moved away before January. Finding a factory building soon proved difficult because we had already purchased the equipment. We demolished over 10 meters of the courtyard wall and merged it with my paint factory to create a large compound. It was a godsend. The original zinc plating factory was to my South, long from east to west and short from north to south. My paint factory was parallel to the east-west factory, and the two factories merged into one, the same length as the north and south ones, resulting in a square-shaped structure.

I found Secretary Zhao of the village party branch and asked to use their zinc plating factory.

Secretary Zhao said three words, "That is great." Within three days, we cleaned up the broken copper and iron in the factory and immediately organized the spraying workshop.

After setting up the workshop, we needed to add three lathes and one cylinder boring machine with a body length of 2.5 meters, produced by the Taiyuan Machine Tool Factory, for 60,000 yuan each, which we could not afford. The old lathes were completely usable, but the cylinder boring needed rough machining with a large tolerance. In 1992, there was no second-hand equipment market and no second-hand equipment dealers; you could not buy what you wanted to buy or sell what you wanted to sell — two small lathes. We did not need to buy new ones. One could only turn the end of the cylinder, and the other was modified to grind the cylinder. Small lathes were easy to find; we purchased one for 500 yuan from an abandoned zinc plating factory and another for 2,000 yuan from a nearby village. It was hard to find a large lathe. I went to Jinan once and twice to Weifang. One lathe was not long enough, and the other was too large. I discussed lathes with friends and acquaintances when we first met. Fortune favors the prepared mind. A friend I had just met introduced me to the machine factory of the Xinwen Mining Bureau. I went there to have a look. There was an old lathe that was perfect for our needs. It was an East German import, priced at 3,000 yuan and of scrap metal. Within a month, I had bought these three lathes.

To spray the cylinders, we needed a heating furnace. After the cylinders were bored, they needed to be heated to 180°C before being powder-coated. The one offered by the Taiyuan Hydraulic Abrasion Research Institute cost 5,000 yuan each. My technician carefully observed and measured the heating furnace in Taiyuan and was confident in replicating it. He suggested we make it ourselves, which would cost only 2,000 yuan. The technician explained that we could build one using refractory bricks, install a steel frame inside, and add heating rods, just like the one in Taiyuan. I agreed, and the technician and two workers spent two days building one. The exterior was brick, and the internal structure was modeled after the one in Taiyuan. After it was made, the technician tested it twice. It turned out that the heating temperature was too slow, and the insulation time did not meet the requirements. We added two more electric heating rods and restructured it twice, but the effect was unsatisfactory. We had to wait for Taiyuan technicians to resolve the issue.

The equipment ordered in Taiyuan was supposed to be delivered on the 20th. On the day of signing the agreement, the head of the institute assured us that it could be delivered half a month early, leaving time for installation. With several calls urging, it was still delayed until the 30th, when the last piece of equipment was completed.

The Taishan light truck, a special vehicle we had bought for delivering paint, made its first long-distance trip to Taiyuan to pick up the equipment. On September 3rd, we returned the equipment and half a ton of coating powder.

On the 4th, two technicians arrived: one from the arsenal, Master Hou, and another from the Shanxi Hydraulic Abrasion Research Institute, Master Mo. Master Hou taught the technique for boring the cylinders, while Master Mo taught the spray coating technique. The plan was to produce qualified products within a week and teach all the processes for this product. Both technicians were very down-to-earth. When offered the option to stay in a hotel, they refused, considering it a waste, and insisted on staying in the southern wing of my house. So I cleaned it thoroughly. It was neither too cold nor too hot in September. The distance from my house to the factory was only a five-minute walk, which pleased the technicians.

On the second day of work, Master Hou went to the lathe workshop. The house was old, but it was cleaned thoroughly. The lathes, switches, and ventilation equipment were arranged as required by Taiyuan. The floor screws for the lathes had been fixed for a month, waiting for Master Hou's guidance on installation. He was the old worker from the arsenal, who had been in the business for over thirty years and was very skilled in mechanical processing. While installing the lathes, Master Hou personally supervised the process. He operated them according to the requirements for processing shell casings. I observed twice. Master Hou squatted down, looking left and right, adjusting the specialized toolings. It took him a whole morning to install the lathes and tools, which were completed by 4 p.m.

After fixing the toolings on the lathes, they needed to be processed again because the sizes of the lathes from different manufacturers varied. The tooling from the arsenal had a uniform size. Reprocessing did not require much work, but it was a challenging task. We contacted several small, local, district-owned factories in Kunlun Town, but none had the necessary machining capabilities. A friend recommended the Boshan Motor Factory, a large state-owned enterprise whose machining capabilities were no less impressive than those of the arsenal. With our friend's guidance, we visited their machining workshop and met the director. The director agreed. After some consideration, he stated that, according to the factory's regulations, they needed to issue a work order from the dispatch room before undertaking outsourced work. After processing, we had to visit the finance department to obtain payment and an exit permit. I replied that they had calculated the hours for such a small job and charged between 700 and 800 yuan.

"If we bypass the dispatch room and don't ask for an invoice, could it be done?"

The director said, "Pay the workers an overtime fee of 300 yuan. Deliver the tooling the next day, and the day after the next day, you could pick it up in the afternoon."

When delivering goods inside the factory, the gatekeeper paid little attention to them. Still, when they left the factory gate, they were very strict. They carefully checked the cargo compartment and cab.

When I went to pick up the tooling, the director's arrangements were seamless. I parked the truck at the corner north of the factory gate, out of the gatekeeper's sight. I left the workshop ahead of time, and later, the workshop foreman used a small cart to transport the tooling to the gate and handed over the internal work order to the gatekeeper, who nodded and allowed the arsenal's tooling to pass after verifying the work order.

The machining workshop was ready, and the cylinders processed met the standards, completing the first step.

Master Mo taught spray coating. As soon as he entered the workshop, he saw the heating furnace. The technician immediately reported that the heating was too slow, taking three hours to reach 180°C. Master Mo promptly explained that we could not use bricks because refractory bricks absorbed and dissipated heat, causing temperature fluctuations. The insulation furnace provided by the Research Institute had two layers of iron plates with insulation cotton in between, heating up quickly and maintaining temperature for a long time. We immediately made the necessary changes.

We purchased iron plates, dismantled the refractory bricks, removed the steel frame and heating rods from the furnace, and rebuilt it according to the standards of the Taiyuan Hydraulic Research Institute. With two layers of iron plates and cotton insulation in between, we worked overtime and completed it in two days. The effect met the requirements, heating up to 180°C in one and a half hours. Twenty-five years later, I realized the usefulness of this method even more. We built two workshops with a steel frame structure. We used seven-centimeter insulation cotton between the iron plates for the walls. One day in July, the temperature was 37°C. I visited the brick-wall workshop and found it very stuffy. When I visited the newly built workshop, I expected it to be hotter, but it turned out to be pleasantly cool. In winter, when it was minus 10°C, I went to experience it again. The tin workshop was warmer than the brick-wall workshop.

After the furnace was modified, Master Mo proceeded to teach the spray coating technique. The first step was sandblasting the cylinders after removing oil stains from the bored inner surface. Young people were reluctant to take on this job because it was considered dirty and tiring. We found three middle-aged farmers in their fifties who had been farming for decades and were skilled with hoes and shovels. But they handled the spray guns clumsily. Master Mo demonstrated twice and taught them hand in hand. Despite the seemingly simple operation, it took a whole morning to teach one of them, an agile veteran farmer.

After sandblasting, the cylinders were weighed, and the weight was noted on each cylinder with chalk. Then, they were placed in the insulation furnace to heat up. Each steel pipe in the cylinder varied in weight, being either slightly heavier or lighter by a couple of liang (one liang equals 50 grams). After powder coating, they needed to be weighed again. The requirement was that the same amount of powder be sprayed on each cylinder to ensure uniform adhesion to the inner wall of the cylinder. For example, if cylinder A weighed 16.3 kilograms and cylinder B weighed 16.5 kilograms, each cylinder would be sprayed with an additional three liang. After spraying, if A weighed 16.6 and B weighed 16.8, the spray gun would be used repeatedly. If it still did not reach the desired weight, three Liang and another round of spraying were needed to ensure the thickness of the powder coating. If the coating were too thin, there would be spots missing when ground, and if it were too thick, the cost would be higher, at five yuan per Liang of powder. The spray coating process was straightforward, and the operation was relatively simple. Quality can be guaranteed if it is done carefully, resulting in qualified products. Master Mo taught for two days, and the three workers finally learned how to spray and coat the cylinders.

The last step was grinding the inner surface. A properly ground cylinder would be smooth and have the same size as a copper-plated cylinder. Our technician made the grinder based on the drawings provided by the Taiyuan Hydraulic Research Institute. We bought a belt lathe produced a century ago for 500 yuan and only used its transmission function. We clamped the cylinders at both ends, made our grinding heads, inserted the grinding bars, and ground each cylinder back and forth seven or eight times. Master Mo personally demonstrated, and a young man with a background in carpentry worked meticulously, ensuring accuracy to the last millimeter. He learned it in two days, and it would take more than 10 days to become proficient. Master Mo was very satisfied.

After producing qualified spray-coated cylinders, we reported to director Sun. He, along with the leasing station master, the factory director, and technicians, came to the site for observation. They stayed in the spray workshop for half an hour and stood by the grinding machine for over 10 minutes. The conclusion was that the local factory had produced high-quality products. The station master and factory director were instructed to install and put them into the coal mines as soon as possible.

At the leasing station of the Zibo Mining Bureau, after several months of trial installations, the effect was very good. Still, the quantity was limited to just over 1,000 per month. This set of equipment can process up to 2,000 cylinders. To expand our business, we targeted coal mines across the province. Deputy Station Master Liu had retired; he was in good health and had extensive experience in the business. He agreed to help me with the business of coal mines across the province. The two of us first visited Longkou Mine, then Shanjialin Mine, increasing the monthly output by 500 each time. Pingdingshan Mining Bureau was large. We went there once and brought back 400 cylinders. Gradually, the business volume increased to over 2,000 cylinders per month.

6.3 Three Gorges Tour

I received a notice from the Taiyuan Hydraulic Research Institute to attend a business negotiation conference in the Three Gorges. I also received a letter from a technician, Old A, briefly stating that I must come to the Three Gorges for business and to discuss personal matters. He reminded me that this letter need not be disclosed to others, and we would discuss matters further in person. The meeting venue is set at the Hongxing Hotel in the Gezhou Dam.

I took a train to Wuhan and a long-distance bus to the Gezhouba Dam. In 1996, it took 38 hours to travel from Zibo to Wuhan, and an additional six hours to travel from Wuhan to the Gezhouba Dam. Finally, I arrived at the Hongxing Hotel on the third day.

The conference attendees came from all over the country, including the Shulan Mining Bureau, Chifeng Mine, Wuhai Mine, Pingdingshan Mine, the Huaibei Mining Bureau, and the Jinxing Hydraulic Prop Maintenance Factory. The conference lasted half a day, summarizing the nationwide development of this new technology over the past two years and discussing its bright prospects for the future. In the afternoon, we boarded a ship to tour the Three Gorges, with the Research Institute covering the expenses.

Boarded a luxurious cruise ship at Gezhou Dam, with two floors and four people per room. It was my first time on such a cruise. After sailing for about 10 minutes, the ship stopped to enter the ship lock chamber. I waited an hour as the ship lock opened, and more than 20 large ships emerged from the lock chamber. I boarded the cruise ship into the lock chamber, watched the lock gate close, and looked up at the sky. The lock towered over us like a chimney, standing more than 90 meters high, with more than 20 large ships neatly lined up, creating a magnificent sight. The two lock gates in front began to move, leaving a large gap. The water level started to rise, lifting us slowly. After about 20 minutes, the lock gates fully opened, and the water inside the lock rose to the level of the river. The ships inside the lock sailed into the Yangtze River.

Unconsciously, the cruise ship arrived at the location of the Three Gorges Dam. Suddenly, the river widened significantly, and as we turned a big bend, a small island appeared in the middle. Excavators and cars were busy working on the island. The guide explained that the Three Gorges Dam had just begun construction, with the barrier built beneath the small island, which would be completely cleared. This stretch of the river was the widest part between the Three Gorges, making it the ideal location for the dam. Sun Yat-sen had dreamed of building the dam, and Mao Zedong had planned it. Still, due to various historical events, the Great Leap Forward, the Three Difficult Years (1959-1961), and the Great Cultural Revolution (1966-1976), it never materialized until Deng Xiaoping's era, when he proposed reform and opening up, and China's power increased significantly. The dam was finally built on the mighty Yangtze River. The guide spoke eloquently, with everyone staring at the river, listening intently.

Ten years later, the dam was completed, raising the water level by over 180 meters, creating a vast lake that stretched for hundreds of kilometers amid the mountains of the Three Gorges. "Close your eyes and imagine the completed dam. Come here when the dam is built. Remember the present scenes and then write about them in 20 years, " I thought, "Twenty-fiveyears later, when I finally want to write about it, I still have not revisited the grandeur of the Three Gorges."

From the small island, we turned a bend, and the river straightened.

The guide called out, "Everyone, look ahead. What special features or scenes do you see on the left?"

We stood on the deck and followed the directions pointed out by the guide. Still, all we saw was a flat mountain with no peaks, nothing particularly remarkable. After a few minutes, the guide pointed at the same mountain, urging us to pay attention.

Suddenly, someone exclaimed, "Chairman Mao, Chairman Mao!" pointing at the mountain.

Everyone saw it clearly – the mountain in front, with its flat top, resembled the late Chairman Mao in the Great Hall of the People. Especially the shape of the head, facing upwards, and the belly protruding, resembles a flag draped over Mao's body. The boat slowed down, and the more we looked, the more it resembled him. The guide continued to explain that no one had seen this resemblance when Mao Zedong was alive. Since his passing, the mountain seemed to have transformed, becoming more lifelike in recent years. During the era of Mao Zedong, nobody dared associate such a thing with him, let alone discuss it, as it was punishable by death. The guide continued, stating that when the decision to build the Three Gorges Dam was announced,

Chairman Mao, as if he had known, had been pleased and manifested himself on this mountain, lying by the riverside, watching the dam's construction.

The boat arrived at Baidi, an ancient city that had been submerged underwater after the dam was completed. It was a must-see attraction. Baidi was a small island with a branch of the Yangtze River running into it, resembling a small lake with the city in its center.

Back then, Liu Bei, in his quest to avenge his second younger brother against the Kingdom of Wu, retreated to Baidi after his failure. The story had been passed down for 2,000 years, deeply ingrained in the hearts of people. Those who were unaware of Baidi in China were few.

Disembarking, we found that the island was not large, with no castle or city walls, only a large temple dedicated to Emperor Liu, where he had entrusted his son to Zhuge Liang. When Liu Bei became the emperor, there were no fewer than thousands of troops and horses and dozens of civil and military officials. This island was not a military, office, or administrative place, but a small desert island. Luo Guanzhong's interpretation is wonderful. Liu Bei retreated to Baidi. Kong Ming (also known as Zhuge Liang) and a group of people went to greet him. It is not true. Interpretation is a drama that cannot be believed as a historical fact.

In the temple, opposite a large hall, Liu Bei is lying on the bed, Liu Chan is kneeling in front of the bed, and Kong Ming is sitting on a chair, listening to Imperial Uncle Liu's account of future affairs. The waxwork is very realistic; in the past, Liu Bei was like this when entrusting his son to Zhuge Liang, also known as Kong Ming. Liu Bei was one of the three Peach Garden sworn brothers, running from place to place, taking refuge with Cao Cao, and defrauding Jingzhou. He allied with the Kingdom of Wu to fight in the Battle of the Red Cliff and finally fled to Bashu (two ancient cities in Sichuan), where he had a firm foothold. But Liu Bei had only been emperor for three years. He passed away when the great cause did not succeed.

"Brother Kong Ming, I entrust my son to you; it's up to you to help him," he might have said.

Exiting the temple, we had free time for exploration. It was the only attraction, with nothing else to see. Standing under a large tree, looking out over the Yangtze River, I reflected. In a few years, the water level on this island was expected to rise by 80 meters, and its surface area was projected to increase by a factor of three. Baidi would remain underwater for thousands of years.

Lost in thought, I realized Old A from the Taiyuan Hydraulic Research Institute was beside me. We had known each other for years, having met three times in Taiyuan to see machines and discuss powder spraying technology. I greeted him when we met in Taiyuan to conduct business.

"Director Yu, you've been doing well these past few years, using seven to eight tons of powder annually. You are a big client." Old A greeted me first.

"Not bad; four to five coal mines use oil cylinders that I repair," I replied, sticking to our professional topics.

I briefed him on the business conditions of several coal mines and our factory's production situation. Old A mentioned that their company produced 100 tons of powder last year, with over 20 factories nationwide using their product, indicating excellent prospects. The profit margin for powder was unimaginable, reaching a ratio of 1:4, with a cost of 1,000 yuan, yielding a profit of 4,000 yuan. They built a six-story building in the development zone using the money earned the previous year.

Although Old A spoke enthusiastically, I was not fully engaged. I was here to enjoy myself, to set work aside for a while. One cannot be consumed by work all the time.

The topic shifted to Old A's family. His parents were alive; his father received a pension, and his mother was a homemaker. His child was in school, typical of an ordinary urban working-class family, living paycheck to paycheck. They have no other income than their salaries.

He asked: "Could we collaborate on something?"

At this point, my heart skipped a beat.

"Collaborate on producing powder for spray painting oil cylinders?" I interrupted Old A. I posed several questions: "How many factories nationwide produce this powder? Was there a patent? If this matter were discovered, how would it affect you? Would you lose your job?"

Old A replied, "There were only two powder production factories nationwide, with one in Tianjin. I was not sure if the Research Institute had a patent for the powder. Still, if we collaborated, I could adjust the formula without compromising quality, and it would not infringe on the institute's patent. The formula used by the factory in Tianjin was similar to the Research Institute, with no conflict. I had a good relationship with my manager; seven or eight people in my unit were familiar with the formula, even if suspicions arose. If asked, we could claim to have obtained it from Tianjin."

It was quite tempting, not for external sale but for personal use, saving hundreds of thousands of yuan annually. Old A's demands were not high, just a small share to support his family.

It was a significant matter that required careful consideration before making a decision.

The cruise ship reached the mouth of the Lesser Three Gorges. We disembarked from the cruise ship and boarded a smaller boat, with about a dozen people per boat, to explore the Lesser Three Gorges. The contrast between the water of the Lesser Three Gorges and the main Three Gorges was striking. The water of the Yangtze River in the main Three Gorges was turbid and slightly yellowish. It was only a little clearer than the Yellow River. But the water of the Lesser Three Gorges was clear and transparent. You could see the riverbed at a glance, with the mountains appearing greener and more beautiful on both sides, like a hidden paradise. As we ventured further in, the air became crisp and cool.

The most famous attraction in the Lesser Three Gorges was the Hanging Coffins. Upon reaching the area of the Hanging Coffins, we disembarked and gathered on a flat area by the riverbank, where we could see several dark spots on the upper half of the mountainside.

There were two high-powered telescopes for tourists to view the Hanging Coffins, with a queue formed, allowing each person one minute to observe. Upon closer inspection, one could see a small cave on the mountain containing a coffin and nothing else, while another was empty. The Hanging Coffins have been featured in numerous books, articles, and television programs. Yet, many mysteries about them remain unsolved to this day.

Over 2,000 years ago, the indigenous people of this area, for reasons unknown, carved caves into the mountain and placed coffins inside. The caves were situated in the most treacherous part of the river valley, on the highest mountain, and in the upper half, with one side of the mountain resembling a knife-edge. The caves were positioned where the water flowed swiftly. The era in which these people lived is believed to be during the pre-urban, pre-agricultural period, commonly referred to as the primitive tribal period. Still, how they managed to place coffins up there remains a mystery.

The caves where the Hanging Coffins were placed were estimated to be over 300 meters above the ground, on the upper half of the mountain, embedded in the cross-section of the mountain, which protruded inward. It is speculated that they drilled caves from the top of the mountain and lowered the coffins down using ropes, but the ropes would not have reached the cross-section of the mountain. Reaching the cross-section without scaffolding would have been impossible; nowadays, helicopters and cranes are needed. Scientists have analyzed and speculated about how the caves were created and how the coffins were placed inside, but the mystery remains unsolved.

The flat ground for viewing the Hanging Coffins was quite large, allowing free movement. After spending time on the boat, constantly looking around, I felt tired and took a half-hour break. After a few steps, Old A approached me, and we started chatting.

"How about what I mentioned yesterday? If you are not interested, I will find another unit. I came to you first because I have had the opportunity to get to know and trust you. If we decide to work together, we can find an excuse to visit Taiyuan and observe the production process. It's quite simple."

Old A seemed anxious, using this trip to the Three Gorges as an opportunity to find a potential partner for collaboration.

"Alright, let's give it a try," I said, not having thought about it for a day, not in a hurry to decide.

Old A was eager to finalize the deal. If I agreed, I would visit the Taiyuan Hydraulic Research Institute to gather more information. If I could benefit from the association with a state-owned unit, I might as well consider it.

6.4 Encountering a Hijack en Route

In 1992, the Weifang-Yantai Highway, a two-lane road, was smooth and gleaming and considered the finest provincial road. Long-distance buses averaged a speed of thirty kilometers per hour. Salesperson Little Zhao and I arrived in Longkou at around six in the evening. After completing the accommodation arrangements, it was nearly seven, too late for dinner. Thus, we proceeded directly to the residence of Chief Wang, the mine manager at Beizao in Longkou.

At the hotel entrance, we found three-wheeled taxis available for hire. Together with Little Zhao, we loaded the specialty products from Zibo intended for Chief Wang onto the luxurious three-wheeler. It was around seven-thirty when we finally arrived at Chief Wang's residence, delivering the gifts with plans to discuss business at the mine the following day. The journey to the mine dormitory area was approximately seven or eight kilometers, which we estimated would take just over 10 minutes to complete. However, shortly after departing from the station, heavy snow fell unexpectedly. As the snowfall intensified, our three-wheeler came to a halt. Despite the driver's attempts to restart the vehicle by kicking and shaking it, it remained immobile. Just as frustration began to set in, a cyclist collided with our stalled vehicle, prompting an outburst from the driver.

"You're blind!" The driver roared.

Sensing the urgency of the situation, we could not stand by.

Stepping out into the snow, we joined forces to push the three-wheeler. However, the luxurious vehicle refused to budge even after considerable effort and pushing for over 10 meters. Walking in the snow, we dejectedly trudged back to the hotel.

Both restaurants were closed there, though the reason remained unknown. In the Jiaodong area, restaurants seemed to shut their doors early in the evening. With our stomachs still empty, we headed to the convenience store. We purchased a bottle of spiced fish, a can of luncheon meat, and a bottle of Longkou Daqu, a Chinese baijiu produced in Longkou, cobbling together a makeshift meal for the night. We decided to brainstorm a better plan for the next morning, after eating a full stomach.

The following morning, we had to rely on the three-wheeler again. Due to the snowy road conditions, we set off half an hour early, ensuring we arrived at the dormitory area ahead of schedule. Navigating through several buildings and units, we managed to locate Chief Wang's residence before seven o'clock. Arriving before he left was essential; it meant the possibility of catching him before he rose for the day. Conversely, arriving late would likely result in missing him entirely. "Bang, bang, bang," we knocked on the door.

From within, a voice queried, "Who's there?"

"A friend of director Zhang from Zibo Mining Bureau," I responded.

The door cracked open, revealing a middle-aged woman who gestured that we could not enter. Without hesitation, I handed over the gifts.

"These are from director Zhang," I explained.

With that, the door was slammed shut, and Chief Wang remained elusive, failing to make an appearance.

At seven-thirty, we entered Chief Wang's office and introduced ourselves, saying, "I'm a friend of director Zhang."

Handing over director Zhang's letter, Chief Wang gestured for us to take a seat. After reading the letter, he casually picked up the phone on his desk, murmured a few words I could not catch, and then settled into his chair behind his two-meter-long desk to review some documents.

After sitting in Chief Wang's office for over 10 minutes, a young man, approximately 1.8 meters tall with a broad face, entered the room and approached Chief Wang's desk.

"Little Geng, this gentleman is from the Zibo Mining Bureau, introduced by my old classmate, director Zhang. He is here to repair the props for us. Please take good care of him and discuss the specifics in the workshop," Chief Wang explained.

Little Geng repeatedly nodded in acknowledgment. "Of course, of course, follow me to the workshop," he said, gesturing for us to accompany him.

On the way to the workshop, we introduced ourselves to each other. Little Geng revealed that he was the head of the support workshop. Wanting to establish a connection, I crafted a narrative on the spot. I mentioned that a few days prior, Chief Wang had visited the Zibo Mining Bureau, where his old classmate director Zhang had invited me to join them. During the dinner, director Zhang highlighted my expertise in hydraulic prop repair, prompting Chief Wang to suggest that I visit his mine. I took the opportunity to inquire if they had any hydraulic prop parts needing repair. It was a subtle way of showcasing my skills while fostering camaraderie.

Repairing hydraulic props was considered the least significant external business of the mine. For the head of the workshop to personally come to the office to receive clients indicated an exceptional level of rapport. Director Geng was determined not to overlook any details. He planned to start by repairing the oil cylinder, followed by the handle during the next visit, and then move on to the base. Given the numerous parts requiring repair, we understood the importance of a systematic approach, tackling each issue one step at a time.

I repaired two batches of oil cylinders to a satisfactory quality. Director Geng asked me to return the handgrips and repair them next time.

That day, I came to Longkou Beizao Mine to deliver the oil cylinder smoothly. I arrived at the support workshop at 3 p.m., unloaded the good oil cylinder, and transported the old handgrips. The previous time, director Geng had agreed to give me half of it, enough for me to pull a cart. Four hundred handgrips weighed two tons. Director Geng took special care because repairing the handgrips of hydraulic props was a simple process with high profits. After loading the truck, I invited director Geng to dinner, but he declined, citing other commitments.

The next day, after breakfast, we leisurely headed back. This trip went smoothly, 300 kilometers in 10 hours. We could return to the factory early. This time, repairing the handgrips, the next trip would be to repair the base, entering into a virtuous business cycle. Three big pieces of hydraulic prop, all done. With just passing Changle's jewelry market, a police car caught up from behind.

"Speed up, there's a police car chasing us!"

"We haven't violated any traffic rules, and all our documents are in order; what's there to be afraid of?" The driver made sense.

The police car started honking, getting closer and closer until it was alongside us. Someone in the police car stuck their hand out, shouting, "Pull over, pull over."

We pulled over to the side of the road, and two people got out of the police car.

"This is from Zibo, right?" They said, standing by the car. "You're transporting scrap metal, and waste metal cannot be transported. Don't you know? We have seen this truck several times in the last few days. How many times is this?"

I hurriedly explained, "This is not scrap metal; these are handgrips from the hydraulic props at Longkou coal mine. We are from a repair plant. We fix them and then deliver them back."

I picked up one of the handgrips to show them. "We're from the enforcement team. Go back, go back."

"Go where?" I pretended not to understand.

"Back to the enforcement team in Changle."

"These handgrips are support parts from the Longkou coal mine.

How could they be scrapping metal? Take a closer look." My voice grew louder as I spoke.

The person trying to hijack the truck raised his voice even more: "I said it is scrap metal, so it is scrap metal. If you don't listen, you'll be fined and confiscated."

After a few minutes of deadlock, the hijacker finally relented, "If you do not cooperate, I will have someone unload the scrap metal, and you will have to pay unloading fees. Believe it or not!"

Being robbed in broad daylight, we would suffer a big loss if we continued to be stubborn. When a scholar encounters soldiers, logic is no longer a reliable guide.

The car stopped in a yard. I followed the hijacker into the office, where an official sat in the big chair opposite the table. I stood and listened to his reprimand. "We have clear regulations. Scrap steel cannot be exported from the country. Any external transport is confiscated."

"These are handgrips from hydraulic props, mechanical parts from the Beizao Mine of Longkou Mining Bureau, not scrap metal, not something from your county."

"No matter where it's from, as long as it passes through our county, it's confiscated."

"These are handgrips from hydraulic props, mechanical parts from the coal mine. They will be repaired and delivered back."

"Our staff has determined it's scrap metal, so it's scrap metal."

"Staff should speak with facts and reason, not just say whatever they want."

"You say it's not scrap metal; it's mechanical parts, so bring proof."

"Fine, I'll return to Longkou and return the proof the next day. That should be possible."

Writing proof was easy. Back in Longkou, when I found director Geng, I was truthful and did not falsify. It was fair and square business. Back at the mine office, I took only a few minutes to finish it.

The next afternoon, when I returned to Changle, the head of the enforcement team was not in the office. After three trips, the captain arrived almost at the end of the workday. I handed over the proof letter with confidence.

"Is this proof fake? There are plenty of places where you can stamp a seal privately."

The captain took the proof letter, glanced at it, and put it on the table.

"What are you talking about? Yesterday, you said to get proof. Today, you say it's fake." I retorted with some annoyance.

"I said whether it's fake or real is useless. We have a business contract; bring out the contract."

The captain stood up from his chair, more agitated, his voice louder, emitting a strong smell of alcohol. With the captain's alcohol not yet dissipated, if we continued, it would only get more tense and difficult to resolve the next day.

Back at the hotel, getting increasingly frustrated as I talked with the driver, I had to devise a solution. Unable to think of a good one, we still could not leave the next day. Feeling anxious, how could I forget Brother Zhong in Changle Machinery Factory? He was an old friend from the hydraulic prop branch factory who could offer us some helpful ideas.

When I arrived at Brother Zhong's home, he had just gotten off work. There was a tavern opposite his home, and we could sit down and talk slowly. Last year, we met at the Zibo Mine Rental Station. It had been almost a year. We were peers, so that words could go together. After a cup of baijiu, we talked about my problem. Yesterday, I met a road robber. I thought I was right, so I was not afraid. I forgot my Brother Zhong in a hurry, and I went to Longkou for nothing; Brother Zhong said frankly. Another two trips could not solve the problem; the truth now was finding a relationship to solve it. It did not matter how much money was spent. It could be simple or complex.

After three cups of baijiu, I calmed down.

Brother Zhong continued to talk, "I can find government officials. The deputy factory director's father-in-law is the director of the county People's Congress. The deputy factory director is my faithful pal, so a phone call can solve this. However, you are fined 500 yuan, and the captain said 2,000 yuan. Could you do him a big favor? A fine of 800 yuan is befitting. More punishment or less punishment, the captain has the final say. He has so much power. The following soldiers know the above leadership."

Brother Zhong had offered the first trick, and I would try it the next day. If it did not work, then I would use the second one.

With friends coming from afar, Brother Zhong was delighted. I was also caught up in the excitement. Our conversation flowed freely. We drank three, four, and five cups, and before we knew it, we were back at the hotel.

Before work, I stood across from the enforcement team captain's office, waiting for his arrival. When he opened the door and went in, I followed immediately. With no one else around, the timing was just right.

"Yesterday, I spoke loudly. Please forgive me; we do have a contract in place. I will go back and get it. It'll take another day."

As I spoke, I approached the captain, quickly slipping an envelope into his pocket.

"How can we do this?"

The captain was taken aback, and I stepped back to the door. "Wait, let's discuss how to handle this."

Exiting the office, I returned to the same spot; about half an hour later, a worker who had "high-jacked" us before came over to inform me that the captain wanted me to go to his office.

I followed the hijacker into the captain's office, where the captain spoke, "Comrade from Zibo, yesterday you got a proof letter from Longkou Mine. These are parts from the mine, not scrap metal. Pay 200 yuan for the enforcement fee, and no fine will be imposed. Be careful and bring your documents next time."

"Thank you, Captain." I nodded and left the office.

Outside, I muttered quietly, "Damn it, what racket."

At Beizao Mine, I received a portion of all three main components of the hydraulic props: oil cylinders, handgrips, and bases, which were delivered twice a month. Business went smoothly for over a year. Chief Wang was transferred to the Bureau of Mines, and the new mine manager reassigned the head of the support workshop. The new manager implemented cost-saving measures, handling small repair parts on-site instead of outsourcing them. The support workshop repaired handgrips and bases internally. The cylinder was repaired externally, and a new maintenance cylinder manufacturer came. I lost a major portion of the business. Sometimes, I would deliver goods and return with an empty car. It continued for half a year. I proposed discontinuing the business, and the new head agreed, settling the repair fees in two installments. And with that, I cleaned wrapped up my business with the Longkou Mining Bureau and Beizao Coal Mine.

6.5 Northeastern Journey

During the Three Gorges tour, I befriended Little Wu from the Shulan Bureau of Mines Machinery General Factory in Jilin. We spent five days together on the same boat, eating, living, and sightseeing. Little Wu loved making friends and singing, with a gentle temperament that matched mine well. We got along well. After spraying the oil cylinder, the powder was put into production, and we used it for some time. It proved to have reliable quality, and I planned to sell two to three tons per month. There was a spray coating oil cylinder process in the workshop where Little Wu worked, and he agreed to use my powder. The previous month, I sent two bags of samples to Little Wu for a trial run.

Little Wu is the chairman of the Mechanics Factory Support Maintenance Workshop Union. He called me the day before yesterday, saying that after several tests, the quality of the powder was fine. I decided to go there and finalize the business.

I took a train to Jilin City and then changed to a bus to the Shulan Mining Bureau. When I arrived in Shulan County, I got off and asked for the address of the Shulan Bureau of Mines.

The conductor smiled and said, "You should have asked earlier.

You missed the stop. Take the return bus and leave at Jishu Town in Shulan."

It turned out that the Mining Bureau named after Shulan was not in the county seat but in Jishu Town. So, I took the same bus back to Jishu.

Together with Little Wu, we visited the factory director, who happened to be his second-oldest brother. We casually communicated in the office. Before I came to the Mechanical Factory, Little Wu had already introduced my factory and our friendship in detail to his elder brother. The factory director agreed to use my powder, and the workshop would decide the price, settlement method, and specific business arrangements, with the factory department only responsible for settling accounts and making payments.

I met with each workshop leader in the workshop office: Director Zhou, deputy director Liu, and Secretary Zhang. Four cadres attended a workshop: two directors, a party branch secretary, and a union chairman. Director Zhou and Little Wu took me on a tour of the workshop. Over 20 mechanical devices were inside, such as punches, latches, and presses. The workshop, where hydraulic props were repaired, including struts and beams for support work, was designated as the support workshop, or Workshop Three, in sequence. The oil cylinder spraying area was at the western end of the workshop. The business just started this year. A metal plate was added halfway to block the dust. The spraying equipment was purchased from the Taiyuan Hydraulic Research Institute and was identical to mine. Director Zhou pointed to a dozen oil cylinders on the ground.

He said, "These oil cylinders were sprayed with your powder, and the quality is very good."

"Is there no oil cylinder repair today?" I casually asked, noticing that there were no workers near the spraying equipment.

Director Zhou replied, "The coal mine has partially stopped production. The coal cannot be sold, so we work two days and rest one."

In the workshop, which was 40 to 50 meters long, over 20 workers were coming in and out; it felt desolate.

At noon, we were treated to a meal at a designated restaurant on the main street outside the factory gate. In state-owned enterprises, the level of hospitality was clear-cut. Leaders from the factory accompanied guests at the Mining Bureau Guesthouse, middle-level staff from various departments, and workshops were arranged at designated restaurants.

The restaurant was situated in a small, two-story building. It did not look fancy from the outside. Still, the rooms upstairs were spacious, with large dining tables that could accommodate over 10 people, equipped with karaoke sound systems, bathrooms, and mahjong tables. There were six of us: me, the sales representative, Little Zhao, and four workshop cadres. The room was too big and empty.

When we entered, a waiter asked, "Director Zhou, are all the guests here?"

"Everyone's here," he replied. "Okay."

Director Zhou arranged for the guests and hosts to take their seats. With six people, there were twelve chairs, two per person, but I doubted it. Just as I was about to sit down, six waitresses came in. There were no formalities or courtesies as they took their seats among us.

I was surprised, but director Zhou explained, "It is a custom in the northeast. Each guest has an accompanying partner. Elder Brother Yu, you're an honored guest, so the waitress will take good care of you and ensure you have a good time."

"Ah, that's how it is. It was my first time experiencing this when six hostesses served six guests."

We were served various northeastern delicacies, including blood sausage stewed with sauerkraut and chicken stewed with mushrooms.

Director Zhou gave a toast, "For Elder Brother Yu, who is visiting the northeast for the first time, our business has started smoothly. We are good friends and brothers. Following the northeastern custom, let's drink three cups, as the three sworn brothers in the Three Kingdoms. Cheers!"

For every guest, there was a wine pot and two small cups. The six waitresses, serving as drinking partners, poured and persuaded us to drink, urging us to eat more dishes. Each time a guest drank a cup, the waitress drank one. After three cups, the deputy director and the secretary were each persuaded to drink three more cups, poured into small glasses holding half a liang, about 25 grams, of baijiu. Not drinking was not an option. Refusing would be impolite to our friends and the business we just sealed. Sitting next to director Zhou and me, the drinking waitress accompanied us, pouring a cup for each sip without hesitation. However, the two waitresses sitting next to Little Wu and Secretary Zhang could not hold their liquor and had to excuse themselves to the restroom to vomit. The first phase of drinking progressed smoothly.

I returned to the toast, thanking director Zhou, director Liu, secretary Zhang, and Little Wu for their warm hospitality. It was my first time in the northeast, where I encountered good brothers, good friends, a smooth arrival, smooth business, and satisfying drinks. I took advantage of such a good wine to offer my thanks, and we shared three cups for everyone. Cheers! Director Zhou did not hesitate and finished three cups promptly. Director Liu wobbled but managed to finish three cups, and Secretary Zhang and Little Wu followed suit. As it reached a climax, we persuaded each other to drink, freely moving around, standing up, moving to the front of someone, and clinking glasses; it was an affectionate atmosphere, and we could not refuse the drink, could not refuse getting drunk. The waitress accompanying me had a strong alcohol tolerance, did not hesitate with each cup, freely toasted, doubled toasts with me, and doubled toasts with Little Zhao. The waitress accompanying director Zhou made a toast to me. The third waitress, who was left, did not get to toast with me and rushed to the bathroom, making loud noises of vomiting.

Little Wu brought the banquet to life with his enthusiastic "Little Poplar Tree" performance. The seats were empty, with some guests holding hands and others leaning in close to one another. One guest refused to drink, while another insisted that he drink. The atmosphere became lively and chaotic as people grabbed the microphone and snatched glasses. It was hard to tell how much time had passed.

My legs felt like jelly, but I knew I could not afford to get drunk or make a fool of myself. Little Zhao helped me back to the guesthouse, and I slept until light.

The next day at noon, director Zhou came to the guesthouse, chatting casually. I was scheduled to go to Jilin in the afternoon and catch the night train to Shenyang. A farewell banquet was arranged for lunch following yesterday's reception. I repeatedly emphasized to director Zhou that the noon banquet should be kept simple, with no formalities, no need for accompanying drinking partners, and that we should speak our minds freely. Director Zhou and I discussed the lunch arrangements, and Little Wu arrived again. We reviewed the business details once more: half a ton of powder per month, receiving the goods, and paying for the former batch. Director Zhou understood the friendship between Little Wu and me, especially since Wu's second elder brother was the factory director. As long as it was for spraying oil cylinders, they would not use powder from other suppliers. "Don't let the water from our well flow to others' fields," as the saying goes.

The farewell lunch was simplified at a small restaurant serving local specialties and northeastern traditional Shaojiu, a special liquor. After three cups, there was no more persuasion or clinking of cups. We chatted leisurely while slowly sipping the liquor. Director Zhou introduced the Mechanical Factory as a county-level unit, directly under the Bureau of Mines, specializing in the production of mining cars, coal conveyors, wind drills, and other mining equipment. They did not produce anything other than mining-related products without considering the problem of selling. With over 600 employees, the factory had an output value exceeding 50 million yuan. Still, it lost over five million yuan last year. The workers had not been paid for three months. Within 100 kilometers, there were no other factories, only coal mines. Workers who wanted to change jobs had nowhere to go, so they had to stay and endure the situation. Many young people had gone to find work inside Shanhaiguan Pass.

Northeasterners were hospitable and loved alcohol. Therefore, the sparing of food and drinking expenses by state-owned factories was not regarded as waste. The factory regulations stipulated that the four cadres in each workshop could sign to entertain guests for meals. The factory had seven workshops and eight departments, including the factory department. There were over 60 people who could sign up to entertain guests. Four designated restaurants were all run by individuals with connections, such as the nephew of the deputy bureau chief or the factory director's brother-in-law, which formed solid relationships. After signing, the bill would be settled at the factory department. There were rules for settling accounts: payment within a month meant the price would not change; payment after two months would incur a 20 percent increase; and after three months, a 30 percent increase would be added. If payment were made after a year, the banquet cost would double. The factory leaders were generous in entertaining guests, accompanying them at lunch and dinner, and even staying to accompany guests the next day. Northeastern hospitality was overwhelming. I have visited state-owned factories in Shandong, where I was only allowed to visit once. In factories to the south of the Yangtze River, unless it were a special business, they would not entertain at all. After completing the business, all the individuals went their separate ways.

Despite the lavish banquets, I could not stay another day. There were matters to attend to in my factory. I headed to Jilin at noon and caught the night train to Shenyang that evening.

The business with the Shulan Mining Bureau Machinery General Factory had begun in 1996. In the first year, everything went smoothly, with half a ton per month and timely payment. But in the second year, the quantity decreased. When Little Zhao arrived, he discovered that they had not used powder from other suppliers. The number of props repaired had decreased as the coal output dropped, and they could no longer afford to pay for the goods as usual. This time, Little Zhao stayed for six days and only managed to bring back 20,000 yuan, leaving a debt of 130,000 yuan. We could not continue to increase the debt and needed to find a way to collect the payment.

6.6 Visit to the Tiefa Mining Bureau

During the journey to Tiefa, I had the opportunity to enjoy a skit performance that rivaled those of renowned comedian Zhao Benshan. Later, on a long-distance bus from Cicun Village to Jinan, I observed that there were ample vacant seats. Interestingly, each row of two seats had only one passenger seat. Five young men boarded the bus through Puji, distributing themselves among the front, middle, and rear sections. One of them, who appeared to be in his early twenties and dressed as a laborer, took the seat next to me, carrying a student bag.

The bus swayed as it moved slowly, and I dozed off in my seat. Suddenly, I was awakened by loud exclamations. The young man beside me was holding a bucket of cola, opening it with his teeth.

One of the guys in front mocked, "Hey, silly bear, have you never had cola before?"

Then he approached and snatched the bucket of cola.

The man beside me handed it over, saying, "Here, have some. Where are you headed for work?"

"Jinan. With a face like a silly bear, can you still find a job?" replied the young man, drinking cola.

"Someone will pick me up at the bus station." He took a sip and muttered, "It's delicious."

Then he tilted his head back and finished it in one gulp. Looking restless, he shook the bucket and exclaimed, "Is there something inside?"

He stared inside, "There's a little bead."

"Nonsense! Let me see what it is." The guy who opened the cola barrel snatched it and took a look inside, shaking it a few times. "There's a little golden bean inside. Shall we open it and take a look?"

The guy nibbling on the cola looked helpless.

"Go ahead, then." The young man who had opened the barrel, holding the cola barrel, shook it a few times, poured out a thing from inside, a glass bead the size of a bean, and said to himself, "I thought it was a small golden bean, but it was a rotten glass bead."

He peered into the mouth of the coke barrel again, "Oh, there's a line of small print; open it."

The young man, chewing on the bucket, nodded. The guy who opened the barrel took out a fruit knife from his bag, made a slit in the lid, lifted it, crying, "Jackpot! First prize, contact number, 0532."

"What jackpot?" the guy nibbling on the barrel asked.

"Make a call."

"I don't have a phone."

"I'll call for you. If we get it, we split it fifty-fifty."

The guy who had opened the barrel was serious. He took his phone from the bag and swiftly dialed, "What? Qingdao. Hold the cola barrel and claim the prize. How much? Repeat that, 20,000 yuan? Confirm 20,000. Sure, alright."

The guy who opened the barrel slapped the guy, nibbling on the cola barrel, "You clueless guy, we hit the jackpot! Twenty thousand, let's go to Qingdao to claim it."

"Where's Qingdao? I have no idea."

"You've got a mouth under your nose; ask someone."

"I dare not go because I have never been far from home." The guy nibbling on the barrel clenched it tightly in his hands.

The guy who opened the barrel continued, "I'll sell it cheap on the bus for you, okay?"

The guy nibbling on the barrel remained silent.

"Is it okay or not? Speak up."

"Sell it, fine."

My drowsiness vanished as I watched such a funny skit. The guy in work clothes nibbling on the barrel had white palms. His face showed no signs of hardship, looking dumbfounded as he mimicked Song Dandan's performance, "My mom said, my name is..."

The guy who opened the barrel stood in the middle of the bus seats, holding the cola barrel high.

"I've decided for him. Who wants to go to Qingdao to claim the prize? I'm selling this prize-winning barrel for 10,000 yuan, half price."

A guy with oily hair and a powdered face stood up from the back seat, pointing at the guy nibbling on the barrel. "I'll take you to Qingdao to claim the prize; we split it, alright?"

"I'm not going. What if you bail halfway? Who will I turn to?"

"What to do? Lower the price again."

"I want cash." "How about taking out 3,000 yuan, 7,000 yuan?"

A man stood up from the front seat, "I do not have that much cash. This Swiss watch of mine is worth 5,000 yuan. I'll give you 2,000 in cash, okay?"

"I don't recognize watches."

A guy stood in the middle, took the cola barrel, and looked inside. "Such a good opportunity, but unfortunately, I didn't bring that much cash. Can you lower the price?"

"Even if we lower it, you can't afford it. What gadget?"

The guy who opened the barrel leaned over to the guy who nibbled the barrel and asked, "How about 5,000 yuan?" He nodded.

"Final offer, 5,000 yuan! Cash only, no trades, don't miss out." They shouted for a few minutes, but no other passengers spoke up.

As the bus passed through Longshan, five young men disembarked, putting on a performance that lasted for over an hour. Despite their efforts, not a single person on the bus was duped.

The visit to Tiefa Mechanical Factory was prompted by director Sun's urgency to prepare for production transfer, settle accounts, and halt operations. Director Zhou introduced the powder business at Tiefa Mechanical Factory, which originated from Shulan Mechanical Factory. Director Sun of Tiefa and director Zhou were close friends, and director Zhou introduced the spray oil cylinder project to director Sun. Moreover, director Sun had a familial relationship with a deputy director of the Tiefa Mining Bureau. With director Sun's commitment to producing qualified oil cylinders and repairing qualified hydraulic props, Tiefa Mechanical Factory secured the exclusive repair business for Tiefa Coal Mine's hydraulic props.

When I had arrived two years prior, the factory had just commenced production. We adopted Director Zhou's workshop technology, which was straightforward and had minimal technical requirements. Within a few months, we were operating smoothly. The sales process remained uncomplicated as long as the powder I supplied maintained a low price and guaranteed quality. Director Sun outwardly represented the Tiefa Mining Bureau Mechanical Factory Branch, but it was his private enterprise. He fully controlled procurement, sales, production, and payment decisions. There was no need for elaborate entertainment, gift-giving, or flattering of various departments such as sales, quality inspection, or finance. Transactions were conducted openly and honestly. Over the course of two years, our dealings progressed smoothly. Payments were consistently made on time, and promises were always kept without delay.

I have only been here once in two years. The route is memorable, and director Sun also left an impression.

The first time I had visited, I had thought I was clever. Arriving at Tiefa Bus Station, I searched for the Tiefa sign. However, after circling, I was unable to locate it. Seeking assistance from the attendant, they pointed to the left and said, "Over there."

Following their directions led me to a dead end without a "Tiefa" in sight. Asking another attendant, I was directed to the right with assurances that it was close by. However, my search still proved fruitless. Seeking help once more, a kind individual informed me that the "Diaobingshan" station was, in fact, Tiefa. It turned out that Tiefa County was located in Diaobingshan. Locals would laugh if you asked specifically for Tiefa. Tiefa did not refer to a single city or town but served as the general term for the entire county. Situated between Tieling and Faku cities, Tiefa County took one character from each of the two cities. So outsiders would ask for Tiefa, but locals call it "Diaobingshan."

Accompanied by salesperson Little Zhao, I arrived at Tiefa Mechanical Factory to settle accounts as arranged over the phone. Director Sun was waiting for us at the factory. Director Sun explained that the Technical Department of the Mining Bureau was preparing to introduce new technology for cylinder lining. It was anticipated that the oil cylinder might be phased out within a year or two, necessitating early preparation. If maintenance of hydraulic props ceased, the plan was to shut down operations and transition to coal transportation instead. To preempt any potential complications with debts, I thought it imperative to settle all outstanding amounts immediately. The total debt amounted to 400,000 yuan, of which the Mechanical General Factory owed director Sun 1.2 million yuan. Fortunately, an agreement had been reached with the General Factory. The 400,000 payments would be redirected to the General Factory, and they would be responsible for disbursing this amount to director Sun. With all necessary procedures completed, the business would have no lingering issues. It was understood that debts owed among friends must be cleared without delay.

With everything agreed upon, we proceeded to complete the formalities of the handover. Director Sun's reputation for trustworthiness was commendable. If a small factory closed its doors, changed contact details, and vanished, tracking them down would be challenging. Given the distance and the absence of communication means, there would be little room for negotiation.

Director Sun and I went to the Mechanical General Factory together. In the finance department, we introduced ourselves, and it was agreed that the General Factory would make the payment of 50,000 yuan. The transfer agreement had been prepared in advance, and all three parties signed and stamped it. I did not bring the company seal, so I had to sign and leave a thumbprint. After completing the handover procedures, I asked the head of the finance department when the payment could be made. The head said there was no specific time and asked me to come at noon the next day.

At eight o'clock the next day, I rushed to the finance office of the General Factory. I had just started working, and the head was very busy. I saw him at nine o'clock, so I asked the head when this payment could be made, in installments or as a single payment. The head's answer was the same as the previous day's. The timing was uncertain, possibly a year or two. Now, there were great difficulties. Workers had not been paid for three months. We would pay as soon as possible if coal sales were picking up. This was vague and indefinite, so I had to wait endlessly for the notice to arrive.

Walking out of the office corridor, a young man caught up from behind, walked alongside me for a few steps, and spoke, "Where are you from, experienced worker?"

"Shandong."

"I'm from Shandong too; we're fellow provincials. What business?"

The young man continued talking, not letting up. "No business; I come here to collect debts."

I ignored him and kept walking.

The young man continued chatting, "This factory will not collapse for three to five years. Out of business, it is hard to collect debts, let alone old debts. You cannot collect debts in one or two years. Don't think about it."

"Tough luck." I ignored him.

"I'll find a way for you. We are both from Shandong. I'll get the money out for you, okay?"

"That would be great." I stopped and observed the young man. Although I could not do magic or read people's faces, I could judge them by their appearance. The young man had bright eyes and a graceful brow, and he looked friendly and straightforward. I had a hunch he was not a liar.

"Let's find a place to talk." I agreed, with Little Zhao accompanying me.

The two of us were not afraid of being taken advantage of. The young man introduced himself. His grandfather had braved the journey to the northeast, and his family had worked in the coal mines in Linyi, Shandong Province. This area was dominated by coal mines, which had been operating at a loss in recent years. Life was not easy at the Mechanical General Factory. To claim money from the General Factory, the director could sign. The deputy director could sign. The Finance director could sign. They could approve it, but one would not get it easily, even if one made several trips. The young man knew a relative of the factory director who could convert the coal into a usable form and sell it to the mines. This method could expedite the payment, but the kickback would be higher, at 30 percent. I agreed to consider it, discuss it, and give an answer the next day. We exchanged phone numbers.

Back at the hotel, Little Zhao and I discussed it and weighed our options. With a 50,000 yuan budget for such a long journey, we had to make two or three trips, spending 7,000 or 8,000 yuan on travel expenses, gifts, and dining out, which accounted for thirty percent. We were unsure if we could achieve 70 percent. It would still be profitable as long as he was not a liar. For both of us, the odds were good. We took a chance.

I spoke with the young man on the phone twice, and we agreed to meet in the corridor of the Mechanical General Factory's office building at noon the next day. I would confirm the payment at the finance department first, get the receipt, and then go to the bank to withdraw the money.

Meeting the young man at the office building, Little Zhao and I found him coming with another man. So four of us went to the finance department together. After confirming my payment of 50,000 yuan, the young man negotiated with the finance accountant to settle the account using coal, and the finance department agreed to handle it. We needed to write a receipt, but Little Zhao had run out of receipts with the finance seal. We could not handle it without a financial seal of approval. We arranged to call the young man again the next day.

There must be a way when a car to be at the foot of the mountain. In the afternoon, I visited the small market, spent 50 yuan, and had my company's financial seal engraved. It was not illegal for me to use it. If our company sent it via the post office, the fastest option would reach us here in three days. I could not wait.

The next day, the finance department accepted the receipt and gave a receipt-received slip. The young man went to the bank with Little Zhao to withdraw money. I remembered the young man's car number. If the receipt were lost, we would call the police immediately. Little

Zhao and I had planned quite meticulously. In 1998, scammers were hard to guard against.

When Little Zhao returned after banking, he came back within an hour, exceptionally smoothly. Little Zhao recounted his heart pounding while riding in the young man's car. Halfway through, it was dangerous for him to get Little Zhao out of the car or beat Little Zhao. Because they were locals, if you called the police, you would not find them immediately. At the bank's entrance, he followed closely behind. In under 10 minutes, the young man received the cash. "Snap, snap, snap," he handed me 35,000 yuan, shook hands, and left the bank separately.

Getting the money back, we understood the whole thing. On the first day, we visited the finance department, received vague answers, and were instructed to return the following day. We came back the next day, but still received unclear responses. I left the office building and "bumped into" the young man who helped me claim the money; it could not have been timelier. The skit director's arrangement was reasonable, and the payment method of state-owned units was truly diverse.

6.7 A Case Resolved by the Court

Yesterday was the summer solstice, and a gentle drizzle began to fall this morning. The temperature was 25 degrees Celsius, and the air was refreshing. Outside the office window, the magnolia tree dripped with crisp raindrops. The phone rang, and my classmate, old Li, wanted to come over for a heart-to-heart chat while it was raining. Welcome indeed!

I also invited four or five old classmates for a small banquet. It had been more than two months since we last met. We chose Santaishan Mountain, a newly opened restaurant with outdoor pavilions where we could listen to the rain and enjoy the view of the mountains while chatting about our recent travels. You went to Qishan Mountain these days, and he went to Lushan Mountain. You shared interesting stories, and he shared amusing anecdotes. It was a delightful reunion.

Lately, I had not been on major trips to rivers and mountains and had no stories to tell. Unknowingly, I started talking about my experience in Tengzhou the day before yesterday, and the more I talked, the angrier I became. A small coal mining machinery factory in Tengzhou ceased operations, owing more than 60,000 yuan. The factory director blamed the Party Secretary, and the secretary blamed the director. They kept passing the buck, saying they had no money to repay the debt. How could this account be settled?

My old classmate Li said, "If there's a place to demand money, how could they forget about it? Let's sue them in court." He had acquired a significant amount of legal knowledge in recent years. He had assisted friends with several debt recovery cases. His work was quite impressive, and a few old classmates looked at him with admiration. Li was willing to help me sue the Tengzhou factory to recover the payment.

It was settled. We would draft the complaint the next day, organize the necessary materials, and proceed to the Tengzhou Court within three to five days to file a lawsuit against this small factory.

The factory was known as the Tengzhou Hongye Coal Mine Machinery Factory. The Tengzhou County Coal Bureau and the local neighborhood committee jointly owned it. Both entities had shares in the factory, along with the director and the secretary. It was neither public nor private, a rather ambiguous enterprise. The Coal Bureau designated the director, and the neighborhood committee appointed the secretary. With a staff of over forty, the factory was divided into two factions: one represented by the director, on behalf of the Coal Bureau, and the other by the secretary, representing the neighborhood committee. There was a two-story office building, a workshop, and a large storage shed, all of which were managed by a well-structured leadership team, including the secretary, the director, the deputy director, the workshop manager, the finance department, the accountant, and the union chairman. The director and secretary worked on the second floor, while the others worked on the first. The secretary drove a jeep, and the director drove a small Jiefang brand truck with a double row, showcasing the state-owned enterprise's style.

When discussing business on the second floor, the director and the secretary had to be present. Their powers were parallel, and neither was superior to the other. I was repairing the base of a hydraulic prop, working with small components that yielded low profits. The director and the secretary kept passing the buck, saying that the business had been operating at a loss for a year and a half. They finally decided to stop the business, claiming it was a bottomless pit. After settling accounts, I was owed over 65,000 yuan for the repairs. When I attempted to establish a repayment plan with the director, he stated that I needed the secretary's approval. After three attempts to contact the secretary with no results, I had no choice but to resort to the court to recover the debt.

My old classmate worked diligently, and within two days, he organized the complaint and supporting documents in an orderly manner, presenting them in a vivid and clear manner. We initiated business from a certain year and month, issuing several value-added tax invoices totaling a specific amount for repair fees. Despite receiving payments, we still owed over 65,000 yuan. The account records served as evidence. We filed the case at the Tengzhou County Court and awaited the court hearing.

One month later, we received a notice for the court hearing. My old classmate and I took a long-distance bus and arrived at the Tengzhou Court on time.

At 8:30, we stood at the entrance of the second trial court, waiting. At eight-thirty, two judges opened the door and entered the courtroom. "From Zibo," one of them asked. "Yes, that's us." "Please have a seat." The judges sat at the front of the court while we sat in the plaintiff's seat. The judges examined the case file, and the room fell silent.

After we waited about fifteen minutes, a woman entered. She was carrying a green messenger bag, smiling as she nodded to the judges and taking her seat at the defendant's table.

The judge spoke kindly. "The plaintiff from Zibo will now present the case."

My old classmate opened the file, stood up solemnly, and read the prepared materials.

"Zibo Baixi Mining Machinery Repair Factory has been repairing the handles and bases of hydraulic props for Hongye Coal Mine Machinery Factory since May 1995. The business has been conducted sixteen times, issuing twelve value-added tax invoices totaling 167,000 yuan. The Hongye Factory has paid 102,000 yuan in repair fees in five installments. Still, it owes the Baixi Mining Factory 65,000 yuan. Despite repeated requests for payment, the Hongye Factory has refused to pay, citing various excuses."

Before my old classmate could finish, the judge interrupted, "Are you a lawyer?"

My old classmate replied, "No."

The judge nodded, and my old classmate finished reading the complaint.

The judge gestured to the woman, "The defendant may respond."

The female lawyer arrived 10 minutes later, glanced at the sky, and took her time before speaking. "Let me introduce myself. I am Lawyer Zhao, representing Hongye Factory. Our two factories had business relations two years ago, and all processing fees were settled. The business has long ceased, and no debt is owed to Baixi Mining Factory. That's all I have to say."

I added, "Playing tricks won't change the fact that the money is owed."

The lady countered, "Let's keep our language civil, shall we?"

The judge intervened, "Could the plaintiff provide proof of the debt?"

My old classmate handed over several sheets of paper.

"Here are copies of the account records from the mining factory, clearly detailing every transaction."

The female lawyer also presented several sheets of paper.

"The accounts of Hongye Factory show that all payments have been settled, and no outstanding repair fee is owed."

The judge asked, "Do the plaintiffs have any other evidence?"

My old classmate replied, "This should be sufficient. Compare it with the accounts of Hongye Factory, and everything will be clear."

The judge remarked, "There's no time to obtain the accounts of Hongye Factory."

My old classmate became agitated, "What kind of logic is this? Can't you judges check the accounts?"

"We are not obligated to do so. It's beyond our scope of work."

I chimed in, "This is outrageous."

The judge stood up, "Court adjourned."

The female lawyer smiled, picked up her bag, and exited the courtroom first.

My old classmate was shaking with anger. "What kind of judges are these? It is unacceptable."

As we walked out of the courthouse, a young judge from the trial approached us.

"I can find a lawyer to help you with this case. If you agree, let's exchange numbers. Mine is..."

The young judge walked away, leaving my old classmate still trembling. "These bastards. They will not fall for your tricks. Ridiculous."

My old classmate had only superficial knowledge of the law, speaking in jargon without real expertise. The judge and the female lawyer were pleased with that. The prepared materials were of no use. From the opening to the end, it took about 10 minutes, not a Guinness World Record, but perhaps the shortest court hearing in China.

The lawsuit ended there, unable to proceed further. Facing the Hongye Factory, the Coal Bureau, the neighborhood committee, two government subordinate units, and their turf was like fighting against the local authorities. Could we win? Even if we did, could we get the money? The 60,000 yuan might all go down the drain, and the best-case scenario might only yield a few scraps of iron.

Sitting in the car on the way back to Zibo, we were filled with frustration. We could not have made the trip for nothing; we had to continue the fight. Only if we went to the court of a business unit could we win the case, as my old classmate had said. The factory case in Tengzhou should be handled in the Tengzhou Court. Initially, we did not consider other factors. Then I remembered something a fellow factory director had once told me. You could sue in the local court if it is processing incoming materials. But we were providing repair services. We had some ideas for filing a lawsuit in the local court, and we were considering whether Zichuan had jurisdiction over the matter. We could go back and learn about it first.

My old classmate had a classmate who was now a member of the court's party committee. Consulting him clarified the main issues.

He said, "For your part, products made from materials supplied to the other party's enterprise must be sued and tried in their local court, which we have no jurisdiction over. If the other party supplies materials and we process them into products, we could sue in our local court, where we have jurisdiction. You repaired parts for Hongye Factory, brought them from their factory, fixed them, and sent them back. They owe you repair fees, and the accounts are clear. You could sue in the Zichuan district Court without any doubt."

With these words, our hearts were suddenly enlightened. We should have discussed this earlier, which would have spared us the trip to Tengzhou.

Once the complaint was submitted to the court, my old classmate arranged for a female judge to handle the case. The judge's husband was the mayor of our town, and we had met at social gatherings, though we were not close. I visited the judge's office, and she warmly welcomed me. With these two layers of interpersonal relationships — her husband managing the factory jurisdiction and her being a fellow alumnus of the court's leadership — my case was straightforward, not complicated, and completely above board, so there was no need for bribery. The judge promised to handle it properly.

The court date was scheduled quickly, within four weeks, less than a month. It took only two and a half months from filing the complaint to the court hearing, compared to the Tengzhou Court's two months. On the day of the hearing, my old classmate and I arrived 10 minutes early at the trial court. Three people were standing at the entrance we did not recognize, probably from the Hongye Factory. The female judge and the court clerk arrived on time at 8:30.

Everyone took their seats, and the judge opened the case file, saying, "The defendant, Tengzhou Hongye Coal Mine Machinery Factory, will make their statement first. Would you like to speak?"

A middle-aged man stood up from the defendant's seat.

He said, "I am the lawyer for Hongye Machinery Factory, Hu. The statement made by Baixi Mining Machinery Repair Factory in the complaint is true. We owe them 65,000 yuan in repair fees. I have brought Hongye Factory's accounts. We should pay Baixi Mining Factory the repair fee of 65,000 yuan. However, our production is abnormal, and we are short of funds. Can we repay in installments or use materials to offset part of the cash?"

Before we could respond, the lawyer for Hongye Factory rattled off her defense, which was the end.

The female judge smiled and said, "You two should negotiate, reach a repayment agreement, and sign it in court. If no agreement can be reached, we will have a second hearing for judgment and execution. Let's end it here for today. Court adjourned."

In a socialist country with Chinese characteristics, two county-level courts using the same civil law reached two different verdicts in a trivial case. The mystery behind this is known to you, me, and everyone else.

As we left the courthouse, Secretary Zhang from Hongye Factory approached us at the gate, taking quick steps. He shook my hand, "Manager Yu, I am sorry. The last time I was in Tengzhou, I received high-level advice, but I made a mistake. Please forgive me. We've had many years of business relationship, not just a business partnership, but also a friendship."

"Last time in the Tengzhou Court, you acted unreasonably and heartlessly over tens of thousands of yuan."

"I regretted it after you left."

"You must be very shocked to receive the summons from the Zichuan court. Do you regret it?"

"How could that be? I truly regret it."

Secretary Zhang's thoughts were unknown, but his words were sincere.

There are two leaders at the Hongye Factory. I do not get along with director Xing; we seem to disagree and are even less compatible at banquets. This Secretary Zhang, however, was easy to get along with and had visited our factory once. Director Xing must have orchestrated the recent lawsuit. He was sharp-tongued. Secretary Zhang was honest and kind-hearted. While both had a say in the factory's operations, director Xing ultimately prevailed over Secretary Zhang.

Having known Secretary Zhang for two years, we got along well, and the agreement was ultimately reached: a down payment of 35,000 yuan in cash, with the remaining 30,000 yuan to be settled by providing steel, liquor, and other items. The whole episode ended in a cheerful atmosphere.

6.8 Buying Machinery

When repairing hydraulic pillars, you cannot just fix the oil cylinder; you also need to address the other components. We need to add repairs for the handlebars and chassis. We contacted the managers of Longkou's Beizao Mine, Xinwen Machinery Factory, Feicheng Mining Bureau Mechanical Branch, and Zaozhuang's Shanjiulin Mine for the handlebar and chassis repair business. A universal lathe must be used to repair, which wastes labor and time. Upon a friend's recommendation, a small factory in Yanzhou had developed a makeshift solution, developing a small machine specifically for repairing bases. It was created by a retired technician, doing it all on his own, cutting labor costs in half compared to the old methods. They had already begun small-scale production, and we planned to purchase a set of them.

My uncle, my cousin's father, whom I affectionately call "Little Uncle (younger uncle)," was responsible for contacting coal mines to repair old equipment. He had very strong business capabilities and had already inquired about where to manufacture makeshift equipment. We were planning to go and order a set.

Knowing Yanzhou manufactured makeshift equipment, I did not ask for a specific address. I went with Little Uncle to the gate of Yanzhou Coal Machinery Factory. This factory fell under the jurisdiction of the Coal Ministry, a large state-owned enterprise, and its entrance was grand.

Standing to the left of the gate, Little Uncle muttered to himself, "Where to find? It is tricky."

I said, "There are three-wheeled taxis across the road".

Give the driver the address, irrespective of distance; getting there is more convenient."

Little Uncle shook his head, confused momentarily, "I only asked for a technician named Xu and did not ask for a surname, or the factory's location. Finding the factory in such a vast staff dormitory with thousands of people, surrounded by rural areas, is extremely challenging. And where should we begin to go?"

In the 1990s, without a cell phone and the exact address, searching for someone in an area was like finding a needle in a haystack. It was preposterous that we were ignorant of the factory name, someone's name, and what the soil machinery factory called, but we only knew that a technician named Xu was involved.

Three gatekeepers at the factory's communication office knew nothing when we asked them. With over 2,000 workers in the factory, the gatekeepers only recognized the factory director, the deputy director, department heads, and certain figures, referring to them as engineers, technicians, and a few hundred technical staff. However, they had no idea about Technician Xu.

Finding the neighborhood committee, we explained that we were looking for a retired worker named Xu, who had set up a small processing factory near the factory to manufacture machinery equipment. The several middle-aged women on the neighborhood committee were very enthusiastic.

After discussing for a few minutes, a woman in her fifties remembered, "Oh, oh," she said twice. "He retired and lived here for a few months. He does not live here now; I heard he is everywhere, helping one factory with their products and assisting another with technical upgrades. He does not have a factory, so you will not find him here. His wife is in Jinan, caring for their grandchildren; their home is locked up."

Little Uncle continued to inquire, "Where is the factory that works with him? Where is it?"

The woman replied, "I don't know."

Out of the neighborhood committee, wandering in the street, we unconsciously reached the end of a small street. It was a commercial street, with shops, cinemas, and schools all concentrated on this street, surrounded by residential areas on both sides. Across the main road was the coal machinery factory, surrounded by cornfields, but no small factories were in sight. There was only one hotel, the coal machinery factory's guesthouse. We decided to stay there for the night and devise a new plan the next day.

Although we racked our brains at night, we could not come up with a viable solution. Obtaining information from Taiyuan without automated exchanges to connect with the post office within a day was impossible. It was Sunday, the next day, and we could not have a call with anyone at the Taiyuan Hydraulic Research Institute due to a rest day.

After finishing a bottle of Erguotou liquor, a traditional Chinese vodka, Little Uncle, in frustration, started singing, "With determination, overcoming all obstacles."

It reminded me of the story about Yu Gong, a foolish older man determined to remove the mountains that blocked his way, namely, the story of Yu Gong Moving Mountains. Suddenly, a plan formed in my mind. We could follow Yu Gong's example, step by step, and thoroughly search every street. I was confident we could find the small factory one day. We would not give up until we succeeded.

The factory dormitory area was quite concentrated, unlike in rural areas, where it is scattered. With four or five streets running in all directions, the factory could not be within the residential area. We started searching from the outskirts of the dormitories. After walking around for a while, we did not find any factories. Outside the dormitories were cornfields, far from the countryside. After walking a few hundred meters forward, we came across a dirt road with a factory producing cardboard boxes. We asked the gatekeeper if there was a machinery factory, but he nodded, indicating he did not know. Near the highway was a larger factory, a chemical fiber factory, a town-run enterprise, but the gatekeepers there also did not know.

From 8 a.m., we walked around the residential area searching for the machinery factory. With the sun overhead, by 10 o'clock, we had not gone far and had reached the endpoint, the coal machinery factory guesthouse. We had just started following Yu Gong's example when we returned to the guesthouse for lunch and planned to expand our search in the afternoon.

Along the highway, there was a small grocery truck.

Little Uncle asked, "Do you have Yunmen brand cigarettes?"

"We don't have Yunmen, but we have Daji brand."

"Give me a pack of Daji."

Handing over the Daji cigarettes, the old lady selling them looked at us and smiled.

"From your accent, you're from the same place wherein Zibo?"

"Zichuan," Little Uncle replied.

"Which town in Zichuan?" "Cicun Town."

"My hometown is Hongshan."

Meeting a fellow townsman while on a business trip is fate."

Little Uncle shook his head.

"Do not mention it. We came to find someone, but we do not know his name. We came to find a factory, but we did not know its name. We only know that Technician Xu from the coal machinery factory retired and started a small factory to make soil equipment. From yesterday afternoon until now, we have heard nothing."

The old lady laughed heartily, "Closing the door and hitting your nose. What a coincidence! We live in the same building. Old Xu and my husband are colleagues and good friends, often together. Please wait a moment; my husband will be here soon. I'll have him take you to the place."

It was a stroke of luck. Little Uncle was so delighted he almost jumped up.

"Thank you, my fellow countryman, it's fateful. I bought a pack of cigarettes from you yesterday, and even purchasing just a whole carton was an option. Today, you've spared me the trouble of traveling ten extra kilometers."

After waiting for about 10 minutes, the older man arrived. Without saying a word, he hailed a three-wheeled "taxi." The older man led the way, with the two of us following closely behind. We walked about five kilometers, entering a village and leaving the dormitory area onto the dirt road. The small factory was at the entrance of the village. It was a small factory of over two acres, and Technician Xu was inside. After explaining our purpose, we entered the office, drank tea, and discussed machinery equipment.

Although it was not Technician Xu's factory, he had the drawings and entrusted the machinery factory to manufacture soil equipment. Technician Xu would then sell them himself, leveraging others' resources to generate profits. This small factory had no name or phone number, and the older man had not brought us here, so if we couldn't find it within three days, we would not be able to locate it.

There was a prototype for the soil machinery repair, and Technician Xu detailed the operating method. After signing the contract and paying the deposit, we returned to pick up the goods in five days. We invited Technician Xu to visit Zibo's Baixi Coal Mining Machinery Factory for guidance.

We needed to add a 30-foot-long lathe to repair the oil cylinder and adopt the new spraying technology. Before spraying, the oil cylinder needed to be bored, but we could not bore it without a lathe. Taiyuan Machinery Factory produced such lathes, each costing over 60,000 yuan, more than our entire year's assets. We borrowed the full 50,000 yuan needed to purchase the spraying equipment. There was no need to buy a new lathe; the old one was perfectly usable. There was only one operation with a large tolerance, allowing it to be machined with a tolerance of 0.1 or 0.2 millimeters. We needed to buy an old lathe as soon as possible.

In the 1990s, state-owned enterprises had yet to undergo significant reforms, while township enterprises were experiencing rapid growth. Private enterprises began to develop, but there was no established marketplace for buying and selling used machinery. This lack of infrastructure made it challenging for those seeking to acquire or dispose of old equipment, as information flow was not smooth, and sellers struggled to find buyers. It was not until after 1995 that the market for second-hand machinery began to take shape.

The spraying equipment from Taiyuan was installed in late August. We had to buy a lathe within two months. Without a lathe, the spraying project could not get started. We relied on friends, connections, and networking to search. The first piece of information arrived: a customer who sold paint sent a letter yesterday, stating that there was a lathe in his neighboring village. I agreed to take a look.

After receiving the letter, we rushed to Sun's village in Huimin County, Zibo. There were no direct buses from Zichuan, so we had to change buses three times and arrive in Lizhuang Town in the afternoon. When we reached Sun's village, there was still a 2.5-kilometer journey to go. There were no pedicabs or bicycles for rent, so we had to take the No. 11 bus, which meant walking a considerable distance. The two of us chatted on the way, and before we knew it, we had reached Sun's village.

Sun had become an official, going from the head of the painting team to the head of the village in Sun's village. When we arrived at his house in the afternoon, it was around four o'clock, and we had planned to check out the lathe first. Sun disagreed, as it was my first time there. As an old business acquaintance and friend, he wanted to be hospitable.

Sun called his wife to buy wine and groceries, and within a short time, his wife brought back a bundle of beer and a bag of vegetables. After looking them over, she went out a few meters and whispered to her husband, thinking I could not hear her.

His wife trimmed vegetables for cooking, Sun opened the canned food, and their seven- or eight-year-old son pumped the bellows. In no time, a table full of dishes was ready. There was a plate of stir-fried leeks with eggs, a plate of canned apples, a plate of canned pears, and a basin of cucumber salad. It was not just one plate of cucumber salad, but a basin, enough for three plates. Sun was generous and enthusiastic, opening five bottles of beer in one go. Each of us was given a big bowl. After a day of traveling by car, we were both hungry and thirsty. Without Sun having to persuade us, we downed two bowls of beer. Stir-fried leeks with eggs, along with home-cooked dishes, went down smoothly. The plate was too small, holding only three eggs at most, so we could not eat much. There were two fruit cans served on small plates, each containing six or seven pieces of apples and pears. Each person had two pieces, leaving two or three pieces left, which we could not finish. The cucumber salad was served in a small basin, with a large portion, so we ate more. When we took the first bite, there was a strange taste, not fishy, but when we listened to Sun, he said it was seasoned with vinegar. We did not know what season it was. After taking another bite and savoring it slowly, we got a piece of egg white, and it became clear. Boiled eggs mixed with cucumber, the egg yolk broken up and mixed in, giving it a strange, fishy taste.

We could not continue eating, and the pace of drinking beer slowed. Sun did not stop and mentioned a local custom in Huiminxian County where people play a finger-guessing game while drinking. The host and guest should drink three bowls for best wishes, gesturing six times and then two times, representing the whole family. After finishing a bunch of beer, Sun's wife went out and brought back another bunch of beer.

Four or five old ladies gathered around the table to wrap dumplings while drinking. Sun explained that it was a local custom. When there were guests, neighbors from both sides would help wrap dumplings, a gesture of utmost respect for their guests. In no time, they wrapped three large baskets of dumplings. They used large baskets, twice the size of the ones in our homes. Boiling the dumplings required a large pot, which the whole family used exclusively for cooking. Next to it was a bellows for heating the pot, which boiled one basket of dumplings at a time. Each basket of dumplings filled a plate with a diameter of 50 centimeters, yielding two plates of dumplings per pot.

After drinking beer and eating dumplings, the dumplings had been boiled for more than an hour, neither hot nor cold, just right. After eating one, it was full of leeks; after eating two, there was no meat; after eating three, there were no eggs or tofu, just leek dumplings. In my forties, it was the first time I had eaten them, and they were refreshing and delicious. I ate more than ten.

We stayed at Sun's house that night, lined up on a platform bed (the traditional style of sleeping arrangements in northern China, where many people sleep together on a long platform), without mosquito nets or electric fans. Sun's wife and child went to stay at the neighbor's house. Three drunken men slept on the large bed. In my forties, it was the first time I had slept like this, two firsts in one night.

Thankfully, I drank so much that I slept well. If I had not drunk, falling asleep tonight would have been difficult. I woke up twice during the night, and it was already bright outside when I woke up. I walked into the small courtyard, breathing in the fresh air.

Sun entertained us for breakfast, bringing a large plate of dumplings from the big table to the small one. He added three small dishes and some vinegar. Yesterday's dumplings were left on the table without covering anything. They had spent the night with flies and mosquitoes. Still, I could not eat them without thinking too much. Sun explained that eating leftover dumplings from the night before for breakfast was a local custom. I made an excuse and declined, saying I was not accustomed to eating breakfast in the morning and usually only drank a glass of water at noon. Sun was hospitable but insisted on serving them. Without any other breakfast options, I did not eat. Sun and my uncle each ate more than ten.

Sun had a bike and met a friend with one too. They rode their bikes while my friend and I sat in the back. It was a flat dirt road with no bumps or slopes, just a roughly four-mile stretch to Zhangjiazhuang Village, where they sold old lathes. The village committee had bought this lathe from a town-run enterprise with plans to set up a factory, but it did not work out. It had been idle for two years and was still about 70 to 80 percent new. I measured the lathe and found that its length was only two meters, which was very suitable. It was a pity it was half a meter short. It was a wasted trip.

Boss Sun felt a bit guilty and did not let us leave. He drank at noon, and by eight o'clock, his sincerity prevented us from attending the banquet at noon. After another half hour of hardship, they sent us to Lizhuang Town. Thanks to Boss Sun, we went back to Zibo.

Coming back from Lizhuang, I went to Jinan to see one, but it was not suitable. The equipment in Taiyuan could not be installed without a lathe. The first process involved boring the cylinder, also known as cylinder boring, and the second process involved spraying.

At a banquet, I met Liu, a salesperson from a nut factory in Zichuan. In our conversation, he mentioned that he had visited Xinwen Machinery Factory the day before and saw two old lathes outside the workshop. He did not know if they were for sale. It was great news! I asked Liu about it, as he had business to attend to the day after. He promised to find out for sure. Three days later, Liu came to tell me that both old lathes were for sale. One lathe was 2.7 meters long, imported, and priced at around 3,000 yuan.

I took a car and asked Liu to accompany me. We set off at four in the morning, aiming to arrive at Xinwen Coal Mine Machinery Factory by eight. It was more than 100 kilometers from Zichuan to Xinwen, with winding roads that were half provincial roads and half rural dirt roads. We arrived at Xinwen Coal Mine Factory at around half past eight.

The old lathes were placed on the side of the road inside the factory. After measuring the lathe, which had a bed length of 2.7 meters, we found it suitable. The main components were still intact, and it could still operate. Liu introduced me to a workshop director, who explained that the lathe was from East Germany, with Soviet experts assisting in its construction in 1956. The lathe had been transported from East Germany and had good quality, having been used for over 30 years. When some parts had broken in previous years and could not be found domestically, they salvaged parts from one lathe to repair the other. This lathe could still operate, even with a few gears removed. It still had two gears left, and it could handle rough machining. I only needed two gears for machining oil cylinders.

After inspecting the lathe, we went to the finance department to make a payment. Liu went ahead, and I followed. When we arrived at the office building's entrance, Liu asked me to wait for a moment while he went to find someone he knew. After about half an hour, Liu returned. The price was 3,500 yuan, as it was a state-owned factory with no room for negotiation. The price was cheap, slightly more expensive than buying scrap iron, but it was acceptable. We paid the money.

When we reached the finance department, Liu stopped and handed me the money, saying, "You don't need to come in." I handed over 5,000 yuan, and Liu conveniently deducted 1,000 yuan and returned the rest to me. Liu tightly wrapped the stack of money with a rubber band and put it into his bag.

I stood at the entrance of the finance department, pacing back and forth. I casually glanced over and saw Liu standing at the desk of the finance department, taking out the tightly wrapped stack of money from his bag. He counted over half of it, about two-thirds, then put the rest back in his bag. Liu handed over two-thirds of the money to the finance staff. Soon, the finance staff handed Liu a receipt, which he crumpled and threw into the nearby trash can.

Back at the old lathe, we prepared to load it onto the truck. The Taishan light truck could carry two tons, but this big guy probably weighed more than three tons. There was a question of whether it could be loaded or not. Liu had good relations with the Coal Mine

Factory, so they used a forklift. I had prepared a pack of cigarettes, and Liu took them. By lunchtime, the lathe was loaded onto the truck.

The forklift arrived, accompanied by the workshop director. The driver asked how heavy the lathe was. According to the manual, the director said it was 4.2 tons, but after removing some parts, it was at least four tons.

"That won't work. If we cannot carry it, and it breaks down halfway, it will be troublesome," the driver shook his head. "It can't be carried," he repeated three times. "We could go back and get a liberation truck to carry it," he suggested.

I hesitated for a few minutes and decided to load it anyway. If the truck broke down, we would find an alternative solution. After loading it, I looked at the Taishan truck. The springs were sagging, but I felt a sense of relief. Where there's a will, there's a way. We returned to the factory without incident.

Slowly drove up and down the hill, and turned more carefully. Thankfully, God helped us. The spring plate and truck held up, and we arrived smoothly back at the factory by 7 p.m.

I needed to add a lathe to work on hydraulic pillars. Zhang, who worked at the factory in Ciyao Town, told me that an old lathe was for sale. His elder cousin knew the place, so we checked it out.

Ciyao Town was a major station on the Beijing-Shanghai line. We took the train from Qingdao to Nanjing, arriving at 3:00 p.m. We stayed at the People's Hotel, where bicycles were available for rent. Zhang and I, along with another salesperson, rented bicycles and followed the map to find the people. We found Zhang's cousin outside a farm machinery factory, working on welding parts in the workshop. After a brief conversation, we agreed to meet at the People's Hotel in the evening for further discussion.

We waited until nine o'clock in the evening, but he did not show up. At half past nine, Zhang's cousin and another young man rushed in, looking like they had been running a long way. They did not bother with pleasantries and immediately talked about the price of the lathe. It was around 3,000 yuan, and they wanted a 500 yuan deposit upfront. They would take us to see the lathe the following day. It was outrageous! Without seeing the lathe and knowing if it was suitable, they required payment up front. I could not agree to that. We needed to negotiate the price first. They said 3,500 yuan, which was even more absurd. It could be a piece of scrap iron or copper without seeing the lathe. These two individuals attempted to make money without understanding the rules of business and social etiquette. Since we came to buy the lathe, we could not afford to offend them. We could not continue the conversation, so we had to play along for now and agreed to see the lathe together the next afternoon.

After they left, we discussed our plan. We decided to take the initiative the next day and search around Ciyao Town. A lathe was a large piece of equipment in rural areas, and many people were familiar with it. Last night, the two guys came to the hotel after nine o'clock. The place where they were selling the lathe was not near the kiln; it was at least five kilometers away. We would search slowly. We would head south in the morning, and in the afternoon, we would go north. If we could not find it today, we would meet up with them again, but we would not give them the extra money until the deal was sealed.

After a breakfast of "youtiao" (deep-fried dough sticks) and "doujiang" (soy milk), we rented two bicycles and set out at seven o'clock. We first headed south along National Highway 104 and stopped to ask along the way.

Traveling along Highway 104, we spotted some villages and decided to ask the elderly locals for information. We specifically targeted those who were not farmers but ran small shops or repair shops, as we believed they would be knowledgeable about the products. A lathe from the 1990s was considered a large machine in the countryside. Whenever we saw a village, we would take the small roads and stop to ask for directions. If we saw anyone driving a tractor, we would stop and ask them for help. We visited five villages located about three or four kilometers south of Ciyao Town. At around 10:15, we took a short break as we were tired and thirsty. After the break, we continued our search in another village to the east in the afternoon.

As we took a few sips of water, a tricycle approached us. The driver was friendly and stopped to chat with us. He waved his hand and brought the car to a stop.

"Excuse me, sir, can you help me with something? I am looking for a lathe nearby. It is for factory use," I said.

"Yes, there is one in Sanlihe Village. They asked me about selling the lathe yesterday," the driver pointed to a village on the left.

"That village, about one kilometer from here. The village head is Sun Xiaoyun. We are quite familiar. Just go into the village and ask the village committee. Everyone knows about it. I won't accompany you."

"Thank you, big brother."

The village head of Sanlihe, Sun, took us to visit the lathe.

As we walked, he said, "This lathe does not have much power. The village does sideline work. We purchased it from someone, used it for three years, and it has been idle for three or four years since then. It's about 70 to 80 percent new."

After a few minutes, we entered a small courtyard. Village head Sun opened the workshop door, and without much inspection, I was quite satisfied. I asked about the price.

"1,500 yuan. It is not negotiable; the village committee sets it. We will not sell for less. Yesterday evening, two young men offered 1,200 yuan, but they did not seal the deal. They're coming again this afternoon."

We quickly made the deal. Village head Sun did not ask for a deposit. I voluntarily paid a deposit of 200 yuan and agreed to come and pick up the lathe at 8:00 a.m. the next day. Village head Sun was so delighted that he promised to find a few people to help move the lathe from the workshop to the street.

Back at the hotel, we packed our bags and checked out. We found another hotel for workers, peasants, and soldiers. During the afternoon, we purposely avoided the company of the two gentlemen and refrained from going to Sanlihe. Engaging in deceptive activities such as playing tricks or cheating for financial gain would ultimately lead to failure.

In the afternoon, we visited the post office to call the factory and arranged for them to come and pick up the lathe the next day. We set off early, bringing two strong workers, poles, gourds, iron bars, iron wires, and thick ropes. We could not afford to miss any tools. We arrived at the hotel for workers, peasants, and soldiers at seven o'clock. We arrived in Sanlihe before eight o'clock and loaded the lathe by ten.

The next day, we drove smoothly, arriving at the Gongnongbing Hotel for workers, farmers, and soldiers before seven and arriving at Sanlihe before eight o'clock. The village head had brought three people, and they had removed the screws holding the lathe in place and laid wooden boards underneath. Our two workers were experts at installing machinery. We planned to move the lathe onto the street in an hour. Everything went smoothly for over 40 minutes, and the lathe was moved onto the street. Half an hour later, it was loaded onto the truck. At a quarter past nine, the lathe was securely fixed, ready for transport.

Village head Sun sent us to the street corner, and we bid each other goodbye. We hurried back to the factory before it got dark.

6.9 Constructing the Factory Three Times

The plastic factory, established in 1982, was in the middle of the village. It consisted of three warehouses, five noodle workshops, and a small courtyard, which was neither crowded nor cramped, making commuting convenient. However, it was not easily accessible for large tractors or cars, which could not enter. Goods were transported to the village entrance using small carts, which could load up to two tons of plastic bars. Cars had to be parked at the end of the alley, and it took four people with small carts two hours to unload the vehicle. After two years in the plastic processing business, the market began to decline, making it difficult to continue. Plans were made to consider producing new products.

At Wendeng Plastic Factory in Zetou Commune, I spent over a year delivering goods and staying at the Supply and Marketing Cooperative Hotel. There, I met Pan Youzhang, a salesperson from Panjiacun

Village, Xujia Commune, in Luwang, Yexian County, Laizhou. We got along well, and sometimes, when waiting for business settlements or collecting payments, we stayed for two or three days. In those days, there was no television, and the commune's headquarters lacked a cinema. During discussions about changing production, Pan mentioned that his fiancée's elder brother worked at Xujia Chemical Factory, where he promoted chemical equipment. I decided to visit and learn more about it.

I made a special trip to Luwang and met Pan's fiancée's elder brother, Wang, the head of the Chemical Machinery Factory. He introduced me to a newly introduced wall paint production equipment that had been recently promoted nationwide. It is used for wall painting in hotels, offices, schools, hospitals, and ordinary homes. This equipment has been produced overseas for over a decade, and its development prospects are quite promising.

Deciding to produce wall paint, I began searching for factory space. The factory did not need to be too large. Still, the yard had to be spacious to transport several tons of materials and products daily.

After searching extensively, I found five donkey sheds belonging to the production team, suitable for accommodating the paint equipment, with a vacant space in front. While navigating cars in and out was a bit inconvenient, it was manageable. After working there for over a year, plans were made to build a compound fertilizer plant to the east, which would block the road to the village entrance. It made it even more inconvenient, prompting the urgent need to find a new location for the factory.

An idle piece of land, located east of the village, is situated north of the galvanized factory. Half of the production team's threshing ground can be extended northward by more than 20 meters and eastward by more than 30 meters, dividing an acre of land into several parts. This way, nine small workshops could be built. It was located next to the village's eastern dirt road, making it extremely convenient for vehicle access. I negotiated with the village secretary to build the factory.

The "Two Committees" of the village (the party branch and

the village committee) had just established regulations this year, encouraging villagers to build factories and develop private businesses. According to the regulations, those who built factories on village land with personal investment and constructed their factory buildings would not need to pay land leasing fees to the village for a period of five years. After five years, the constructed factory buildings, offices, warehouses, and all other buildings on the land would belong to the village. If they were to continue using them, they would need to sign an agreement with the village committee.

Since there were village regulations, I followed them and signed an agreement with the village committee to build the factory. Despite running losses for the past two years and accumulating debts of over 70,000 yuan, I opted for a simple approach to save on building expenses.

The village's construction team was hired, and I covered the labor costs while personally purchasing the materials. Although the nine rooms were considered factory buildings, they resembled simple sheds, which were much simpler than the houses in which ordinary people lived. We bought miscellaneous wood from the market and had carpenters process it. Large beams and braces were welded together using triangular iron pieces. We purchased bamboo poles from Boxing County, eight meters long. We used them to support the ridge beams, saving two-thirds of the cost of wood and half the cost of cement ridge beams. We built a guard room and five open sheds.

Three rooms were designated for paint production, with five rooms prepared for adding new products. An office was added six months later, and hydraulic jack repair was undertaken. On the day the paint factory relocated, managers from both the old and new factories, along with relatives and friends, came to congratulate us. Two banquets were held to celebrate the occasion. With the new factory area completed, production commenced.

It required space to repair hydraulic jacks and upgrade spray painting technology. After calculations, it was determined that more than 10 rooms were needed to accommodate the equipment. Five days later, the galvanizing plant to the south of our factory was relocated, creating an opportunity for us to merge. We knocked down a wall without altering the main entrance, effectively combining the two factories. We found the village party committee secretary, Zhao, who readily agreed to the proposal, as the location had been idle for some time and merging the two factories seemed a suitable option.

The electroplating factory was a village-run enterprise, originally a workshop for porcelain electrical accessories. In the 1960s, it only conducted electroplating, hence the name. Twenty years ago, it was renamed the Porcelain Electrical Accessories Factory. However, locals still referred to it as the electroplating factory. I had visited a few times before but had not observed it closely. Now that we had considered taking it over, I took a closer look. The three northern rooms were built in 1968, measuring 2.5 meters in height and 4 meters in width, resembling warehouses more than factory buildings. The southern side had four open sheds, three of which had walls on three sides and were used as warehouses, while the remaining side was open. These dilapidated sheds were put into use, but we still needed five more rooms.

Before spray painting hydraulic jacks, it is necessary to sandblast to remove oil and rust stains. Two small rooms were needed, attached to the southern wall of the warehouse. The warehouse was set up like a lathe, with the first process being the boring of oil cylinders. The sandblasting room was conveniently located adjacent to the lathe. There was a large pit on the south side of the warehouse, previously used by the galvanizing plant to treat wastewater. Eight cement slabs were placed over it, serving as a cement floor and the foundation for the building. Instead of burying the pit with soil, this method saved labor and time, and a few young workers could handle the construction. No lime or cement was used; yellow soil was mixed to form mud, bricks were laid, and two rooms were completed in three days with six bamboo poles and four reed mats. The windows were not installed, and the door opened onto the south wall of the warehouse.

A door was opened on the east side of the warehouse, creating the appearance of two separate rooms from the west and east, with a passage in between. The construction of this building was relatively good, measuring 3.5 meters in height and six meters in width, with large windows and doors that could accommodate two lathes.

For grinding oil cylinders, two separate rooms were built. Grinding required the use of kerosene for cooling, resulting in dirty oil spills on the ground, which posed a fire hazard and needed to be kept away from other factory buildings. A small vacant area to the east was suitable for two factory buildings. Given the success of building the previous rooms, we decided to undertake the task ourselves. The original ground was hard, so we did not need to dig foundations. The rooms were built two meters high, three meters wide, and five meters long. We bought four old windows and one old door from Xiguan Big Bazaar in Zichuan and completed the construction in three days. The walls were coated with a yellow mud painted white, and the floor was laid with red bricks, making the workshops visually appealing.

The transformation of the southern open sheds was a major project that required hiring a construction team. The building was at risk of collapsing. The southern wall was originally made of adobe. It had been patched up partly with adobe and partly with brick for over 20 years. It needed to be rebuilt. The back wall resembled a map, with blue bricks in one place, red bricks in another, and some original adobe. After years of exposure to smoke and fire, there were four windows of varying sizes, and the purlins were on the verge of snapping. A few years ago, the village committee had planned to relocate the factory, so they had been making do. Converting the southern open sheds into regular factory buildings was more labor-intensive than constructing new ones.

The southern open sheds were transformed into standard factory buildings, with the front wall rebuilt using red bricks and cement and the surface plastered with cement mortar and painted with exterior wall paint. New doors and windows were purchased, and the roof, beams, and rafters were replaced. The concrete floor was polished, resulting in a completely new look for the workshop. In preparation for expanding production, the hydraulic jack's handles, bases, plugs, and other small components were moved here. Since the coal mine was a state-owned enterprise, it was more expensive for workers to handle these minor repairs than to buy new ones. Relocating them to a small factory made it easier for the workers, and the leaders had baijiu to drink and cigarettes to smoke. Making it a win-win situation. The southern open sheds had to be built properly.

Within a month, the factory renovation was completed. The original triangular small workshops and the newly constructed small factories formed a square. Then, we prepared to install lathes and spray equipment. In another month, the new project would officially start production.

Over the next two years, the hydraulic jack repair business expanded to other cities, including Pingdingshan, Huaibei, Xuzhou, and Datong. With the workshop becoming increasingly crowded, another large workshop was needed. In the northwest corner of the factory, there was a vacant area outside the wall, covering over 200 square meters, where residents had been dumping garbage. Inside the compound were three small houses on the north side, short and narrow, making it impossible to install machinery and equipment. These were demolished, and the space was added to the northwest corner, providing enough room for 10 factory buildings. With the business expanding in recent years and its debts paid off, it was necessary to increase factory space to accommodate the production growth.

I approached the village committee building, where the secretary and the director were in their office. They had been in office for less than two months. After explaining the need for additional workshops, I expected not just their support but also their enthusiasm. Unused and neglected land could be turned into factory buildings, improving the village's appearance, increasing revenue from land leasing, supporting enterprise development, and earning the leaders a good reputation. They should have responded promptly and unconditionally, just as their predecessors did. However, quite the opposite happened. For over 10 minutes, neither the secretary nor the director spoke in support, citing the need to consult higher authorities. Currently, obtaining land approval is a complex and challenging process. The Bureau of Land and Mines must complete the formalities before construction can begin. I asked how long it would take to obtain land approval.

The director hesitated before replying, "It could take six months, maybe even a year."

A few days before, we could still greet each other warmly when we met. Still, as soon as they became junior government officials, they began to put on airs. After saying that, I returned to the factory.

Last Wednesday, I attended an economic work conference organized by the town government. Secretary Wang of the town party committee made a statement during the meeting, emphasizing that if projects and funds were available, they should be utilized without hesitation. If any difficulties arise, the government will provide comprehensive support. Occupying a few acres of land was not a problem; it would be acceptable for everyone to take possession of the land first and then obtain government approval. The government was obligated to help with land approval. With the secretary's speech, I gained confidence. Disregarding the village leaders, I proceeded with constructing the workshops.

Just as the foundation was being excavated, the director arrived unsteadily.

"Construction cannot begin without approval. How could you start without it?"

"The foundation has been dug, and the bricks, tiles, and stones have all been delivered. What do you suggest we do?"

Fuming with anger, I could not hold back and retorted sharply. Unable to back down, the director approached me, whispering, "Invite Sun, the Land and Mines Bureau director, to dinner in a day or two. It will be easier to discuss things."

Without explicitly stating it, inviting the bureau director to dinner and offering a small gift could help facilitate progress. Economic development is like a rolling wheel; the director could not stop it.

The dinner with the bureau director was arranged at Santaishan

Mountain Restaurant. It was the best restaurant in town. Inviting the director of the local mines, we must choose a restaurant that befits his status. We could not go to a small restaurant. I arrived at the restaurant at eleven o'clock, and the room had already been booked. The village secretary and director arrived shortly after. As I stood at the kitchen door, ready to order, a minivan pulled up, and three people got out. Leading the way was my cousin from my aunt's side.

"Cousin, it's been a long time since we last met." Before I could say anything, my cousin spoke up first.

"Cousin has been busy recently; which department have you been transferred to?"

"Just making do at the government office. Later, at your banquet, let's have a couple of drinks."

"I'll order the dishes first and have a couple of drinks."

I went to the kitchen to order the food while my cousin went upstairs. It had been over half a year since we last met, so we would catch up and have a couple of drinks together at the gathering.

After ordering the food, I entered the room. My cousin was already seated and stood up immediately. The village director took the opportunity to introduce him, pointing at my cousin.

"Let me introduce you. It is Sun, the director of the Land and Mines Bureau."

He then pointed at me. "This is Mr. Yu, the factory owner."

My cousin burst into laughter. "So, it's my cousin who's treating us today."

The village director was dumbfounded.

"You know each other? You're cousins, and you didn't say anything earlier."

"We wanted to enjoy snacks and drinks — no need for formality. Congratulations to my cousin on his promotion. Director Sun, please take the seat of honor."

"Don't make fun of your cousin. Let's have a couple of drinks as brothers."

With the guest and host seated, we chatted about daily affairs. After several drinks each, director Sun made his statement. The bureau could approve my cousin's occupation of over 200 square meters of unused land. Construction could begin now, and the approval process would continue concurrently. The Land and Mines Bureau would fully support it, hoping for the expansion and prosperity of my cousin's enterprise. The village secretary and director had no response. The argument they had presented earlier was easily invalidated.

The new workshop was 30 meters long and 10 meters wide. Unlike the rural residential-style adobe workshops of the past, it was constructed in the layout of a standard factory. It had the appearance of a real factory workshop. The business of repairing hydraulic jacks expanded over the next few years. Still, by the late 1990s, national coal production had declined significantly, resulting in the suspension of hydraulic jack repairs. The workshop had shifted to producing automobile alternators for several years before switching to manufacturing medical infusion bottle caps. But that is a story for another time, a tale from many years later.

6.10 The Lawsuit with a Happy Ending

On my office desk lay a letter from the Jinan Intermediate People's Court. Upon opening it, I found several printed pages detailing the lawsuit filed by the Taiyuan Hydraulic Research Institute against the Baixi Mine Machinery Repair Factory for intellectual property infringement in the production of cylinder coating powder. Among the papers was a court summons from the Jinan Intermediate People's Court. I had to consider strategies to deal with this situation.

Big Master A from the Research Institute shared the powder formula with me. Still, I was unable to replicate it exactly. If there were a patent in the Research Institute, engaging in a lawsuit over it would be embarrassing and costly. Big Master A assured me that the formula had been modified slightly. There would be no repercussions, given his good relationship with the institute director in the state-operated unit. As expected, I received the lawsuit within a year. It was my first encounter with such a situation, and I needed to remain calm and clear-headed.

Sitting at my desk, I was consumed by messy thoughts. Workshop director Little Chen entered without a word from me; he approached my desk, looking at the lawsuit documents instead of reporting on internal factory matters.

"The lawsuit comes from Jinan Intermediate People's Court?" Little Chen asked.

"Yes, it's troublesome," I sighed.

"No worries," Little Chen lifted his head confidently.

"What's the witty plan?" I inquired.

"Remember what I told you before? You might have forgotten. My second young uncle is a judge at Jinan Intermediate People's Court." Little Chen explained.

"Your uncle by blood or marriage?"

"By blood. My dad is the eldest. My second uncle was assigned to the court after retiring from the army. He's now the head of a trial division, just a small official in the court."

I breathed in relief. "That's fantastic. There's always a way out. Let's head to Jinan the next day."

"I'll call my uncle tonight. If he's not on a business trip and stays in Jinan, we'll go there tomorrow."

The next day, we arrived at Jinan Intermediate People's Court at 10 o'clock in the morning. Informed by the guard, Little Chen's uncle answered the call, knowing his nephew had come. The guard directed us to the third office on the second floor. It was the first time Little Chen had come to court.

Within a small room was a desk, two chairs, and a three-person sofa in Presiding Judge Chen's office. Little Chen introduced me as the factory director with a case needing Presiding Judge Chen's help. Presiding Judge Chen gave us a warm reception because he treated us as fellow townsmen, friendly. Then, without much small talk, we discussed the case.

I carefully explained our relationship with the Taiyuan Hydraulic

Research Institute, the powder formula, and the event that was taking place. I expressed confusion over the allegations of infringement and patent protection.

Presiding Judge Chen listened attentively, nodding along. When I finished, he chimed in.

"In cases like these, stay calm. Intellectual property lawsuits are complex, with intricate procedures that differ significantly from those in regular debt-related cases. The first step is to verify whether there's infringement. Understand the scope of protection for the patent on this product. Not every material in chemical products is protected by patents. For instance, common additives like calcium starch are not subject to patent protection. Out of 10 materials, only two or three might be protected. If you modify any of these, the product will not be produced. Firstly, determine if your modifications fall within their patent protection."

I explained, "We modified additives and kept two main ingredients."

As I spoke, Presiding Judge Chen made phone calls and answered a few calls himself.

He then pointed to Little Chen and said, "This case belongs to the Second Civil Division of the People's Court, which Little Zhang charged. It is not a big issue. As they came from Taiyuan for the court, let's delay it. It will not be finished within one or two years. Does your younger brother know any lawyers? They might have solutions. Meet with your younger brother this afternoon; understand the situation first, and take it slow. It's a fellow townsman's matter; I'll do my best."

Feeling reassured, we left the courtroom feeling relieved. We had not been to Jinan in Shandong Province for over a year. The loose-packed beer, Baotu Spring Beer, was very refreshing, and its Bazirou Pork was delicious. Bazirou, a popular delicacy in Shandong cuisine, was a stewed pork fillet with fat and lean meat. The steamed buns named after the founder's nickname, "Caobao," were delicious. We decided to enjoy a meal and then visit Little Chen's brother to discuss strategies in the afternoon.

Half a month later, after we returned from Jinan, I joined a lunch gathering with my friends at Santaishan Restaurant, where I drank more than half a liter of baijiu. After returning to my office, I sat on the sofa and dozed off. Two people, around 50 years old, wearing jackets and each carrying a briefcase, entered. They did not appear to be businesspeople or government officials.

"You're director Yu, right?" one with the slightly chubby figure said, then I nodded. "Heard a lot about you; this is our first meeting."

The thinner one followed, "The Taiyuan Hydraulic Research Institute assigns us to discuss the infringement of our coating powder."

I remained silent, and the chubby one continued, "It looks like you've had quite a bit, director Yu."

"There's nothing much to discuss. I have not infringed on your intellectual property or utilized your technology. China is vast, and what you have, others might have, too. I learned it from Beijing and Tianjin, and it has nothing to do with you."

Emboldened by alcohol, I spoke more forcefully. Alcohol was indeed a good thing. I was at my best at eight or nine-tenths drunk. Words I usually struggled to say flowed smoothly, logically, and endlessly.

Since I was drunk on endless talk, occasionally excited or angry, they never mentioned the infringement again. Instead, they began to roam around my office.

When they seized a moment of my pause, one asked, "Director Yu, can we visit your home?"

"Well, certainly, let's go."

My home was situated in the center of the village, just a short distance from the factory, approximately 300 meters away. As we passed by, we saw a house with wedding lanterns hanging outside and two red flags inserted.

"Wedding flags fluttering," muttered one of the Taiyuan men.

"The red flag roused the serf, halberd in hand, while the despot's black talons held his whip aloft."

"Oh, director Yu can still recite Chairman Mao's poems," the chubby one remarked.

"Northern landscapes, snowflakes swirling for thousands of kilometers, gazing at the Great Wall inside and out..." "Impressive. Surprisingly, you can recite so fluently," The chubby man commented as we walked.

After reciting the poem, "Snow," we entered my house. I lived in the west wing, while the bedroom and study were at the southern end. There was a small living room which was over 10 square meters. I invited the visitors to sit down. While I was still semi-drunk, they did not mention the main issue; instead, they chatted about poetry.

"Director Yu, you're well-versed in Chairman Mao's poetry," one of them remarked.

"People who lived through the era of the Cultural Revolution can recite quite a few. It is not boasting; we could recite over 30 poems by Chairman Mao at that time. But I have forgotten some in recent years. Please excuse my rustiness." I replied. "You can recite many Tang poems, too, right?"

The chubby Taiyuan man seemed quite interested and continued to discuss our poems. I recited Li Bai's poem with the help of alcohol.

"From a pot of wine among the flowers, I drank alone. There was no one with me — Till, raising my cup. I asked the bright moon to bring me my shadow and make us three. "

After reciting a few lines of Li Bai's drinking poem, the Taiyuan visitors applauded enthusiastically. The door to the adjacent room was my small study, which was left open, revealing four or five bookcases. The Taiyuan visitors walked in, inspecting my book collection.

"Let's take a look at director Yu's books."

"Please, the collection of books isn't relevant — just a hobby of mine. Feel free to come back tonight if you would like to read," I said.

The two Taiyuan visitors walked around the bookshelves, touching this book and that. They conversed among themselves and concluded that director Yu was not just a wealthy landowner or nouveau riche, but a literate and morally upright businessman.

Standing aside, I suddenly remembered to ask for their names. "May I ask for your names?"

"I'm surnamed Zheng, given Zuo Liang, Zheng Zuoliang."

He was slightly older and chubby, quiet and gentle, and had the appearance of an intellectual.

"I'm Wu Zhengchun."

He was thinner with the appearance of a worker.

The two Taiyuan visitors did not sit down or drink water. Instead, they circled the room before leaving for the Zichuan Hotel. We agreed to meet again the next day at noon at Zichuan Hotel for further discussions.

The next day at Zibo Hotel, I apologized to the Taiyuan visitors because I had been intoxicated and had spoken out of turn the previous day. The two visitors praised me, thinking that I was a bumpkin. However, they were surprised that I was quite knowledgeable, a cultured businessman well-versed in the poetry of Mao and Tang, and had a substantial collection of books. I explained that I could not have recited those poems without a few drinks, as I was constantly busy with work and rarely had time for reading. After a brief conversation, we began discussing the matter of the powder spraying.

Zheng Zuoliang handed me his business card and introduced himself as an engineer at the Taiyuan Branch of the Institute of Chemical Engineering, the Chinese Academy of Sciences, and an amateur lawyer. He explained they were neighbors with the Research Institute and did not charge legal fees. Additionally, they assisted in various lawsuits. Wu Zhengchun was the office director of the Hydraulic Research Institute and represented them as the plaintiff in this lawsuit. Both were sincere and straightforward, explaining that they had come from the Jinan Intermediate People's Court, where they met with the presiding judge. The judge advised them to try to negotiate before the trial. If an agreement could be reached, it would be for the best. If not, then the trial would proceed. They hoped to settle amicably, given their longstanding business relationship and personal connections. The lawsuit demanded a settlement of 500,000 yuan. After much consideration, they were willing to settle for 200,000 yuan. If we refused, they would proceed with the trial in Jinan.

Before arriving at the hotel, I reminisced about the scene from yesterday afternoon. They looked around the factory and came to my house to inspect the residence, assess the household items, and estimate the assets. It is not common sense to pay a visit before filing a lawsuit. We visited the Jinan Intermediate People's Court and met with a judge. The judge sided with us during the conversation because he may encounter some difficulties. It depended on the situation before discussing whether it was favorable.

After Lawyer Zheng finished speaking, I said there was no infringement; "We did not use your formula and compensate, let alone 200,000. We cannot back down; if we admit fault, it would confirm infringement. Patent infringement was the key. As long as it involves patent rights, we will certainly compensate. It's just a matter of how much we can't admit."

Lawyer Zheng smiled faintly, not in a hurry, and spoke slowly.

"We have evidence. Without solid evidence, we would not have come to Jinan to file a lawsuit in Shandong. The material you used is our patented H_2O, which was purchased from Kunshan Chemical Factory through a longstanding relationship we have maintained. All other materials were purchased from our suppliers, and the proportions of materials purchased match our formula. We know how many times you have made a purchase and how many tons you have purchased. We obtained samples from your products, which are sold to Shulan (Jilin), Tiefa (Tieling, Liaoning), and Wuhai (Inner Mongolia Autonomous Region). We have analyzed them and found that they are identical to our formula. Let's discuss how much compensation you will pay; we will not be too harsh. After all, it's been a business relationship of many years."

I repeated the prepared arguments.

"We obtained the formula through my friends from a subsidiary Research Institute in the Tianjin Hydraulic Pillar Testing Center. The institute is located on Shenyang Avenue, Tianjin. They were engaged in cylinder spraying half a year before you. They now supply to the Zhengzhou Mining Bureau, Qitaihe in Heilongjiang Province,

Shuangyashan, and over a dozen other units. As for the formula, it is largely similar; we did not know whether Tianjin learned from you in Taiyuan or vice versa. Several main materials were the same: corrosion-resistant, wear-resistant, and irreplaceable. We had evidence, but confirming who bought the formula is difficult. The names of workers in state-owned units cannot be disclosed. Let's see how far the lawsuit goes. I could not back down, yet I continued to hold on. If you want to prosecute, I will keep you company."

Unable to continue the discussion, Lawyer Zheng and I went outside for a few minutes after a stalemate and returned to the room.

Lawyer Zheng said, "We'll return to Taiyuan first, report the situation to the institute's managers, and discuss the next steps before we talk again."

Lawyer Zheng concluded, and we gave him an out.

"Goodbye, see you again," we said as we left the room.

The first round ended in a draw; we had to keep going. The other side was a state-owned unit with great power and influence, and I lost the battle. Losing is not only about compensation, but also affects our business. We had to think of a way for the Jinan Intermediate People's Court to cut off Taiyuan's retreat. We strive to avoid going to court and aim for a resolution at the second meeting.

We went to Jinan again, this time with Little Chen. Then, we found his cousin and recounted the situation and discussions with the Taiyuan plaintiffs. We analyzed their attitude and how to respond next.

His cousin said, "The two plaintiffs from Taiyuan came to the Jinan Intermediate People's Court and talked to Judge Zhang. We don't know the details, but Judge Zhang will likely favor us and try to help."

We met Little Chen's cousin this time and paid the lawyer's fees. We could not just talk empty words to ask for Judge Zhang, so we entrusted his cousin to handle it. We treated him to dinner and bought cigarettes and alcohol. No matter how much it costs, the company would reimburse it. We can manage the lawsuit without losing, dragging it out for two or three years, or forcing Taiyuan to withdraw it. His cousin readily agreed to try his best to get the lawsuit withdrawn.

It was Little Chen's cousin's first encounter with an intellectual property case. He had only just begun promoting national intellectual property protection. The legal aspect of this was imperfect and inconsistent in many ways, and the courts were still in the early stages, leaving loopholes to be exploited. The judge's decision played a significant role in the outcome, particularly in determining whether to accept the samples. Taiyuan had already sent samples of our production; whether the court accepts them was another matter. They can come to the factory for samples or determine whether the samples sent from Taiyuan were acceptable; there was plenty of room for maneuvering. We stayed calm, waited for Taiyuan Hydraulic Research Institute to come, and engaged in psychological warfare, beating them mentally. We did not take the initiative; we waited for them to make the first move. Little Chen's cousin spoke confidently with assurance and gained more than the last time we came to Jinan.

Seven days before the Jinan Intermediate People's Court hearing, I received a call from Lawyer Zheng in Taiyuan, asking me to meet at the Zichuan Hotel the next day.

Coming before the court hearing, actively seeking negotiation, and conceding significantly more than the conditions discussed during the first meeting would not be possible otherwise.

Before visiting Zichuan Hotel, I discussed it with my second-youngest brother, director Chen, hoping to settle the matter this time. We all conceded that finding a compromise could not be pushed too far, as we were wrong. We agreed to compromise on a few tens of thousands of yuan. Then we unified our thinking for the meeting.

During the meeting, Lawyer Zheng clarified the institute's viewpoint.

"Whether you admit it's our institute's formula, we are certain it is a fact. You can use the powder produced, but you cannot infringe on our market share or sell it to others. As for who taught the formula from the institute, we have an idea, but cannot confirm it. If we reveal it, no one in the institute will punish the formula leaker, but it will serve as a warning to others not to spread it further. As for the amount of compensation, let's negotiate."

I agreed with the first point about using the powder for personal use. We would not compete with the institute in the market or withdraw from it. As for the Tianjin market, we would take a portion, jointly seizing the Tianjin powder market. As for who guided the production, I was evasive; no one came to teach; they did not have to believe it. If someone were to come to guide me, I could not say it was a matter of character. We would rather spend tens of thousands more than betray friends. Please understand.

"Without saying it, we can guess most of it. It is not hard to guess because three people know the formula. Just want to confirm it," director Zhou said. "To be honest, we visited your factory and home last time. We were there to determine how much money you earn from selling the powder and assess your financial situation to see if you can afford the amount we listed. If you are well-off, we'll come to file a lawsuit with a background. Honestly, the Governor of Shanxi is an old classmate of our institute's director. It would have escalated if our manager had not sought out the institute director. Our manager is reasonable and understanding, and you two have worked well together. Unpleasant incidents happen with mutual understanding. Building a factory is not easy, but destroying one is even more challenging. We do not want both sides to suffer losses. Let's discuss and come to an agreement." Lawyer Zheng, being an intellectual, spoke sincerely. The institute manager listened to him. Unlike the institute's lawyer, who spoke on my behalf, I got along well with him.

"You two are old cadres, knowledgeable and reasonable. You have come to discuss this matter with me twice, and I will not argue anymore. I am willing to handle it immediately and put my main energy into my business. You are a large state-owned unit; I am a small business owner. I will make as many concessions as I can. Let's handle it well and resolve it."

Without discussing relationships, he emphasized the importance of human emotions. As I spoke, I thought today's matter was easier than last.

I deliberately changed the subject and discussed the history of the Zichuan District, the ancient city, Pu Songling, his manuscripts discovered in Shenyang, his current residence, and the Fox Fairy Garden that was built. The two of them were quite absorbed in listening. After I finished talking about Pu Songling and was about to talk about the ancient city's history, Lawyer Zheng interjected.

"Manager Yu spoke wonderfully. Let's get back to the main topic. Up to this point, let's lay our cards on the table. Before coming, we discussed it. Given that our business cooperation has been smooth over the past two years and that we have maintained harmonious relations between our people, we have made a major concession by not pursuing compensation and settling the lawsuit. You will pay off 90,000 yuan owed to the institute. Can you accept this condition?"

It was beyond expectation. Before we arrived at the hotel, I estimated that it would cost between 70,000 and 80,000; if it did not exceed 100,000, we agreed to settle the lawsuit and not prolong it. Dragging on for a few years, we would lose tens of thousands of yuan. The compensation turned into repaying the debt, which I fully accepted. There was no reason not to accept it. Debts must be repaid sooner or later. Refusing to pay is equivalent to defaulting on the account and disregarding professional ethics. This small lawsuit did not happen and ended dramatically.

We signed an agreement that was paid in three installments. Still, we did not remember the exact date, which was the end of December 31, to pay off a total of 91,000 yuan, plus an item that could not be paid on December 31, resulting in double repayment, totaling 182,000 yuan.

After signing the agreement, we solemnly treated the two Taiyuan guests to dinner at the top restaurant in Zichuan, Puquan Grand Hotel. We ordered brand-name dishes: Fotiaoqiang (steamed abalone with shark's fin and fish maw), braised shrimp, steamed rainbow trout, and famous Zibo dishes like suguo (a stew of various foods) and doufuxiang. Appreciating Zibo's liquor culture, we toasted the guests with two cups first, then served them two more shots three times until they were no longer drunk. We returned to the factory with the two Taiyuan guests in a Shenyang Jinbei or Golden Cup van (a van used for both passengers and cargo). Still, I did not remember what time it was. We sealed them with official seals on three copies, then took them back to Taiyuan and stamped them with official seals. One paper would be mailed back. The two would withdraw the lawsuit from the Jinan Intermediate People's Court the next day. It was a small lawsuit with a happy ending.

In the gap of the official seals, Lawyer Zheng spoke a few words to me separately. He would depart from Jinan for Qingdao the next day, while director Zhou would return to Taiyuan. Zheng would stay in Qingdao for two days, then stop in Zichuan district for a day on his way back to Taiyuan to discuss a matter with me. He warned me not to go on business trips and to wait for him at the factory. He saw me drunk and wrote a note and left it on my desk. I was quite puzzled.

6.11 Assembling Hydraulic Props

6.11.1
I pulled a cart loaded with repaired handles and bases across Weishanhu Lake. It was quiet on Weishanhu Lake, where my beloved "pipa" (a traditional Chinese musical instrument) echoed. Reeds stretched endlessly, and fishing boats dotted the waters. I have seen this scene countless times in movies and TV shows. Weishanhu Lake, a place where immortals reside, is in the south of the lower reaches of the Yangze River. But today, as I arrived at Weishanhu Lake and crossed two bridges. Into the lake, there was a large area of barren beach on both sides of the bridge. There was a pond of water, a patch of blue and black, and a patch of yellow. People occasionally saw a group of ducks jumping around. Alas, where is the legendary Weishanhu Lake?

I was delivering handles and bases to Datun Coal Mine for the first time. The Datun Coal Mine's coal machine factory, under the leadership of director Hao in the support workshop, had specifically requested my presence.

The full name of Datun Coal Mine was Shanghai Datun Coal Electricity Company. It was a coal mine built by people from Shanghai, and the coal extracted here was sent to power plants in Shanghai. It was not under the jurisdiction of the Ministry of Coal. I had been doing business with them for over six months, delivering several batches of prop parts. I had made the journey once before, taking a train from Xuzhou and then transferring to a car, accompanied by director Hao from the support workshop. Director Hao was from Shanghai, and his home was on Huangpi Road. When I mentioned that my grandfather worked on Lianyun Road and lived on Longmen Road, director Hao said his home was nearby. It seemed like we were second-hometown folks, which brought us closer. Our first meeting was warm and pleasant, and the business went smoothly. While the salesperson accompanied the delivery, I had not been there until now.

After crossing Weishanhu Lake and entering Jiangsu Province, it took about half an hour to reach the Datun Coal Machine Factory. When we arrived at the gate, it was almost closing time, so we stayed at the guesthouse.

The next day, I went to the workshop to unload the repaired handles and bases and reinstall the old parts. I chatted with director Hao about personal matters before discussing business matters in the office. Director Hao mentioned that the mine had recently achieved a record production, with coal production increasing by 20 percent. As a result, the coal machine factory needed to keep up with improvements to enhance efficiency and add a few new underground accessories. These accessories would be allocated to our workshop for beam and roof support. Although the parts were not large and the process was not complicated, the workload was significant, and there were not enough workers available. Workers could not work overtime every day. Over the past few days, I would have thought their factory could repair oil cylinders, handles, and bases. Why not take a step further and assemble hydraulic props to earn extra money? They could send the major components to us for refurbishment and handle the minor components themselves, such as springs, plungers, and gaskets, by purchasing them directly from the manufacturers. Once the props were assembled, they could be directly delivered to us. So they could save them time and effort while allowing them to earn more. Director Hao's idea intrigued me. I thought it was worth a try.

Director Hao took me to the workshop, where we had an assembly station for props. It was semi-automated with manual operation. There were three or four pieces of equipment and seven or eight workers. Two people lifted the oil cylinder, and two lifted the plunger. One person installed the handle, and another installed the base. It was not complicated. Once assembled, the props were pushed to a testing station for pressure tests. If they passed, a certificate of approval was affixed to their records.

I agreed to director Hao's proposal to try it back in the office. Although I was not confident about assembling props, I knew all beginnings were difficult. Before attempting assembly, we needed to organize the parts and see if the assembly was feasible. I promised to call director Hao back in 10 days.

I returned from Datun Coal Mine, and I could not stop considering whether to proceed with the assembly project. The first step was to consult a technician because technical clearance was essential. Assembling props was not a simple task. It was equivalent to introducing a new product. The second step was establishing a makeshift workshop and investing in several pieces of equipment, which would require considerable money, as this work was done for just one customer, assembling 100 or 200 props a month. Workers worked three days and rested two. They would be challenging due to labor shortages and potential work slowdowns. After pondering for a few days, I still could not decide. So, I decided to talk to the leasing station manager.

I have been doing business with the Zibo Mining Bureau Leasing Station for four years. There have been two changes of station managers during that time. The current manager, Manager Jia, was transferred from Dongli Coal Mine over six months ago. He is two years older than I, and we get along well. I went to him to discuss and seek advice on the situation at Datun Coal Mine. The leasing station had over 80 employees, but it was small, so the manager was not too busy. I did not need to make an appointment in advance to see him.

Manager Jia's office was on the second floor. When I entered, he was sitting at his desk drinking water. "Boss Yu, why do you have time to visit me today? It's been a long time since you last came." Manager Jia hurriedly came to greet me at the door. "Just some free time; I'm dropping by to see you. let's chat." Manager Jia grabbed a cup, poured me some Longjing tea, and then handed me a cup of water. Manager Jia said, "You have not been here in over two months. Have you been busy?" I said, "I cannot come often and do not want to trouble the manager. This month, I went on a business trip to Pingdingshan in Henan Province and Huaibei in Anhui Province. Finally, I sorted out the business there. "There's a problem at Datun Coal Machine Factory. Can you think of a solution?" "Sure, if I can help, I will." The old Datun Coal Machine Factory support workshop props are sent to our factory. The old pillar was dismantled and assembled, and then we tested it and sent it to the whole prop. Is this job easy to do or not? Is this work feasible?" I went straight to the point with Manager Jia.

Manager Jia is straightforward when discussing work matters. "I'm a layman. I do not understand. You should go to the workshop and carefully observe whether it's feasible." "I know you're not an expert, but it's not a technical issue I'm concerned about. I want to understand the investment, equipment, market, and other aspects of the situation." I followed up on Manager Jia's response. "Observing the workshop is easy; you can come anytime you want. I'm considering whether a small factory like mine can do this." As I spoke, two guests entered the office. I could not remember which company they were from. Manager Jia introduced them to director Zhai from Changle Machinery Factory and director Zhong. They were here for business discussions, so I left to visit the assembly workshop.

I had visited the assembly workshop before. But today, I paid more attention. The workshop was approximately 20 meters long and eleven to twelve meters wide, featuring a long workbench in the center. Two people were oiling cylinders, and two were lifting plungers. Someone was measuring handles, and another was examining plungers. Four people were gathered around two assembly machines, installing plungers and handles. It was a semi-automatic manual operation, without the use of automated assembly machines. I walked to the south end of the workshop, where two testing machines were testing assembled props. Workshop director Little Sun greeted me warmly, "Boss Yu, do you come here to guide our work?" "I come here to learn something. Manager Jia's office has guests, so I came out briefly." I chatted with director Sun while waiting for the technician, Little Wang, who had come to find him. "Elder Brother Wang, please tell me which part of the hydraulic prop is the most important?"

"The cylinder and the plunger. If the cylinder has no air holes and the plunger doesn't leak air and can withstand pressure without moving, it's 100 percent good." Little Wang was a technician and an old acquaintance of mine. He supervised the quality testing of repaired cylinders. "I'm going to repair bases for Xinwen Machinery Factory. I'll take the opportunity to discuss assembling props with him." I used the repair of bases as an excuse to invite Little Wang to discuss the assembly of props. Just as we were talking, Office Assistant Little Zhang came to call us for lunch.

At noon, the four factories gathered for a banquet. Manager Jia hosted the event, with director Zhai from Changle Machinery Factory serving as the guest of honor. I, along with director Xin from Tai'an Electroplating Factory, acted as a deputy guest. We were joined by the deputy station manager and the deputy secretary, making a total of eight people at one table. We were all from companies related to hydraulic props. Director Xin from Tai'an was a new client introduced by me. His main business was electroplating, particularly copper plating for cylinders, and he also repaired small components of props. Changle Machinery Factory produced hydraulic props and had been doing business with the leasing station for many years. When the Mining Bureau purchased new props, the leasing station was responsible for inspecting and storing them. Then, we leased them to various coal mines. Director Zhai was talkative and influential in the industry. He shared insider information and industry news. After a few rounds of drinks, we toasted each other and exchanged business cards. I also knew the cadres of a large factory and met a few friends.

6.11.2

On Sunday, director Sun and Technician Little Wang from the assembly workshop were invited to discuss the assembly of hydraulic props. Director Sun mentioned that for small batch assembly, "we did not need to add much equipment. We could make do with the existing lathes and drilling machines. I could only take advantage of poor conditions to do things. It would be labor-intensive for the workers, but they could manage to assemble them. However, for pressure testing, we must use proper equipment. It was the final and most critical step. The testing equipment was expensive, costing tens of thousands for a set. We couldn't afford it since it was only sold in bulk." Little Wang assured us that there were no technical issues. He would ensure the inspection of parts and the measurement of data. Although he understood the assembly process, having not personally done it, he would do his best to assist.

I suggested starting by accepting the batch of props from Datun Coal Mine Machinery Factory and assembling them to the best of our ability. Then, we would explore other coal mines to see if there was a demand for prop assembly. If there were, we would borrow money to buy equipment and establish an assembly workshop. If not, we will stop after completing this batch. Assembling this batch relied heavily on director Sun and his team. Our factory workers were not familiar with the process. Director Sun readily agreed. He planned to start by having a few people dismantle the props on Sunday. Without a proper dismantling machine, they would have to make do with makeshift equipment, which would be labor-intensive and slow.

As for assembly, we would have to rely on traditional methods.

We could assemble a dozen props daily with four or five workers. I promised to pay the workers double wages for their efforts. We could only repair three prop components: the cylinder, handlebar, and base, as director Sun knew. For items like the fire pillar and plunger, two repair shops in Tai'an, Shandong Province, specialize in them. We would send the old parts to them for repairs. As for the seven or eight small components, such as springs, rubber rings, and leather packing, we would discard the old ones and purchase new ones. Director Sun was familiar with the manufacturers, so everything was ready; we just needed to decide and get started.

The final major challenge was conducting the oil injection and pressure testing after assembling the props. The testing equipment cost tens of thousands, which we could not afford. We could only rely on the manufacturers to test the props for us. I believed the problem would be solved if I approached Manager Jia at the leasing station for assistance.

One day, I found Manager Jia and said, "I have a hydraulic prop assembled from old parts that I would like to test for compression on your site. Can you help with this task?" After I finished speaking, Manager Jia pondered for a moment, "I am afraid I cannot help. You are assembling a prop from old parts, and our site also uses old parts for props. If you come to test it here, it will not be easy to differentiate between yours and mine. When dismantling old props from the mine, we may end up with five or seven pieces after taking apart ten; the exact number is uncertain. If you bring one to mix in, troublemakers might fabricate issues. I have two supervisors above me, the factory director and the Production Department leader from the Mining Bureau. If someone complains, who can tell if the prop on the testing platform belongs to you or me? It's difficult, so I can't help with this task." I thought it was simple, but Manager Jia made it seem more complicated: "On Sunday, lock the workshop, leave the testing area separate, and don't mix."

Before I could finish, Manager Jia continued, "In a state-owned factory, decisions are not made by one person alone. It might be allowed if it were your factory. Still, here we have deputy agents, deputy secretaries, and a group of officials, some of whom are related to the bureau leaders or are friends, able to meet with department heads and deputy bureau-level officials. Even if we handle it today as an internal matter, the bureau leaders might find out the next day. I have heard about many such messy situations; this minor matter truly cannot be resolved; I beg your pardon". I was stuck, unable to argue further. "I've got it," Manager Jia muttered to himself, "Changle Machinery Factory produces new props with many test machines. A few days ago, we were dining together. Director Zhai is in charge of production, while director Zhong serves as the workshop manager. You know each other. I'll make a call, and if you go there, you should be able to get it done." I replied, "I will give it a try. If it doesn't work out, I'll think of another solution."

I went to Changle Machinery Factory to discuss testing the hydraulic props on my way to the Beizao Mine in Longkou (a mine in Longkou County in Yantai, Shandong Province). The factory director, Zhai, and director Zhong warmly welcomed me. After I told them my requirements, they readily agreed to assist, and a weight was lifted off my shoulders.

The preparation work for assembling the props had been completed. 100 props were received from Datun Coal Machinery Factory; the old props were removed, and the oil cylinders and handles were quickly repaired within the factory. I went to Sunjiazhuang Village in Tai'an, where I met Boss Sun. About a dozen workers were in a small, authentic village-run factory. Still, they seemed indifferent and not enthusiastic about the order. The first batch of 30 fire props required the salespeople to make two trips and stay overnight before they were pulled back. With the main components ready and the small parts purchased, they were now waiting for director Sun to bring in the personnel for assembly.

There are thirteen coal mines under the Pingdingshan Mining Bureau in Henan province, with an annual output of millions of tons, making it one of the top 10 mining bureaus in the country. After more than a year of business relations, they inquired about assembling props. The Mine Bureau's machinery factory was a subsidiary that repaired props, roof beams, and various parts for underground tunnels. Since they were too busy with maintenance work to care, I wondered if there was a business opportunity for installing props. After finding the factory director, we spent over an hour discussing it. They did not have plans to outsource the assembly of s. Returning from Pingdingshan, I visited the Huaibei Mining Bureau's Machinery Factory in Anhui. The factory directors were aware that they did not have enough work to do and did not outsource assembly. Passing by Xinwen Mine Machinery Factory in Tai'an, Shandong, I went to talk with the directors, finding no opportunities. Returning empty-handed, I finally stopped at Laiwu Coal Machinery Factory in Shandong. When I was about to return to Zibo after seven days, I could not stop thinking about it.

Laiwu Coal Machinery Factory had no business. Still, I knew Engineer Pu and Chief Nian, who were from the same hometown in Zichuan, Zibo, Shandong, as I was. I had sought their advice on technical issues twice before. They had once visited my factory in our hometown. We were not only fellow townspeople but also friends. Over lunch, we discussed the latest and old news in the coal mining machinery industry. I first talked about assembling for Datun Machinery Factory. Elder Brother Pu was an expert in hydraulic technology and was enthusiastic to help with any challenges. Elder Brother Pu grew increasingly enthusiastic as he spoke.

Five years ago, when the technology was quite mysterious, Elder Brother Pu was among the first to learn about maintenance: how to dismantle the old, clean it after dismantling, repair damaged areas, weld, and replate if the coating was lost. These tasks were performed by professional machinery factories, not at the coal mine, where he was only familiar with using them. Over the past few years, Elder Brother Pu has learned all these tasks and can handle them in both large and small factories. He mentioned that assembling old parts was more difficult than assembling new ones, as old parts had been used multiple times. Multiple repairs and wasted time can easily lead to quality issues. Using old hydraulic props may seem convenient, but producing new ones poses no problems. However, the challenge lies in selling them due to the high capital investment required. "If you can secure some funding, I can introduce the new props for you." Elder Brother Pu straightforwardly suggested. "That sounds simple," Chief Nian continued, "If we can get the funding, production will not be an issue. However, the real challenge lies in sales. As a subsidiary of the Mining Bureau and supplier to coal mines, they cannot purchase products from small factories. With the recent decline in the coal industry, the sales of props have been poor." Elder Brother Pu made a valid point: "Introducing a new product will not yield benefits in just a year or two". It is a long-term investment. Things change over time. Who knows, maybe the coal industry will turn around in three years." As the two alternated in speaking, I could only listen and was gapless for a response.

Returning from Laiwu Coal Machinery Factory, the prop components, handles, and bases for Datun Machinery Factory were all repaired, and the small parts were purchased. They were only waiting to bring back the phosphating fire props from Sunjiazhuang Village to begin assembly. They planned to finish assembly in about half a month, conduct testing, and deliver the first batch of props

After returning, I had a recurring dream of hydraulic props being loaded one by one onto trucks. During the day, the image of the new props in the workshop flashed in my mind. I could not shake off the idea of the new props from Laiwu mentioned by Elder Brother Pu. Three days later, I visited Changle Machinery Factory to conduct pressure tests on the props and to inquire about their production and sales.

6.11.3

After purchasing two sets of tableware produced in Zibo, a Jinbei brand van with a double row of seats loaded with 30 props, I visited the Changle Machinery Factory for pressure testing today. I booked it over the phone yesterday; Factory director Zhai and Chief Engineer

Zhong were at the factory.

I arrived at Changle Machinery Factory at 10 o'clock. Chief Engineer Zhong went to the workshop to arrange the testing, while I had tea in factory director Zhai's office. At noon, he was not busy, and we chatted. I indirectly guided factory director Zhai in introducing the production and sales of hydraulic props. The last time we were at the Kunlun Leasing Station, we had divergent ideas due to the cacophony of voices from too many people. Still, today, Factory director Zhai was quite enthusiastic about the detailed explanation of the props.

Changle Machinery Factory was a county-owned factory and a large collective enterprise. It consisted of four workshops: the first for tractors, the second for agricultural machinery, the third for tricycles, and the fourth for hydraulic props, externally referred to as the Changle Machinery Factory Hydraulic Prop Branch. They were planning to establish a fifth workshop to produce jeeps. Hydraulic props had been in production for five years but had not penetrated the market well. They only sold 4,000 to 5,000 props per year. Over the past two years, the company's performance has been unsatisfactory, largely due to the decline in coal sales. Establishing the prop workshop went through many twists and turns. It took more than a year to obtain the production permit. Domestic prop factories were all large state-owned enterprises under the Ministry of Coal, which received a green light to pass wherever they went. County-owned factories were at a disadvantage and had to rely on connections and fabrications to obtain the permit. Without this permit, people dared not buy props in coal mines, and sales were impossible. I had heard that obtaining permits in recent years had become easier, but who would bother with that when the coal mines were in a slump?

I asked about the investment. Since the Factory director, Zhai, personally handled it, he remembered it clearly. They spent a total of just over 1.2 million yuan on the following equipment: two lathes, a grinder, a boring machine, a set of casting equipment, a set of phosphating equipment, a press, a testing machine, and numerous other small pieces of equipment. It was the minimum investment. The monthly output ranged from 400 to 500 units, and they subsequently added several more machines. It was hard to calculate the working capital. It could take two months or half a year to recover the payment, and the output size was uncertain. Factory director Zhai was open to all my questions and showed no concern about my inquiry regarding the market. He just drank tea in his seat and chatted casually. Suddenly remembering an important matter, I said, "I need to go to the workshop to see the arrangement of the hydraulic prop testing." I walked outside. "Sure," he replied. The factory director, Zhai, got up and saw me at the door.

The hydraulic prop workshop was behind the office building. As I entered, Chief Engineer Zhong was talking to two workers on the side. "Chief Zhong, I'd like to visit your workshop and learn something," I said. "Please come in; there's not much to learn," he replied. The workshop is approximately 60 to 70 meters long and 40 to 50 meters wide, with machines arranged sparsely in the center. As we visited, Chief Engineer Zhong explained the processes: cylinder processing here, bore drilling there, this lathe for one end, that lathe for the fire pot, and edge grinding here. When we reached a small furnace, Chief Engineer Zhong stopped. "We just switched to an electric furnace and cast handles on the base; previously, since we used coal, the oil grime couldn't be dissipated out of the workshop. We perform electroplating on the cylinders and apply phosphorization to the fire-stage posts at this facility. They are all done in this workshop, with a metal partition separating the processes. We arrived at a workstation in the east; here, the props were assembled semi-automatically: conveyor belts brought the components over, starting with the cylinder, then the handle, base, and fire post. Once assembled, they undergo pressure testing. If they pass the testing, they're stored; if not, they're disassembled until they meet the requirements, ensuring a hundred percent pass rate." Chief Engineer Zhong concluded that they manufacture major components like cylinders, fire posts, and handle bases.

In contrast, smaller components, such as three-way valves, springs, and rubber rings, are outsourced. Before he could finish, the quitting bell rang. I asked Chief Zhong how the testing of the props was arranged. He said, "We'll finish testing in two days, and you can pick them up the day after."

We returned to the office building with Chief Zhong. The factory director, Zhai, was waiting for us at the door. The factory had a canteen, and director Zhai arranged a sumptuous lunch for us. The topic of hydraulic props dominated the conversation at the banquet. I learned a great deal about hydraulic props during my visit to the Changle Machinery Factory, which expanded my knowledge and horizons.

6.11.4

I returned 30 props from Changle Machinery Factory and will deliver them to Datun Coal Mine the next day. I will accompany the shipment by car. It was the first time I had delivered complete props, so I wanted to hear their feedback: any quality issues, whether the specifications matched, and the main indicators. The testing at the major factory showed no problems. Different manufacturers may focus on minor components, which could be overlooked. If there were any problems, the production would correct them next time. I wanted to understand the assembly of props in the latter half of this year.

It was already after work when I arrived at Datun Coal Mine Machinery Factory. I had dinner with director Hao in the evening and discussed the arrangements for the next day. Pressure testing of the props takes a considerable amount of time. With 30 props, testing one by one would take a day. I could not wait, as I needed to load the props. We would initially test two props. I honestly told them about the testing at Changle Machinery Factory, and there were no quality issues. Director Hao suggested adding 50 more, increasing the quantity gradually. Although he is from Shanghai, his straightforward northern character shines through; he speaks his mind.

The next day, we unloaded the props, and the quality inspector inspected each one, checking if the handle bases were securely installed, the cleanliness of the appearance, and the pressure testing.

While we loaded the props onto the truck and left, they thoroughly inspected each one. After the inspection, the quality inspector concluded that the overall quality was good, and the assembly of various components met the technical requirements; however, the cleanliness did not meet expectations. There were oil stains and grime on the props, which had not been cleaned properly. They requested that we take them back and clean them thoroughly, and they could only accept the items. I stood by the truck, feeling embarrassed. It was our first delivery, and now we had to return them. Besides the transportation cost, it was a blow to our pride. Director Hao noticed my embarrassment and intervened, "We did not clarify things properly first. You are responsible for maintaining the cleanliness of the workshop. I wish this won't happen again, Manager Yu." He saved face for me. The quality inspector remained silent, focusing only on the pressure testing and assembly. I had not cleaned the oil from my hands or the dust from the truck, making the props look dirty. It was nothing like a properly assembled prop. "Next time, we'll ensure they're spotless and dressed in new clothes," I said regretfully. It was a basic oversight; how could I forget about cleanliness?

On the way back, we stopped by the Hongye Coal Machinery Factory in Tengzhou, Zaozhuang, Shandong. There was no business today, so we chatted about the coal mines in the Tengzhou area, their scale, and their annual production, which ranges from tens to hundreds of thousands of tons. In neighboring counties, such as Zouxian and Sishui, there were also county-owned coal mines. I visited a few, but there was not much demand for complete prop repairs. The secretary at Hongye Factory was not in his office, and the factory director, Xing, was at home. We chatted for about half an hour, discussing county-owned local coal mines. Dawu Mine in Tengzhou is the largest, about 20 kilometers from the county seat. Sometimes, unintentional remarks can lead to new opportunities. I decided to visit Dawu Mine.

At Dawu Mine, we found the mine repair workshop. They used props for the entire external repairs. The volume was not significant, around 300 units per month. I proposed offering complete prop repairs, but the price they quoted was only half of what Datun Mine pays. They were using Hongye Mine Machinery Factory's services, and we could not poach their customers. The repair fees they quoted leave no room for profit. We did not discuss it further and left.

Returning from Datun, I could not calm down. Assembling over 100 props per month was not sustainable. Disassembling old props required two workers working with their hands, and they could only disassemble three in a morning. With a prop disassembly machine, they could do fifteen. It used a simple workstation to assemble, with two workers assembling two props in the morning. A regular factory with semi-automatic machines could assemble ten. As a legitimate product, purchasing a disassembly machine, setting up an assembly workstation, acquiring a lathe, and investing in a pressure testing station would cost approximately 300,000 yuan. However, with these additions, producing only 100 monthly props would not be worthwhile. Moreover, pressure testing props could not be a long-term commitment to Changle Machinery Factory.

I must visit more coal mines and explore opportunities for assembly. I could not go to state-owned mines; they had their repair workshops. There were many local coal mines in the province, so I would start with those. Linyi in Shandong had two coal mines; according to the salespeople, they used props for a year before the repairs were made. I visited a Labor Reform Mine in Weishan, Jining, Shandong, where some customers were not expanding, and it was challenging to navigate the procedures for entering and exiting the mine.

The Jinbei van approached Laiwu. On the way back to Zichuan in Zibo, Shandong Province, I must pass by the entrance of the Laiwu Coal Machinery Factory. I stopped by and planned to chat with Elder Brother Pu, brainstorm ideas, and develop solutions. Pu had been in the coal industry for most of his life and was well-versed in its intricacies. Local coal mines were established relatively recently, primarily during the reform and opening-up period in the 1980s. Their equipment was rudimentary, and the costs were economical. It is hard to make money from their mines. State-owned mines had more resources and businesses, and there was profit to be made, considering the benefits of winning, dining, and gifting. Pu advised doing business with large state-owned mines rather than local small ones. Assembling old props was not a long-term solution. If I want to stay in this industry and profit from it, I should focus on producing new props. Without capital, I could borrow or partner with others to achieve my goals.

To get millions of yuan was difficult, but it was also feasible. When we discussed applying for a production permit, I visited the Changle Machinery Factory. Pu was well-connected there since he helped with the paperwork. Factory director Zhai and Chief Zhong were good friends of mine. I accompanied Factory director Zhai to the Tianjin Hydraulic Prop Testing Center to apply for the permit. However, the center can not handle permits for collective enterprises. So we'll go through the provincial Coal Bureau and the Coal Department. It took a year and a half to get the permit. Regarding private enterprises unable to obtain permits, Elder Brother Pu suggested finding a collective enterprise to collaborate with. If we encounter any difficulties, he will lend a hand.

After returning a few days later, the town government held an economic symposium. The directors and managers of the top 10 taxpayers' factories, the secretary, the mayor, the deputy secretary, and a dozen leaders attended. I was one of the leaders in the top 10 enterprises. The secretary began by stating that the symposium would not have a specific agenda, but would instead discuss the economic performance of the first half of the year, plans for the second half, and any difficulties or issues that had been encountered. The government would provide full assistance. He also encouraged sharing excellent products or projects; everyone would work together to promote them. As others spoke, I considered whether to mention hydraulic props. If I did, everyone would chime in, but they were all outsiders who could not offer much help. It would become fodder for their jokes. I decided not to bring it up during the meeting but to discuss it separately with deputy secretary Zeng afterward. After the meeting, I walked to the back and spoke with deputy secretary Zeng about hydraulic props. We arranged to discuss it in detail the next day.

The next day, deputy secretary Zeng came to the office. I explained the hydraulic props in detail. They are used in coal mines to replace wooden props. After the workforce was finished, the props were dismantled after a year or half a year, repaired, and then reassembled for reuse. Shandong had two hydraulic prop factories: the Tai'an Coal Machinery Factory and the Changle Machinery Factory, each producing between 20,000 and 30,000 units annually. There were 106 mining bureaus and thousands of coal mines nationwide, with hundreds of local coal mines operating across the country. They consumed millions of props annually, and the market was promising. Establishing a small-scale factory with one workshop and 10 acres of land, equipped with the necessary equipment, could produce 10,000 props annually, with an estimated investment of approximately 2 million yuan. The key difficulty was obtaining a production permit. Without it, products could not be sold or used in coal mines. The Coal Department reviewed the application and underwent the approval process at the Tianjin Hydraulic Prop Testing Center. Private enterprises could not obtain permits, but collective enterprises can. We discussed the possibility of a joint venture with the town government, with the town holding the majority stake and me holding the minority stake.

Secretary Zeng agreed on the spot that a joint venture was feasible. I would report it at the town's working meeting the next day. The specifics of the joint venture, including its scale and next steps, will be discussed in detail over time. The town government was currently lacking good products. Both the Party Secretary and the mayor would approve of this advice.

I explained that I could not report it immediately because the town government's approval for the product is one thing, but whether we could obtain the production permit is another. I must go to Beijing and Tianjin to see if we can obtain the permit. If we could, then we could discuss the next steps. If not, everything was in vain.

6.11.5

Heading to Beijing and Tianjin to handle the permit, I sought a guide
to lead the way. Vice Chief Wang from the leasing station was an
expert on it. I might contact him since he mentioned he was acquainted
with someone in the hydraulic prop management departments of
Beijing and Tianjin. While on the road inside the leasing station's
factory, I ran into Vice Chief Wang, who was processing internal
retirement. According to regulations from the Mining Bureau, cadres
at or above the section level retire at the age of 55, after which they
still get salaries without working, with the option to continue working
until the age of 60, when they formally retire. During this period, it is
feasible to work or not. When we talked about hydraulic prop work,
Vice Chief Wang was ecstatic. He had long been acquainted with Zou
and Liu, directors of the Coal Department, who managed the property.
They had attended meetings and dined together. They knew a few
people at the Tianjin Prop Testing Center, but were unsure who would
issue the permits. They were eager to assist me with the procedures for
obtaining a permit. One needed a letter of introduction and a reason
to enter the Coal Department. Vice Chief Wang promised to arrange
a letter of introduction from the Mining Bureau, and we planned to
depart the following week.

First, we visited the Tianjin Hydraulic Prop Testing Center to see the
process for obtaining permits. Vice Chief Wang had visited twice and
was familiar with deputy director Zhang and Engineer Wang. On the
day of our visit, director Zhang was out on business while Engineer
Wang was in the office. We explained our purpose to Engineer Wang,
who was talkative and familiar with the permit process. He explained
that approval needed to be obtained from the Coal Department first.
Still, he was not sure of the specific procedures. Once the approval
was secured, we could apply for the permit at the experimental center.
Before applying for the permit, the workshop had to be completed,
and all the necessary machinery for manufacturing hydraulic props
had to be procured. Parts of the props should be processed, and a batch
of props should be finished. Then, a team led by the center's deputy

director, along with several engineers and technicians, conducts an on-site inspection at the applicant's factory. They would inspect whether the workshop met the required standards and whether the machinery could meet the requirements for manufacturing hydraulic props, conducting inspections for each piece of equipment. They would also inspect the materials used for manufacturing the props one by one, including checking the strength of the steel materials, the quality of the components, receipts, and testing reports, to ensure that they met national standards. If they could not confirm on-site, they would return the materials to the testing center for further examination. The second step would involve selecting five manufactured props and sending them to the center for testing compression, acid and alkali resistance, and aging resistance, which would take about three months. If all the tests passed, they would issue a production permit, which would take approximately six months. Engineer Wang provided detailed explanations of the permit process, drawing from his firsthand experience as an on-site inspector and recalling various data. As long as the Coal Department approves, we will obtain the permission, regardless of how long it may take. We should understand the procedures for building the workshop and follow the standards to ensure that the first inspection passes. They could be replaced if the machinery and equipment did not satisfy the requirements. If the materials were subpar, we could switch suppliers. All of these could be solved. Selecting one from five installed props, how could it fail the testing? Obtaining this permit would not be difficult.

The next day, we headed to Beijing. The Coal Department was located on the north side of a main road. I did not remember the exact road, but I knew it was a five-story building with two armed guards at the entrance. There was a room to the right for applying for entry permits. Vice Chief Wang handed over the introduction letter and our work permits. We filled out two forms, one for entering and one for exiting, and kept another for exit.

We found the department we were looking for, the Coal Machinery Division, on the second floor. When we asked for director Zou's office, a staff member led us to the second-to-last room on the right. Director Zou was in his office reviewing documents. When he saw us, he was momentarily surprised. Vice Chief Wang introduced himself, mentioning that he was from the Zibo Mining Bureau and was responsible for props. They had met and dined together at the Zibo Mining Guesthouse last year. Director Zou tapped his forehead, recalling the encounter, and invited us to sit down. Vice Chief Wang pointed at me, introducing me: "This is Mr. Yu, the factory director of Zibo Mining Factory. We have been in business relations for many years. He is a friend of director Xiao and a classmate of deputy director Jiang. We seek your advice on whether a certain product could be produced."

"Please, go ahead," director Zou said, putting down the documents as a staff member brought us two glasses of water. "Mr. Yu's factory produces handlebar bases for hydraulic props, supplying them to Tai'an Coal Machinery Factory and Changle Machinery Factory for many years."

We had prepared these words before coming, referring to the props. "They also produce beams for underground use and pressure pumps. They've been in business for many years." "You're doing a good job. Is your enterprise state-owned or a township enterprise?" I continued, "It's a township enterprise." "Has it been restructured?" Director Zou asked.

"No, it hasn't. The Township Economic Commission directly manages it."

"In several provinces to the south of the Yangtze River, township enterprises are being transformed into private enterprises, which are called private enterprises in new terms." Director Zou remarked. As he worked nationwide, he knew more than us.

It was almost lunchtime, and we had not gotten to the point yet, so Vice Chief Wang quickly interjected, "Director Zou, we are here this time to seek your approval for producing hydraulic props. Mr. Yu's factory has the necessary conditions to produce props. They can start production without any existing workshop and machinery additions."

Director Zou paused for a few seconds, took a sip of water, and said, "Collective enterprises cannot be approved to produce props. All prop production is done by factories subordinate to the department."

Vice Chief Wang interjected, "The Changle Machinery Factory is a county-run factory, a large collective enterprise that has been producing props for four or five years and has been quite successful."

"Five years ago, I wasn't in charge of this area, so I don't know how it was approved. Nowadays, the department's regulations are very strict, and township enterprises aren't approved."

"Can we go through the interpersonal network in the city and get a county-run certificate?"

"Fabricating documents won't work. The reason it has not been approved is that the coal industry has been in decline for the past two to three years. It is the first time since the country's founding that some mines have been shut down partially or completely. With the coal mines in a slump, fewer props are needed naturally. The coal machinery factories are also struggling. There's no reason to approve Tai'an and Changle near Zibo. Township enterprises cannot be approved on a temporary basis. Let's wait two or three years, see how the situation develops, and wait for changes in national policies."

Director Zou glanced at the clock; it was time for us to leave. I said a polite farewell, "Director Zou, we understand. We will not bother you anymore. Thank you. If you pass through Zibo, welcome to enjoy Boshan cuisine."

Exiting the gates of the Coal Department and returning to the hotel, Vice Chief Wang and I continued to discuss today's events. Just a few days ago, I had my mind set on hydraulic props, oblivious to the looming crisis in the coal industry. It was difficult for Zibo Coal Mine to pay salaries, and the entire northeast province was partially shut down. How did I spend the past two months solely focused on props without considering how to sell them and recover the funds? Vice Chief Wang shook his head, "Director Zou enlightened us. Even if it were approved, we would still be unable to do it. The coal industry cannot operate in order within two or three years. I have worked for 30 years and have not encountered this situation before. At Lingzi Mine in the west of Zichuan district, the coal piles are burying the roads. At Bucun Village Mine in the southwest of Zhangqiu, near Jinan, the coal piles are not being watered, leading to spontaneous combustion. At Xiazhuang Village Mine in Zichuan, workers are paid in coal, with five tons allocated per person. Who will buy the props? Let's put this aside now and focus on repairing the existing props."

Vice Chief Wang suddenly realized, "I do not support producing hydraulic props."

After returning from Beijing, I found deputy secretary Zeng. I recounted the events before and after our visit to Tianjin and the Coal Department, providing a detailed account of the experience. This product, hydraulic props, was not allowed by policy; the procedures were not approved, and there was no market, as the coal industry continued to decline. It was not feasible to proceed. Deputy Secretary Zeng understood. We had just started without investment or loss.

The market is unpredictable, and fortunes can change. Two years later, the coal industry experienced a resurgence, with coal prices rising steadily every month. Four years later, in 2002, there was a sudden surge, and coal prices soared from 150 yuan per ton in the 1990s to 800-900 yuan per ton. Demand for hydraulic props rose accordingly. Over a dozen manufacturers of hydraulic props emerged, with seven in Kunlun Town and six in Tai'an in two years. Director Xin supplied plated oil cylinders with an annual output value of 500 million yuan. Director Sun, who had previously worked in a village-run factory, established his prop factory with an annual output value of 300 million yuan. It only took two months to obtain a production permit. With the dissolution of the Coal Department, there was no need for approval. Everyone showed their capabilities.

There is no medicine for regrets, and it is never too late to act. As the saying goes, " Got up early but missed the morning collection. "

6.12 Ringing the Bell to Settle Accounts

6.12.1 Collecting Iron Plates in Huaibei
The Coal Machinery Factory of Huaibei Mining Bureau is located in the northeast corner of Huaibei City. Setting off by truck from Zibo, we take the first right turn after entering Huaibei and will arrive there. I made the acquaintance with Manager Lin of the coal machinery factory at a banquet in Longkou Beizao Coal Mine. Since we were seated close, it was convenient to conduct a conversation. Director Lin was very interested in the repair of hydraulic pillar oil cylinders using spraying technology. We made an appointment to bring some sprayed cylinders to Huaibei Machinery Factory for a trial installation. Upon returning from Beizao Coal Mine, we loaded 50 repaired oil cylinders onto a truck and headed to Huaibei Coal Machinery Factory.

When we arrived in Huaibei, it was already past six o'clock in the evening. We checked into a hotel and were about to visit director Lin the next day. Director Lin was the head of the pillar division of the General Factory, overseeing one workshop. A workshop manager was present in the workshop, and director Lin was in charge externally. When the truck entered the workshop, director Lin, the quality inspector, and two team leaders gathered to inspect the new oil cylinders. "They're shiny and in good condition," someone remarked. After the quality inspection by the quality inspector, which included measuring the inner diameter and checking the smoothness, all 50 cylinders were deemed qualified and unloaded. They would be installed on pillars later in the day. In this workshop, using traditional repair methods, only 50 percent of the old oil cylinders could be reused, with the rest treated as scrap steel. With spraying technology, over 90 percent of the damage could be repaired, resulting in significant cost savings. The workshop operated under a contracting-out system. We signed the contract at noon, agreeing that the cylinders would be used underground for six months without bubbling, peeling, or coating loss, with no issues for one or two years. The price per cylinder was five yuan higher than Zibo's, but the round-trip transportation costs were covered. We brought back 100 cylinders. After three months of underground testing, business operations were normal. We used medium-sized trucks to transport either 300 or 200 cylinders per trip, maintaining normal business operations.

Business went smoothly for two years. In November 1996, director Lin sent a letter through a salesperson, inviting me to accompany the next oil cylinder delivery. I went to Huaibei Coal Machinery Factory with the oil cylinder delivery truck a few days later. After unloading the new cylinders and reloading the old cylinders, director Lin would not let me return with the truck. Instead, he invited me to stay for an extra day. That evening, we went to a wild game restaurant on the outskirts to enjoy a drink, where we savored a variety of wild delicacies, including stewed wild pheasant, braised pheasant, and roasted wild rabbit.

Since director Lin was at his office in the afternoon, he invited me to discuss a matter with him. A few days earlier, a senior leader from the Zibo Mining Bureau had mentioned that a factory in Huaibei was under construction to adopt a new technology for lining oil cylinders in Taigu County, Shanxi Province. The factory director visited two days ago, mentioning that their equipment would be operational in December. The senior leader specifically requested the adoption of the new technology, leaving no room for refusal. Afterward, there was gossip that the factory director responsible for lining the cylinders was a relative of a bureau chief. Director Lin apologized, acknowledging our excellent cooperation and the absence of any quality incidents. He felt uneasy about suddenly discontinuing it. But we could continue collaborating on other components of the pillar.

The lining of the oil cylinders was postponed until March of the following year, when we could supply to Huaibei Coal Machinery Factory. My sprayed oil cylinders ceased supply in May, and the accounts were settled, with 63,000 yuan owed for processing fees. Director Lin promised to pay in installments, with the full amount paid by the end of the year.

Director Lin was a straightforward person, very decent, and

promoted leaders from the workshop. He had never accepted bribes or gift cards. If he received anything, it would be left outside the door. For local specialties like Zibo porcelain tableware, which is worth around 100 yuan, he would accept one or two pieces. Our business relationship was very harmonious. Although he ended our cooperation, the General Factory would make the final decision, and he could not afford to do so. After two months, the continued decline of the coal industry made funds even tighter.

Director Lin tried many ways to resolve the payment, but it could not be done. He called me to his office to discuss it. Straightforwardly, he told me they could not pay now, and the workers had not received wages for two months. The General Factory had a batch of iron plates that could pay the debt. If we could accept it, they would settle the payment at once. The price would be whatever they paid for it, without markup. Director Lin took me to the warehouse to inspect it. The plates were suitable, so we completed the paperwork that afternoon, and the delivery would be made in the coming days.

They remained unsold after returning the iron plates and stacking them in the yard. Some engineers from Taiyuan saw them and thought they were suitable for making water heaters. Several months later, they were transformed into water heaters. I detailed this extensively in Chapter 7.

6.12.2 Obtaining the Truck in Pingdingshan

The processing capacity for spray oil cylinders has improved rapidly, from an initial 400 per month to over 1,000 per month, and we can now easily handle up to 1,500 per month. With the supply unable to meet production demands, my uncle-in-law, Sun, and I sought business opportunities. We invited Section Chief Sun to write a letter of introduction on our behalf. We went to the Pillar Repair Branch of the Zhengzhou Mining Bureau. They were unfamiliar with the technology of spray oil cylinders and paid no attention to us. After treating us to lunch, they politely sent us on our way.

Since our visit could not be in vain, we headed to the Pingdingshan

Mining Bureau, which is closer to Zhengzhou. After visiting the Shaolin Temple, we set off for Pingdingshan.

We identified the Hydraulic Pillar Repair Factory, which is affiliated with the Pingdingshan Mining Bureau. The Mining Bureau did not directly manage this factory. Still, it was operated by a labor service company run by a collective of workers. With the reform and opening up, many cadre family members working in coal mines had transitioned to urban residents. They were encouraged to set up factories if they could not find jobs in cities. Many cadre descendants who were unable to gain admission to junior colleges or technical secondary schools stayed at home and remained unemployed until they were temporarily employed as workers in factories owned by family members, with management cadre members transferred from various departments of the Mining Bureau. After finding the office, we met with director Qi, who had just been transferred from the Mining Bureau Newspaper less than a month ago. Director Qi had been working at the newspaper for 20 years. He was now appointed as the director of the repair factory. He seemed a bit confused about the situation.

After obtaining a university degree, director Qi was assigned to the Mining Bureau Newspaper. He enjoyed discussing history and literature. Although I did not have much formal education, I could still keep up with the conversation. After chatting about various topics for over an hour, we finally got to the point and discussed the hydraulic pillar oil cylinders. Director Qi was unable to grasp the concept, so he called deputy director Zhuang, who was in charge of production and technology. Deputy director Zhuang understood immediately. He had heard of this technology and was familiar with the process. He assured us they would try it since we came from Shandong and sounded confident. If the quality was good, they could collaborate with us. Sparing no effort in searching for it, after just a few minutes of discussion, the deputy director agreed to give it a try, and director Qi immediately approved. He asked us to send 10 samples. If the trial installation were successful, they would start replacing old oil cylinders, and business would commence.

Two months after the trial installation, director Qi called us to say they were ready to receive a truckload. We arranged for a liberation truck. My uncle-in-law, Sun, took two workers to Pingdingshan and returned 250 old oil cylinders.

We made four deliveries in two months, and the quality feedback was excellent. The pillars could be used underground, and the processing fees were paid promptly. However, during the last delivery, deputy director Zhuang said they needed to pause temporarily and wait for further instructions. It was normal for business relationships to encounter setbacks, so we waited a month without receiving any notification. Our salesperson then went to Pingdingshan and learned that the factory had already installed spray equipment and was about to start production. Our salesperson learned the message from a technician whom he knew. It dawned on us that when we visited two months earlier, they had already ordered the equipment and used our products for testing. As a result, the testing was qualified, which accelerated their process.

We made two more deliveries, and deputy director Zhuang provided an explicit explanation, announcing that the business was now closed.

During the six months of business dealings, I visited the deputy director twice and briefly. The impression was not deep. However, according to my uncle-in-law, Sun, the small factory had around 40 to 50 employees, and the leaders had intense internal strife. Director Qi had his faction, and deputy director Zhuang had his. The latter was more knowledgeable about business and held real power. Director Qi had connections within the bureau and was responsible for its finances. I got along well with director Qi, with whom I had meals twice, and deputy director Zhuang was aware of it, which might have influenced the outcome.

After concluding the business, we owed a repair fee of 52,000 yuan. Director Qi agreed to pay it in two installments. Still, the deputy director Zhuang found fault deliberately and refused to process it. It was dragged out until the end of the year. Deputy director Zhuang assumed his position when director Qi was transferred elsewhere. I visited him once, but he was not in the office at the time. After waiting for a day with no sign of him, I finally found his dormitory with exquisite Zibo tableware in the evening. However, he refused to meet me.

The Taiyuan Hydraulic Research Institute organized an annual conference, inviting equipment purchasers and powder coating manufacturers. Factory directors and managers were taken to Wutai Mountain for sightseeing. During the conference, I met director Zhuang from Pingdingshan. At the evening banquet, I seized the opportunity to sit at the same table as director Zhuang. After a few cups of liquor, director Zhuang became talkative and animated. I had no chance to interject. After the banquet, I drunkenly grabbed director Zhuang for a photo. The next day, we visited Pingdingshan, and we became friends. We exchanged greetings from time to time. Regarding business, he agreed to settle the outstanding repair fees.

Before the Spring Festival, my uncle-in-law Sun and I went to Pingdingshan again. This time, as soon as we entered the factory gate, director Zhuang spotted us and warmly welcomed us into his office. He accepted the high-end tableware we brought and invited us to dinner that evening to discuss the payment arrangements for the next day.

The next day, we negotiated the payment in director Zhuang's office. First, he briefed us on the current situation of the Mining Bureau. With the decline in coal production, wages could not be paid on time, making it difficult to settle debts. The repair fees owed by various mines for pillar repairs were also outstanding. Pingdingshan Mine No. 8 had a Jiefang truck, which was half-new. Taking over the truck would cover part of the debt, and the remaining amount could be paid off over time. We went to see the truck before finalizing the price.

Pingdingshan Mining Bureau had twelve coal mines. A narrow-gauge train with passenger carriages ran past here. It was smaller than regular trains, making it convenient to visit various mines. Director Zhuang assigned the office director to take us to Mine No. 8 to inspect the truck. The fare for buying tickets on the bus was five mao each, regardless of the number of stops. Workers with commuter cards did not need to buy tickets. It took about half an hour to reach Mine No. 8, and the station was close to the mine. The truck was parked behind the mine office building. The director found the head of the transportation team. The head stated that the truck had been in operation for five years, transporting goods between various mines. Due to the downturn in the coal industry this year, it was no longer needed. It was still in good condition since it had not been used for long-distance trips. The head started the car and drove around in a circle for a dozen meters.

When we returned from No. 8 Mine, it was not yet time to clock out. Director Zhuang was waiting for us in his office. We wrote off 30,000 yuan for the truck, and the remaining amount would be paid by check in one lump sum. Director Zhuang was straightforward in his approach, which I appreciated. I estimated that selling the truck back would not cost much money, but it would help clear all the debts. It was a good outcome. I agreed to the director's suggestion for handling the business relationship.

The next day, we received all the documents and keys for the truck and settled the payment in the afternoon. When we returned, I assigned the driver to transfer the account and drive the car. To date, our business dealings with the Pingdingshan Mining Bureau have been successfully concluded.

6.12.3 Obtaining the Triple-Function Valves in Xinwen

Station chief Wang, whom I had greeted before his retirement, became a consultant in our factory after he retired. After completing his retirement formalities, he started working. His schedule was flexible: he could come to work whenever there was an event without limitation on attendance time. On this particular day, we had arranged to visit the Suncun Mine Repair Plant in Xinwen. Station chief Wang was responsible for this task, which involved repairing the handles and bases of hydraulic props. We had been doing business with them for over a year, but it was not smooth sailing. We took a long-distance bus from Boshan to Laiwu and then transferred to another bus. When we arrived at Suncun Village, it was around 11:00 a.m.

We went to the repair plant in the afternoon, but the Director was not in his office. I had only been there once before, so I was not familiar with the director. It was a small plant with about 40 employees, and the director had the final say. Station chief Wang and I toured the workshop and waited until the director returned around 3:00 p.m.. In front of me, he reprimanded station chief Wang, stating that the handles we had sent last time had quality issues. The repair fees could not be recovered when they were sent to the mine for repairs. The quality was unstable. Station chief Wang could not interrupt him. Now that the business was not going smoothly, they settled the accounts and discussed further business matters later. The director agreed to settle the accounts the next morning with the accountant. After leaving the office, Station chief Wang cursed, "This guy is hard to deal with. Every time we deliver goods, he deliberately finds fault with them. After settling the accounts the next day, I will resign and find a better job."

As we left the factory gate and headed towards the hotel along the road, we saw three policemen standing by the roadside checking for licenses and license plates for motorcycles. We walked about 30 meters along the road and saw two policemen standing in the middle, each holding a whip and walking back and forth on the road. We stopped to see what they were doing. Shortly after, a motorcycle sped down the road, and one of the police officers with the whip rushed forward, took a few quick steps, and lashed the driver with the whip. The young man riding the motorcycle leaned forward, and the whip struck his back. The motorcycle wobbled, getting out about 20 meters, and crashed by the roadside. The policeman chased after it, but before he could catch it, the young man quickly picked up the motorcycle and fled. It was like an excellent close-up view in movies, but it was reality, not a movie.

We realized that the three policemen ahead were the first checkpoint. As the police officers waved their hands to signal a stop for inspection, obedient drivers pulled over. In contrast, bold drivers rushed through without hesitation. The two policemen were at the second checkpoint. When the bold drivers from the first checkpoint arrived, the police officers would point them with the whip, and then they would stop. If someone had been even bolder, they slowed down as if to stop, and then suddenly accelerated past the police. If they were whipped accurately, they must fall half-dead.

We discussed the scene we witnessed in the afternoon for a long time during dinner. Recalling law enforcement in the 1990s, it was not much different from the current situation in the United States, where police deal with African Americans.

The next day, we went to the repair plant to settle the accounts with the director. The repair fee owed was 33,000 yuan, which was paid in full. We were happy, but the director said, "We do not have the cash, so we'll use parts to cover the bill! We have a batch of triple-function valves, brand new, and we'll give them to you at the original price to clear the debt." There was no room for negotiation, and further delay would make resolution difficult.

We were taken to the warehouse by the warehouse keeper to inspect the triple-function valves. Station chief Wang, being knowledgeable in this field, picked up two and examined them. It was impossible to repair old triple-function valves to meet the quality standards. If sold, they would only be worth half the price.

Back in the office, the director insisted on using the price of new triple-function valves to settle the account. What could we do if we disagreed? Next time, they might offer even worse parts than triple-function valves. Reluctantly, we agreed to settle the account. However, we would take whatever we could salvage from the triple-function valves, even if it were only worth 3,000 yuan.

The triple-function valves had been in the warehouse for over three months without being sold. They were now just a pile of scrap iron, rusting away. During a gathering with old friends, I met director Chen from the Mining Bureau. Halfway through the drinks, I remembered the triple-function valves and handed over the problem to him, my old friend.

Chen was three years younger than I, and we were old family friends. We lived about 50 meters apart in our hometown. Since we took our respective jobs, we have met less frequently. However, we still had a lot to discuss when we got together a few times a year. He had worked his way up from an ordinary worker, with each step bringing him closer to success. His father was also an ordinary worker with no connections, relying solely on his ability. From an accountant in a coal mine to the director of the Audit Office of the Mining Bureau, he had worked diligently, adhering to his principles and demonstrating good business acumen. When it came to triple-function valves, director Chen had no idea about what they were.

After explaining it twice, he understood that these were parts for hydraulic props used in the mines. They could be dismantled underground, repaired, and reused on the pillars. He assured us that this batch was guaranteed to be in use. Since it was a minor matter, the bureau could not intervene directly. But it should not be ignored, even if it was not easy to help. After a few drinks, the decision was made to proceed, with or without official support. With the bonds of friendship and loyalty strengthened by alcohol, it was a good decision indeed. After three cups of wine, we stopped discussing and agreed to take action. It was decided: it would be done.

After rechecking the triple-function valves and making necessary repairs, they were sent to a coal mine and sold at the original price. We did not incur any losses and successfully cleared the debt.

6.12.4 Obtaining Coal Tickets in Feicheng

I received a call from Manager Gu, the manager of the pillar division at Feicheng Mining Bureau's Machinery Factory, instructing me to settle the payment the following day. Manager Gu was efficient and reliable, consistently keeping his promises throughout our two-year dealings. Every time goods were delivered, cash or checks were arranged promptly and kept in the drawer. If anything were difficult for us to do, Gu would help us solve it upon our first visit. It was seldom to find someone like him to help us in large state-owned factories.

Supplying powder coating to the Feicheng Pillar Division Factory for spraying, at a rate of half a ton per month, was a standard practice, with prices set accordingly. Manager Gu was the sole authority for delivery and payment. The deputy manager was only responsible for workshop production, with no involvement in external business, pricing, or delivery quantities. At lunchtime, he was accompanied only by drinks, and his business ran smoothly.

Due to the powder coating issue, we had a legal dispute with the Taiyuan Hydraulic Research Institute. After the lawsuit was settled, a slight adjustment was made to the formula: the original grinding powder was replaced with quartz powder, which showed no difference in experiments. The assembled pillars did not have any quality issues. After the formula change, we delivered half a ton to Feicheng. During its use, workers reported that the oil cylinders sprayed with the powder were harder to grind on the grinder, taking several minutes longer than before. During the second delivery, I accompanied the delivery to discuss the situation with Manager Gu and the deputy manager. The workers reported that the hardness was greater than before and the grinding time was longer, but there were no other issues. I suggested that there might be a problem with the purchased materials without mentioning the formula change, knowing it myself.

A month later, the salesperson returned from delivery, stating that a new deputy director in charge of outward business had taken his position. We must follow his arrangement when we delivered the powder there next time. Manager Gu was solely responsible for payment. According to the factory manager, the new deputy director was about to take over from Manager Gu.

When this batch of powder was not used up, the bad news came that quality issues had arisen. I hurried to the workshop, where five oil cylinders were stored, surrounded by Manager Gu, two deputy managers, and a quality inspector. The inspector used a flashlight to examine the inner wall of the oil cylinders and found fine hairline cracks. The deputy manager explained that this issue had never occurred before, and the grinding strips had been checked and found to be in good condition. Not every strip had cracks; sometimes, only one strip out of a day's production had one crack, and the previous day's shift had produced two. Various reasons were analyzed, but I understood that the problem lay with the quartz sand, and I was unable to reveal it. I immediately stated that all wasted powder and labor costs would be compensated, unused powder would be returned, and new powder would be provided. I ensured there would be no further issues.

However, the returned powder still resulted in two oil cylinders with fine cracks. The new deputy manager contacted a powder factory in Tianjin and sent half a ton there. Manager Gu wanted to help, but could not; the new deputy manager was preparing to take over and was quite assertive, effectively ending our business relationship.

In Manager Gu's office, we spent a considerable amount of time talking. After two years of business, our relationship was cordial, marked by mutual understanding and apologies, but we ultimately had to part ways. The 80,000 yuan owed would be paid back before Manager Gu retired. At last month's Mining Bureau meeting, all unit leaders and financial personnel attended. It was decided that external business transactions would no longer be settled with cash but with coal tickets from any coal mine. According to the deputy manager, my payment would be split into two installments. However, Manager Gu disagreed and prioritized my payment over others, settling it all at once.

Yangzhuang Coal Mine had good-quality coal, making it easy to sell. Manager Gu arranged for coal tickets from Yangzhuang Mine. To cover 85,000 yuan owed, he issued three tickets. It was considered easier to sell three than one; having one ticket might pose difficulties. Manager Gu explained in detail that two brokers at the entrance of Yangzhuang Mine's sales office specialized in buying coal tickets on credit, deducting 15 percent or 20 percent of the total amount. Negotiations had to be gradually settled to ensure the buyers were not scammers who might easily agree on a fair price. Then, they would exchange cash and tickets at the bank simultaneously.

I had a fellow villager in the Yangzhuang Coal Mine. I found him, and he knew the deputy sales manager at the sales office, who, in turn, had an external salesperson. With one phone call, the external salesperson arrived in 10 minutes and accepted the three tickets at the highest price, with a 15 percent transaction fee. Then my fellow villager and I chatted in the office while drinking tea. Within an hour, the external salesperson returned with a bag of cash, counted it in front of us, and handed it over to my bag.

Now, looking back, the business in Feicheng was possible.

6.12.5 Obtaining the Agreement Signing in Kunlun

A military factory in Taigu transitioned to civilian products and developed a new technology for lining oil cylinders. Using the method of making artillery shell casings, they produced iron barrels two sheets thick, which were then rolled onto the inner diameter of the oil cylinder and coated with a rust inhibitor. This method, simpler than spraying, saved half the cost and replaced the traditional one. The leaders of Zimining instructed the leasing station to adopt this new technology. The leasing station had already adopted the spraying method, causing dust to fly during oil cylinder sanding. Workers wore gas masks and used kerosene to cool down, resulting in a messy mixture of oil and water on the floor, as well as a harsh working environment. This dirty and tiring work, coupled with the communal dining and the lack of guaranteed job security, made workers reluctant to work. With the new technology, oil cylinder lining and iron barrel rolling were completed, and a professional factory did the final coating. Under pressure from the leaders, the workers were willing to cooperate.

Within two months, the oil cylinder lining process at the leasing station was put into production. My supply of sprayed oil cylinders ended three months later, at the end of 1996. Since 1991, we had cooperated for six years, during which the relationship between departments was good. However, I had only met the factory director once since he had arrived a year ago. After settling the accounts, I owed him 250,000 yuan in processing fees, the largest receivable in our small factory, which had around 20 employees. In previous years, the leasing station's finances had been independent, and the station chief could arrange processing fees. However, with the arrival of the new factory director, financial matters were centralized, and all payments had to be approved by him. If he did not approve, not a single yuan could be obtained.

I went to see the factory director for the payment. As soon as I knocked on his office door, the office manager blocked my way, went inside to inquire, and came back to say there was a meeting at noon, and no visitors were allowed. On my second visit, I went to the finance department first, and the head of the department went to the factory director's office and came back saying that he was about to leave. I discussed my thoughts with the head of the department, taking into account the factory's financial difficulties, and the payment was not rushed. I suggested meeting the director face-to-face to discuss the payment plan in installments over time. Blocking us outside the door, with no end in sight, the director of a large factory could not behave in this impolite way. The head of the finance department shook his head without saying a word and saw me to the door, whispering, "Find another way."

I had known the head of the finance department for four or five years, having shared meals twice through an old friend, director Chen, at the Mining Bureau, which broke the rules by allowing a single payment. We got on well with each other, but the regulations changed with the arrival of the new factory director. His words had a hidden meaning when he said to find another way. What other way? Through legal means, going to court with the help of my old friend.

Elder Brother Qin worked in the court. We had known each other for over 20 years. In the 1970s, we met when we were both private teachers. In the 1980s, he transitioned from the school to the court, becoming a judge, and our relationship continued. I asked him about it, and he said he was the chief judge in Zhangzhuang Town and could handle cases independently within his jurisdiction. I explained the situation regarding the debt owed by the leasing station in detail, based on six years of business relations, using only the account books, with no other receipts, bills, or agreements. Although there was no clear evidence, the account books provided some insight. If we opened a court session, they might deliberately delay the trial and mess up the account in six years. Holding two court sessions would take half a year. We needed to get a promissory note, but they certainly would not write one. My old friend said a statement of account would suffice, just as effective as a promissory note, serving as evidence. We could find a way to get a statement of account with a suitable excuse.

I approached Kang, the director of the town government audit office. I told him the truth, asking for help in obtaining the payment. We obtained a statement of account using the excuse of auditing village-run enterprises. Our factory's business license had a red hat imprinted as a "village-run enterprise." Sending someone else to impersonate an auditor might lead to inaccuracies in professional terms. It could easily expose us, so I asked director Kang to go, which would be legitimate and ensure success. Before going, I communicated with the head of the finance department. However, I did not explicitly state it, making my intentions clear. The accountant accompanied Kang, and the department head gave the green light to pass, allowing the statement of account to be processed without the director's approval. We successfully obtained it.

Without serving a summons before the trial, the court had the right to freeze the defendant's bank account when the defendant was unaware. One day, a friend from inside the bank called to inform me that 300,000 yuan had been transferred to the factory's account that afternoon. I immediately informed my old friend at the court, suggesting that the next day, as soon as the bank opened for business, the account must be frozen. I took the chief judge and another judge to the bank. We arrived at the bank within 10 minutes of opening. As we went to the manager's office, the judges presented the authorization letter explaining the reason for the account freeze. The manager was very polite. When offered Longjing tea and handed Taishan cigarettes, he said, "Just started work; let me sort out the accounts first, and then do it." He went to the back office. After sitting for about a dozen minutes, the bank manager returned from the counter, saying, "We can proceed now." The two judges went to the counter, and the bank manager stayed and drank tea with me. A few minutes later, the judges returned, saying, "The account is frozen, and there's no money in it." As the judges were unaware of the internal report, I could not mention it in front of the bank manager. When we left the manager's office, I called my old friend, "The 300,000 yuan in the factory's account has been transferred out. Please come immediately." A few minutes later, my old friend, the chief judge, arrived and went to the bank manager's office. He said firmly, "We know very well what is going on. There was money in the factory's account, but now it is gone. You just started work, and how did you transfer it? Investigate it thoroughly."

The bank manager said, "I don't know, let's check in the counter room." The chief judge followed him into the counter room, and I followed behind. The cashier took out the transfer slip. "It was transferred yesterday, and there's only 115 yuan left in the account." Transfer slips were handwritten, with random dates, and both sides had insiders. The chief judge was angry, shouting in front of the bank manager, "Whoever received the account freezing notice and transferred money without authorization, I will investigate it at the head office and deal with it legally." But it was useless. There were clear rules back then, as well as latent rules.

In the No. 2 courtroom of Zichuan Court, both the original defendant and I arrived, along with Wang, the accountant, and the deputy station chief, Liu, and the office director, Wang, who were now defendants. The four of us smiled and shook hands, having had business relations and friendship in the past, but today, we were all in court together. The presiding judge asked deputy station chief Liu, "Is your factory owed 250,000 yuan in payments to the mine repair factory? Did you write the statement?" "Yes, the debt on the statement of account is entirely correct, but it's very difficult to repay now. The workers' wages cannot be paid. Could we postpone it a bit? Give us some time." Deputy station chief Liu's attitude was sincere, and the presiding judge continued, "You two should negotiate and come up with a repayment plan. Once the plaintiff agrees, seal it with a stamp to make it effective."

"I'll strive to pay it off in three months, in three installments." Deputy station chief Liu put aside his usual demeanor as deputy station chief, took my hand, and said, "old relationships, old business, old friends. Please postpone it and get through this difficult time. Do me the honor, and I'll be able to report back." I compromised for six months, but deputy station chief Liu still did not agree. I pretended to leave. "What you say doesn't matter; you don't have the final say. Let's settle it in court next time." Deputy station chief Liu stood up to block me, "When I came, the factory director instructed me to talk to you about our factory's difficulties. Please understand. I promise to repay it all within a year." Deputy station chief Liu reluctantly revealed his bottom line.

The presiding judge signaled me to approach, and I did. "If we have another court session, there are two months away. It won't make much difference, just a few months away from six months, and we can sign the agreement happily, leaving it at a year." My old friend told me this, and it made sense. To give deputy station chief Liu some face, we signed the agreement.

Deputy station chief Liu was prepared, and the agreement was ready, with only blank spaces for repayment dates and amounts to be filled in and signed by both parties. Once we filled it out and signed, the clerk took it to be stamped. After six years of business, it all came to a cheerful conclusion with the signing of a business agreement.

6.12.6 Circular Steel Collection in Shanjialin

Deputy director Wang was acquainted with the director of the Shanjialin Coal Mine Machinery Factory. They had been friends for many years. When Wang had retired and joined our factory, his official title was consultant. However, our small factory had little to employ consultants and do business. He therefore reached out to the Xinwen Coal Machinery Factory and visited the Shanjialin Machinery Factory in Zaozhuang. Shanjialin needed maintenance support, and out of consideration for our longstanding friendship, they allowed us to take on part of the work, specifically repairing the base. Business went smoothly for over a year. However, when a new director took over the factory, things changed. Unsure of how to proceed, Elder Brother Wang and I decided to go to the factory to assess the situation.

A few days ago, Elder Brother Wang went there, only to find out that the old factory director had been transferred due to approaching retirement, replaced by a new director. The new director took a lukewarm attitude, and they only allowed us to repair the base. Without handles, the profit margin was already low. With further reductions in quantity, it was no longer worthwhile to continue the business. Rather than wait to be dismissed, we decided it was better to terminate the business early. Elder Brother Wang and I agreed to visit Shanjialin Machinery Factory to terminate the business and settle the accounts.

Over the past year, we had conducted repair business totaling over 80,000 yuan. We had been paid 50,000 yuan in installments, but were still owed 36,000 yuan. After settling the accounts, the new factory director was vague about when payment would be made, possibly in a few days, citing financial constraints. The Mining Bureau had some round steel available to be distributed to each factory to offset the accounts; if we agreed, the transaction could be completed in a few days. Although the amount was not substantial, chasing after payments incurred us a few thousand yuan in travel expenses. We decided to accept the round steel. The factory director agreed to settle the account in a single payment. We decided to visit the Mining Bureau warehouse, where we found various types of round steel. We needed to select the steel with the best sales potential as quickly as possible.

That afternoon, we went to the Zaozhuang Mining Bureau warehouse. We presented a letter of introduction from the Shanjialin Machinery Factory. The warehouse keeper opened the door of the warehouse. The warehouse was vast, with a large outdoor area filled with a variety of materials. After explaining our situation, we were led to the area with the round steel. He indicated several available types. I took note of the manufacturers and models, including A18, B20, and 22, among others. These were used for electrical porcelain components. So we decided to ask the electric porcelain accessories factory which models were available.

Upon returning, we contacted Zhao, the director of the electrical porcelain accessories factory. We introduced the manufacturers, models, and types of round steel. We explained that those were large, state-owned factory products of high quality. There were about 20 tons. We asked if they could accept them. He was willing to accept them, like Hanxin assigned soldiers, as much as possible. He specified that they needed types 20 and 22.

A couple of years younger than me, Zhao graduated from school in 1966 and became a member of the commune. On the other hand, I had graduated from junior high school in 1968. I then returned to society, becoming a member of a communal living arrangement. The team leader had asked us to walk cattle on my first day of work. The production team gelded a cattle, and the newly gelded cattle could not lie down and had to keep walking. We were young and inexperienced. We took over the cattle at noon and handed them to the keeper, Grandpa Zhao, at midnight. We had no watch at the time, so we estimated the time approximately. Then we went home to check the time, and the factory director, Zhao, called the old keeper after midnight. I led the cattle back and forth from the feedlot to the keeper's door.

Director Zhao stood at the keeper's door, knocked, and called, "Grandpa Zhao, Grandpa Zhao."

There was a reply, "I heard."

No longer called, standing at the door, about half an hour later, Grandpa Zhao had not gone out.

Director Zhao knocked on the door and called again, "Grandpa Zhao, Grandpa Zhao."

"Wait a moment. I'm coming."

More than an hour out, it had been half past one. Walking the cattle took seven days; in the last two days, Grandpa Zhao was called twice but did not come out. Director Zhao unlatched the big door and quietly entered. Looking through the crack in the door, Grandpa Zhao was drinking from a wine cup. Grandpa Zhao was moody; to the younger generation, he beat and scolded, and even the captain was somewhat afraid of him — no more screaming. After more than two hours, he was coming out to take our class. Zhao was accommodating, agreeing to take the steel and emphasizing the need for prompt payment. Wang went to Shanjialin to settle the accounts, aiming for a quick and efficient resolution to our business with Shanjialin Machinery Factory.

6.12.7 Cash Collection in Yima

Little Tian, a business representative from the Yima Mining Bureau Support Maintenance Factory, called to inform me that he would be going to Weifang on a business trip. And on his way to Zibo, we arranged to meet in my office at the agreed-upon time. Little Tian arrived with a friend, and we spent the afternoon touring Pu Songling's Former Residence, a national-level scenic spot in Zichuan. After our tour, we had lunch at the Liaozhai Restaurant in Pujiazhuang, where we toured the hometown of Pu Songling, enjoyed local food, and had a great time.

At the dinner table, we discussed business with the Yima support maintenance factory. Little Tian informed me that the support maintenance factory had stopped production for three to four months due to a sharp decline in coal production at the Yima Mining Bureau. The bureau had held meetings, instructing each coal mine and unit to find ways to maintain their production and ensure workers' wages. The support maintenance factory was being restructured and sold off entirely, with the mine car factory acquiring it. The former directors had been reassigned, and all machinery and personnel were transferred to the mine car factory. And no cadres, small or large. They were moving these days and needed time to attend to the business and settle their accounts.

I had not visited the Yima support maintenance factory in six months. They did not have a dedicated business representative, so I contacted them alone. Little Tian was a conscientious worker who handled transactions promptly and efficiently. Our business dealings had been clear and straightforward, despite our visits being limited to twice a year and a half. The first was to contact the business, and the second was to express gratitude for his dedication to our transactions. After the factory ceased operations, Little Tian called me twice to urge me to settle the remaining accounts. However, due to various reasons, I had inadvertently delayed for almost half a year.

Little Tian assured me that the remaining payment was settled upon his return to Yima. I would go to the Yima Support Factory.

Taking the Qingdao-Lanzhou Express Train, I arrived at Yima Station at 4:15 in the morning. The station was shrouded in darkness, with no lights inside or outside. About seven or eight passengers stood in the middle of the square, waiting for taxis. Because of the late August chill, they huddled together, shivering in their T-shirts. After about 10 minutes, a small minivan taxi arrived, accommodating approximately seven or eight people. We paid five yuan each for the ride to the city, with passengers indicating when they wanted to get off along the way.

Arriving at the hotel, I rested briefly before leaving at 8 a.m. Then, following the address Little Tian provided, I headed to the new location of the support factory. I hailed a van taxi on the roadside — a communal minibus from Yiwu — which did not follow a fixed route but traveled in one direction, picking up and dropping off passengers as needed. The Yima Support Factory had relocated to the mine car factory, about 10 kilometers from Yima, the last stop for the van taxi.

Upon arrival, we inquired about the mine car factory, and the driver pointed to the left, indicating the third workshop. After a couple of turns, I arrived at the factory gate. A large sign read "Yima Mine Car Factory" beside the gate. I asked the guard about the newly relocated support factory, and Little Tian hurried over upon hearing my voice, leading me to the office of the factory director. Little Tian briefed the factory director on our business dealings, but the director listened without comment. When I inquired about the remaining payment, the director replied vaguely, citing uncertainties about when production would resume and financial constraints. With nothing further to discuss, Little Tian and I left the office without finishing my cup of water. We walked along the main road of the factory, passing by four or five large workshops, all eerily empty. Little Tian explained that the factory produced mine cars and conveyor belts for use in various mines operated by the Mining Bureau, as well as for sale to external customers. The Yiwu Mining Bureau had twelve coal mines, producing nearly 10 million tons of coal annually. However, with the recent downturn in the coal industry, the factory's future was uncertain, and wages in the car factory were in trouble. Even a small sum of 30,000 yuan became difficult to collect.

Back in Yima City, Little Tian and I shared a beer bottle while discussing the plan to settle the remaining payment. Upon returning from Zibo, Little Tian had contacted a colleague of his father's who worked in the finance department. Although Little Tian's father had left the finance department seven or eight years prior, they maintained their friendship. Little Tian's contact was a deputy director responsible for transferring payments from various mines to the support factory. He agreed to help with our case. Although it was difficult to withdraw cash directly, payments could be transferred through several channels, albeit with additional costs. I proposed a 20 percent fee, amounting to 6,000 yuan. Little Tian agreed and said it might take a few days to finalize the transaction. Without Little Tian's ingenious plan and connections, it would have been impossible to recover this small sum even after eight years.

With nothing much to do in the small town, we browsed a bookstore. One of the Xinhua Bookstores mainly stocked children's books, with a few classics and limited new releases. Among the books, I spotted one titled Tough Journey in Culture, which piqued my interest. It was my first time encountering the author, Yu Qiuyu. Flipping through the pages and examining the contents, I found the topics intriguing — The Taoist Priest's Towers, Tianyi Pavilion Amidst

Wind and Rain — and decided to purchase a copy. I returned to the hotel with the book, awaiting good news from Little Tian.

Back at the hotel, I read through the book's preface: "This book is a collection of essays written by Professor Yu Qiuyu during his lectures and research trips at home and abroad in recent years. The book's main theme is exploring cultural essence and life's mysteries through natural landscapes." It was my first time reading lyrical travel essays, starting with the renowned West Lake.

I was both unfamiliar and familiar with West Lake. While I had never visited it, I had heard its name countless times and read about it in various books. Reading the essay on West Lake, I followed Professor Yu's journey through its scenic spots — White Pagoda, Sudi Causeway, and the moonlight on the lake — all of which were vividly described. Although I could only imagine walking along the causeway and admiring the moon's reflection on the water, I felt like I was strolling with him. The collapsed Leifeng Pagoda, immortalized by Lu Xun's writings, was set for reconstruction. Still, I wondered if it had been completed yet.

Learning about the "Tianyi Pavilion," the largest private library in China with the longest retention time, I realized I might not be as cultured as I thought I was. Still, I loved books and enjoyed visiting bookstores and libraries. Years later, when I visited Ningbo City, Zhejiang Province, I visited the Tianyi Pavilion after completing my business. The two-story old building stood with its doors tightly shut, devoid of tourists. I walked around it in the drizzle, spending over 10 minutes gazing at it before taking a photo.

Staying in the hotel for two days, I leisurely read through the book, visiting Dunhuang, Dujiangyan Irrigation Dam, Dongting Lake, and Mount Tianzhu, as mentioned in the essays. Seeing these places in person was far better than reading about them repeatedly in books. In the coming years, I would travel across China with Professor Yu's book, exploring every corner of this vast land.

On the third day at ten, Little Tian entered the room with the words, "It's done."

"Thank you, it must have been quite a hassle," I replied. "I spent two days constantly contacting people and urging them. I had to make four transfers between factories and withdraw the money in three separate installments."

I took the money and treated Little Tian to a nice meal at noon before heading to Luoyang. Then, I caught the evening train back to Zibo.

6.12.8 Cheque Receipt in Wuhai

During a trip to the Three Gorges, I met Mr. Sun, the director of Wuhai Coal Mine Machinery Factory. Sun confirmed the equipment for oil cylinder spraying, which was scheduled to start production soon. Back through a call, one month later, the spray oil cylinder process was put into production. He agreed to use my products if the powder quality met the requirements. And if the state-owned factories conducted business at the same price as private factories, he would be willing to deal with private factories.

Two bags of samples were sent by train freight with other goods. Upon receiving the feedback, we confirmed that the experiments were successful and the quality was good. One ton of goods was shipped, and we immediately arranged for a salesperson to Wuhai to meet the director of the support maintenance workshop and various other officials. Although the director of the state-owned factory agreed, lower-level leaders posed challenges. They found faults, making it difficult to conduct business. The salesperson followed up and provided services, adhering to an unwritten set of rules that included giving gifts to the workshop director, the deputy director, the storage keeper, technicians, and quality inspectors. Only when all these matters were handled could the business be considered complete.

Over the course of two years, the salesperson visited twice without incident, and shipments were made. Invoices were sent, and cheques were received smoothly. With the national coal situation in decline, Wuhai experienced a greater decline than developed coastal areas, operating at a semi-shutdown status with very little coal usage. During the settlement, it was found that half a ton of powder was unaccounted for. The storage keeper at Wuhai Machinery Factory was unable to locate the goods. Sun promptly made arrangements to investigate the matter further. A few minutes later, the workshop director arrived. "This is director Yu from the Zibo Powder Factory. We were unable to locate the half-ton of powder sent here. Tomorrow, we'll send someone to the railway station to investigate and ensure it's sorted out." After giving instructions, he instructed the workshop director to treat us to lunch.

The next day, the workshop director prepared a double-row truck and took me and the storage keeper to the railway station. At the freight office, we submitted the bill of lading from Zibo Freight Station. Since the storage keeper often handled shipments, he was familiar with the freight office staff. The leader of the shipping team opened a large iron cabinet and searched for over 10 minutes until he found the bill of lading for this batch of goods. The bill of lading bore the signature of the storage keeper. The storage keeper apologized profusely, "I'm sorry, the goods were returned, but the bill of lading got lost, and I forgot to account for it." We made a copy of the bill of lading and completed the necessary procedures at our office. So the storage keeper went across the street to the railway station and made a copy. The workshop director signed off upon returning, and we completed the paperwork. A half-ton of powder was found, and the workshop director was pleased to have resolved the issue in front of the factory director's friend.

At noon, I treated everyone to lunch. On the way to the restaurant, I contemplated the smooth resolution of the powder issue. To express my gratitude to the workshop director and storage keeper, I bought each a carton of cigarettes. There was a shop next to the restaurant where I bought the cigarettes.

"Give me four cartons of Zhonghua cigarettes," I requested.

"Few people here smoke Zhonghua cigarettes," the shopkeeper replied.

"They cost 20 to 30 yuan a pack. What other brands do you have?"

"We don't sell such expensive cigarettes." I continued, "What's the most expensive brand?"

"Local tobacco, called Congrong, is thirteen yuan a pack."

"I'll take eight cartons."

"One carton sells out within half a month. It is the first time I have seen such a large buyer. I'll go to the tobacco company immediately to take the cigarettes, and I'll be back in an hour."

In the late 1990s, small business owners in regions like Jiangsu and Zhejiang smoked Zhonghua cigarettes. In contrast, ordinary workers smoked Nanjing cigarettes, costing 20 to 30 yuan. The regional disparities were significant. Two hours later, after finishing our meal, I took the workshop director to the cigarette counter.

"Take my eight packs of Congrong cigarettes," I said to the salesperson.

The salesperson hurriedly explained, "Sorry, the person who takes cigarettes hasn't returned yet."

"I'll pay the bill now. Prepare a bill of sale, and I'll return to pick them up after work."

"Thank you, thank you, Mr. Yu."

The workshop director took my hand and held onto it for four or five minutes. I felt unsteady on my feet, supported by the storage keeper.

Upon returning to Wuhai, I wasted no time preparing the invoice. I sent the salesperson, Little Shi, to settle the account. The next day in Wuhai, the account was settled, and a check was issued, which Little Shi brought back.

6.12.9 Lathe Receipt in Shulan

I visited the Machinery Factory of Shulan Mining Bureau, staying at the bureau's guesthouse because the other hotels were deemed dirty and unsafe. This time, it was November 20th, and Zibo had just started heating, with temperatures dropping to minus two or three degrees Celsius. The morning in Jishu Town was minus seventeen degrees Celsius. Walking to the machinery factory took over 10 minutes, and I hurried along, shivering. Director Zhou sat alone in his office inside the workshop. His office is located at the front of the workshop, separated from the rest by a wooden partition. It features four desks that offer a view of the entire workshop. Five or six workers dismantled the support columns in the thousand-plus-square-meter workshop, which was warm but desolate.

I asked director Zhou why only a few workers were in the workshop. With a sigh, director Zhou explained that workers were marked present if they showed up for work and only half-present if they did not. They came if they wanted to, resulting in a semi-shutdown state. This situation persisted for three or four months, and the leaders of the Mining Bureau were helpless. The workers had not received wages for half a year.

"What about the workers' livelihoods?" I asked director Zhou.

"They find odd jobs elsewhere. They steal from the factory to sell things if they can't find work."

"What about future production and wages?" I inquired.

"The leaders of the Mining Bureau say they can only take one step at a time. Typically, this is the peak season for coal sales, but it is not showing an increase this year. The machinery we produce is specifically designed for use in coal mines. If coal can't be sold, our factory has to shut down."

Business had been interrupted for half a year, and no payments had been made this year, resulting in a debt of 130,000 yuan. I approached the factory director. He said to wait until winter, when the coal market would improve, to pay part of the debt. However, when winter arrived, the situation worsened instead of improving. Hope for payment was dashed. Director Zhou accompanied me to see the factory director. Seated in his office, the factory director was alone, sipping tea. Unlike previous years, there was no continuous flow of people, no work reports or signatures, no people coming and going. After chatting for an hour about the factory's production, the factory director admitted he had no solutions, only waiting. Unable to make the payment, he apologized. Finally, he remembered there was a small Jiefang truck, four years old, which he could use to pay off part of the debt.

Director Zhou showed me the truck, which was in good condition. I decided to take it and asked for the price at the office. The factory director quoted 20,000 yuan, saying that other factories also wanted it, but he did not provide it. The next day, arrangements were made to have the truck transferred immediately.

Back at our factory, I sent Little Shi, the salesperson, to handle the matter. In seven days, he drove the Jiefang, or liberation-brand truck, to Shulan.

Furthermore, I regularly called director Zhou to stay updated on the machinery factory's situation. With a remaining debt of 110,000 yuan, we could not afford to wait until we went bankrupt. Director Zhou explained over the phone that the Mining Bureau's actions were legal. Still, the machinery factory was not an independent economic entity. If the machinery factory went bankrupt, it would not be the one to go bankrupt; instead, it would be the Mining Bureau, which was directly under the leadership of the Coal Department, a state-owned enterprise, that would go bankrupt.

Director Zhou called to inform me that production had stopped. I rushed to the Shulan Machinery Factory with Little Zhao. In the evening, I met with director Zhou, who explained that a meeting of workshop directors and above had taken place two days prior. The factory director had conveyed the leadership's decision from the Mining Bureau to cease production for reorganization. They planned to introduce new products, no longer solely producing machinery for coal mines, but to expand into new markets and products. Existing machinery that could be used would be retained, while those that could not would be disposed of. With this opportunity, I planned to settle the account with some machines.

When I met with the factory director the next day, I fabricated a story about expanding production to manufacture handles and bases for support columns, which would necessitate the use of several lathes. We did not have the funds to purchase them, so I asked if they had any old lathes they were not using that they could give us instead of payment. The factory director did not immediately respond, but picked up the phone on his desk.

"Hello, could you ask little Xing to come to my office?"

Shortly after, Xing, the head of the machining workshop, arrived.

The factory director instructed, "Take Mr. Yu to the workshop to see the lathes earmarked for disposal."

I was familiar with Xing; we shared a few meals at director Zhou's invitation. Accompanied by Xing, we visited the workshop, where rows of machines — lathes, milling machines, grinders, and presses — were lined up, with approximately 40 or 50 marked for disposal. After inspecting three lathes, Xing estimated that they were worth over 100,000 yuan. Still, he did not know the exact prices. I requested three, and even though the price was higher than the debt owed, it could not be lowered.

In the director's office, Xing listed the serial numbers and models of the three lathes. The head of the equipment department came to check the prices, totaling 126,000 yuan. The factory director asked how much was owed: the debt was 113,000 yuan, while the lathes were worth the debt and another 13,000 yuan. Then the head of the equipment department and Xing left the office, leaving only me and the factory director.

I touched the red envelope prepared from the pocket, stuffed it into the director's pocket, saying, "These three lathes are the best choice for me to clear the debts. Although I have more than 13,000 yuan in debt, I hope you can offer me a lower price for them. For the sake of our relationship, can we pay less for them?"

He pondered and asked himself, "How should we settle the accounts? We could write them off as scrap, but we cannot write off just one side of the transaction. We could account for them as depreciation."

After a few minutes of silence, he concluded, "You could go to the finance department this afternoon to take lathes."

I handled the account settlement procedures, and director Zhou assisted me in finding a truck. We aimed to load and transport the machines by truck within two or three days. Xing accompanied me to the workshop to determine how to transport the lathes from the workshop to the main road inside the factory. Since the lathes were not together and were wedged among dozens of other machines, one lathe was brought out directly with a forklift. The other two could not be reached with a forklift, so we used a crowbar to move them into position before lifting them out with the forklift. We paid the workers for moving the lathes and offered a tip to use the factory forklift. I gave director Zhou 500 yuan and told him to use it to pay the workers, and if it was not enough, I would add more.

"It won't take more than half a day. The rest can have a meal by paying less money to the workers. We are all good friends here," director Zhou assured me, and everything proceeded smoothly as promised.

The next day, I arrived at the workshop at 8:00 a.m.. Shortly after, director Zhou arrived with four workers, each carrying a sledgehammer, a pry bar, and a toolkit. Moving the first lathe to the middle of the workshop road took over an hour. With experience, the second lathe was moved out in half an hour, and the third lathe only required the screws to be removed without needing to be relocated. The forklift operator Wu was a friend of director Zhou's who agreed to help. By 10:00, all three lathes were out of the workshop, neatly arranged on the roadside.

Wu's friend found a truck for us. Since there were no designated freight trucks in northeastern China at the time, finding a truck was challenging, and there was a risk of losing the cargo along the way. On the third day, we found a large Jiefang truck transporting goods to Shandong. Thanks to connections, we trusted that it would be reliable, and it promised to deliver the lathes within five days.

The Jiefang truck transporting the lathes had smooth sailing, and on the afternoon of the fourth day, it arrived at the gates of our factory.

CHAPTER 7
MANUFACTURING HOUSEHOLD WATER HEATERS

7.1

Engineer Zheng Zuoliang had returned after completing his work in Qingdao. This time, his identity had undergone a significant change. No longer was he the legal adviser of the Taiyuan Hydraulic Research Institute; instead, he had become a partner in the Baixi Mine Machinery Repair Factory and my friend.

We chatted for a whole morning, and Engineer Zheng began by discussing the lawsuit, recounting the entire story from start to finish: Last year, Zheng had become aware that we were producing powder, and our previous usage was normal, about half a ton per month. Suddenly, for two months, we ceased using powder. Upon inquiry, it was discovered that we were producing it ourselves. He suspected that someone from the Research Institute was aiding us. Still, we did not pay much attention to it since it did not directly affect us. However, a few months later, two clients from the institute stopped purchasing powder and inquired about buying it from other manufacturers. At that time, there were only two powder producers nationwide, one in Tianjin and the other in our Research Institute. Both had maintained separate clientele for many years. Since we competed in the market, the leaders were quite upset. They dispatched individuals to several suppliers of raw materials. They found that we purchased materials from them in quantities and proportions identical to their formula requirements. Without much investigation, it became clear that someone within the institute had leaked the formula. Exposing the mole in court would be difficult, and the institute's leaders had conversed with him several times regarding the protection of intellectual property. Lawsuits in this realm could be arduous, especially for someone with limited legal experience. Unlike economic disputes with clear amounts and easily discernible evidence, intellectual property lawsuits involve considerable judicial discretion. Determining whether there had been infringement, gathering evidence, and determining the amount of compensation were all challenging tasks. It could drag on for three to five years, resulting in losses for both parties. Moreover, the defendant's economic strength must be considered. Even if the lawsuit were won, recovering money might prove difficult, rendering it unnecessary.

When the lawsuit was filed in the Jinan Intermediate Court, Zheng proposed to the institute's leaders that they visit the factory to assess its economic strength and integrity. Continuing the lawsuit could lead to financial difficulties since the factory had a certain scale and was valued at millions. Upon entering your factory, they first inspected the workshops. They noticed that there was no decent building, which did not indicate a profitable enterprise. Given the factory's weak foundation, they wanted to see your living conditions. Was it a villa? An apartment? Upon arriving at your home, they found it to be an old farmhouse with average furnishings and no precious wood furniture. At that moment, they abandoned the idea of pursuing the lawsuit further.

Upon meeting you, the institute's leaders' initial impression was not that of a country bumpkin or a rich man, despite your inebriation. Upon entering your home and seeing numerous books, they understood your interests, establishing a connection. With shared interests and a love for reading, you could engage in meaningful conversations. Upon returning to Taiyuan, I relayed to the institute director what I had seen and heard. Given our longstanding friendship and my role as his legal adviser, he was receptive to my perspective. I emphasized that filing the lawsuit in Jinan, close to Zibo, would lack a geographical advantage, making it easy for you to leverage connections. Dragging on for three to five years might lead to no resolution, resulting in losses for both parties. Given our longstanding business relationship and good personal rapport, the factory director, influenced by someone in the institute, preferred to pay a sum rather than betray someone within the institute. Even if the culprits were identified, they were all old colleagues from the institute. Could they be fired? How could they be disciplined? Withdrawal of the lawsuit was the best course of action.

Zheng's kindness and persuasion convinced the institute's leaders to drop a protracted intellectual property lawsuit.

Upon the first visit to the factory, they observed two stacks of iron plates in the courtyard. Upon the second visit, the iron plates remained unmoved. I informed Zheng that the iron plates were from Pingdingshan, intended to settle the account, and were being prepared for a discounted sale. Upon approaching the iron plates, Zheng inspected them carefully and inquired about their thickness. Three millimeters. I suggested using these iron plates to aid in the production process. During the second visit, before returning to Taiyuan, he mentioned something, but I did not pay much attention to it. Upon returning from Qingdao, Zheng sincerely assisted in producing household heating stoves, recognizing the promising market prospects and potential for further product development.

Zheng's friend, an engineer from the Taiyuan Boiler Factory, spends his spare time researching household heating stoves. He has assisted in establishing several factories in the suburbs of Taiyuan, which have proven profitable. Zheng explained that stoves are seasonal products, with sales lasting three to four months each year, yielding high profits. The materials for each stove cost approximately 100 to 150 yuan, while the market sale price ranges from 400 to 500 yuan. With a large market and improving living standards, every household could use one. The lifespan of a household heating stove is around five years, making it a short-cycle, disposable product. Scaling production could result in stable and lucrative earnings compared to providing repair parts for coal mines, offering both speed and stability.

Zheng has visited several small household heating stove factories in Taiyuan, noting their modernized workshops and semi-automatic production lines, which are capable of producing hundreds of units sold across the province daily. These industries have experienced significant growth over the past five to six years, with ample room for further market expansion. Repairing coal mines poses significant limitations and challenges to earning money freely. Zheng proposed starting modestly with basic equipment, such as a sheet metal cutter, a rolling machine, and several welding machines, which would require an investment of around 20,000 to 30,000 yuan. It would open up the market and expand the factory buildings to invest in production lines.

Zheng's suggestions were logical and practical, sparking interest. With available workshops, factories, and iron plates, engaging expert assistance could enable immediate production. Throughout a single afternoon, half of the decision was made.

Further market research would precede the final decision.

7.2

Accompanied by the paint delivery truck, we first went to Boxing County, Binzhou City, Shandong, to take a look. Three local sundry shops in Boxing County sell paint and start selling stoves after autumn. I have seen them in previous years. One of the shops has quite a presence and is a major seller of stoves. Our first stop was at the Lujia local sundry shop. Today, we did not discuss paint-related matters; instead, we talked about household heating stoves. When I arrived in June, it was not the season for selling stoves, but there were still four or five left from last year, stored in the backyard. Boss Lu took me to see them. They are locally produced and sell for 550 yuan each for medium-sized stoves and 620 yuan each for large ones. Boss Lu explained that they started stocking up in September, with October and November being the peak sales months. Sales dropped off in December, and in January, they stopped altogether. In previous years, they had sold between 70 and 80 stoves per season. Last year, they sold over 120 stoves to an installation team. There were dozens of stove sellers in the county and surrounding areas. They estimated they could sell over 1,000 stoves a year because the percentage of households in the county using heating was low, less than 10 percent. As a result, over the past two years, ordinary households had begun using stoves, and the number of users was increasing annually. Hence, Boss Lu was willing to sell stoves for us.

The next day, we visited Wangcun Town in the Zhoucun District. There were six paint dealers in Wangcun, two of which sold household stoves. Wangcun Town was industrially developed, with four state-owned enterprises nearby. Because the residents' living standards were relatively better than in other towns, they had started installing household heating stoves in recent years. During that time, installing a set of household heating stoves, including the heating radiator, iron pipes, and installation fees, cost over 2,000 yuan, which was too expensive for ordinary families to afford. We first visited the local sundry shop of Boss Bi, the largest sundry shop in Wangcun Village, which sold stoves after the autumn harvest. Boss Bi was straightforward, and we often had a couple of drinks together. He assured me that he would sell our stoves. Then, we visited the second shop owned by Boss Bai, which was slightly smaller than Boss Bi's but had been in business for many years. They started selling stoves just last year and sold over 20 stoves in a season. It was not bad. Because he collaborated with a small installation team, giving them a 10 percent kickback on stoves sold to them, he earned less. Still, he allowed the installation team to make a profit. Every shop had its way of doing things, and it was hard to do business if they did not see a benefit.

After visiting more than 20 shops, they recognized the idea of selling paint and stoves and agreed to be our distributors. With over two months of sales time, the goods were sold out. It was time to settle the bill.

We dispatched salespeople to various towns and large villages in Zibo, adopting the traditional method of selling paint by setting up a network and visiting every household in each area. In this way, I spent 10 days with three salespeople. However, most sales agencies for household heating stoves were tied to designated manufacturers. They were unwilling to add new stove varieties, as people preferred established brands. Despite our efforts to persuade them by highlighting the advantages of our new stoves and offering cash upon sale, some were still reluctant, citing the space constraints posed by the stoves. Eventually, we managed to convince around 20 distributors. Although thousands of households used stoves, there were even more manufacturers in the Zibo area, as our sales staff discovered. Whether they would succeed or not remained uncertain.

Engineer Zheng urged me to go to Taiyuan and meet Engineer Yang.

Engineer Yang was a retired employee of the Taiyuan Boiler Factory who had spent many years researching household heating stoves. He had helped several small factories in various counties in Taiyuan. It was essential to meet him in person and make a decision soon, as June was already upon us and we had only three to four months of production time left. Engineer Zheng also intended to take me to visit a small boiler factory where Engineer Yang served as a consultant.

Upon our arrival in Taiyuan, Engineer Zheng arranged a factory tour for us. There was a train from Zibo to Taiyuan every day, arriving at six o'clock in the morning. Engineer Zheng arranged for a minivan to pick up me and Workshop Manager Little Chen first to tour the factory, and then we met Engineer Yang.

The factory was located in the suburbs of Taiyuan. It took about an hour for the minivan to reach there. We stopped in front of a factory with a sign that read "Taiyuan Hongguang Boiler Factory." The gate was electrically operated, and upon entering, we turned left and saw the office building. There was a three-story building with mosaic exterior walls and a red-glazed tile roof. Inside the office building, a marble floor, crystal chandeliers hanging from the ceiling in the corridor, light yellow wallpaper on the walls, and large windows with brown trim. The factory director's office was on the second floor, and Engineer Zheng took us in. After exchanging pleasantries, the factory director made a phone call. Then, a young man in work clothes entered the room. "Take Engineer Zheng and the two guests to the workshop," the factory director said straightforwardly.

We followed the young man to the workshop, whom Engineer Zheng introduced as Section Chief Liu from the sales department. This workshop produced low-pressure boilers for government agencies, schools, and factories, which were used for heating drinking water, bathing water, and other purposes. Boiler models ranged from 100 to 1000 kilograms, with more than a dozen varieties, each capable of holding between 100 and 1,000 kilograms of water. These boilers were mainly sold throughout the Taiyuan province, with over a dozen sales outlets outside the province and an annual sales revenue of 50 million yuan. Section Chief Liu guided us through the entire production process, from material cutting to welding and assembly, providing detailed explanations along the way. After visiting this workshop, we saw the production line of household heating stoves.

The household heating stove workshop occupied only half the space of the low-pressure boiler workshop, but the production process was similar. Section Chief Liu explained that only five varieties of household heating stoves were designed for ordinary household use. Their sales range spanned 200 kilometers from Taiyuan, resulting in high shipping costs and low profits for household stoves beyond that distance. The annual sales revenue was 7 to 8 million yuan, earning a small profit to maintain the overall expenses of the factory. The main profits came from the low-pressure boilers. Section Chief Liu led us around as we spoke, explaining everything in detail.

We were treated to lunch in the factory canteen, which was more luxurious than a three-star hotel.

In the afternoon, we met Engineer Yang. The decision regarding this product, whether to proceed or not, would be made in the afternoon.

Engineer Yang was already waiting for us when we returned to the hotel. His home is not far from there. Engineer Yang said nothing when we entered the room, so Engineer Zheng asked me to speak.

"Factory director Yu, please discuss your impressions of the boiler factory from the morning visit."

"Starting from when we entered the factory gate, it didn't feel like a typical factory, and when we entered the office building, it was even more extraordinary, more luxurious than the hotel. The products and production process were ordinary, but the profitability was extraordinary, and the factory was thriving."

I spoke whatever came to mind, and Engineer Zheng continued, "This factory was built based on Engineer Yang's technology. It has been five years now, and the factory has undergone five renovations. The demand for products exceeds supply. Not to mention the amount of money Engineer Yang has earned, he spent more than 300,000 yuan on building the factory gate and over 800,000 yuan on constructing office buildings. Who would be willing to spend so much money on a township factory? Just think about it, director Yu. Please let Engineer Yang introduce his new product."

Engineer Yang was wearing a blue work uniform and had dark hands that did not resemble those of an engineer.

He said loudly, "Factory director Yu, Engineer Zheng has told me you are considering producing the household heating stoves. This year, I designed an energy-saving household heating stove, which has yet to be produced. There are many varieties of household stoves on the market. Still, the mine features an inner chamber with two layers, circulating water twice inside, which saves 20 percent of coal consumption. By developing new products focused on energy conservation, ordinary people recognize the importance of conserving coal when burning stoves. If they can save one-fifth of the coal, it is remarkable. I plan to apply for a patent to secure a market position, deterring others from copying it. The appearance needs to be aesthetically pleasing. Most stoves on the market are round, but we can make ours square. I've almost finished the drawings."

Engineer Zheng interjected, "Household stoves are easy to produce. Factory director Yu, today, I brought you to see the boiler factory, not to produce household stoves. I have discussed this with Engineer Yang and decided to assist you in introducing a product. Look far ahead and set ambitious goals. Produce household stoves in the first year and low-pressure boilers in the second year. Start with the 100 models and introduce a few varieties each year. These are long-term products with stable demand and high profits. That's the purpose of today's visit, can you understand?"

Engineer Yang added, "The production process for low-pressure boilers above 100 models is similar to that of scaled-up household stoves. If we can handle the small ones, we can handle the big ones as well. Engineer Zheng is right. We have discussed it. Start small and aim big. We'll do well with small stoves this year and help you with the big ones next year."

Engineer Zheng invited me to Taiyuan to broaden my horizons by visiting the boiler factory and urged me to change from coal mine maintenance to boiler production. They talked about boilers in turn. It had already been over 10 years since the reform and opening up. Industries had developed rapidly, with factories becoming increasingly modern. Both workers bathed, and the workshops were heated using boilers. Government agencies and schools are building new facilities, all of which require boilers. With the current pace of social development, living standards double every seven to eight years, and the demand for household items increases accordingly. Five years ago, household stoves were the main product of the Hongguang Boiler Factory. Still, two years later, small boilers surpassed household stoves, unexpectedly overtaking them. It is time to make a decision! As for compensation, Engineer Yang explained on their behalf before I even asked: three sets of drawings for the three types of household heating stoves, each valued at 2,000 yuan, totaling 6,000 yuan for the drawing fees. Engineer Yang would go to guide production, and the duration was uncertain, so we would pay him double the salary plus that of two workers. As for the future, it is subject to negotiation. After we made money and made a fortune, according to profit drawing, it is up to you to raise more or less.

Engineer Zheng said, "Factory director Yu, whether to proceed is up to you today. If you do not choose to proceed, it is like making a friend. You have come to Taiyuan for a tour, and if you choose to proceed, go back and prepare the machinery and equipment."

There's no reason not to proceed. One was a warm-hearted matchmaker, actively facilitating and helping a friend. The other was an engineer who did not demand much and had readily available products. We had ready-made iron plates, two large stacks, sites, workers, and technicians. It was decided that we would produce household heating stoves.

7.3

After returning from Taiyuan, we started preparing the mechanical equipment. We needed a plate shear machine to cut the plates for the stove cores, which had to be cut precisely and neatly, and a rolling machine to roll the plates into cylinders. We also needed a bending machine since we designed the stoves to be square-shaped. We decided to start with these three major pieces of equipment. Other equipment, such as welding machines and pliers, was readily available for purchase.

I took Technician Master Zhao with me to the Zichuan Plate Shear machine factory to select a suitable model for our use. Once selected, they would deliver the machine to us. After leaving the plate shear machine factory, we visited the Banyang Machinery Factory to inspect the rolling machines. We examined several models, but they were expensive, priced at 4,000 to 5,000 yuan each. Technician Master Zhao suggested we inquire about used ones, which could also be used. If we could not find any, we would consider buying new ones. As for the bending machine, the plate shear machine factory had some. Technician Master Zhao found it quite simple, and since becoming a fitter for his entire life, he was confident that he could make one himself without needing to buy it.

When we returned from Zichuan, Technician Master Zhao pointed to the oil cylinders in the yard and said, "Aren't these ready-made rollers for the rolling machine?"

The oil cylinders were steel pipes, approximately a meter long and 12 centimeters in diameter, slightly thinner than the rollers we had seen. There were three or four unused motors and two old gearboxes. We could make a rolling machine for just a few hundred yuan with welding and assembly. Technician Master Zhao was confident he could make the rolling machine himself.

Back in the office, Technician Master Zhao and I continued discussing machinery. We finalized the rolling machine and ordered it immediately. The plate shear machine required precise cutting of the plates, something Technician Master Zhao was not confident he could do himself; therefore, we decided to purchase one. After a phone call, the plate shear machine factory immediately arranged for delivery. The bending machine was simple; the iron plates used for the stove casing were only 0.7 millimeters thick and did not require a motorized bending mechanism. With a simple press, we could bend them ourselves without buying a machine. With these three pieces of equipment determined, along with some small tools and devices, we would buy what we could and make the rest ourselves. Technician Master Zhao also requested an assistant, so I arranged for one from the workshop the next day.

We set up a temporary workshop shed on the west side of the yard to shield us from rain and sun without occupying the main workshop, and we planned to work there for about six months. We plan to expand production and construct a new workshop next year. We would consider producing small boilers two years later.

The next day, we needed to buy the necessary machinery and equipment. Coupled with the machinery we had made and the assistance of Technician Master Zhao, the plan was to complete it within 10 days.

As agreed, Engineer Zheng accompanied Engineer Yang to our factory on the appointed day. Engineer Yang brought three sets of blueprints for stoves of various sizes, drawn according to standard specifications. Three workers were called in from the workshop, with Technician Master Zhaoleading the way and Engineer Yang giving instructions. We started production on the same day. Engineer Yang personally drew lines on the iron plates and cut and rolled the furnace liner. At the same time, Technician Master Zhao supervised the workers in welding. We started by making two samples of each stove type. The stove cores were designed to hold two layers of water, welded with three layers of iron plates to heat up quickly and cool down slowly. Engineer Yang applied for a patent in the name of our factory for this part of the stove. Most stoves on the market have only a single layer of water in their core. The exterior was square-shaped, with cotton insulation between the core and the casing. Our design allowed the core to heat up quickly and dissipate heat slowly while the casing was spray-painted with a light yellow color. Our household heating stoves were unique from the inside out, aiming for an auspicious start in the market.

Engineer Yang worked tirelessly from the start of the workday until the afternoon, never leaving the production site. He drew lines on the iron plates, worked alongside the workers, and even helped lift the stoves, effectively doing the work of several workers. In the first four or five days, we produced two to three stoves daily, gradually increasing to seven or eight per day. As production progressed smoothly, Engineer Yang felt reassured. After working for half a month, we paid Engineer Yang the agreed-upon blueprint fee and wages, not withholding a single yuan. Before leaving, he stated that if we encountered any technical difficulties, he would be available to assist us at any time. Engineer Yang was an outstanding engineer, a senior technician, and a hardworking eighth-grade worker. Among the technical experts we had encountered, he was the best.

Starting production in August, we gradually delivered stoves to various sales points over the next two months. With three salespersons rotating, some sales points received three or four stoves. In contrast, others received seven or eight, with a maximum of 10 stoves in a single location. By mid-October, we had run out of iron plates, so we stopped spending money on purchasing more. We decided to halt production. We delivered 230 household heating stoves over a period of two months and settled accounts after another two months.

7.4

By the end of November, we had nearly sold all the stoves, prompting the salespersons to start settling their accounts. However, a few days later, they reported that sales were far below expectations. Some shops did not sell stoves, while others only sold one or two. Settling accounts with these shops did not take much time, as the amounts involved were small.

Salesperson Little Zhao reported that the Limin Store in Puji Town had closed, and its owner, Boss Sun, had relocated. We had delivered six stoves to the store, but it was unclear how many had been sold. Since these six stoves were worth over 3,000 yuan, we could not just let them go for nothing. We needed to find out where Boss Sun lived. As they say, "A monk may run away from the temple, but he can't escape his fate." We decided to visit his home.

After gathering some information, we learned that Boss Sun was from Sunjiazhuang Village in Puji Town, four kilometers away from Puji. One day, I went with Little Zhao to Sunjiazhuang Village, where the vehicle was delivering paint, and stopped at the village entrance. We asked around on the main street, but nobody was there.

"What's Boss Sun's full name?" I asked Little Zhao.

"His name is Sun Weibin."

We took a few steps forward and saw an older man standing at the entrance of an alley.

We approached him and asked, "Excuse me, where does Sun Weibin live?"

The old man replied, "I don't know."

"Is he from this village?"

"I've never heard of him."

Just then, a middle-aged man approached us.

Little Zhao asked him, "Elder Brother, do you know where Sun Weibin lives?"

"There's no one by that name in our village."

We might have misheard. We went through an alley and circled back from another street. As a young woman approached us, Little Zhao asked again, "Big Sister, is there someone named Sun Weibin in this village?"

The young woman stopped and hesitated momentarily before saying, "Yes, here we called him Da Binzi or Big Bin."

"Is he Sun Weibin?"

"Yes, around here, people don't usually use full names, only nicknames. We're neighbors, so I know him as Sun Weibin."

"We need to speak with him about something. Could you take us to his place?"

The young woman replied firmly, "He is not at home. The whole family went out for business and locked up the house."

Little Zhao continued, "Where did they go?"

"I don't know. I heard Sun's family settled down somewhere."

It was a wasted trip, and the fate of the six stoves remained unknown.

Salesperson Old Zhao had contacted over a dozen dealers to sell the stoves. Only two shops were open: one sold one stove, and the other sold four. The shop that sold four stoves was located in Wulitang village on the outskirts of Yidu City. Old Zhao had visited three times, but the owner was unreasonable. He refused to settle the bill properly, claiming it was a one-time deal. The litigation was rejected because the money was insufficient. Old Zhao was fed up and decided to take me along to figure out a solution and get as much money back as possible.

We stopped by the small shop while passing through Wulitang to deliver paint. Upon entering, the middle-aged owner sat silently on a footstool, refusing to stand up or speak. He recognized Old Zhao and knew we were there to collect payment, but he ignored us. Standing opposite him, Old Zhao said, "This is my boss. Let's settle the payment for the stoves today."

The middle-aged owner lifted his head slightly and said, "I am short on funds. I'll pay you whenever I have money."

I could not contain my anger and interjected, "You cannot just say that. Set a deadline for payment. You cannot keep delaying it. Set a schedule if you can't pay it all at once."

The middle-aged owner replied angrily. "Who knows when I'll have money? When I do, you are not around. When I don't, you show up."

Old Zhao was getting frustrated. "We've come so often, and you're still being unreasonable. How many times do I have to come? You're trying to cheat us!"

"So what if I don't have money? Do you want to fight? You want to curse?"

The middle-aged owner stood up, glaring with his sleepy eyes. "If you don't reason with us, let's go. We will not offer you a 2,000 yuan discount for nothing. We'll find a way to get it back."

I pulled Old Zhao out of the shop.

Sitting in the car, Old Zhao's hands were still shaking.

"We can't let that guy off easy. Giving him 2,000 yuan for nothing? We have to figure out a way to get it back."

I remembered Elder Uncle Wang, who worked at the Yidu Industrial and Commercial Bureau for 30 to 40 years, specializing in dealing with small traders like this. He had retired and lived in Yidu. I had visited his home before, and we strongly bonded as fellow villagers. I suggested we seek his help. After unloading the paint, I found my elder uncle Wang and explained the situation.

Without hesitation, he said, "Let's go. We can't let these guys get away with it."

Back at Wulitang village, we re-entered the small shop. With Elder Uncle Wang leading the way, Old Zhao spoke up first, "Boss, set a deadline for the payment today."

After the owner could say "no money," elder uncle Wang stepped forward, grabbed his collar, and pulled him outside. "Let's go, let's find a place with money."

The middle-aged owner was stunned. Old Zhao explained from the side, "This is a retired cadre from the Yidu Industrial and Commercial Bureau, my fellow villager. If you hurt him, you'll have a hard time."

Elder Uncle Wang continued to pull him outside, and the owner relented.

"Who said I wouldn't pay you? Just not today."

"If you don't pay today, I'll take you to the bureau." Elder Uncle Wang didn't let go and asked again, "Are you going to pay today?"

"Yes, yes, let me go out and borrow some." Elder uncle Wang let him go, and the middle-aged owner went out, turning right. After waiting about fifteen minutes, he returned with a bundle of cash and handed it to Old Zhao. "Count it. It's 2,160."

Old Zhao counted it; it was exactly the amount for the four stoves, not a penny less.

There was another troublesome account. Two receipts were missing for stoves delivered by Little Pan. One shop acknowledged the receipt but returned it since they had not sold the stove. Another shop had received five stoves but refused to acknowledge receiving eight. Little Pan visited twice, and the shop still had three stoves. The owner only admitted to receiving three and refused to acknowledge the other five. Little Pan and the warehouse keeper double-checked and confirmed that eight stoves had been sent. The warehouse keeper accompanied Little Pan on another visit, bringing the account book and the stubs from the warehouse, but it was of no use. The shop only returned three stoves without receipts. It was a case of being unable to reason with them despite being in the right.

We settled all accounts before the Spring Festival. We sold eight stoves, but we were cheated out of 11. The remaining stoves were gradually retrieved. The sales points were small, and with no sales for most of the year, we were unable to occupy them. The retrieved stoves filled every nook and cranny of the workshop, and two rows were lined up in the yard.

After wasting human resources and losing iron plates, we had been busy for half a year without much to show. We decided not to continue the following year. For the unsold stoves, we thought of a solution. We contacted several installation teams for stoves, offering a steep discount and only charging them half the material cost. We sold half of the remaining stoves in three months. The rest could not be kept for another year, so each employee was given one to help alleviate the factory's troubles.

CHAPTER 8
THE EMERGENCE OF SHOE POLISHING MACHINES

8.1 Finding a Product

In 1993, my younger brother, who was two years younger than me, resigned from the town-operated ceiling fan factory where he worked and then teamed up with a few friends to start his own factory. Due to various reasons, the partnership dissolved, and he returned home to find another product.

That year, I was involved in two projects: wall coatings and hydraulic pillar repairs. My second younger brother returned home with plans to expand production and scale up. However, the sale of coatings was geographically limited. The production process was straightforward, and the products were offered at affordable prices. However, the shipping costs were high, which accounted for 20 percent of the total price. Sales were limited to an area within a 100-kilometer radius. Coating factories were located in all counties and towns, resulting in fierce competition and minimal profits, which made expansion difficult.

Repairing hydraulic pillars required dealing with state-owned coal mines posed significant challenges. Hydraulic pillars include oil cylinders, fire pillars, handles, and bases. The structure was easy, and it was not complex to repair them separately. Each component was unique, and its maintenance requirements varied accordingly. The oil cylinders needed to be plated, the fire pillars required to be phosphate, and the plane and mill were used to repair the handles and bases. We could only handle two or three types without adequate equipment to repair all components. Product repair should first obtain the necessary parts from the manufacturer and then send them back after the repair is complete. If we pulled back more parts, we needed to work overtime; on the contrary, we must stop production and wait. We had leeway to regulate production, but we lacked a production initiative for maintenance.

The production value of repair parts was low. Since our customers were large state-owned enterprises, the reception standards were high. They could easily give small gifts on holidays. But for small factories, it was a big expense. It was dissonant for a small factory to deal with a large state-run organization. It was a large expense that could not be written in the accounts. It has proved to be even more challenging to perform repairs and expand the business simultaneously.

With no prospects for expanding either of these two projects, we began searching for new products.

After discussing with my second younger brother, we considered electrical products. A friend mentioned that there was demand for both single-strand and multi-strand wires. Still, we were unable to find the necessary technical expertise. We could only give up.

During those years, a government initiative encouraged schools, government agencies, and the public to establish factories. A friend was seeking eyeglass manufacturers to treat myopia in primary school students. My second younger brother had connections with a factory operated by the Shandong Provincial Household Electric Appliance Company, located in a lane off Taoyuan Road in Jinan. The factory produced glasses for treating myopia and also manufactured several children's toys. The factory director was deputy manager Wang of the Provincial Household Electric Appliance Company, who had visited the ceiling fan factory and knew my second younger brother. I had met Wang before and found him to be straightforward, without the airs of a government official. After discussing with my second younger brother, we decided to visit Wang to explore potential products suitable for us. My second younger brother made arrangements over the phone and set up a meeting with Wang.

We arrived at the Provincial Household Electric Appliance Company factory on the appointed day at about 10 o'clock. After exchanging pleasantries, we got down to business in Wang's office. Wang was a graduate of Shandong University of Technology and majored in electrical engineering. He had worked his way up from a clerk to the deputy General Manager of the Provincial Household Electric Appliance Company as a technical expert. Having visited electric appliance factories throughout the province, he was well-versed in all types of electric products, from small electric shavers to large appliances such as fans and refrigerators. Wang explained that it was not easy to manufacture such products. Though they might seem simple, with plastic, metal components, and an electric motor, they were not much different from larger products in terms of complexity. Although seemingly small, they required a complete set of components. Wang's frankness was evident as he shared his experiences managing a factory for the past three years, where they had been unable to find a suitable electric product. Appliance companies had the money and the market. Professionals and technical personnel could be found; who can match? But when you did it yourself, you would realize it was not as easy as you thought. Without a solid social foundation, it was impossible to compete effectively, and the factory still lacked a flagship product.

As we were talking, Wang fetched a small device from his office behind him. It was approximately a meter tall, featuring a chromium-plated rod and a motor located underneath. At both ends of the motor were two red and black leather covers.

"What's this?" I asked Wang.

"Last month, the company leaders went to Europe for a study tour and saw it in a shop in the UK. They asked the salesperson what it was, and he said it was a polishing machine. With this, you do not have to bend over to polish your leather shoes. Press the button, and the shoes will be polished to look like new. It is not available in China, so we bought two," Wang explained. "I'm thinking of producing this product. It's not complicated — I've dismantled one, and it's just a motor, a vertical rod, a switch, and two leather covers."

Deputy manager Wang pointed to the shoe-polishing machine and provided a detailed introduction.

"Have the leaders decided to produce this product?" I asked Wang.

"The general manager has agreed. We are planning to conduct market research and explore new factory sites," Wang replied enthusiastically.

"How far have the preparations gone?" I inquired further.

"We've already sent people to Zhejiang Province to contact motor manufacturers. We'll handle the plastic components by buying two injection molding machines. And we are contacting manufacturers to produce switches and leather covers," Wang spoke confidently. "We've dispatched personnel to several major cities in China, but we haven't found shoe polishing machines yet. It's very convenient for home and office use, and the prospects for development are promising."

My second younger brother had worked in the fan factory for over a decade, rising from a worker to a deputy factory manager overseeing production. He was very familiar with fan production processes. A ceiling fan had one motor and three blades. He could produce fan motors, so dealing with the motor for the shoe polishing machine was a piece of cake for him.

After inspecting the shoe polishing machine, my second younger brother asked Wang, "Can I handle the motor for the machine? I'm fully confident I can do it well."

Having visited the ceiling fan factory and seen its production workshops, Wang was familiar with my second brother's capabilities and immediately agreed to collaborate with us using our motor. What a coincidence to have such cooperation! It did not take much effort to find the product. We returned home to prepare for the production of the shoe polishing machine motor.

8.2 Prepare the Establishment of Yongtai Electrical Appliance Factory

Having ordered the production of shoe polishing machine motors, we immediately began searching for a suitable factory. The factory area, covering more than 2 mu (approximately 0.134 acres), produced coatings and repaired hydraulic pillars, and was already overcrowded, with its courtyard filled with oil cylinders and paint buckets; no space was available to move out of the six newly built workshops for repairing oil cylinders.

To the south of the paint factory were four small factories. A flouring milling factory at the southern end had been closed for three months, so its flour milling machines had been sold off. With an area of 2 mu, the small courtyard had eleven workshops in the north and six western rooms, making it suitable for motor production. We approached the village secretary, and the matter was quickly settled.

The factory building where the flour milling machines were moved had been demolished, with potholes on the ground. The place passed through by the flour milling machines had been torn apart, with few walls left. Therefore, the building required renovations, including relaying concrete floors, repainting walls, and redoing ceilings, as the old look needed to be updated.

There was one office, and two more were added. The courtyard gate was in bad condition, so it needed to be removed and replaced with a new one. The yard had been cleared and cleaned thoroughly. The motor factory for shoe polishing machines was under construction after more than 10 days of hard work, and it was neat and orderly.

Once the factory building is complete, we should obtain the business license and commence production. Naming the factory was the first step, and choosing a suitable name that ensured smooth operation was essential. Since the reform and opening up, naming has become a consideration. Once banned from sale after Liberation, the naming books were grandly shelved again. I bought one and occasionally read it. Despite its feudal and superstitious nature, the book was well-reasoned and well-argued, with examples. After pondering for a few days, we devised two factory names: Yongtai (永泰) and Huatai (华泰). Then, we needed to visit the Industrial and Commercial Bureau to obtain the necessary licenses. Still, we had to ensure that no two individuals in the same industry shared the same name. Before Liberation, my grandfather had owned a small shop in Shanghai named "Yongshengtai General Store" (永昇泰料 货店). His name was "Zhensheng" (振昇), with "zhen" (振) being the seniority in the family and "sheng" (昇) the given name. He had named his grandchildren accordingly. If there were a boy, he would be named "Guotai" (国泰) as seniority in the family and "Tai" (泰) as the given name, so the shop was called "Yongshengtai". I still recall my visit to Shanghai in 1960. Inspired by my grandfather's shop name, I consulted the naming book and carefully reviewed it. After calculating the strokes, we found that the strokes of "Zibo Yongtai Electrical Appliance Factory" (淄博永泰电器厂) were auspicious, our first choice. If there were any duplicate names and they could not be approved, we could use "Huatai." We submitted the name to the Industrial and Commercial Bureau. We confirmed that no other factories were named "Yongtai" nationwide in the electrical motor industry. Thus, we confirmed that our factory was named "Zibo Yongtai Electrical Appliance Factory." There was a factory in Zhejiang called "Huatai," our peers. The boss was the same age as me. We ate together a few times and supplied motors to several main engine plants. We were rivals, but we had a joyful reunion.

We did not need large machinery, as we had just started producing motors. We bought two punch presses, lathes, and other small devices and machines. Liuwacun Village, a neighboring village, served as a production base for punch presses, with over 150 manufacturers. They could deliver the punch presses as soon as we called them. Since we did not have enough money to buy new lathes, we went to the recently established old machinery market in Zhangqiu. We purchased two lathes, which cost only as much as one new lathe and were still in good condition. We gradually acquired various small machines and equipment, including electric welding machines, drilling machines, aluminum casting machines, coil winding machines, and lacquer dipping machines, totaling over 10 types. We bought one piece for each type and produced it in small quantities. Once production increased, we would gradually add more mechanical equipment.

To start production, we needed capital first. We spent around 50,000 yuan renovating the factory building and other trivial things. If not calculated in detail, we needed more than 50,000 yuan for machines and equipment, which could be settled later. We still needed an additional 40,000 yuan, as 100,000 yuan was urgently required, and 60,000 yuan had been raised by ourselves.

I approached Little Qi, a credit officer at the Rural Credit Presses.

He looked helpless and explained that funds were tight and the bank's loan quotas had been used up. Suppose the unit or individual who had repaid the loans did not renew them and could transfer the loans to me. Currently, the remaining loan was less than 10,000 yuan. In recent years, private lending had gained popularity, resulting in a decline in bank deposits. The interest rates for private lending were high, but borrowers would still take out loans despite the high interest rates if the need were urgent. Taking advantage of this opportunity, the township government established a credit fund in the name of a foundation, offering high interest rates to attract personal deposits and lending at similarly high rates. It disrupted normal banking operations and led to a decline in bank deposits, resulting in a credit crisis.

From the period of the production team, we began to associate with the Rural Credit Cooperative. Our team had a side business and began dealing with them again. We borrowed 3,000 yuan, which was a big loan in 1979. The entire brigade had few loans, making us the first team in the commune to receive a large loan, an exception granted by director Zheng of the Credit Cooperative. We started our factory in 1982. Little Qi, a credit officer, was responsible for this area. He was virtuous, frank in drinking, and efficient in his work. We got along well; he constantly lent us 2,000 or 3,000 yuan. The coating equipment investment cost 20,000 yuan, so I approached Little Qi, who consulted the head of the Credit Cooperative. The head stated that individual loans should not exceed 10,000 yuan. After discussing it for several days, Little Qi made an exception and lent me 20,000 yuan. The loan was approved because the Credit Cooperative recognized me as a reliable borrower. We had to wait despite excellent credit, this year, if no funds were available. There were many individuals in need of loans, while a few no longer renewed them after repaying the loans. After waiting more than 10 days, Little Qi called to inform me that the 20,000 yuan was ready. Priority was given to customers with good credit, and I applied for a loan of 20,000 yuan, but the remaining shortfall still needed to be addressed.

One day, I went to Kunlun and noticed a two-story building with a sign for the Urban Credit Cooperative. I called an old classmate in Kunlun and learned that it was a newly established bank organized by the government.

My family friend and fellow townsman, Teacher Chen, was known as Grandpa Chen due to his ancestral ties. He ran a small factory in Kunlun, and we had maintained a close friendship between generations. After completing my business at the rental station, I went to his small factory for tea, where we discussed the Urban Credit Cooperative. Teacher Chen spoke confidently, saying that he knew the director and was friends with Little Fang, the credit officer, with whom he often socialized. I mentioned the shortfall in producing shoe-polishing machine motors. I asked if Little Fang could loan us tens of thousands of yuan. Teacher Chen immediately rode his bicycle to the Credit Cooperative. Since it was not far, discussing matters in person was better than doing so over the phone.

Shortly after, Teacher Chen returned, saying, "Little Fang will be here soon. I mentioned it to him, and it should be fine." Teacher Chen poured water for me without sitting and continued, "Little Fang is reliable, honest, and straightforward. He does what he says and does not beat around the bush. Discuss it with him when he comes; it won't be a big problem."

"When was the Urban Credit Cooperative established?" I asked Teacher Chen. Its operations began in March or April, mainly serving individual small factories. It is quite convenient," Teacher Chen replied.

We discussed various business matters for over 10 minutes. When Little Fang arrived, he was of short stature with a dark complexion, but wore a smile on his face. I introduced our products and the operating conditions of our factory, and Teacher Chen encouraged me. We discussed two products: a hydraulic pillar and expanding production for shoe polishing machine motors. Our products had good sales prospects, but we lacked sufficient funds, so we urgently needed tens of thousands of yuan. Little Fang did not say much. He mentioned that funds could not be allocated solely to major clients, as the Credit

Cooperative had just been established and had been operating for less than three months. Small loans were also available to support small factories and individual business owners. He promised to arrange a loan of 30,000 yuan for us, solving the major problem of insufficient funds at that time.

With the factory building issue resolved and half the space allocated for motor production, we needed to expand our product range. We would buy the necessary machinery and equipment and handle what we could. We were almost ready. The first step was to start production, and now that we had enough funds, everything was falling into place. We had the right timing and location, but were short on workforce.

Producing motors differed from producing other industrial products. With the guidance of an experienced engineer, we could quickly start production. While motors were not complicated, they required expert guidance to produce qualified products. However, it would take some time to master motor production. The Second Young Brother had worked as a deputy factory director at the ceiling fan factory, so he had a good understanding of motor production. Without skilled workers, workshop managers, and technicians who understood the business, producing qualified products would take at least six months. It might only take two or three days to learn tasks like winding and pressing wires, but doing them neatly and efficiently, with a 99 percent success rate, would take two or three months. Even for small processes like inserting paper, drilling holes, or screwing bolts, a process was also needed. If we could recruit experienced management personnel and skilled workers from the motor production industry, it would take one to two months at most to produce qualified motors. However, it would take at least half a year if everyone were a newcomer.

The Second Young Brother inquired everywhere, gathering the chief technicians and workers who had been laid off or resigned from the ceiling fan factory, to expedite the production of shoe polishing machine motors. Information spread quickly with the small land area of Cicunzhen Village nearby. In just a few days, they managed to gather several factory officials from the ceiling fan factories, including workshop director Little Chen, technician Little Wang, wire-pressing workers Little Li and Little Zhang, totaling seven or eight personnel. With every position filled, the team was assembled. With the team assembled, we were ready to kick-start the production of the shoe-polishing machine motors.

8.3 The motors started manufacturing

The shoe polishing machines' motors were similar to those used in ceiling fans, with no differences in the housing, rotor, and stator. The second younger brother was well-versed in the entire motor manufacturing process. With some modifications in appearance and speed, he swiftly organized the components. If we could make it ourselves, we would outsource it. Seven or eight seasoned workers from the ceiling fan factory were recruited, and preparations were made in an organized and efficient manner. The plan was to produce motors within two months and establish mass production.

The motor casing was made of cast iron. There was a foundry in the neighboring village. They could produce prototypes within half a month by providing them with samples and drawings. Silicon steel sheets were used for the stator. We approached several hundred processing plants in the nearby town with forging facilities. Two or three agreed to produce the molds within half a month. They could stamp out dozens of stators in a day.

While the rotor shaft appeared simple to manufacture, it required high precision and accuracy to ensure optimal performance. Since the shoe polishing machine motor operated with minimal load and rotated for only a few minutes each time without overheating or overloading, the pass rate was 100 percent. The main focus was controlling noise, ensuring proper fit between the stator and rotor, and between the shaft and bearings. The precision required for this small shaft was higher than that for larger motor shafts. The tolerances at both ends where the bearings were installed were extremely tight, and the concentricity was high. The threads for screwing on the polished sleeve, with one end rotating clockwise and the other counterclockwise, were something small factories could not handle. The Third Branch of Boshan Electric Motor Factory could handle it, but their prices were outrageously high. Zichuan Boiler Factory had a machining workshop. However, they could only lathe the shafts and mill the threads; they lacked grinding machines. We had to find another manufacturer for grinding. The Second Branch of the Kunlun Mining Bureau General Factory could grind them, but each shaft cost three yuan. For a small shaft slightly thicker than chopsticks, the total processing fees from both factories amounted to eight yuan and 2 mao. We were unable to negotiate the price down, despite visiting over a dozen factories.

Manager Master Wang at the rental station recommended a factory in Tianjin that specialized in machining various types of motor shafts. I went to Tianjin and immediately found the state-owned factory producing shafts for various machinery and motors. They had over 100 varieties. I showed them the samples and drawings, and after careful calculation by their planner, they quoted five yuan and three mao per piece. They promised to deliver within half a month. We placed an order for 5,000 units, paid upfront, and signed a contract. I returned home joyfully. A week later, I received a call from the factory stating that, after I had left, the workshop director had recalculated and found that they could not produce them at that price, as it would incur losses. If we still wanted to proceed, we had to sign a new contract with an additional one yuan per piece. What a sham! A state-owned enterprise failed to fulfill its obligations. I had to come up with another plan.

My third younger brother returned from Shanghai to visit our parents. During a chat, the difficulty of machining motor shafts was mentioned. He suggested visiting the hardware market on Sichuan Road in Shanghai, where a wide variety of machine parts could be found. Upon returning to Shanghai, he would check if they could machine motor shafts.

My third younger brother worked at the New World Department Store, located near Sichuan Road, just two streets away, which took about 10 minutes to walk. After returning to Shanghai, he called back and said he had contacted several stores. Some said they could machine the shafts based on the provided drawings. I took the samples and drawings to Shanghai. My third younger brother accompanied me to the hardware market on Sichuan Road, where we found a shop with a large storefront run by someone from Wenzhou. The boss examined the drawings and samples, confidently stating that they could do it very well, guaranteeing it would be 100 percent accurate according to the drawings. They would provide a quote the next day, waiting for the calculation from the Wenzhou factory.

The next day, as I wandered down Nanjing Road toward Sichuan Road, I arrived at the hardware store before eleven o'clock, the agreed-upon time to discuss the price. The small boss greeted me with a smile, offered me a seat, and served tea. I had already mentioned the quantity of motor shafts required yesterday, around 4,000 to 5,000 per month, and the quantity would determine the price. After finishing a cup of tea, the small boss waited for me to speak.

"Have you calculated the price?" I asked.

"Yes, the factory has calculated it. We are quoting the lowest possible price, without padding, based on the quantity. It's two yuan and seven mao per piece, with an invoice."

I could not believe my ears. The accent between the north and the south was different. I asked again. "Is it two yuan and seven mao per unit?" I gestured with two fingers.

"Yes, two yuan and seven mao. I'm not lying."

"Let's make it an even two yuan," I joked with the small boss.

"You earn one fen less per unit. If you think it's unfair, you can check other stores." The small boss replied calmly, without a hint of panic.

The price was one-third of what I was paying. I had heard that the people of Wenzhou were sharp in business, but to this extent? How could northern industrial products compete?

"Let's not haggle over the price, but the quality must be guaranteed."

"If there's one piece that doesn't meet the standard, we'll have to

replace ten. We will deliver within seven days after placing the order."
We made a deal that the first batch of 500 pieces was for testing. Then
we signed the contract. I brought two copies of the contract, one for
each party, and signed and sealed them. The six-month-old problem
was finally solved.

As for the motor casing, we found a foundry in Shangjia Town.
It was an old factory that had been in operation for over a decade,
specializing in the casting of pig iron. After machining, there were
always pores, which were filled with putty and painted over, making
it look decent. After finishing the first batch, we sent it to the Jinan
Shoe Polishing Machine Factory for inspection. It was qualified. The
technical department requested that the casing be brighter for a better
visual effect. The progress was slow upon returning to the foundry
to discuss the pores issue. While the larger pores were reduced, the
smaller ones persisted. Once, when some casings were laid next to a
pile of discarded oil drums, it was discovered by chance that the outer
diameter of the oil drums was almost the same as that of the motor
casing. It was found to be a perfect fit after measuring with a caliper.
With three or four threads turned off the outer diameter and a few
threads off the inner diameter, it was just right for a motor casing. It
was beautiful, made of steel, shiny and bright. After a light coat of
paint, it looked better than the motors bought from Zhejiang by the
Jinan Shoe Polishing Machine Factory. With the horsepower increased,
motor production was ramped up.

8.4 Shoe Polishing Machine Offline

The mass production of the shoe polishing machine motor was
completed, and three batches were delivered to the Provincial
Household Appliance Company's shoe polishing machine factory. All
of them passed the quality inspection, making manager Wang very
satisfied. The newly built Luokou factory had started operations, and
Manager Wang invited us to visit, introducing us to the facility. The
new factory was situated west of Luokou, a considerable distance from

the city center. There were no public buses, and the taxis could not find it. It is a desolate area, and people must drive to this newly built industrial area. So, we borrowed a Santana from a friend and headed straight for the shoe-polishing machine factory.

Following manager Wang's directions, we easily found our way, as I was quite familiar with Jinan. Turning right from Beiyuan Road at the Long-Distance Bus Station, we took the Jinan-Luokou Road towards Luo Kou. When we reached a gas station, we turned left and walked west along a newly paved asphalt road until we reached the end of the road, which was the shoe-polishing machine factory.

Manager Wang led us on a tour of the new factory, introducing it as we walked. The Provincial Household Appliance Company purchased over 40 acres of land in the previous year. In the first phase, one workshop will be constructed; if it is successful, another workshop will be built the following year. Eventually, three workshops could be constructed on this land. As we entered the workshop, which had been in normal production for a month, we saw three injection molding machines taking up only a third of the space. The plastic bases, motor end caps for the shoe polishing machine, and seven or eight other components were produced on these three injection molding machines, with a monthly capacity of 5,000 units. After inspecting the injection molding machines, we followed manager Wang to the second floor, where a 30-meter assembly production line was installed. Seven or eight workers were assembling shoe polishing machines, and two of them installed switches at one end of the line. My younger brother did not accompany us; he stopped at the production line to observe. He caught up with us only after we had left the workshop.

Upon returning to the office, manager Wang explained the company's design plans and development strategies to the team. Before building the factory, the company sent staff to conduct market research in several major cities in Shandong Province, including Qingdao, Yantai, and Weifang, as well as cities near Shandong such as Tianjin, Beijing, and Shijiazhuang. After a month of negotiations with the managers of several large department stores, it was clear that there was a market for small household appliances. Initially, 2,000 units would be sold in each city, with the number gradually increasing to 5,000 to 6,000 units in the second year. With a population of 100 million in the province alone, and another 100 million in neighboring areas, the potential market demand of 200 million people translates to approximately 100,000 units annually, making it quite achievable goal. The plan was to gradually expand to other regions nationwide, to sell half a million units in the second phase and one million units in the third phase. Two workshops would be sufficient to meet the production capacity of one million units per year. In contrast, the third workshop would be used to produce other household appliances. The industrial land to the factory's north would be developed further in a few years to accommodate future expansion.

After listening to manager Wang discuss the grand vision, I asked if there were any other manufacturers in other parts of the country. I heard that a company in Fujian was preparing to produce and had already bought a batch of shoe polishing machine motors from Zhejiang Electric Machinery Factory. Manager Wang went on to say that the Chinese market is too large. They are located in the south, and we occupy the northern market, making it difficult for us to meet together. Hurry up and expand motor production. You two may not be able to supply motors next year, but I guarantee a timely power supply. Manager Wang is steady and capable, not just someone who talks big but does not follow through on practical things.

Reflecting on manager Wang's ambitious vision after returning from the shoe polishing machine factory, I realized that the Provincial Household Appliance Company was no novice in the household appliance market. They would not rush to conclusions mindlessly but rather adapt to social progress, economic development, and rising living standards. With the increasing demand for daily small household appliances, such as shoe polishing machines, the main component of which was the motor, being able to produce motors meant being able to produce shoe polishing machines, which made it seem like a straightforward task. We agreed when I shared my thoughts with my younger brother, especially after he visited the shoe polishing machine factory's production line. It led us to consider the production of shoe polishing machines as a promising prospect.

If we were to establish a production line for shoe polishing machines, we would need to register our trademark and independently explore the market. It could lead to conflicts with manager Wang and challenge his authority. After discussing with my younger brother, we decided to approach manager Wang and propose cooperation to avoid conflicts and foster mutual development. If manager Wang disagreed, we would look for alternatives. After determining the plan, we would visit manager Wang in Jinan soon.

During the second visit to the shoe polishing machine factory, when we met manager Wang again, we exchanged pleasantries before turning to the topic at hand. I laid out our proposal, expressed my admiration for his visionary goals from our previous conversation, and explained how we had prepared to expand motor production after our return. Given the market size, I suggested a joint production of shoe polishing machines. We could install an additional assembly line in one of the workshops. They could utilize our motors, and we could utilize their plastic components, thereby merging the two into one. manager Wang pondered for a few minutes after hearing my proposal, then said, "Your suggestion makes sense. We can consider it. However, I have superiors to whom I report. I'll have to present this matter to the company's top management for approval before discussing the specifics of a joint venture."

After hearing manager Wang's response, it was clear that he agreed. A mutually beneficial collaboration between the two factories would create a win-win situation. We waited for manager Wang's response.

A few days later, the phone call came, confirming manager Wang's agreement to the cooperation between the two factories. The details would be further discussed, and both parties would sign the agreement in Jinan.

In manager Wang's office, we had a heartfelt discussion about the collaboration. Manager Wang explained that the company's general manager had approved the collaboration. He emphasized that it would be a joint production of shoe polishing machines, not a partnership or joint venture. The two factories would independently handle production and sales without interference from each other. I raised my hand in agreement and supported this mode of cooperation.

Regarding the pricing of components, the motor prices had already been set. Still, there was no pricing list for plastic components. Manager Wang sent someone to inquire about other plastic factories. Typically, the pricing for plastic components would be 120 percent of the raw material price, including mold costs, mechanical depreciation, management fees, wages, and taxes. For example, if the raw material costs 10 yuan per kilogram, the product price would be 22. Two factories shared the same trademark, despite being part of the same company and having two separate production bases. Since there was no price list for plastic components, both factories would calculate the component costs based on their usage, and the total amount would be offset against each other. Other costs, such as the company's trademark, would not be charged separately. Before my visit, I had considered using the company's trademark. I wondered how much we would pay for each shoe-polishing machine. Manager Wang graciously agreed to waive any fees associated with using the company's trademark. We fully agreed with manager Wang's terms, and the Provincial Household Appliance Company's shoe polishing machine factory registered trademark "Lu Wenhua (or Shandong Culture)" would be shared by both factories. The production addresses would be listed separately in the instruction manuals, as would the after-sales service contact numbers, ensuring clarity and no interference between the two entities.

The sales territories would not overlap; demarcated areas were agreed upon. Manager Wang had a plan: in the first year, the Jinan Shoe Polishing Machine Factory would focus on sales in Jinan, Qingdao, Yantai, and Weifang. The Yongtai factory would cover Zibo and its surroundings.

Tai'an and Binzhou, as well as other cities, would be excluded for the time being. In the second year, sales would be expanded province-wide, with the Yongtai factory adding two or three more cities. Mutual communication would be essential for sales outside the province; both factories would avoid entering the same city, and no sales agreements would be made without mutual consent. A gentleman is always ready to help others attain their aims; that is settled, then.

This trip to Jinan was even more rewarding, providing us with additional momentum to move forward with the Provincial Household Appliance Company.

8.5 Advancing into the Market

With the main components of the shoe polishing machine sorted out, including small parts such as the fur cover, handlebars, and packaging boxes, we took matters into our own hands by contacting subcontractors and finding electroplating factories. We could not rely on the Jinan Shoe Polishing Machine Factory because dealing with state-owned enterprises would only cause manager Wang more trouble. After two months of preparation, the shoe polishing machine was independently assembled and put into low-volume production, ready to be pushed into the market.

The first step was approaching various department stores in each district and county, leaving no stone unturned. We first visited two major shopping centers in Zichuan: Hualian Commercial Building and Dongfang Commercial Building, located on either side of Xiguan Bridge. After finding the managers, they agreed to sell our products on a consignment basis. We arranged space for four or five machines on the shelves, with payment due after the sale. Business representatives were dispatched to Zhangdian and the municipal government headquarters to secure agreements with five or six large shopping centers. Within a month, department store shelves in various districts and counties of Zibo were adorned with a new product — the shoe polishing machine.

Advertising was essential to raise the product's profile. We visited the Zibo Daily newspaper office to ask about the advertising department. As we entered, the doorkeeper informed us that the advertising department was not located in the newspaper office, but two streets to the west, in another courtyard. After finding the advertising department on the second floor of the courtyard, the staff warmly welcomed us. I laid the instructions on the table, and a young man in his thirties took out several newspapers with advertising rates and explained them to us. Full page, half page, quarter page. The minimum number of appearances for a full page was fifteen, costing 12,000 yuan, while a half page cost 6,000 yuan. For smaller sizes, the rates decreased proportionally, with an eighth or tenth of a page, plus a few lines of text, costing at least 8,000 and 6,000 yuan, respectively. The details were explained meticulously, from determining the size of the advertisement to designing the layout, text, and slogans. Upon hearing the cost of the advertisement, I felt a sense of apprehension. We had organized production with a loan of 30,000 yuan. How could we afford to spend thousands on advertising? Moreover, advertising was not a one-time event; it had to be repeated multiple times. After pondering for half an hour, I negotiated with the young man from the advertising department. Eventually, I settled on a text-only advertisement, without images, appearing fifteen times a month for 3,000 yuan. I hoped that readers in Zibo would take notice. In those days, with few computers and no WeChat, many people still relied on newspapers for information. A week later, the advertisement was published. We received responses that showed its effectiveness, with inquiries began to pour in.

One day, as I sat alone in the office drinking tea, a Tianjin-made van pulled into the courtyard, and two people in suits and leather shoes got out, carrying briefcases on their way to the office. They did not look like government officials or salespeople. I greeted them at the door, invited them to sit on the sofa, and served them two cups of Longjing tea. After drinking the tea, he took a business card from his pocket and handed it to me with both hands.

"Ah, a reporter from the Luzhong Morning Post. Welcome,

welcome," I said, taking the business card from the table and handing it back to him.

8.5 Entering the Market

"Director Yu, may I ask if the electric shoe polishing is the product of your factory?" the journalist inquired, eyeing the small courtyard and dilapidated factory buildings skeptically.

"We've just developed this new product, the only one of its kind in the country," I fired back, my voice climbing with unshakable certainty, syllables ringing clean. I had never heard of the Luzhong Morning Post. The journalist must be a con artist trying to create a scene. "But since they can't take money from me, let's see what trick they have up their sleeves today," I thought.

The journalist was astute enough to be well aware of my skeptical attitude. As he handed me his business card, he took several newspapers from his briefcase calmly.

"This is our newly established newspaper from last month. Please have a look, director Yu."

"In which street in Jinan?" I only saw the four-character "Luzhong Morning Post" on the card, without the address.

"We're not in Jinan; our newspaper is based in Zhangdian District, Zibo," the journalist replied. As I looked at the newspaper, I examined the business card again, revealing the journalist's name: Miao Lu.

Journalist Miao explained his purpose. He had seen our advertisement in the Zibo Daily about the electric shoe polishing, and he was impressed. He admired our bold innovation, which reflected the times. He offered to publish a few free advertisements for us in the Luzhong Morning Post, with the layout to be discussed if we agreed. Why should we not agree? It was like a pie delivered to our doorstep. Miao pointed to a quarter-page advertisement in the newspaper and suggested starting with that, featuring a photo of the electric shoe polishing and a few advertising slogans. I retrieved a ready-made image from the warehouse and a box containing the electric shoe polisher, which featured a beautiful image. It caught the eye, designed by the Jinan Electric Shoe Polishing Factory, with a smiling woman gently pressing the switch as she polished a red high-heeled shoe. Miao immediately agreed to use this image.

"What advertising slogan should we use?" Miao mused aloud as he paced around the office.

After a few minutes of silence, I suddenly remembered the phrase "Returning with fragrant horse hooves after trampling flowers." I said, "Gently press, and your shoes are polished brightly."

The image of the beautiful woman pressing the switch on the handrail, her hands shining the shoes, was just as the horse returned with fragrant hooves after trampling flowers.

Miao clapped his hands in approval, saying, "Excellent! Let's use this slogan; it fits the scene perfectly."

After finalizing the advertising slogan, we had two cups of tea. Although I invited Miao to lunch, he insisted on leaving because the newspaper had just been established, and there was much to do. We agreed to visit the newspaper office soon.

One afternoon, on my way back from the Linzi Construction and Installation Company, I stopped by the Luzhong Morning Post to visit Journalist Miao. It was newly established, renting an old telecommunications building. From the Center Road to the Xingyuan Intersection, after turning north at the intersection, the Telecommunications Bureau in Zibo was located from the 1960s to the 1970s. I remembered Miao's instructions that he go for interviews in the morning and stay at the newspaper office in the afternoon.

After confirming, I found his office on the second floor. Miao was organizing his articles as I entered the office.

"Please have a seat! Have you received the newspapers we sent you?"

"Yes, I have. The layout looks great."

"I wonder how the public is reacting. " Miao said, getting straight to the point.

"The municipal government values the Luzhong Morning Post greatly. They have drawn key personnel from the Zibo Daily to help with the newspaper. The plan is to make it the second-largest newspaper in Zibo, with plans to expand to surrounding cities. That is why it is named Luzhong, not limited to just Zibo." Miao explained, and I listened attentively.

After discussing the newspaper, we talked about continuing to publish advertisements. The price was lower than the Zibo Daily, approximately one-third less. Ultimately, we agreed to pay only a quarter of what the Zibo Daily charged for the same space, with additional discounts. The advertisement would be published twice a week for three consecutive months. Miao was the director of the advertising department, so there was no need to negotiate with anyone else over the pricing. After signing the agreement, I headed back to the factory.

With advertisements in two newspapers, my friends suggested advertising on television, as it had a wider reach and a faster impact. After inquiring, the production cost for a video was tens of thousands of yuan, with each airing costing tens of thousands more. Even the simplest video, with a minimum number of airings, would cost over 100,000 yuan. This was beyond our budget. Instead, we decided to use a subtitle advertisement on television, which flashed for a few seconds, costing 5,000 yuan. It was affordable and effective. The information would spread with the television appearance, and the electric shoe polisher would officially hit the market.

With newspaper advertisements done and television commercials aired, patience was key. Rome was not built in a day; progress would come gradually.

The electric shoe polishers sent to various department stores received positive feedback. Zibo Department Store called to inform us that the first batch of 10 machines had sold out and requested an additional 20. It was the first one to call for goods. Soon after, Boshan Department Store requested more machines and purchased ten. Hualian Commercial Building and Dongfang Commercial Building in the Zichuan district each sold two. At the same time, sales in Linzi District were good, with eight machines sold between the two stores. Similarly, Huantai County and Zhoucun District also sold several machines. The sales momentum was promising.

In December, Zibo Industrial and Commercial Bank held its annual meeting and purchased 80 machines as year-end bonuses. Huayan Trading Company, managed by the town, bought 30 machines as gifts. At the same time, the Town Economic Commission purchased 40. The Credit Cooperative Agency bought 20 machines, and several factories in Kunlun Town and Zichuan district visited clients, purchasing over 10 machines each. Sales soared in December.

One day at the end of December, a Santana car arrived. Two individuals exited the car and entered the office, questioning whether it was indeed the electric shoe-polishing factory. They seemed skeptical but interested in purchasing machines and asked if we had them in stock. When asked how many they wanted, they estimated around 300 machines. They looked around eagerly and asked if they could visit the workshop. We could not let go of such a big buyer. Our production workshop for electric shoe polishers was not located in the same compound as the office; this compound was used for hydraulic prop repair and coating production. I led them out of the compound gate and walked 200 meters south to the electric shoe polishing workshop. Upon entering, they nodded in approval repeatedly and accompanied me back to the office, smiling. They were from the thermoelectric plant of Sinopec Qilu Petrochemical Company, purchasing 300 machines for their year-end meeting awards and gifts. They had not come prepared to take the machines immediately. Still, they placed an order, paying a deposit of 10,000 yuan, with delivery scheduled for the tenth of next month. It was the largest order yet, and my heart raced. After seeing off the customers, I sat down and had a cup of tea. We had a meeting in the afternoon to discuss ways to increase production.

We sold 2,300 machines during the two months before the Spring Festival. By the 25th day of the twelfth lunar month, there were still customers coming to pick up machines, and we worked overtime until the 28th of the twelfth lunar month before closing for the holiday. During the Lunar New Year, as we visited family and friends and businesses exchanged New Year's greetings, some customers came to buy machines, and we set aside 200. After the accountant finished the books, we saved 12,000 yuan. Over the past 10 years, since I established the factories, this was the first time we had savings at the end of the year. We had been financially tight every year, from producing coatings to repairing hydraulic props. Still, we were worried about having enough work after the New Year. This year, the accountant happily announced that we could purchase materials for the next two months using our current savings.

With a successful opening year for electric shoe polisher production, we planned to expand production next year and venture beyond Zibo, entering the national market.

8.6 Sudden Changes

After the Spring Festival, we sold over 20 shoe polishing machines in January. Still, there were hardly any sales from March to June. Major department stores had no inquiries. With 500 machines in stock, cash flow was tight, and we could not afford to keep excessive inventory, so production was temporarily halted. It had been six months since I last visited the Jinan Electric Shoe Polishing Machine Factory. I decided to take the truck to Jinan to understand the situation and exchange ideas.

I knocked on the door of the vice general manager Wang's office, but there was no answer, and the door was locked. Next door was director Cao's office, and he was speaking with another cadre. After their conversation, director Cao informed me that vice general manager Wang was absent that day because he was accompanying his daughter to see a doctor. I had a chat with director Cao about the market situation. Sales in the first half of the year were not optimistic. Those in Qingdao and Yantai were minimal, far worse than expected. Only a few hundred machines were sold in over a dozen major stores in Jinan. Store managers reported that few were buying out of their own needs; most were prizes or small gifts. We planned to expand into the southern market, as the economy was more developed in the Jiangsu and Zhejiang regions. We explored the markets in Suzhou,

Wuxi, Changzhou, and Shanghai. Director Cao, a cadre of the Shandong Provincial Household Electrical Appliances Company, had a down-to-earth attitude and was chosen by vice general manager Wang to set up the Electric Shoe Polishing Machine Factory. We chatted until eleven o'clock, but the vice general manager Wang still had not arrived. It seemed he might come in the afternoon. I had to go to the city to buy an internal micrometer, so I returned in the afternoon.

I arrived at the Electric Shoe Polishing Machine Factory at 2:00 p.m. However, vice general manager Wang still had not shown up by three. In those days, there were no mobile phones, so I did not wait any longer. There was no urgent matter to discuss, so I returned another day.

It has been almost a month since I returned from Jinan without seeing vice general manager Wang. I decided to visit again. Upon entering the Electric Shoe Polishing Machine Factory, I found vice general manager Wang's office locked. Fortunately, director Cao was there.

I asked, "Vice general manager Wang is not at work today. Is he on a business trip?"

"Let's talk in the office." Director Cao replied. He led us into the office. After a few minutes of silence, he poured some water for us. "Vice general manager Wang is in the hospital. On the day you came last time, he felt dizzy and cold, and his daughter accompanied him to see a doctor. The doctor recommended a CT scan. When the results came out, the doctor did not let him see them and asked him to return the next day with a companion. His wife went with him the next day, and the doctor advised him to be hospitalized. When he asked about his condition, the doctor initially refused to say, but eventually told him he had a brain tumor. His legs weakened when he heard this, and he was unable to walk down the stairs. His wife and the driver, Little Zhang, helped him downstairs. He was very generous in ordinary times, but collapsed when he found out he had cancer. He has been in the hospital for a month and hasn't shown any signs of improvement."

I added, "It has been a month. Wang's condition seems severe."

Director Cao was the deputy general manager, Wang's vice, in charge of production. Vice general manager Wang was the vice general manager of the Shandong Provincial Household Electrical Appliances Company, as well as the secretary and factory director of the Electric Shoe Polishing Machine Factory. With a higher rank than the factory director, he was usually referred to as the manager rather than the director. Director Cao was the deputy director, and he was usually addressed as director Cao when vice general manager Wang was not at work. Director Cao was now in charge of the work.

Upon hearing that vice general manager Wang was hospitalized, I felt it was necessary to visit the hospital. I went through Zhongshan Park to the Provincial Hospital. On the twelfth floor in the oncology ward, vice general manager Wang lay in bed, looking completely different from a month ago. He was thin, his eyes barely opened, and his voice was barely audible.

"I can't pull through... I cannot," he whispered.

"Hang in there. You will be discharged in a few days. There are good medicines now, and you'll recover soon."

I tried to offer comforting words, but he shook his head with tears in his eyes. I could not stay by the patient's bedside for long. After just over ten minutes, I hurriedly left, feeling a mix of indescribable emotions.

Three years before, my younger brother had introduced me to the factory on Taoyuan Road. The first time I met manager Wang, he was tall, about 40 years old, in his prime, and had just been promoted to deputy General Manager of the household appliance company. With his youthful vigor, he walked with confidence and spoke with authority. He had the demeanor of a cadre, a friendly face, and was approachable. I accompanied Teacher Chen to purchase glasses for the prevention and treatment of myopia used by students; manager Wang not only lowered the price to the lowest point but also offered us a banquet at noon.

Two years ago, manager Wang had moved to the new factory in Luokou in Jinan, investing in shoe polishing machine production, borrowing to build the factory and expand the market, rallying a new army in the household appliance industry. In the first year, we rooted ourselves in the middle parts of Shandong Province. We planned to expand into the northern and Southern Jiangsu, eastern Zhejiang, and western Zhejiang markets in the second year. In the third year, we had entered the three northeastern provinces. What a grand blueprint with ambitious goals, expecting to occupy the national market within three years. It was very uplifting and inspiring, but unexpectedly, the coach was bedridden on the way out. Just as the saying goes, "Man proposes, and God disposes."

One year ago, manager Wang helped me set up the shoe polishing machine, supported me, and hung up the "Lubin" sign. Just as I stood firm, just as I began to develop the market, just as I spread my wings to take flight, just as the flowers began to bloom, but before they bore fruit, manager Wang, unable to oversee, left us suddenly. Leaving the gate of the Provincial Hospital, I could not calm down for a long time, hoping for a miracle from heaven.

One day, a car carrying plastic parts for a shoe polishing machine returned from Jinan. The salesperson who accompanied the car told me that manager Wang had passed away two days prior. It had only been 20 days since I had visited him in Jinan. It was less than two months from hospitalization to departure — too fast, according to what the salesperson had heard from the caretaker at the Jinan Shoe Polishing Machine Factory.

I delivered 200 motors a month later, planning to bring back 400 plastic parts. However, I only managed to retrieve 100. The salesperson explained that the workshop's production was abnormal, and raw materials could not be obtained.

I rushed to the Jinan Shoe Polishing Machine Factory to see what was happening. On the day of my visit, I did not see director Cao; he was on a business trip. Workshop director Dongye discussed the situation in the factory with me. Since manager Wang was hospitalized and stopped coming to work, it had been three months. The factory was in chaos, operating for three days and closing for two. He could not handle it. He was honest, reliable, and capable of managing production. Still, there was a gap in his ability to manage the overall situation. He was too busy running around, unable to develop a comprehensive plan. Previously, manager Wang had traveled several times a month to manage the market in other locations. He would leisurely drink tea in the office and make a round in the workshop. He was relaxed as if he had nothing to do. With chaos in the factory, the deputy Manager Cao could not even hold a cadre meeting. I heard the company sent a new factory director, but he had not arrived yet. We would see how to proceed next. Director Dongye spoke for over an hour. Other leaders in the factory did not recognize me, and I did not stay long. After listening, I left the factory.

What worried me was how cooperation would proceed once the new factory director arrived. Would they agree to use the trademark? Could the components still be exchanged? How would market sales be allocated? Could conflicts be resolved smoothly? Changing the leader would bring numerous problems, and preparations must be made well in advance.

Little Fan from the shoe polishing machine factory had worked at the household appliance company seven or eight years ago, and my younger brother was familiar with him. They had some interactions before. After the shoe polishing machine factory was established, he was transferred from the company to serve as the deputy manager of the sales department, where he was responsible for business development. I had met him at the Electric Shoe Polishing Machine Factory. One noon, he suddenly came to see me, so it must be something important. Luckily, I was not on a business trip.

Little Fan had graduated from university and been assigned to the Provincial Household Appliance Company. Being assigned to a provincial-level unit during the planned economy era was a mark of excellence, as he was an outstanding and highly talented student. He excelled in his work at the shoe-polishing machine factory. When he visited that day, he did not stray from the topic, speaking about shoe polishing machine sales before discussing the current situation in the factory. Following the illness and passing away of manager Wang, deputy manager Cao served as the head for several months. Still, he proved unable to handle the role effectively. A new factory director, an administrative cadre with no industry experience, was transferred to the company. Despite working for over two months, he had not grasped the essentials. He was worse at managing than deputy manager Cao, completely clueless, putting on the airs of a senior company executive, reciting meeting protocols and official documents, and criticizing others with sound arguments, but unable to offer solutions for business development. He often got stuck after a few sentences in his speech. Bank loans were overdue by two months, and despite frequent visits from the bank presidents to urge payment, the new factory director was at a loss, sighing in his office. Little Fan pointed out that at this rate, the factory might close by the end of the year. There were no young cadres like manager Wang, who understood both the business and management and were diligent and practical in our company. Several deputy general managers were nearing retirement age. At the same time, the department heads were good at boasting and discussing national policies. Still, they could not run a business.

After discussing the factory's situation, Little Fan explained the purpose of his visit today. From picking up shoe polishing machines from our factory to managing sales in shopping malls and downtown areas under his responsibility, it was effortless to sell a single brand, complete sales, and settle accounts. He needed details on the sales policy, shipping, commission, and compensation fees. His sudden visit caught us off guard, having been made without prior preparation or precedent. He made his demands and conditions known first, then returned to Jinan. My younger brother and I discussed it. He could earn more, and I could sell more shoe polishing machines. It would be a win-win situation, so we agreed to sign the agreement next time.

Little Fan's timely arrival provided even more timely information. Just a few days ago, my younger brother and I were casually chatting, thinking that even if a new factory director took over, we could still manage for a year or two at worst. We anticipated some coordination issues in our respective businesses, but did not expect such rapid changes. Little Fan was an insider; he saw things clearly, whereas we saw them superficially. Regardless of the circumstances, it is wise to prepare early.

8.7 Double Harvest after the Trip to Ningbo City

When we produced the electric motors for the Jinan Electric Shoe Polishing Factory, our business license listed the scope of operations as electric motors, electric shoe polishers, and their parts. With prior preparation, I added electric shoe polishers to the scope of operations; there was no need to change the license. We used the Jinan Electric Shoe Polishing Factory's trademark but operated independently of it. We needed to register another trademark separately. The accountant went to the Industrial and Commercial Bureau to register a Yongtai trademark.

There were eight plastic components on the electric shoe polishers. Unable to wait for the Jinan Electric Shoe Polishing Factory to cease production, we immediately searched for a plastic processing factory. Customization requires time, with the quickest turnaround being two to three months. There were many plastic mold factories and plastic processing factories in Zhangqiu District, Jinan, Shandong Province, so we started by searching in Xianggongzhuang Town, Zhangqiu County. We discovered the largest plastic factory in the area, which produced molds and plastic parts. As amateurs, we relied on their cost calculations. We brought 10 samples of plastic parts, we weighed them, and calculated the costs. After factoring in mold costs, we found that the total costs for the three major plastic components were twice as much as the Jinan Electric Shoe Polishing Factory. Unable to order, we visited two more plastic factories with similar prices. Prices varied by 10 percent up and down among plastic and mold factories in the area, so we decided to seek another manufacturer.

Leveraging the Sinopec Qilu Petrochemical Company in Linzi

District, many plastic processing factories have emerged. Several customers of our coating had extensive connections, so we asked them to introduce us to some plastic factories. My first stop was at the Linzi Construction and Installation Company. We met Manager Liu, who had worked for over 30 years since he was sixteen, and had a wide network. After I explained my purpose to Manager Liu, he immediately set aside his work. He took me to a plastic factory across from the Dongfeng Railway Station. The factory owner was familiar with Manager Liu. I placed the three major plastic components on the table, and the factory owner called a technician to weigh them.

"How many pieces do you need monthly?" the factory owner asked me. I did not exaggerate the numbers and gave a conservative estimate.

"3,000 to 4,000 pieces per month," I replied, not entirely truthfully.

"That's too little. One shift can produce between 700 and 800 parts. Three to four shifts will cover the monthly demand. Manager Liu is an old friend of mine, so I cannot refuse."

The factory owner thought the quantity was too small, so the price would not be low. He would not disclose the price unless I asked. Being from the north, he took pride in himself and felt embarrassed about refusing a friend's friend. After a few polite words, he calculated the price later and passed it on to me through Manager Liu.

A few days later, Manager Liu informed me of the price, which was a few fen higher than in Xianggongzhuang Town.

We have approached several plastic factories for the three small plastic parts of the switches. The larger ones declined, citing the small size of the parts. In comparison, the smaller ones struggled with the processing complexity and the high technical requirements. Unable to find a processing factory around Zibo, we turned to Little Fan to find out which company Jinan Electric Shoe Polishing Factory sourced from in the south. Many plastic factories in the north closed down each year. At the same time, Wenzhou City of Zhejiang Province dominated the national market. Little Fan provided the address of the plastic switch factory, and I made a special trip to visit it.

Since plastic switches needed to be sourced from Zhejiang Province, there was no need to wander around for several large plastic components. Crossing the Yangtze River, we would procure all the plastic components.

My old classmate, Li Yinjian from the Zibo Plastic Fourth Factory, provided the contact for a plastic processing factory in Zhejiang Province, located in Changhe Town, Cixi City. I transferred from Hangzhou City to Ningbo City by train, got off at Yuyao County, and took a bus directly to Changhe Town. Following the map, I found the plastic processing factory — an ordinary rural gate, a small courtyard with no factory sign, occupying about half a mu of land. After scanning the surroundings — a dozen houses, with only one functioning as an office — I met the owner, a thin man in his thirties with a Southern physique. A few days ago, my old classmate had asked a friend to make a call ahead so the owner would know I was coming. After examining several samples of electric shoe polishers' parts, he brought out a scale and weighed each one separately.

He spoke in stiff Mandarin and said, "It will take about a month to make the molds. When the molds are finished, you can ask for them anytime."

"I need the prices to be accurate from the start. I have come from Shandong Province," I replied, watching him calculate the prices for each item using a calculator.

"Don't worry about the prices. They will not be too high. Let me see. This one costs 5.3 yuan, this one costs 2.2 yuan, and these two together cost 7.5 yuan. That is a total of 11.1 yuan. We'll round it down to 11 yuan for the set," he said casually, undercutting Jinan's prices by three yuan.

I tried to bargain, saying, "How about rounding it down to 10 yuan?"

"Boss, I'm not lying to you. I have already offered the lowest price. Your friend recommended you so that I will not charge much. There are several plastic factories nearby. You can check them out and choose the one that suits you best. It is okay," he said, with a Southern demeanor but a northern style. With matters reaching this point, we signed the agreement.

Within an hour, the business was completed. Seeing such a large price difference between the north and south for a small plastic part, I wondered what tricks they had employed to achieve this disparity. The owner led me on a tour of the plastic processing factory, which had four injection molding machines in a tall building to the west. Pointing at the two larger machines — each weighing 300 grams — he explained that they were for larger components, while the two smaller ones — each weighing 200 grams — were suitable for my parts. Moved to the southern side, 10 manual injection molding machines were lined up, operated without motors, with the smallest being vertical. Making a few grams of small plastic parts involved heating the electric furnace, injecting plastic granules into the mold, manually pulling it down, waiting a few seconds, and then releasing it. The upper mold automatically retracted when released, and the product was ready.

When I picked up two small plastic tubes, the owner pointed and said, "These are pen shafts."

In the northern room, eight female workers sat, each with four boxes in front of her. There were four different small plastic tubes. All I could hear was the sound of "boop, boop," as the workers quickly assembled pens. The owner picked up two and handed them to me, explaining that they were for export to European countries.

"How many orders do you have in a month?" I asked the owner.

"We just make them. Foreign trade companies come regularly to collect them. There are over a dozen factories involved. The foreign trade companies manage the orders," he replied.

"And how much profit do you make per pen? A few jiao?" I asked.

"Haha, a few jiao? It is less than half a fen," he chuckled.

A small factory produced small products, exported to Europe, making fractions of a few fen — this was what rolled in from the gold and silver mountains. We Zibo folks used to look down on such small products. Sent to Jiangsu Province and Zhejiang Province, they laid the foundation for many future large enterprises.

"Let's have lunch with some Shaoxing Yellow Rice Wine," the owner insisted, but time was tight, so I could not stay. I rushed back to Ningbo City the next day to confirm the switches.

After breakfast, I took the No. 8 bus to its terminal in Ningbo overnight. Asking a passerby, I learned that the plastic factory was still quite a distance away, about five kilometers, located in the Yinzhou district in Yin County. I had no choice but to take a taxi. Afraid the driver might not understand northern dialects, I handed him a written address slip. The starting point was by the lake, and the car circled the lake for a while before turning onto a cobblestone road. After about three or four meters, it stopped at a small village intersection.

The driver said, "This is the village."

An older man stood at the intersection. After asking twice and receiving clear directions, I walked down the alley to its end, where the plastic factory was located.

I arrived at the end and followed the cobblestone road for a few minutes. Then there were two brand-new large red doors.

As I entered, a middle-aged woman greeted me, and I asked, "Is this the plastic switch factory?"

"Yes, yes, please come in," she replied.

It was a family-run factory, and there was no sound of machinery. I sat down on the sofa in the living room. A young man in his thirties came in.

"It's hard to travel by train from Shandong; I received a call from Little Fan and knew you were coming," he said as he made tea. "This little village is quaint and beautiful, with Taihu Lake ahead and green mountains behind."

I struck up a conversation.

As I drank tea, the young man left and returned shortly with two switches.

"Are these the switches you need? The ones used on shoe polishing machines?" he asked.

"Yes, exactly. My factory produces shoe polishing machines, and we used to source the switches from the Jinan Electric Shoe Polishing Machine Factory. I only discovered recently that your factory produces switches," I replied.

"Why aren't you sourcing the switches from Jinan anymore?" the young man asked.

"We collaborate with the Jinan factory for the shoe polishing machine production. I produce the motors, while the Jinan factory produces the plastic parts. Our collaboration was going well, but after manager Wang passed away, there have been significant changes in the factory," I explained.

But before I could continue, the young man interjected, "Manager Wang passed away? What happened?"

"He had malignant tumors," I replied.

"We only met once. Wang was a good person. Such an early death, such an early death."

The young man shook his head and said nothing further.

Our business negotiations went smoothly. Since the switches we needed were standard, we did not need to renegotiate quality and price. We agreed to meet again to finalize the deal. I decided to purchase directly from his factory, establishing a new business relationship. The young man assured me he could fulfill orders promptly and satisfactorily. After half an hour of discussions, the young man showed me around the workshop.

We turned from the corner of the west building and entered another courtyard. There were three rooms for assembling switches, with six female workers assigned to each assembly room.

There were many varieties, so I asked the young man, "How many types of switches do you produce?"

"Over 30 varieties," he replied.

"Could I take a look at your plastic products workshop?" I asked.

"The plastic parts are sourced from other factories; I only produce copper sheets and do not engage in plastic products," he said, leading me to three rooms on the right.

Inside were six small punching machines lined up, with six female workers operating each machine. They were stamping various copper pieces, all for switches, ranging from thin to thick, measuring half a centimeter or more, in both square and round shapes, mostly copper with some aluminum.

After the workshop tour, we walked into the courtyard and saw orange trees in the distance.

"Let's look at the oranges," the young man invited.

"Sure."

Leaving the village, we arrived at the foot of the mountain. The terraced fields on the mountainside were neatly arranged, with rows of orange trees, thick as fists, densely packed with oranges. The branches were pressed down like carrying poles. Following the narrow mountain path, we reached the halfway point on the mountain. There were no orange trees further up, just dense bushes. It was the first time I had seen such an orange grove. Here, there were no rocks or weeds, just good mountains and treasure mountains.

After seeing the mandarin grove, I checked the time. It was almost 10 o'clock. I bade farewell and prepared to return to Ningbo.

"Don't leave yet. Would you like to taste Ningbo cuisine?" the young man insisted, not letting me leave. He insisted we have lunch.

"It's still early for lunch. It will not be late if I go back to Ningbo now," I said.

"Workers here start at six in the morning, have lunch at 10:30, finish work at 15:30 in the afternoon, and go home to play cards," the young man explained. "Let's have lunch now."

We did not enter the living room; instead, we went straight to the dining room. There was no distinction between guests and hosts. We sat casually. Six people were at the table. After about 10 minutes, the dishes were served. These were local, quite different from those in Shandong. They are prepared casually," the young man said as he arranged the table.

There were two bottles of Gu Yue Long Shan, a brand of Chinese liquor, on the table. The young man opened them and poured the wine, saying, "This is Shaoxing Old Wine. Are you used to it?" "Yes,

I'm accustomed to it. I have had it in Shanghai before. It tastes very good. I have had Shikumen yellow wine and loose yellow wine in Shanghai," I replied.

Dish after dish was served: steamed fish, braised spare ribs with preserved vegetables, marinated pork, and marinated yellow croaker. The young man offered me food, saying, "Try the steamed fish. Is it not prepared this way in Shandong?" I took a bite and found it quite salty, unlike the other dishes, which were not salty at all. The vegetables were light and lacked saltiness.

I casually asked, "What are the characteristics of Ningbo cuisine?"

The young man replied, "Ningbo cuisine is original and authentic, neither sweet nor spicy."

"Do people in the south mostly eat sweet food?" I asked.

"Sweet dishes are mostly in Suzhou, Wuxi, and Changzhou. Shanghai slightly prefers sweetness, but Ningbo has no sweet dishes," the young man explained.

He kept urging me to eat and drink, and three of us at the table were drinking. The two bottles of Gu Yue Long Shan were almost empty. The young man toasted me, and we finished both bottles of old wine. I had a feeling I had drunk a bottle myself.

After finishing our meal and drinks, it was not yet noon. The young man arranged for a van to take me back to the hotel in Ningbo. In the afternoon, I would be heading to Shaoxing. This trip involved placing an order for plastic components and switches, as well as visiting the hometown of Lu Xun.

After entering grades five and six, I knew Lu Xun was China's greatest writer, occupying the top seat among writers. In our Chinese language textbooks, we read "Hometown," "From the Hundred Herbs Garden to the Three Tastes Schoolhouse," and "The Story of Medicine." Mysterious and profound, we seemed to understand them, but not quite so, for example, why Hua Laoshuan and Hua Xiaoshuan, a father-son pair, ate buns with human blood to cure the son's sickness? "Hometown" was easy to understand; Runtu and Shuisheng, two characters in Lu Xun's story "Hometown", caught fish by the sea and caught sparrows in the courtyard. "From Hundred Herbs Garden Three Tastes Schoolhouse" was more interesting, where children played and memorized their lessons. During the 10 years of the Cultural Revolution, from 1966 to 1976, Lu Xun was elevated to the status of a deity, a great literary figure, a revolutionary, and a thinker. Anyone disrespectful to Lu Xun, mocking him, would be labeled as a capitalist lackey or a member of the Cultural Gang of Four (a group of influential Chinese cultural figures from the 1930s whom Lu Xun satirically referred to for their dominant roles and behaviors during that time), who were all to be overthrown. No matter how the winds of society changed, Lu Xun's literary status remained unchanged. Regardless of scholarly attainment or fame, Lu Xun was revered by the world. Stepping down from the pedestal, Lu Xun remained an extraordinary writer in the history of Chinese literature.

Visiting Lu Xun's hometown had been a longstanding wish of mine. Walking through the streets of Shaoxing, there were few people in the morning. After breakfast, I unknowingly strolled to the scenic area. Since the scenic area opened late, I wandered the main street first. The old street had not changed much. In 1995, it seemed that the winds of reform had not blown in. The buildings on both sides of the street were two or three stories tall, with a few scattered new buildings; however, none exceeded 10 stories in height. The big trees and sidewalks along the street looked unchanged for decades. When I reached the entrance of Lu Xun's hometown, the gate was still closed. It did not open until eight-thirty. Xianheng Tavern, where Kong Yiji drank old wine, stood on the street. It was not the small tavern of the past where "four wen or pennies (wen, 文 , modern Chinese monetary units of measurement) bought a bowl of wine, standing by the counter, drinking hot and taking a rest." The tavern had expanded into a five-star restaurant. No one stood and drank anymore, and the gates were tightly shut before work hours.

The gate slowly opened, and the waiting tourists streamed in. The entire street was lined with buildings from Lu Xun's "Hometown," still built to resemble the old model. Lu Xun's family house was sold to the descendants of Zhu Wengong. Still, after Liberation, it was reclaimed by the government and converted into the Lu Xun Former Residence Memorial Hall. The entire street had no grand mansions of high-ranking officials; instead, it featured ordinary courtyards with small gates and low houses, possibly the residences of low-income families from 100 years ago.

Lu Xun's former residence was an ordinary Jiangnan-style house. Two rows of houses, without grand halls with high platforms, without flying eaves and carved beams of phoenixes (凤凰 , a sacred bird in ancient Chinese myths and legends) and "qilins" or Chinese unicorn (麒 麟 , Kylin or kirin, a mythical creature from ancient Chinese lore, symbolizing good fortune, peace, and prosperity). Lu Xun's grandfather's official position was not very prominent, and there was not much money to build a grand mansion, so it fell into disrepair.

After visiting Lu Xun's old house, I walked further. I arrived at the famous Hundred Herbs Garden, about an acre in size, Lu Xun's childhood paradise. It was still the same old place; the trees and flowers were less impressive. The trees planted were not valuable, and the flowers were not colorful; it was just an ordinary rural courtyard. I did not see "the emerald green vegetable plots, the smooth stone well railings, the tall soapberry trees, the purple-red mulberries, not to mention the cicadas singing on the leaves, the fat yellow wasps resting on the cabbage flowers, and the agile skylarks suddenly soaring up into the sky" as described in "Hundred Herbs Garden." The layout of the Hundred Herbs Garden was inferior to that of an ordinary park in Jiangnan. It seemed to be unmanaged. I felt very disappointed. For those who had studied in high school, literature enthusiasts, who wouldn't remember the Hundred Herbs Garden?

From Lu Xun's former residence, the sign read, "Heading east from the door, less than 500 meters away, after crossing a stone bridge, you arrive at my teacher's home. Through a black bamboo door, the third room is the study, with a plaque in the middle that says: Three Tastes Schoolhouse." The description in Lu Xun's books had not changed. Arriving at Three Tastes Schoolhouse, I found a room with a long table in the middle and six chairs; the layout of Lu Xun's childhood classroom remained unchanged. Standing under the plaque of San Wei Shu Wu, or the Three Tastes Schoolhouse, I looked at the private schoolhouse where Lu Xun studied. It was not only an ordinary house, but also a famous one that had gained widespread recognition.

A visit here should not be in vain, so I bought a souvenir — folding fans sold at the entrance — and had them inscribed on the spot. After giving my name, a poem was written on the fan beginning with each character of my name. The poem I was given read: "Mr. Yu arrived in the south of the Yangtze River at a time when the spring was bright and beautiful, the country flourished, and the people prospered with blessings and longevity."

Even Kong Yiji could not be forgotten. Xianheng Tavern had opened its doors. Kong Yiji, dressed in a gray robe, stood somberly at the door, holding a wine glass, watching the beautiful women and handsome men come and go. Gone were the curved counters, the warm water for wine, and the bowing shop assistants at the entrance. Instead, there was a long, dazzling glass counter with two young female servers inside. The spacious hall had several small tables that could seat four people each. It was just 10 o'clock, the store had just opened, and there were no customers. I wanted to buy a plate of fennel beans, a plate of boiled bamboo shoots, and a bowl of hot Shaoxing Old Yellow Wine, sit at a small table, and slowly savor them. However, being alone, I no longer wanted to imitate Kong Yiji.

Kong Yiji was one of Lu Xun's most representative works. Who in China or among overseas Chinese doesn't know about Kong Yiji at Xianheng Tavern? Its influence is immense and unmatched. The Xianheng Tavern before me had modernized, reaching a five-star level. It was no longer the old Xianheng described by Lu Xun. There was a huge contrast between the Three Tastes Schoolhouse and the Hundred Herbs Garden. I wonder what the descendants of Lu Xun and Kong Yiji would feel about this.

To the right of Xianheng Tavern was the Xianheng Tavern food specialty store, specializing in Xianheng food products. There were fennel beans, boiled bamboo shoots, pickled vegetables, and marinated chicken and duck. After visiting Xianheng, I could not leave empty-handed, so I bought several packets to enjoy at home.

This trip to Zhejiang was a double harvest. I successfully purchased shoe polishers and their components, fulfilled the dream of visiting Lu Xun's former residence, and took a bus back to the factory according to the planned schedule.

8.8 Heading to Shanxi, Hebei, and the Three Northeast Provinces of China

The "Yongtai" trademark had been approved, and the shoe polishing machine could now break out of Shandong Province and expand nationwide. The Jinan Electric Shoe Polishing Machine Factory was semi-paralyzed, and our cooperation with them had come to an end. Parts had been exchanged, accounts settled, and there were no strings attached. The next step was to increase production and expand into neighboring provinces.

Jinan Electric Shoe Polishing Machine Factory entered the markets in Tianjin and Beijing last year. My factory had just ended its cooperative relationship with this factory, so we could not encroach on them. However, Taiyuan and Shijiazhuang were viable options. They were both provincial capitals, so the market potential should be good.

We have been doing business with the Taiyuan Hydraulic Research Institute for three years. With familiar faces and places, we needed to proceed cautiously in the market. We have only dealt with commercial departments for over a year, so our experience was limited. We should take it one step at a time. I brought along our salesperson, Little Zhao, to Taiyuan. Mr. Sun, the director of the institute, arranged for Little Wang to drive a van and take me around the department stores. Little Wang knew which stores were big and which were small, so we started with the largest one in Taiyuan, Hualian Department Store. We found the manager of the electronics department. With Little Wang's introduction, the manager read the specification and quickly agreed to consignment without hesitation, with payments settled monthly. The first store went smoothly, so we continued. At the second store, Dongfeng Mall, we found the business manager after waiting an hour. After establishing a relationship, they agreed to let us be their agents. Unfortunately, the manager was not available at the third store, and this staff member was unable to make a decision. It was already close to noon. Sun had prepared a banquet, so we decided to try again in the afternoon.

We could not trouble Little Wang in the afternoon, so we made arrangements to continue the next day. We visited three more stores the next day and successfully signed contracts. There were only six major department stores in Taiyuan, so we managed to cover most of them. We did not bother with small stores.

When delivering the shoe polishing machines to department stores, nobody was aware of them, so we needed to conduct some publicity and advertising. However, our factory was not large, and we did not have a lot of capital. Hence, advertising in provincial capital cities was out of our reach. I lamented about this to Little Wang, and he said that his father worked for the Taiyuan Evening News and might be able to help. We found the newspaper office and spoke with Little Wang's father, explaining our advertising needs. I had experience placing text ads in the Zibo Daily, so I suggested a simple text ad without graphics or large banners. Little Wang's father, who was the head of a certain department, quoted us a price of 2,600 yuan. If it proved effective, we could consider expanding to include graphics or television commercials, taking it one step at a time.

With the Taiyuan business sorted out, we headed straight to Shijiazhuang. Although I have passed through Shijiazhuang several times by train, this was my first time entering the city. After checking into a hotel, I started asking around. I purchased a city map and inquired with the hotel staff about the major department stores in the area. I learned that five large department stores were located in different parts of the city. Armed with our product manuals, we hailed a Tianjin-Dafa taxi and started visiting each one. Negotiating business was smooth, with agreements for consignment without the need for bargaining. We needed to be wary of scams and ensure we did not lose any shoe polishing machines. Settlement depended on sales, so the contract was easy to sign. Priced at 209 yuan each in the market, we purchased them for 160 yuan each, resulting in a profit of 49 yuan per unit for the department stores. We planned to stay for two days, but finished our business in one day and signed contracts with four stores. One store intentionally made it difficult for us. It could not make just one demand, offering a single price for 10 units and another for 20 units. If they could not sell five units within several months, we would be required to pay for occupying the counter space. They were not on the right track. We were bound to be fooled if we dealt with them, so we stayed two nights before returning to prepare for delivery.

We purchased spray powder from the Taiyuan Hydraulic Research Institute every month, typically around a ton, or approximately 600 to 700 kilograms. At that time, there were no delivery trucks, so we had to rely solely on trains for transportation. Typically, it took 10 days for goods to arrive from Taiyuan to Zibo Station. Still, it occasionally arrived in as few as seven days. Once, however, it took half a month. We inquired with the Taiyuan freight depot, and they assured us the train had departed on time. We frequently picked up goods, so the warehouse staff at Zibo Station were familiar with us. We were unable to locate the delivery after waiting two days and rechecking the warehouse, including reviewing the receipt records. We then contacted Taiyuan Station, and they advised us to check with other stations in Zibo. We checked Zhoucun Station, the largest freight depot in Zibo, first, but found nothing of interest. Next, we checked Zichuan Station, also to no avail. Finally, we found it at Boshan Station. With the spray powder unavailable, production halted for five days. On another occasion, the shipment was sent to Jinan and mistakenly unloaded there instead of being transferred to Zibo. Mistaken deliveries were common in the 1990s, and it was difficult to hold anyone accountable.

When delivering the shoe polishing machines to Taiyuan and Shijiazhuang, using trains was not an option. We used our own Jinbei minivan for transportation. This van was very old and had numerous problems, but there was no need to worry about it breaking down in the Zibo area. However, I was worried about crossing the Taihang Mountains this time. Since I had a vehicle, I could not hire someone else's. I gathered my courage and decided to transport the shoe polishing machines to Taiyuan, bringing back a ton of spray powder, which proved to be a cost-effective decision.

With the arrangements in Taiyuan and Shijiazhuang settled, we prepared to head to northeast China. The northeast was vast and rich in resources, once the leader in heavy industry nationwide. However, by the 1990s, it had fallen behind. Anyway, a lean camel is bigger than a horse. The market demand volume was better than that in the Central Plains and Northwest China. We planned to test the market for shoe polishing machines in the Northeast before moving to Central China and the Jiangnan region, which is located to the south of the Yangtze River.

When selling shoe polishing machines in the northeast, we considered sending relatively stable sales representatives who were familiar with the local customs. Selling products requires understanding local habits and customs. After much consideration, I thought Old Zhao would be the most suitable candidate.

I informed Old Zhao to come to the office to discuss the sale of shoe polishing machines in the northeast. I briefed him on the department stores in Taiyuan and Shijiazhuang, as well as the agreed-upon prices. Old Zhao shared his thoughts, pointing out that the northeast's opening-up process was relatively slow, with the planned economy still predominant. It differed from the south, where markets opened earlier and more rapidly, resulting in sellers quoting high prices and buyers haggling fiercely. In the northeast, proceeding steadily and following the traditional route of state-owned enterprises was crucial. I agreed with Old Zhao's assessment. For the first trip, we would only visit the three provincial capitals: Shenyang, Changchun, and Harbin.

After an hour of discussion, we settled on selling shoe-polishing machines in the Northeast. Prices would be the same as those in

Taiyuan, ranging from 200 to 220 yuan per unit. We would not sell for less than 200 yuan or more than 220 yuan. We could not sell at a high price. We would offer the department stores a price of 160 yuan per unit, bypassing agents and dealing directly with the stores, with a focus on major department stores rather than scattered sales points. Each city had three or four large shopping malls, and we did not distribute multi-point sales. The method of transporting the shoe polishing machine to the northeast depended on the specific situation, and we made the necessary arrangements accordingly. Old Zhao was prepared to depart for the northeast within two or three days.

Ten days later, Old Zhao returned from the northeast. He had contacted eleven department stores in the three major cities — four in Shenyang, three in Changchun, and four in Harbin. All were state-owned department stores that had not undergone restructuring. We arranged for consignment sales and managed deliveries to the store warehouses ourselves.

The round trip was over 3,000 kilometers, and sending goods by train was the most cost-effective method of transportation. Sometimes, when chatting with friends, the topic of missing goods on trips to the northeast would come up. Despite purchasing insurance guarantees from the stations for hundreds or even thousands of yuan, tracking down missing small items was often impossible. Collecting insurance payouts proved to be even more challenging. Warehouse staff at the department stores were not responsible for receiving goods, so salespeople had to handle it themselves. Staying in large cities meant they could not always commit to a specific delivery time, sometimes taking five or six days or even ten. In those days, there were no trucks for delivering goods.

What could we do? We eventually decided to take our old and ailing Taishan 130 truck to the northeast. Old Zhao arranged for the vehicle to be serviced, a process that took two days to complete. After three days of trial runs to ensure it was in good condition, we sent it with two drivers, accompanied by Old Zhao, to deliver the shoe polishing machines to the northeast.

8.9 Exporting Shoe Polishing Machines to Singapore

I received a phone call from someone who greeted me with three or four "Nihao" (formal hello), which did not sound like a Chinese person. In 1996, when digital phones had only been installed for two years in Zibo, Chinese people didn't usually start a call with "Ninhao." The caller, from Singapore, with an office in Zichuan, invited me to discuss exporting shoe polishing machines to Singapore. He provided the office address: Zihong Road.

As arranged, I found the office on the second floor across from the gate of the Zibo Mining Bureau. At the appointed time, a young man in his thirties was waiting at the door and led me into the office. A middle-aged man in his forties sat behind the desk, dressed in a navy blue suit, coffee-colored leather shoes, and with neatly groomed hair. As I entered, he hurriedly stood up, walked two steps quickly, and shook my hand, inviting me to sit on the sofa. He handed me his business card, which listed him as the manager of three companies, Mr. Huang. He had a typical northern Chinese face. I reciprocated by offering my business card and introducing our company and its products. After I finished, Mr. Huang began speaking in Mandarin, although not entirely standard, but clear enough to understand, for he did not have a Cantonese accent. He explained that their company had offices in Zibo, where they purchased local specialties, including porcelain, glassware, and silk products, from Zhoucun. They sold these products in Singapore and other Southeast Asian countries. A few days ago, he saw our shoe polishing machines at the Zibo Department Store. He thought they were excellent products with good market potential in Southeast Asia. He asked if we could cooperate with them to promote our shoe polishing machines in Southeast Asia.

I replied, "That sounds great; we can cooperate."

"Do you have the production capacity? The Southeast Asian market is quite large. If I place an order and you cannot fulfill it, there will be fines," Mr. Huang said seriously.

"How many units do you estimate you can sell per month?" I asked him.

"Two to three thousand units per month should be no problem," Mr. Huang nodded, answering my question.

"To meet your requirements, as long as we sign the agreement, we will prioritize supplying your orders over domestic market demands to secure your supply," I assured him straightforwardly.

Mr. Huang was pleased and stood up from his chair, pacing around the office.

He pointed to the young man beside him and said, "This is my general agent, Little Liu. He will handle the business. Let's schedule a visit to your company. We'll draft an agreement, submit it to headquarters for approval, and once approved, we'll sign the official agreement. You need to ensure a steady supply of goods."

"Please rest assured, Mr. Huang. We do what we say. I can guarantee it with 100 percent," I replied firmly, addressing the concerns of the Singaporean businessman with certainty and determination.

My face did not change color, and my heart did not beat faster. Mr. Huang was very satisfied and arranged for Little Liu to visit our factory the day after the next day for an on-site inspection.

Little Liu arrived in a Xiali sedan and found our shoe polishing machine factory. Instead of going to the office, I took him to the workshop to see the production process in action. Little Liu was quite surprised to see such nice and practical shoe polishing machines being produced in several simple workshops without the use of modern machinery. He commented several times on how impressive and uncommon it was.

He looked around and pointed to the motor, asking, "Where do you purchase the motors from?"

I replied, "We produce them ourselves. Let me show you in the front workshop later."

"Where are these plastic parts produced?" Little Liu picked up the base of the shoe polishing machine.

"We buy them from a subsidiary of Jinan Electronics Company," I explained.

After touring the assembly workshop, I took Little Liu to the motor workshop. We went through the process from motor casing to winding, pressing, and aluminum casting of the rotor. Finally, we arrived at the assembly workbench.

Little Liu wondered, "Is this how the motors are produced?"

"The process for large and small motors is similar. A stator, a rotor, put them together, and when powered, they rotate." I explained.

"The main component of the shoe polishing machine is the motor. The shoe polishing machine is not good if the motor is not good." Little Liu muttered to himself.

I added, "As long as the factory tests are qualified, the motors will not break down. It only takes 10 to 20 seconds to polish a shoe, at most one or two minutes at most. The motor won't be strained or break down for many years."

"If the quality is guaranteed and the shoe polishing machine won't break after a few uses, then we can rest assured. After visiting your motor workshop, I am now more confident. I'll report back to manager Huang."

Little Liu was relieved that his quality concerns had been addressed after visiting the motor workshop.

After the workshop tour, we returned to the office. Little Liu mentioned production capacity, inquiring whether we could guarantee a monthly supply of 3,000 to 5,000 units. I replied slowly, explaining that the motor was the key to the shoe-polishing machine's production. We could produce 100 motors daily, with a monthly capacity of 3,000. If there was a demand, we could add two more lathes and a dozen more workers, producing another 100 motors daily. The Southeast Asian market could not be developed in a month or two. With expanding markets and guaranteed funds, we could increase motor production to 10,000 units per month without any issues.

Regarding plastic components, we could produce 500 pieces daily. With two additional assembly workers, we could assemble 200 units daily. The plastic components and assembly were also 100 percent guaranteed. After hearing my explanation, Little Liu had no further questions.

Little Liu informed us that the tasks assigned by Manager Huang had been completed for the day. He planned to draft an agreement that we would sign. The agreement would then be sent back to Singapore headquarters for approval. After approval, it would be returned to us for our signatures to finalize the agreement. Once the order was signed, the company would assign a quality inspector to reside in Zichuan. The inspector would visit our factory periodically to ensure the product quality remained top-notch. The goal was to achieve a 100 percent pass rate with no quality issues for every 10,000 units produced.

At this point, I interjected and said, "We have been selling our products in the Zibo area for over a year now, and we have sold over 7,000 units. I'm happy to report that we have not encountered a single quality issue, maintaining a 100 percent pass rate."

The draft agreement was ready, and Little Liu brought it for my review to see if any modifications were needed. As the saying goes, "The customer is always right." Therefore, the servant must comply with their wishes. The agreement outlined terms such as delivery time, delivery location (Qingdao Customs), placing orders, and delivery within a few days, as well as penalties for breaches of contract, including a fine of 200,000 yuan for setting up a second sales company in Southeast Asia. The final important clause was about pricing.

Little Liu had the authority to set the price. During his visit with Manager Huang, he had already inquired about the price of the shoe polishing machines at the Zibo Department Store. That was the selling price, and the purchase price was not fully known. The retail price was 208 yuan per unit, and my estimated cost price was around 160 yuan per unit. Little Liu made a pretty good guess. "With a gross profit of 25 percent per unit, you sell them to us for 155 yuan each," Little Liu proposed.

"Little Liu, I do not agree to this price. I strive for 160 yuan. The Zibo Department Store sold it for 160 yuan. You could verify it yourself if you don't believe me." After a brief pause, I continued,

"Let's not argue, Little Liu. I can offer you a rebate of two yuan per unit, making it 160 yuan per unit."

"I add one yuan for each piece, and the discount will be three yuan for each."

"All right, it's a deal. Three yuan each."

The price was 160 yuan per unit, including shipping to Qingdao Port. From Qingdao to Singapore, the shipping costs would be covered by Manager Huang. The draft agreement was finalized, and I signed it. Manager Huang sent it back to headquarters.

A few days later, headquarters called, requesting five sample machines. Upon receiving the samples, headquarters would make a decision. Little Liu sent the address in Singapore, requesting direct shipment.

I had never handled overseas shipments before, so I called my old classmate Shi Jun, who worked in foreign trade in Qingdao. I asked her for help. Shi Jun and I had been classmates from the first grade of primary school to junior high school. We had both graduated from the Worker-Peasant-Soldier University, and she was assigned to the provincial foreign trade department. I brought the five shoe polishing machines and went to Qingdao. The company had moved from Huaihai Road to Shanhaiguan Road. I presented Mr. Huang's business card and the receiving address in her office. She carefully examined the English content on the business card, which indicated that it was a general merchandise trading company. She checked the import and export information for Singapore but was unable to find this company. My old classmate utilized her business credentials to arrange for the shoe polishing machines to be sent to Singapore under her name, saving over 2,000 yuan in shipping costs. Shi Jun accompanied me to Zhongshan Park and the Badaguan in Qingdao, also known as the Eight Great Passes. We returned home and waited for good news.

After waiting for half a month without any response, I contacted Little Liu. He replied that there was a lot of business at headquarters and no need to rush. Another half a month passed, and Little Liu's phone was off, indicating it was out of service. I went to the Zihong

Road Office, but it was closed. The dust on the door and windows was thick. The shop's owner next door said it had been closed for a month.

8.10 Calculating Income Tax

I received a notice to calculate income tax at the factory. In previous years, the accountant would take the accounts to the town tax office. After the calculation, the factory director and accountant would be notified to go to the tax office. The tax officers would list item by item which expenses were not compliant, which were considered profits, and the total profit. According to tax laws, 30 percent of the profit was subject to income tax. The accountant noted the accounts were at a loss. Yet, the tax officers could still calculate profits, identify profits, and find many more. Our factory's accounts for last year neither suffered a loss nor made a profit, yet we still paid 30,000 yuan.

The previous year, my first visit to the tax office required over 50,000 yuan. The tax officer showed me the audit records, which listed 50,000 yuan for this repair expense and 20,000 yuan for this expenditure, totaling eight items. These could not be categorized as expenses but as profits, totaling over 170,000 yuan. According to the 30 percent tax, the income tax amounted to 51,000 yuan. I was dumbfounded. The amount doubled from last year. This year, we lost and were unable to raise this money. Negotiating the amount seemed fruitless. On the second visit, the tax officer stated that after rechecking, they were able to categorize several expenses for us. Therefore, we only needed to pay over 40,000 yuan. I disagreed. What to do? How could I forget to treat them? I hosted a top-notch dinner the next evening, and we drank heartily, with a small gift for each person. On the third visit, the tax officer took out the audit list, pointing to it and saying they had consulted with the leaders and managed to categorize two more items. After recalculating, we owed 10,000 yuan less, 30,654 yuan. Were we satisfied now? Unable to argue further, we got 5,000 yuan more than last year and agreed to sign. The accountant took back the books, completing the income tax payment for the year.

Over the past two to three years, small factory directors and tax officers had taken their considerations into account when calculating income tax. The previous year, our enterprise had paid 30,000 yuan in income tax. This year, they planned to charge 40,000 yuan, but calculated it would be up to 70,000 yuan. Prevailing over the opponent in the first encounter, we waited a few days to see their actions. If we did not comply with the unwritten rules, you should at least pay an extra 50,000 yuan. Over the past few years, the small factory directors have come to understand that it increased early but did not generate a significant profit. When dealing with tax officers, we could not be too stubborn. After a few days, things settled, and both parties were happy.

At nine o'clock, two tax officers from the town tax office arrived, Little Qu and Little Liu. I knew them but had never had any dealings with them.

In the office, Little Qu said, "This year, there's a new method for calculating income tax issued by the bureau leaders. Each area has been reassigned. Little Bai and Little Zhang, who handle your factory's area, are being reassigned to Zhangzhuang Village, and we'll handle the calculation for your factory." Having known them for three or four years, we had not collaborated professionally. I brought out Longjing tea and made a cup for each of us.

I replied, "Director Zhai, director Zhang, it has been tough for enterprises over the past few years; please consider that."

When speaking to tax officers, we were required to address them by their titles, using "Director Zhang" and "Director Li." It sounded more respectful, and the tax officers found it pleasing to the ear.

After finishing a cup of tea, Little Qu stood up and walked to the shoe polishing machine beside the door while I poured water. He carefully examined it.

"Director Yu, what's this gadget?"

"A shoe polishing machine produced by our factory." I went over, pressed the handle switch, and extended a foot, "Swish, swish." It started spinning.

"Try it." Little Qu extended his coffee-colored leather shoe, and he polished it to a shine.

"Good stuff, good stuff, not low in technical content; you invented this?" I said, "I learned it from the provincial household appliance shoe polishing machine factory, benefiting from their expertise."

Little Qu looked at the shoe polishing machine and muttered, "Not bad profit, high-tech product, good, good." Returning to the sofa, he sat down. "Director Yu, here's the plan for today. I will be at your factory, while Little Liu will go to the electrical porcelain accessories factory. He aims to finish by noon, with two more factories to handle in the afternoon."

"Alright, I'll ask Accountant Wang to bring the books."

Accountant Wang had already placed the books on the table and hurried over, saying, "Director Zhai, everything's ready."

After these two factories finished calculating income tax, we prepared for a lunch banquet.

I said, "Director Zhai, there are two restaurants in the village, one east of my factory and the other west. Which one would you like to go to?"

"Director Yu, please pay attention to our positions. Since we are the work clothes, we cannot go to a restaurant. Let's eat something simple."

"Come to my home; altogether, there is no need for formalities with two accountants. There are six people. Is that okay?"

"Sure, the simpler, the better. We can't drink too much at noon because we still have work in the afternoon."

Little Qu agreed sincerely. Accountant Wang went to the restaurant to order dishes.

The restaurant served eight dishes, which featured high-end farmhouse cuisine: stir-fried rice with small chicken, fried bean worms, and braised pouting fish. We drank heartily and ate to our heart's content. Since we had to calculate income tax for two more factories in the afternoon, we could not drink too much. There was no finger-guessing game — a drinking game at feasts, no finger pressing. Just over an hour later, the lunch banquet ended.

It got dark early in winter. Without having dinner yet, Accountant Wang and I got into the Jinbei minivan, which was equipped with five shoe-polishing machines. We visited Nanhe County, located in Tai'an. Following the map, we found Little Qu's house. The gate faced east, with lights in the yard. Accountant Wang and I stood outside the gate, swinging it a few times. We called out softly, "Director Qu, director Qu." After a few minutes, there was no response from the yard. Accountant Wang pulled the two round rings on the gate and banged on it to make a sound heard inside the house. Then we continued to call, "Director Zhai."

After waiting five or six minutes, we heard the sound of the door opening. But when we listened closely to the door, there was no sound. Accountant Wang found three bricks and threw them into the yard from the wall. The people inside the house could hear the bricks hitting the ground. We shook the gate and knocked on it again. When we peeked through the crack, the lights inside the house were bright. There must be someone inside. What was the matter? Perhaps Little Qu forgot that we had been appointed to deliver the shoe polishing machines in the evening. We stood at the gate for over 40 minutes, checking the time. Maybe as guests were inside, it was not convenient to open the door? It was hard to figure out the reason, so we did not wait any longer and decided to come again the next day.

On the way back, our stomachs were growling. We had not had dinner yet. When we reached the halfway point of the alley, a car came from the opposite direction. But the alley was not wide enough for both to pass, so we reversed to the alley's end to give way. The car opposite was driving very slowly, with the director Wang of the Credit Cooperative Agency sitting in the passenger seat. Since I sat in the back of the Jinbei car, I could see him clearly, but the director Wang could not see me. The Credit Cooperative Agency also calculated income tax at the end of the year. When the Credit Cooperative Agency's car passed, I turned the car around and followed behind. The Credit Cooperative Agency's car stopped behind Little Qu's house, and director Wang got out of the car carrying a bag, followed by loan officer He carrying another bag. I got out of the car quietly, far away from them, and followed them to the back of Qu's house. When walking to the west end of the small north house, they turned south and climbed a small hill with a small door at its summit. "Bang, bang, bang." Director Wang knocked a few times. Upon closer inspection, I found a window on the north wall of the small north house, facing the small side door. After two or three minutes, "creak, creak," the door opened. Little Qu invited them inside.

Back to the car, shortly after, the Credit Cooperative Agency's car drove away. We also arrived at the Credit Cooperative Agency's parking spot and went to the small side door, knocking twice. As we heard a cough inside the house, I knocked twice more, and Little Qu came out, opening the door.

"Director Yu, I apologize for the long wait; it's been tough for you!"

Following Little Qu inside, we put down the shoe polishing machines. Little Qu grinned, saying, "It seems like someone was at the front door just now. Was it you? Sorry, sorry."

"We promised to deliver the shoe polishing machines; we couldn't break our promise."

Little Zhai poured the tea in a hurry, but we did not sit down; we stood there for two or three minutes.

"No need to sit. Our car is parked by the roadside. Director Zhai, please rest early." Accountant Wang and I left the house through the back door and returned to the car. Since we had not had dinner yet, we went home in a hurry.

On the way to Taiyuan, I first stayed in Shijiazhuang. In Shijiazhuang, several malls displayed shoe polishers, but accounts had not been cleared for a year. Salespeople had visited twice or three times, selling only a few machines and promising to clear the accounts. In the morning, I visited two malls, where I found that they had sold 15 machines. I collected 2,400 yuan in cash, returned the remaining machines, and settled accounts at both malls. In the afternoon, I visited two other malls, where I found they had sold eight machines, and then I collected 1,300 yuan in cash. The managers of the four malls all had the same response: The shoe polishers occupied the counter space and warehouses with no buyers, which affected the sales of other electronics. After a year and two months, the shoe polishers were withdrawn from Shijiazhuang.

The next day, I took a train to Taiyuan. Since it was not a holiday, there were not many people, so I bought a seat ticket and checked in. After the train had stopped, passengers on board alighted first, and the 10 or so people waiting to board stood orderly at the door. When I boarded, two passengers were in front of me. I followed them as they entered the carriage and tried to find my seat using the ticket. Then, a young man hurried towards me and said, "You're stepping on my ticket."

Without thinking, I instinctively lowered my head and lifted my foot. The young man, carrying a coat with one hand, brushed past my shoulder and squeezed past me. I did not notice him dropping his ticket.

Behind me, the salesperson, Old Zhao, tugged at my arm, saying, "The guy in front of you just reached towards your chest."

Before I found my seat, I reached into my suit pocket, but it was empty.

Old Zhao rushed back to the door to chase him, but the train attendant saw the young man get off the train. The young man snatched the money from the shoe polishers in a year in Shijiazhuang. Careless, how careless I was! It was over 3,000 yuan, a thin stack of money I put in my pocket for convenience, considering it took no space. With a suitcase and a handbag, I thought it was not worth putting them in. But the thief was so cunning. With just a brush past, in two or three minutes, it was not second to a magic show. Over 20 years later, I still remember that young man.

Taking the Dafa van, a joint venture between Tianjin and Japan in Taiyuan, I finished visiting six stores in the morning. Four malls refused to stock shoe polishers, and two agreed to clear the accounts and remove the shoe polishers from the shelves. In the afternoon, Little Wang from the Research Institute and I went to Hualian

Shopping Mall first. We went to the warehouse to check where eight shoe polishers were stored. Then we went to Dongfeng Mall and found the manager and the storekeeper. We cleared the accounts after loading the unsold shoe polishers onto the truck. It was already past five in the afternoon.

Driving the van, Little Wang took Old Zhao and me to the Research Institute. An older man rode a motorcycle on the opposite side at a crossroads. Paying no attention to the traffic lights, he collided with Little Wang's van. Both vehicles were crossing the intersection at a slow pace. The older man and his motorcycle fell to the ground. Old Zhao and I exited the van to support the older man. The older man did not touch the van; he lay on the ground, unharmed, with no injuries to his hands or feet. He pretended to be unstable on his feet, and the motorcycle's mudguard was bent from the collision, but it could still be driven. The older man was unreasonable, demanding 1,000 yuan to repair his motorcycle and have his injuries checked at the hospital. It would only cost tens of yuan to replace the mudguard. The older man had not even scraped his skin; what injury would prompt him to go to the hospital? Around a dozen older men and women were present, some praising him, and some criticized him. In the end, we gave the older man 500 yuan.

There is a saying in folk culture that misfortunes never come alone. I was robbed in Shijiazhuang and extorted in Taiyuan. Although the losses were small, they were coincidental. Sitting in Little Wang's car on the way back to the Research Institute, I was reminded that three years before, when my wife was beside the paint grinder cleaning the filter net, just 10 minutes after starting work in the morning, she was accidentally hit by the filter net, fracturing her arm. This machine had been grinding paint for seven or eight years without injuring any workers. On the fifth day after my wife left the hospital, another female worker fractured her arm in the same place while cleaning the net in the same position on the grinder. Afterward, this grinder had been in operation for nine years until it was discontinued, and it never caused a single injury to a worker again. Some social phenomena, minor illnesses, and disasters seemed reasonable and coincidental, scientifically explained as the result of work errors or improper arrangements. Witches believed it was caused by geomancy. I was hapless in Shijiazhuang and Taiyuan, so I left. The shoe polishers took about a week to retreat from these two provincial capitals.

Zibo Department Store was the largest in Zibo during the 1970s and 1980s, thriving for over 20 years. By the mid-1990s, several new malls had been built, surpassing its scale, but it still held considerable influence. The first choice when promoting shoe polisher machines was the Zibo Department Store. The home appliance department was on the first floor, now contracted out, with Manager Sun in charge. He had the final say in business dealings, with simple procedures and high efficiency. In the first year, they sold over 1,000 shoe polisher machines, the most in Zibo. Payments were made promptly. In the first half of the following year, only 100 units were sold. Even during the peak season at the end of the year, sales were not as strong as they were the previous year. According to Manager Sun, home appliance sales were generally poor that year, not just shoe polisher machines, but the washing machines and air conditioners had experienced a greater decline. Two more malls were opened in Zhangdian District, Zibo, specializing in home appliances, and intensifying competition. People preferred new things, so the Zibo Department Store underwent a layout change, featuring clothing categories such as leather goods, children's wear, and women's wear on the first floor. At the same time, home appliance shopping places were moved to the fourth floor. Manager Sun withdrew from the home appliance contract.

Manager Sun called to clear the business and settle payments. I went with the salesperson, finding Manager Sun still in his original office. There was a lot of follow-up work. The goods sold on consignment could not be sold, so the client took them away. The distributed home appliances were stored in the warehouse for later processing. The shoe polisher machines were consigned, with 10 unsold units brought back. After selling and settling the accounts, the remaining payment owed for the shoe polisher machines was 103,000 yuan. Manager

Sun promised to repay a portion of the accounts in cash and use home appliances to offset a portion of the accounts. The warehouse keeper had not been coming to work lately. Then, we could go to the warehouse and randomly select household appliances according to the notice.

Two days later, I received a call from Manager Sun. He told us to take a truck to the Zibo Department Store to pick up home appliances. Arriving at the warehouse, the warehouse keeper had received a notice that we could pick up any item and load it onto the truck for checkout at the office. There are only two little duck washing machines, two Haier air conditioners, and one drive, with no more televisions. Then we installed these four big ones. Just launched dozens of microwave ovens, piled up in large quantities, and luxury goods priced at over 2,000 yuan per unit, similar to washing machines and televisions. We took five of them. They were not very useful, so we used them as gifts. Kitchen disinfection cabinets have various uses, so we have selected 10 of the most notable ones. We did not bring back any other small items that were useless. After being selected, we went to the office to settle the bill. With the accounting, we paid 36,000 yuan for home appliances. Manager Sun promised to provide 30,000 yuan in cash within a few days, with the remaining payment to be divided into several installments. He settled over a year ago. Having worked at the Zibo Department Store for over 20 years, Manager Sun was a trustworthy individual. He kept his promises, making him a good client.

Two months later, I accidentally switched to Zibo TV while eating dinner and watching TV. The screen showed a building engulfed in flames, with several fire trucks spraying water onto the scene. The host explained that the Zibo Department Store had caught fire at 2:35 p.m. that afternoon, with firefighters working to extinguish the blaze. The mayor, district Party Secretary, and district head were at the scene directing operations.

A few days later, I went to Zhangdian specifically to see the Zibo Department Store. Both inside and out, it was charred, with windows and doors in disarray, surrounded by barriers. News reports stated that the fire originated on the ground floor and subsequently spread to the roof. The first floor sold inflammable items, including leather jackets, sweaters, cotton jackets, and various types of clothing. The fire was intense, and the entire building was burned to ashes. Manager Sun's office was destroyed, and his phone was disconnected. Since then, he was nowhere to be seen, and the debt owed was incinerated, too.

A year later, passing by the Zibo Department Store, it remained in the same burned state, abandoned and neglected.

Several years later, the Zibo Department Store underwent a complete renovation, both inside and out, showcasing a new look for the 21st century. Its clumsy appearance before the fire was completely gone, rebranded, and stepping into the new century.

Several malls in Zhoucun and Boshan sold a few dozen units. The Huantai and Linzi shopping malls wholesaled a few hundred units. Most shops had no inquiries. In the Zibo area, it was popular for a year and a half, but by the third year, several malls were unwilling to display them on their counters. Because they occupied the space without selling, it was time to close the shop.

Over 100 were sold in the three northeastern cities after two years of selling. Calculating the profits, they could not withstand the travel expenses of the salespeople. It was also time to close the shop.

Colonel Uncle, a retired military officer turned businessman in Beijing, was my good neighbor and fellow villager. He gathered a few friends to sell shoe polishers in Beijing. In the capital of China, with countless billionaires, selling a few thousand shoe polishers should have been easy. For some unknown reason, this product, praised by everyone who saw it, was displayed in Beijing for over a year, yet it only sold a few dozen.

From production to discontinuation, it took a total of three years. Imported from Europe, it was said to be a good product, but it did not adapt well to the Chinese market. It could not take root and blossom. The market did not accept it, and the people did not like it.

There were grand plans with radio, newspapers, and advertising.

Monthly plans were set at 10,000 units, increasing to 20,000 units, then 30,000 units per year, with an annual production range of 300,000 to 500,000 units. Sales routes were planned for Shandong, Hebei, Shanxi, Beijing, Tianjin, and the northeast, followed by Jiangnan, or the southern part of the Yangtze River.

Man proposes, God disposes, like a momentary bloom of a fleeting flower — three whole years of jumping around, all in vain.

EPILOGUE

Before the autumn of 1981, the Cicun town commune convened a Three-Level Cadre Conference (comprising cadres from the district, communes, and production teams). It announced the implementation of the household contract responsibility system in rural areas, whereby land would be allocated per capita based on labor, allowing individual farming while retaining the organizational form of production teams. Distribution policies remained unchanged, as did the regulations of the People's Commune.

In our Cicun commune, the land allocation rule was as follows: males received 10 mu (approximately 0.66 acres) of land. In comparison, females received eight mu (approximately 0.53 acres). Each male laborer managed 10 mu of the land, while each female laborer managed eight mu. Each village determined its allocation based on available land, avoiding a one-size-fits-all approach. After the autumn harvest, the land was distributed to households. Each village should determine its production quotas and work points per mu of land. Land quality was categorized into three levels based on productivity. For instance, irrigated fields producing two crops a year yielded wheat at a rate of 300 catties (approximately 165 kilograms) per mu and maize at 500 catties per mu, setting a standard of 800 catties annually for first-class land. Rain-fed fields, reliant solely on natural precipitation, yielded wheat at 200 catties per mu and maize at 400 catties per mu, totaling 600 catties annually for second-class land. Thinly soiled areas suitable for only one crop per year, such as sorghum or sweet potatoes, were classified as third-class land. They remained fixed once production targets were set, barring major natural disasters. After harvesting, the amount of grain one should share and the amount one should hand over to the production team would be calculated according to the number of mu of land one had contracted, with the rest being theirs. Work points were calculated based on land quality, with first-class land earning 300 labor points per mu, second-class land earning 200 labor points, and third-class land earning 100 labor points. At the end of the year, the income distribution followed the methods of production teams, with each work point corresponding to a certain amount of money. For instance, our team changed from a ratio of three labor points for every seven catties of grain to four labor points for every six catties, with grain accounting for 40 percent and population size for 60 percent of the distribution. Production teams remained intact, and the People's Commune retained its structure.

The Three-Level Cadre Conference instructed the convening of general meetings for commune members to solicit opinions. Decisions could be made based on specific circumstances in dispute or dissent. Without such meetings, news of land distribution spread throughout the streets and alleys. During the general meetings, there was no debate or dissent; all members unanimously agreed to distribute land to households.

According to the accounts of previous generations, establishing the People's Commune and collectivizing land faced significant resistance. Some individuals stayed in their fields for three days and nights, refusing to return home. Others surreptitiously brought their cattle back from the team's custody at night. The most stubborn opponents of collectivization were forcibly taken to their fields, where the seeds of the production teams were sown. However, during this land distribution, there were no such diehards; everyone was delighted. After the production teams completed harvesting and measuring the land, it was distributed to the households. Adults and children went to the fields together to plant wheat, completing the task several days earlier than in the era of production teams.

During the era of production teams, there were the "Three Autumn Battles." A stage was set up at the village entrance, a loudspeaker was installed, and a Three Autumn Command was established. With flags flying and songs filling the air, we responded to the call of the Central Committee of the Communist Party of China, ensuring that the People's Commune would successfully sow wheat before the frost descended.

In our production team, after measuring all the land, it was determined that each male laborer would receive four mu of land and each female laborer three mu, based on the labor force available at the time of planting. With over 40 mu of the land remaining, it was distributed as private plots among all team members, including those who worked in communal factories or village enterprises and had not received land. Along with their original plots, each person would receive slightly over 3 fen (approximately 0.3 mu) of land. A family of five could harvest around 1,000 or 800 catties of grain annually. Those who had contracted land were satisfied, and those who could not were dissatisfied.

With land distribution to households for a year, rural life underwent significant changes, including a surplus of grain. The most noticeable change was in the diet, shifting from pancakes as the staple to steamed buns, with pancakes becoming a side dish. Vegetables became a regular part of meals, and although meat and fish were still scarce, they were consumed more frequently. While life did not undergo a complete transformation in just one year, the most basic livelihood problems were addressed. With food security assured, agricultural work proceeded smoothly, with three months dedicated to harvesting and planting. With spare time available, people explored ways to earn additional income, with some engaging in household handicrafts and others involved in trading. No longer were farmers solely dependent on farming from sunrise to sunset; they were now free to work at their own pace.

After two years of land contracting, in 1983, the central government issued a document initiating comprehensive rural reform, which included the household contracting system, the dissolution of production teams, and the end of people's communes. The land in rural areas was distributed on a per capita basis, regardless of gender, age, or labor capacity, with each person receiving an equal share of the land. In the autumn of 1983, the land was redistributed after the harvest. After planting wheat on the newly allocated land, the assets of the production teams were divided among the members. Cattle, donkeys, and pigs were sold at market value, while pigsties and warehouses were sold to members of the commune. Tools such as carts, plows, rakes, baskets, pots, and pans were distributed by drawing lots. In just three to five days, the production teams that had operated for 25 years disbanded, and the People's Commune exited the stage of history.

In the commune, farmers in village-run factories no longer received work points; instead, they received wages. Commune members became workers with guaranteed livelihoods. For those who previously worked in the fields, after completing their agricultural duties, they found themselves unemployed. Recognizing that fortunes would not fall from the sky, they opened small workshops, traded goods, and started small factories, signaling the budding of capitalism in rural areas.

I was an unemployed farmer. I purchased the smallest extrusion machine from the production team, but I struggled to operate it. I purchased two additional extrusion machines within a year to expand production. However, the good times did not last long; the products did not sell well. After struggling for over three years, I stopped production and changed my career path.

I then ventured into producing wall coatings, a new product. In the first two years, things seemed promising, and I managed to keep the business afloat. However, fierce competition arose as the product's simplicity and low investment attracted many others. Dozens of new competitors emerged within several dozen kilometers, intensifying the struggle. When I thought I understood the market dynamics and was ready to produce, the cost of raw materials began to rise. The price of the main material increased from 2,600 yuan per ton, gradually climbing by 200 to 500 yuan each month, reaching 6,000 yuan after six months and 10,000 yuan after a year. Despite losses, I persevered, learning from the experience of dealing with recycled plastics. During market downturns, I could not afford to stop production and had to find alternative means of survival. A year later, fortunes changed; surrounding small factories closed down, and the price of the main material began to fall gradually. Slowly but steadily, I recouped the losses incurred.

Lack of foresight leads to immediate worries. I could not wait until the products declined in popularity before seeking new opportunities.

During the prosperous period of coating production and sales, I expanded my factory and invested in hydraulic pillar maintenance. Making money from state-owned enterprises was relatively easy, so I explored new technologies and found sources of goods. Starting from Zibo coal mines, I traveled to Longkou, Xinwen, and Feicheng in search of opportunities, visiting various mining bureaus within the province and venturing beyond its borders. I visited mining bureaus in Yima, Datun, Xuzhou, Shizuishan, Wuhai, Tiefa, and Shulan, where I dealt with coal mines for eight years.

Maintenance work was cumbersome, so I had to find new products to replace the old ones. I discovered shoe polishers, imported from Europe and previously exclusive to domestic markets, by the Provincial Household Electric Appliance Company. With confidence, I borrowed money and invested, securing the support of the Provincial Household Electric Appliance Company. This time, I made a significant investment to open new markets and shift my business philosophy. From entering markets in Shijiazhuang and Taiyuan, skirting around Beijing, to venturing into the northeast, I painted a grand vision and dreamed big. Unfortunately, the good products could not adapt to the local markets, and the good times did not last long. After three to five years, it was time to close that chapter.

During this period, I experimented with several small projects. I blew plastic bottles, welded household stoves, and produced paint-drying agents, fan switches, and car dashboards. After trying various options, I was not sure which industry to focus on or which product would stand the test of time.

From the dissolution of the production team to the new millennium, 20 years passed imperceptibly. Two decades passed without any major upheavals or extraordinary challenges, without achieving anything remarkable or falling into deep despair. As the saying goes, crossing the river by feeling the stones, I went with the flow. I just rushed forward year by year without goals or directions.

Over the past 20 years, I have had joys, troubles, delights, and depressions. Even now, I still miss those times.

When the production team disbanded, I delivered the first batch of goods. I planned to reach my destination in one night, but my tractor broke down, delaying me for two days. Tractors were prone to issues in those days, and I might reach my destination on the third day. Frustrated and anxious, it was my first time delivering products, and I encountered a big problem. It seemed luck was on my side. A person appeared unexpectedly on the road and bought the goods, offering an extra 200 yuan per ton. I lost sleep that night because it was a happy one.

The old formula could not keep up with the market, and it was hard to eat and sleep. One day, a professor from Wuhan came knocking with a new formula, turning the tide in the coating market. It became a local brand for three to five years.

There were not many joyous occasions, and the days of anguish were long.

When producing wall coatings, I took out loans to buy equipment and borrowed money to purchase materials. In the first year, just as I was expanding into the market, the Great Cold arrived early, freezing the coatings solid like Spring Festival rice cakes, necessitating a costly redo. I had to raise funds to buy materials and paint drums; without them, production would halt, putting me in dire straits. Securing bank loans without collateral was futile, and the more poorly I managed the business, the further my friends and family distanced themselves from me. I could not give up, despite the difficulties. I desperately sought assistance and managed to borrow 5,000 yuan, an unforgettable struggle.

In the early 1980s, government departments had relatively less control; however, as the 1990s arrived, regulations and management systems were implemented. We had to pay various administrative fees, leaving us confused and frustrated. Today, we had to pay a certain percentage to a management unit; the next day, we would have to pay another percentage to another unit. Overpaying resulted in losses, while underpaying led to strict scrutiny. Soon, fees were introduced for river and water resource management, and if we refused to pay them, it led to lawsuits. Then there were education surcharges, urban and rural construction fees, environmental management fees, and numerous other charges — small amounts of money but big worries. Taxation was the most headache-inducing; tax collectors, department heads, and bureau chiefs had the final say. Policies changed yearly, and one had to comply, overtly or covertly. Even if one's accounts were meticulous, they could still find problems and demand payment. Overtly entertaining officials or covertly giving bribes, from top to bottom, one had to bend over backward and push through; if one didn't, how could one survive without a stable job?

There were fewer days of anguish and more moments of joy, though failures outnumbered successes. From land redistribution in 1981 to producing shoe polishers, I ventured into seven or eight different products over a 17 to 18-year period. Initially, I was unsure of what I was doing or how to operate a factory. Growing up in the countryside, I experienced the people's communes, where people pushed carts to work and wielded hoes in the fields; I had no idea about factories. For the first few years, I bounced from one thing to another, abandoning one product for another on a whim. After seven or eight years, I gradually came to understand some key principles and accumulated valuable experience. Through repairing hydraulic pillars and getting to know people in coal mines, I gained insight into enterprise culture and management methods. Producing shoe polishing machines introduced me to the wider market, social interactions, and commercial culture, teaching me about products and society. I was over 40 by this time, realizing I could not rush headlong into things. I needed to steady myself, reflect, and focus on one product.

In the late 1990s, I produced constant-pressure generators for tractors, replacing old-fashioned generators, and the market boomed for two or three years. However, my product was only on the market for less than two years before prices plummeted and the market became saturated. Thus, I had to withdraw from the market. I then set my sights on automotive generators and resolved to persevere. I started supplying generators for agricultural vehicles and large tractors. I began visiting diesel engine factories because these generators were components of diesel generators and required mass production. Despite being seemingly insignificant, the generators required three to five years of refinement and development. For the first three to four years, the main factories did not approve, and I suffered losses year after year. However, after 2000, the quality improved year by year, and the generators received praise from the main factories, becoming standardized. In the 20 years after 2000, I focused single-mindedly on producing automotive generators. I developed into a considerable-scale enterprise.

From my earliest memories, I experienced the people's communes, ate at communal canteens, and witnessed the Great Leap Forward, the three years of natural disasters, and the 10 years of the Cultural Revolution. I then returned to the countryside and farmed for over a decade, drifting along with society for 30 years. During this time, I had no personal goals, and I felt powerless to control my destiny. If they told one to be a teacher, one went straight to school; if they told one to be an accountant, one came back to record accounts and distribute grain. Confined within one's area within two and a third mu, one could not move around freely or act recklessly.

With the fall of the Gang of Four and the onset of the 1980s, rural areas underwent tremendous changes, returning to the right path of history and bursting forth with tremendous energy. By establishing factories, opening shops, and venturing worldwide, every ordinary person could determine their fate and live freely. These 20 years were the most memorable, the most promising, and the most significant segment of my life.

There were many 20-year experiences from 1981 to the new millennium. These 20 years crossing the century mark were a period of great social change and the most important 20 years of my life. I wrote them down with nothing else to do and named it "Twenty Years of Chopping Wood."

Before putting pen to paper, I thought the trivialities of life must be recorded and written. Were they worth remembering? Was it useful to record who experienced these troubles and trifles? In the vast river of history, these trivial matters were like drops of water in the ocean. Ordinary people had nothing worth writing about; they had no biographies. Wang Dingjun once said, "Biographies of important figures are written for ordinary people, while biographies of ordinary people are written for important figures. One of the regrets in this world is that ordinary people do not write memoirs, and even if they do, important figures won't read them." After reading these words, I decided not to write.

A philosopher once said, "There are trillions of leaves in the world, and none is the same. The lives experienced by hundreds of millions of people are all unique." My experiences, life, and these 20 years may seem ordinary. Still, upon reflection, there are aspects worth remembering despite the effort it takes to recall them. Although not extraordinary or earth-shattering, there are some moments that others may not have experienced.

Writing memoirs requires sincerity. Over the past 20 years, I have experienced numerous ups and downs, and I cannot just jot down everything. I must pick and choose what to remember, reflecting the true social conditions of the time, being objective and realistic without embellishment or fabrication. Recording these experiences can enlighten society and future generations, promoting social progress and guiding people along the right path.

Writing memoirs requires time and energy. Writing and learning, I would pause for several days, pondering and contemplating, before continuing. Clumsy and slow, I wrote intermittently, and after two years, I finally finished, breathing a long sigh of relief.

After resting for a few days, I will have to push myself again, whip myself into action, and complete the established plan, weaving together the events and stories of the past few decades into a coherent narrative. And finally, I finished the book.

About the Author

Guotai Yu, born in Zichuan District, Zibo City, Shandong Province, has led a diverse life as a farmer, teacher, accountant, and entrepreneur in China.

About the Translators

Jicheng Sun is an Associate Professor of English at the School of Foreign Languages, Shandong University of Technology. He pursued his English studies at the Department of English at Shandong Normal University (1988-1992), the Institute of American Modern Literature at Shandong University (1995-1999), and the Department of English at Peking University (2001-2007). Email: jichengsun@pku.edu.cn.

Yingrui Gong is a Professor of English in the School of Foreign Languages at Qingdao University. She studied English writing and translation at Ocean University of China (1991-1995), Shandong University (1996-1999), and Shanghai International Studies University (2006-2009).

About the Proofreaders

John Drew, [B. A. (New Brunswick); M. A. (Chicago); Ph. D. (Cambridge)], a poet and tutor in Cambridge, UK, earned his PhD in the English Department at the University of Cambridge. John has taught poetry writing at various universities worldwide, along with his wife, Rani Drew, who teaches drama writing and performance. His notable works include the poetry collection *The Chorus of Birds* (Cambridge Poetry Workshop, 2010) and *India and the Romantic Imagination* (Oxford India, 1987). John is a world traveler, having been educated on scholarship at universities in four different countries and serving as a full-time university lecturer in Canada, Singapore, China, and Hungary, in addition to teaching at universities in six other countries. He has also worked as a journalist and a postman.

Hal Swindall is a native Californian with a Ph.D. in comparative literature from UC Riverside (1994). He is a vagabond English professor around East Asian universities in China, Korea, and Malaysia. His main academic research interests are late nineteenth-century European literature and art. Still, he has become interested in Chinese literature, Korean Buddhist art, and similar studies during his time in East Asia. He has also translated academic and journalistic French articles, in addition to writing some of his own journalism on East Asia.

www.ingramcontent.com/pod-product-compliance
Lightning Source LLC
Chambersburg PA
CBHW021210130626
46554CB00004B/1165